Palgrave Studies in European Union Politics

Series Editors
Michelle Egan, American University, Washington, USA
William E. Paterson, Aston University, Birmingham, UK
Kolja Raube, KU Leuven, Leuven, Belgium

Following on the sustained success of the acclaimed European Union Series, which essentially publishes research-based textbooks, Palgrave Studies in European Union Politics publishes cutting edge research-driven monographs. The remit of the series is broadly defined, both in terms of subject and academic discipline. All topics of significance concerning the nature and operation of the European Union potentially fall within the scope of the series. The series is multidisciplinary to reflect the growing importance of the EU as a political, economic and social phenomenon. To submit a proposal, please contact Senior Editor Ambra Finotello ambra.finotello@palgrave.com. This series is indexed by Scopus.

Editorial Board:

Laurie Buonanno (SUNY Buffalo State, USA)
Kenneth Dyson (Cardiff University, UK)
Brigid Laffan (European University Institute, Italy)
Claudio Radaelli (University College London, UK)
Mark Rhinard (Stockholm University, Sweden)
Ariadna Ripoll Servent (University of Bamberg, Germany)
Frank Schimmelfennig (ETH Zurich, Switzerland)
Claudia Sternberg (University College London, UK)
Nathalie Tocci (Istituto Affari Internazionali, Italy)

Felix Biermann

The Battle for Authority in European Defence Cooperation

Felix Biermann
Ludwig-Maximilians-Universität
München
Munich, Germany

ISSN 2662-5873 ISSN 2662-5881 (electronic)
Palgrave Studies in European Union Politics
ISBN 978-3-031-30053-0 ISBN 978-3-031-30054-7 (eBook)
https://doi.org/10.1007/978-3-031-30054-7

© The Editor(s) (if applicable) and The Author(s), under exclusive license to Springer Nature Switzerland AG 2023

This work is subject to copyright. All rights are solely and exclusively licensed by the Publisher, whether the whole or part of the material is concerned, specifically the rights of translation, reprinting, reuse of illustrations, recitation, broadcasting, reproduction on microfilms or in any other physical way, and transmission or information storage and retrieval, electronic adaptation, computer software, or by similar or dissimilar methodology now known or hereafter developed.
The use of general descriptive names, registered names, trademarks, service marks, etc. in this publication does not imply, even in the absence of a specific statement, that such names are exempt from the relevant protective laws and regulations and therefore free for general use.
The publisher, the authors, and the editors are safe to assume that the advice and information in this book are believed to be true and accurate at the date of publication. Neither the publisher nor the authors or the editors give a warranty, expressed or implied, with respect to the material contained herein or for any errors or omissions that may have been made. The publisher remains neutral with regard to jurisdictional claims in published maps and institutional affiliations.

Cover illustration: Magic Lens/Shutterstock

This Palgrave Macmillan imprint is published by the registered company Springer Nature Switzerland AG
The registered company address is: Gewerbestrasse 11, 6330 Cham, Switzerland

Paper in this product is recyclable.

Acknowledgements

Writing this book was an intense time for me that pushed me to my limits and enabled me to grow, both intellectually and in character. Part of that development process is embodied in this book—the other part is safely stored away. I am grateful to many people. To some for opening up new possibilities for me. To others for having created the conditions for these possibilities. To all of them for accompanying me along the way, encouraging me, supporting me, challenging me, and helping me not to take myself too seriously.

First, I would like to thank my two doctoral supervisors, Moritz Weiß and Berthold Rittberger. Moritz, thank you for having had the courage to offer me, a lateral entrant, the chance to prove myself in academia. This leap of faith still means a lot to me; it keeps me motivated and provides me with the courage to leave my comfort zone. The direct way in which you formulated expectations, your helpfulness and your unsparing but well-meaning honesty gave me a boost and drive. Without your guidance and support, without you believing in what I do, I would not have succeeded in accomplishing this book. Berthold, I thank you for finding the right balance between challenging and supporting me, which helped me strike the difficult balance between contentment and discontentment with the quality of my work. You exemplify every day what it means to sacrifice and devote oneself wholeheartedly to the cause. In this you are my role model and helped me push my boundaries in small but regular steps. Thank you!

I would hardly have been able to cope with the challenges of this intense time if I hadn't had companions who were in the same situation. My dear colleagues, you always had an encouraging word—you shared my anger and joy, you were there when it was time to celebrate or to come to terms with a situation. Whether in the office, in the Eisbach, at the Chinese Tower—it's been a blast! Thank you, Benjamin Daßler, Stefan Jagdhuber, and Vytautas Jankauskas. Ben, your reflective, pragmatic nature helped keep me grounded and your great suggestions showed me new ways of doing things. Stefan—thanks for everything, my sparring partner. Your friendship and dependability mean a lot to me! Vytas, thanks to you I had mostly "everything under control."

Furthermore, I would like to thank my colleagues Raphaela Hobbach, Rainer Hülsse, Andreas Kruck, Veronika Ohliger, Dovile Rimkute, Laura Seelkopf, Yves Steinebach, Hilde Van Meegdenburg, Bernhard Zangl, and Eva Ziegler for the great working atmosphere, the always constructive comments, and their open doors. Furthermore, I thank Aurora Bergmaier, Zita Köhler-Baumann, Melina Mekhail, and Felix Rüchardt for their great research assistance! My work has also benefited from important influences outside the institute—I thank Kenneth Abbott, Christopher Daase, Jennifer Eriksen, Christian Freudelsperger, Philipp Genschel, Cathérine Hoeffler, Stephanie Hofmann, Markus Jachtenfuchs, Andrew Moravcsik, Frank Sauer, and Duncan Snidal for taking the time to engage with my research and for their valuable comments, which greatly helped me structure and sharpen my argument.

While it sometimes felt that way, fortunately, the years did not consist merely of work. Compensation was therefore even more important, and I was able to use this time well to recharge and get important new impulses. I thank my dear friends Benjamin, Benedikt, Colin, Chiara, Franzi, Géraldine, Hendryk, Julian, Moritz, Katharina, Philip, Raphaela, Stephan, Ruth, and Teddy for bringing other thoughts and so much joy into my life. And I would like to thank Anja for being by my side for long periods of this time. You gave me strength and confidence—I owe you so much. Finally, I would like to thank my family. Nora, Renate, Bertram, Diana, and Jürgen, you are the condition of the possibility— through your unconditional support. Your warmth and love have taken me through situations of aimlessness, rescued me from holes in motivation, and allowed me to get through phases of depressed self-confidence. Thank you from the bottom of my heart! Lisa, you endured years with me in the office and beyond, experienced all the ups and downs, and steered me through them. I couldn't have done it without you. I thank you for being by my side. Hannah, my sunshine, your smile and laughter remind me of what is really important every day—I love you both.

Contents

Part I Introducing the Problem

1 Introduction   3
  The Innovation: European Defense Cooperation
  as a Regime Complex   7
  Researching the CSDP—Filling the Gaps   8
  Broadening the Perspective, Sharpening the Focus   11
  The Theoretical Argument in Brief   15
    Types of Interinstitutional Relations   15
    Causal Pathways to Authority Distributions   17
  The Empirical Findings in Brief   19
    Integration: The WEAG/WEAO and the EDA   20
    Marginalization: The EDA and OCCAR   21
    Fragmentation: PESCO and Regional Defense
    Cooperation   22
    Resilience: PESCO Withstanding Competition   22
    Confronting Alternative Explanations   23
  Plan of the Book   26
  References   27

Part II Concepts and Theory

2 Authority Relations in Regime Complexes — 37
 The Emergence and Consequences of Regime Complexes — 40
  What Is a Regime Complex? — 40
  How Do Regime Complexes Emerge? — 44
  What Are the Consequences of Regime Complexity? — 46
 Reducing Complexity: A Typology of Authority Distributions — 49
 A Typology of Interinstitutional Relationships — 54
 Summary — 57
 References — 58

3 Struggling for Authority in Regime Complexes — 63
 Sources of Dissatisfaction — 65
 Contestation and Power — 68
 Condition I—Go-It-Alone Power — 71
 Condition II—Membership Preference — 75
 Explaining Authority Distributions — 80
 Summary — 83
 References — 86

Part III Explaining Authority Distributions in the European Defense Complex

4 European Defense Cooperation and Member State Preferences — 93
 Research Design and Case Selection — 94
 Member State Preferences on European Defense Cooperation — 99
 References — 106

5 Integrating the WEAO into the EDA: Toward a European Armaments Agency? — 111
 Stagnation in Armaments Cooperation — 113
  Dissatisfaction: The Principle of "juste retour" — 115
  Reform Attempts Blocked—OCCAR and the LoI — 116
  The Trigger: The Franco-British Initiative at Le Touquet — 119
 The Threat of Exclusion: "There Will Be Peer Pressure" — 122
 Membership Preference: Welcome to the Club! — 126
 Integration of the WEAG/WEAO into the EDA — 131
 Summary — 133
 References — 134

CONTENTS　　xi

6	The Marginalization of the EDA: False Premises, False Promises?	141
	Dissatisfaction: Spirits That They've Summoned, Their Commands Ignore	144
	Reform Blockade: Resistance on All Fronts	147
	The Trigger: Avant-Gardist Resignation	149
	The Threat of Exclusion—The Avant-Garde Goes It Alone	151
	Membership Preference—Six Is Company, Seven's a Crowd	154
	Formalizing Marginalization: The Administrative Arrangement	157
	Summary	161
	References	162
7	The Fragmentation of European Defense Planning: PESCO's Deep Sleep	169
	Buried Alive	172
	Contested from the Outset	173
	Blocking PESCO	176
	Minilateral Regional Cooperation	179
	Sustaining Minilateralism	181
	The Europeanist Reaction	186
	Fragmentation—The Least Common Security and Defense Policy	188
	Summary	191
	References	193
8	PESCO's resilience: Jumpstarting the bandwagon	199
	Taking Stock: Europeanist Dreams and Atlanticist Reality	202
	Leaving Them Alone—The Atlanticist Coalition After Brexit	204
	The Europeanist Trump Card—A New Need for European Defense	208
	PESCO's Resilience—Awakened by the Bandwagon	211
	Summary	218
	References	225

Part IV Assessment

9	**Confronting Contenders**	235
	Neorealism and CSDP Institutions	238
	Neorealism and the EDA	239
	Neorealism and PESCO	242
	Neofunctionalism and CSDP Institutions	246
	Neofunctionalism and the EDA	247
	Neofunctionalism and PESCO	250
	Summary	253
	References	254
10	**Quo Vadis, CSDP?**	261
	Interinstitutional Relationships in Regime Complexes	264
	The CSDP Between Preferences and Power	268
	Avenues for Further Research: Endogeneity, Marginalization, and the Future of the CSDP	270
	References	275

References 279

Index 315

About the Author

Felix Biermann is currently Senior Manager for Strategic Projects at acatech - National Academy of Science and Engineering in Munich, Germany. He wrote this book during his time as an Assistant Professor at the University of Munich. He holds a bachelor's in philosophy and economics, a master's in Public Policy, and received his Ph.D. in International Relations from the University of Munich. His research focuses on European integration and disintegration processes. His work on the topic has been published in leading journals such as the *Journal of Common Market Studies*, the *Journal of European Public Policy*, the *Journal of European Integration*, and *West European Politics*.

Abbreviations

AA	Administrative Arrangement
BoS	Board of Supervisors
CEDC	Central European Defence Cooperation
CFSP	Common Foreign and Security Policy
CSDP	Common Security and Defence Policy
DTIB	Defence Technological and Industrial Base
EATC	European Aircraft Transport Command
EC	European Community
EDA	European Defence Agency
EDEM	European Defence Equipment Market
EDTIB	European Defence Technological and Industrial Base
EEAS	European External Action Service
EII	European Intervention Initiative
EMU	European Monetary Union
EP	European Parliament
EU	European Union
EUROPA MOU	European Understandings for Research Organisation, Programmes, and Activities
FCAS	Future Combat Air System
HI	Historical Institutionalism
HR	High Representative of the Union for Foreign Affairs and Security Policy
IDET	International Defence and Security Technologies Fair
IR	International Relations
LI	Liberal Intergovernmentalism
LoI	Letter of Intent

MALE RPAS	Medium-Altitude, Long-Endurance Remotely Piloted Air System
MoD	Ministry of Defense
NAD	National Armaments Director
NATO	North Atlantic Treaty Organization
NORDEFCO	Nordic Defence Cooperation
OCCAR	Organisation Conjointe pour la Coopération en matière de l'Armement
PESCO	Permanent Structured Cooperation
PSC	Political and Security Committee
QMV	Qualified Majority Voting
R&T	Research and Technology
RCI	Rational Choice Institutionalism
SME	Small and Medium-sized Enterprise
TEU	Treaty on European Union
V4	The Visegràd Group
WEAG	Western European Armaments Group
WEAO	Western European Armaments Organization
WEU	Western European Union

List of Figures

Fig. 1.1	The regime complex of European defense	14
Fig. 2.1	Typology of interinstitutional authority relationships	55
Fig. 3.1	Go-it-alone power	73
Fig. 3.2	Membership surplus—transaction cost trade-off	79
Fig. 3.3	Theoretical pathways to interinstitutional relationships in regime complexes	84
Fig. 5.1	Process leading to the integration of the WEAG/WEAO into the EDA	113
Fig. 6.1	Process leading to the EDA's Marginalization through OCCAR	143
Fig. 6.2	OCCAR and EDA - operational budgets 2002–2012	151
Fig. 7.1	Process Leading to the fragmentation of European defense planning	170
Fig. 7.2	2010 Defense expenditure per group as percentage of total EU-27 defense spending	183
Fig. 8.1	Process leading to PESCO's resilience in light of competitive regime creation	201

List of Tables

Table 1.1	Theoretical framework	18
Table 3.1	Explanatory framework	80
Table 4.1	EU member state positions regarding deepened European defense cooperation	101
Table 4.2	EU member states' defense expenditures 2004–2016 (US $m at 2015 constant prices)	104
Table 8.1	PESCO-Projects, Lead nations (L), and Participants (P)	219

PART I

Introducing the Problem

CHAPTER 1

Introduction

In 2022, the question of how the security and defense of Europe should be organized became more topical than it had been for a long time. When Russia launched its war of aggression against Ukraine in February of that year, for many it marked a watershed moment (a *Zeitenwende*, a turning point in history, according to German Chancellor Olaf Scholz) as far as Europe's security environment was concerned. Even those member states of the European Union (EU), such as Germany itself, which had not up to then stood out as being among the most inclined to high military spending swiftly pledged to increase their defense expenditure massively (SIPRI, 2022). Besides this EU-wide impulse to step up defense spending, the outbreak of a war on the EU's border also prompted member states to reconsider and tighten their alliances. European defense had, after all, been considered a collective endeavor at least since the 1998 Anglo-French St. Malo declaration, which served as the "launch-pad" for the EU's Common Security and Defence Policy (CSDP) (Bickerton et al., 2011, see also Salmon & Shepherd, 2003; Weiss, 2011).

Interestingly, however, at the time of writing EU member states have still not turned the war situation into a window of opportunity for strengthening their Defense Union. In fact, European defense cooperation under EU auspices has not even become a hot and high-priority topic on the Brussels agenda. What we have witnessed instead has been the

© The Author(s), under exclusive license to Springer Nature Switzerland AG 2023
F. Biermann, *The Battle for Authority in European Defence Cooperation*, Palgrave Studies in European Union Politics,
https://doi.org/10.1007/978-3-031-30054-7_1

strengthening of a different security institution; the North Atlantic Treaty Organization (NATO). In the weeks preceding the outbreak of the war, it was already evident that the EU member states, not to mention EU institutions, had been sidelined by the United States and Russia (Le Monde, 2022), who were negotiating (without much success) in Geneva. Consequently, as far as the Europeans were concerned, their NATO membership soon became the only way to gain information about, and have a say in, the talks that were supposed to de-escalate the situation on the Russian/Belarusian–Ukrainian border. EU member states appeared, therefore, to have accepted a new reality—NATO is the dominant security framework for Europe. Even the traditionally neutral states, Finland and Sweden, decided to apply for NATO membership. As of 2022, the European Union appeared weaker than ever in the field of security and defense.

This raises the question of why EU member states have invested enormous effort in the creation of various European security and defense institutions only to avoid using them when the security environment actually worsens. Neorealism (Mearsheimer, 2014, 2018) seems to provide an easy answer: Whenever the security environment worsens, EU member states seek to tighten their alliance with the world's most powerful state, the US, and forget about strengthening EU institutions with the aim of achieving what Brussels (in)famously called "strategic autonomy" in security and defense (Fiott, 2018; Politico, 2021).

But such explanations are premature—for three reasons. First, it remains unclear why the Russian annexation of Crimea in 2014 did not prompt a similar institutional choice and strengthening of NATO at the expense of European security and defense institutions. The security environment, threat level, and power distributions appear inadequate to explain EU member states' institutional choices. Second, the reversal of neorealist hypotheses does not seem to hold. When the European security situation was stable and the outlook positive in the 2000s and early 2010s (Rasmussen, 2010, para. 7), attempts to strengthen European defense cooperation and create a credible European Defence Union were equally unsuccessful. Finally, and most importantly, the success and failure of European defense-institution-building should not, and cannot, be evaluated at the level of the CSDP vs. NATO. Rather, individual European defense institutions demonstrate considerable variation in their viability and effectiveness that neorealism cannot explain.

This variation is exemplified by two institutions that were supposed to be the cornerstones of the EU's security and defense: the European Defence Agency (EDA) and Permanent Structured Cooperation (PESCO). The EDA and PESCO have several similarities. First, the proposals for both institutions emerged during the European Convention and were subsequently included in the Constitutional Treaty (European Union, 2005). Second, both institutions are flexible in design, allowing for project-based differentiation in cooperation. Member states intending to work together more closely can do so without relying on the consensus of those that do not wish to participate. As instances of "differentiated integration" (Leuffen, Rittberger, & Schimmelfennig, 2013), these institutions are designed to bridge differences in member state preferences and capabilities and thus lead to convergence over time without being limited to "lowest common denominator" solutions (Moravcsik, 1993, p. 501). Preferences are especially intense in the area of security and defense, a core state power (Genschel & Jachtenfuchs, 2014), since states are deeply concerned about their national sovereignty (Koenig-Archibugi, 2004; Wagner, 2003). Third, and relatedly, both institutions were "born amid considerable controversy" (Howorth, 2004, p. 5) and contested from the outset. While some states preferred deeper EU integration and independent EU capabilities, others emphasized the primacy of NATO and were thus opposed to taking any steps that could potentially undermine the alliance. Considering their common starting situation, their similarities in timing, design, and the challenges they face, we should be able to expect both institutions to have comparable prospects of fulfilling their mandates and becoming the centers of authority in the issue area where they are supposed to operate. Yet the EDA and PESCO's institutional development, importance, and ability to fulfill their formal mandates could hardly be more different. To remedy the fragmented nature of the EU's defense sector, which was characterized by system duplication, excess capacity, interoperability problems, uncompetitive industries, and capability shortfalls (Hartley, 2011; Hill, 1993; Mölling, 2015), the EDA was created in 2004. It integrated the pre-existing Western European Union (WEU) institutions, the Western European Armaments Group (WEAG) and its subsidiary body, the Western European Armaments Organization (WEAO). It was mandated with four main tasks: to develop European defense capabilities, create a competitive European defense equipment market (EDEM), enhance the effectiveness of research and technology

(R&T) in the defense sector, and promote and enhance European armaments cooperation (Council of the European Union, Art. 3). Over the last decade, the EDA has arguably been successful in contributing to improved capabilities (Dyson & Konstadinides, 2013, 89–9) and played a role in strengthening the EDEM as well as R&T cooperation (Britz, 2010). However, when it comes to the supreme discipline of organizing Europe's hard power, armaments cooperation, the EDA has remained in the passenger's seat. Large armaments cooperation programs, such as the Tiger helicopter, the transport aircraft A-400M, or the recent undertaking to build a European drone, have consistently been organized outside its framework. Multilateral programs like those are managed within OCCAR, an exclusive institutional framework outside the EU, and thus escape control by EU institutions and the majority of EU member states. As far as its function as a European armaments agency is concerned, the EDA has been marginalized.

PESCO's development, meanwhile, has been almost the perfect inverse of the EDA's. With the Treaty of Lisbon, signed in 2007, the EU member states formally created the possibility of activating PESCO for those states "whose military capabilities fulfill higher criteria and which have made more binding commitments to one another … with a view to the most demanding missions" (European Union, 2010, Art. 52(6)). However, the member states then decided not to cooperate through PESCO but through mechanisms outside the CSDP framework, mostly in regional fora such as Nordic Defence Cooperation (NORDEFCO) or Central European Defence Cooperation (CEDC). Instead of creating a flexible but coherent institutional framework for military planning by activating PESCO, they fragmented European defense planning into a variety of bilateral and regional defense cooperation frameworks. This situation persisted for almost a decade. Only in November 2017 did the Council formally establish PESCO (Council Decision establishing Permanent Structured Cooperation (PESCO) and determining the list of Participating Member States, 2017). Despite its decades-long suppression, as soon as it was established the EU member states were able to agree on a total of 34 collaborative projects to be conducted under the PESCO framework (Council of the European Union, 2018; PESCO Member States, 2018). PESCO thus proved to be resilient and is now even considered the first step toward a European Defense Union (Reuters, 2017).

How can we account for this much variation in institutional success as demonstrated by two very similar institutions in a similar issue area? In more theoretical terms, how can we explain states' choices to use or sideline the institutions they have created? This book will answer these questions both in theoretical terms and for the EDA and PESCO specifically.

THE INNOVATION: EUROPEAN DEFENSE COOPERATION AS A REGIME COMPLEX

The key argument advanced in this book is that to explain an institution's success in terms of it being used to tackle problems that fall within its formal mandate, it is necessary to consider that institution's environment. When states decide not to use an institution, this does not imply that they forego cooperation altogether. In most cases, states make institutional choices and use alternatives instead. When EU member states decided not to use EU institutions to cooperate on defense issues, they strengthened NATO. Similarly, both the EDA and PESCO were subject to institutional competitors—the WEAG/WEAO and OCCAR in armaments cooperation, bilateral and regional frameworks such as NORDEFCO or the CEDC in the case of defense planning. The EU member states had different institutional options for cooperation. This situation, in which states have several overlapping institutions at their disposal, is specific neither to the CSDP nor to the EU. It is, in fact, part of a general trend toward an ever-denser network of international institutions that form regime complexes. Examining the EU's CSDP institutions through the lens of the burgeoning literature on regime complexity (Alter & Meunier, 2009; Alter & Raustiala, 2018; Biermann et al., 2009; Gehring & Faude, 2013, 2014; Raustiala & Victor, 2004) offers the tools to analyze specific EU institutions in relation to their institutional environment—both inside and outside the EU. This study argues that the CSDP institutions should be treated as contested international institutions in a regime complex. An analysis of their varying success in acquiring authority in relation to their competitors, benefits by employing accounts of regime complexity rather than more traditional theories of European integration, especially Liberal Intergovernmentalism (LI), (see Moravcsik,), for while LI convincingly presents analytical reasons, such as the unanimity requirement, why the CSDP institutions have generally proven largely ineffective, this literature does not account for the variation between them. I argue that the *formal-legal authority* delegated to individual CSDP institutions does not necessarily imply that any particular institution is actually used by its member states and thus possesses *relational authority* (Lake, 2009, 2010). Therefore, institutions with the same level of formal-legal authority may demonstrate different levels of relational authority. Applying the regime complexity literature to the EU and understanding the CSDP as a regime complex rather than a system of differentiated integration can add considerably to our understanding of the conflicts and dynamics characterizing cooperation in the realm of European defense.

Researching the CSDP—Filling the Gaps

This book adds a new perspective to research into the EU's security and defense policy, which, during the last 30 years, has been driven by a desire to identify the gaps between the EU's soft and hard power (Hyde-Price, 2006; Manners, 2002), or between what it was expected to do and what it was able to agree on doing (Hill, 1993; Toje, 2008). Consequently, the creation of the CSDP and its institutions have often been analyzed in relation to its ability to narrow these gaps. However, the CSDP's success in this regard remains subject to contradictory evaluations. I argue that the existing literature focusing on the EU member states' ability to agree neglects an important aspect: variation in the actual use of the respective CSDP institutions, constituting its relational—and relative—authority (Lake, 2009, pp. 28–33).

In 1993, Christopher Hill identified the often-quoted "capabilities–expectations gap" between the EU's—at that time, the European Community's (EC)—foreign and security policy ambitions and its actual ability to pursue them. He described the EC's capability shortfall along three dimensions: the ability to agree, resource availability, and the political instruments at its disposal (Hill, 1993, p. 315). Even though Hill remained vague as to exactly whose expectations remain unfulfilled, it is hard to deny that the EU's security and defense policy regime during the 1990s proved largely ineffective in coping with conflicts and crises even in Europe's immediate neighborhood. The EU's heavy reliance on US support in dealing with the Yugoslav Wars is a case in point.

It was not only the lessons learned from these sobering experiences that prompted EU member states to agree to make their security and defense policy more efficient (Shepherd, 2015, p. 67) and to take steps to close this gap. They were subject to enormous functional pressure to rationalize and modernize their national defense and security sectors due to exploding technology costs (Augustine, 1997), shrinking defense budgets (Platteau, 2015), increasing competition on the international defense market (Gholz & Sapolsky, 2000), and a changing international security situation that brought new threats such as hybrid warfare, terrorism, cyberwar, and humanitarian crises.

EU member states and their respective defense industries have therefore faced an increasing demand for cooperation (Weiss & Biermann, 2018). Since the late 1990s, after years of defense-industrial and military cooperation in various institutional setups outside the EU, including NATO, the member states have been trying to establish a European framework to organize coherent security and defense capability building. By creating a European Defence Technological and Industrial Base (EDTIB) with harmonized standards, interoperable systems, and a competitive EDEM, they attempted to establish affordable and effective European security of supply that would stop them having to rely on imports.

In this connection, the Franco-British St. Malo Declaration served as a "launch-pad" for the EU's CSDP (Bickerton et al., 2011). First established as the European Security and Defence Policy by the Nice Treaty of 2001, it had its name changed to the *Common* Security and Defence Policy by the Lisbon Treaty of 2007. Scholarly evaluation of the CSDP's significance is mixed. Views range from descriptions of the CSDP as potentially "one of the most significant transformations in recent world politics" (Weiss, 2011, p. 3) to the perception that it "achieved little more than the creation of a new layer in the EU's already complex institutional system" (Rynning, 2011, p. 24). How can these contradicting evaluations of the new institutional framework be explained?

European integration theory contributes to a better understanding of these diverging accounts. Börzel (2005) highlights the distinction between the "level" and "scope" of integration, which can account for some of the ambivalence in judgments concerning the CSDP. Integration can evolve unevenly along these two dimensions (Börzel, 2005, p. 231). The delegation of decision-making to EU institutions and the pooling of decision-making within them do not necessarily go hand in hand (Hooghe & Marks, 2015). While the member states have relocated the regulation of European defense cooperation to the EU level, the CSDP is almost purely intergovernmental; supranational actors such as the European Commission, the European Parliament (EP), or the European Court of Justice (ECJ) hardly play any role.[1] This implies that decision-making is almost exclusively organized by unanimity vote in the Council and its subordinate bodies such as the Political and Security Committee (PSC). With the formal establishment of the CSDP framework and the agreement on new EU-level institutions such as the EDA and PESCO, EU member states have thus created the institutional potential to consolidate their security and defense.

However, focusing on the *ability to decide* on the efficient production and use of joint capabilities, in other words on the scope of integration, presents a different picture. With the establishment of the CSDP, the "capabilities–expectations gap" referred to above has been transformed into a "consensus–expectations gap" (Toje, 2008). While the EU may have made "notable improvements in terms of its resource availability, as well as the instruments at its disposal," its ability to agree has not been enhanced (Toje, 2008, p. 121). The intergovernmental character of the CSDP, with its requirements for unanimity and its tendency to deliver lowest common denominator outcomes (Moravcsik, 1993), has promoted a gap "between what the EU member-states are expected to do in the world and what they are actually able to agree upon" (Toje, 2008, p. 122). By creating the CSDP, the EU member states transferred a significant share of defense-related authority to the European level. For all that, as many scholars have correctly pointed out, policymaking in the realm of the CSDP remains largely intergovernmental (Dyson & Konstadinides, 2013; Rynning, 2011) and is very likely to stay that way (Wagner, 2003).

Importantly, with the Treaty of Lisbon EU member states created the institutional potential for defense- and security-related cooperation at the EU level that allows for *flexible cooperation*. The EDA and the PESCO framework in particular can be understood as tools for differentiated integration (Leuffen et al., 2013), inasmuch as they were established to allow groups of willing member states to intensify their cooperation without relying on the unanimity requirement. This, at least formally,

---

[1] There is some evidence to the contrary, however, which suggests an increasing influence of the European Commission in the realm of security and defense. This evidence will be discussed in the next chapter where a neofunctionalist account of defense integration is presented.

facilitates the decision-making process by overcoming stalemates in situations where state preferences diverge. This *variable geometry* approach, which allows for both horizontal (membership) and vertical (degree of pooling) differentiation across policy areas and institutions (Biermann, 2022; Schimmelfennig et al., 2015), can be interpreted as an attempt to narrow the consensus–expectations gap.

But when it comes to explaining why the EDA has never been used as an armaments procurement agency and why PESCO was only activated a decade after its formal creation, the limits of liberal intergovernmentalism become apparent. While the "consensus–expectations gap" can contribute to explaining why there is no single joint procurement project in the EDA involving *all member states*, it cannot establish why no EDA procurement project involving only a *group of willing member states* exists either. OCCAR, an exclusive, 6-member[2] organization outside the EU, manages these procurement projects. The same holds for PESCO, where unanimity was never required to activate the framework. Nonetheless, for a decade, the EU member states preferred to establish new frameworks outside the treaties before PESCO eventually gained new momentum in 2017. In other words, even though groups of EU member states were willing to cooperate, the flexible CSDP institutions were not always used.

Beyond the question of whether creating the CSDP institutions in the first place was not an achievement in itself, we should ask whether an institution that is potentially endowed with the formal-legal authority to regulate an issue area also possesses the relational authority to do so—relational authority being understood as "a political construct created and sustained through practice" (Lake, 2009, p. 20) that is additional to the formal authority granted to the institution. An institution's de facto authority, its ability to fulfill its mandate, actually depends on its member states' willingness to make use of it, to allocate their political and financial resources to it. Thus, at least for some institutions, there seems to be a third gap between their formal and relational authority.

Broadening the Perspective, Sharpening the Focus

By asserting that the divergence between the level of and scope for integration is the main factor behind inefficiencies in the CSDP, integration

---

[2] The members of OCCAR are Belgium, France, Germany, Italy, Spain and the United Kingdom.

theory overlooks one of the most important realities in European defense cooperation: There is a lot of cooperation going on; it simply does not always take place inside the EU framework. Armament cooperation is organized in OCCAR, and during PESCO's period of deep sleep, defense planning was coordinated regionally. These alternative institutions outside the EU possessed relational authority, while the CSDP institutions were only loci of formal-legal authority. An exclusive focus on EU institutions and neglect of cooperation frameworks outside the EU has prevented us from understanding the conditions under which an institution is actually used in accordance with its mandate. To explain why the EDA never gained a foothold in armaments cooperation while PESCO finally became the center of authority in defense planning, I argue that it is necessary to broaden the perspective offered by liberal intergovernmentalism and to consider international institutions beyond the EU.

Building on prior attempts to pin down the consequences of regime complexity for the CSDP in general (Hofmann, 2009, 2011, 2018), I argue that it is necessary to sharpen the focus on the level of the "elemental" (i.e., constituent) (Raustiala & Victor, 2004, p. 279), institutions of the European defense policy complex. Treating the CSDP as a unitary alternative to NATO, as has been done, and thus neglecting the various bi- and minilateral cooperation frameworks outside these two regimes does not allow for a detailed understanding of the elemental institutions' relative positions in the institutional environment. We need a broadening of perspective as compared to European integration theory (and to consider institutional alternatives beyond the European Union). We also need a sharpening of the regime complexity literature's focus to determine the differences in the relative authority of elemental institutions. Only then will we be able to observe the variation in authority distributions across different regime complexes and, in a second step, to theorize the conditions under which a specific institution that is added to a complex becomes the new center of authority in an issue area.

Stephanie Hofmann's (2009, 2011, 2018) work emphasizes the need to consider the "institutional environment" when trying to explain the existence and design of the CSDP (Hofmann, 2011, p. 102). She demonstrates that the overlap in mandate, membership, and resources of the CSDP and NATO "matter[s]" (Hofmann, 2011), as it crucially influences the effectiveness of both institutions. Drawing attention to interinstitutional relations, which are mediated by their member states (Hofmann, 2018), is important for understanding the dynamics at play when states decide which is their preferred institutional setting for cooperation. Member states differ in being either single or multiple members, that is, members of only one institution or of several. Being a multiple member enables states to engage in additional strategies, such as forum shopping or hostage taking, which they can pursue in order to shape cooperation and enhance or reduce institutions' effectiveness (Hofmann, 2018).

Hofmann's broad focus on the CSDP as a unitary institution, however, runs the risk of overlooking variation between the elemental institutions in the complex. Focusing on the EU–NATO dichotomy and thereby cutting out the various institutions outside the EU and NATO – OCCAR as a competitor to the EDA or the Nordic Defense Cooperation (NORDEFCO) as a competitor to PESCO, for example—obscures the important differences in the relative positions of CSDP institutions within the institutional landscape. The European defense complex not only consists of two overlapping regimes, the CSDP and NATO, but has an architecture consisting of many overlapping elemental institutions. These can be bi- and multilateral agreements, such as the Franco-British Lancaster House Treaty and PESCO, or international organizations, such as the EDA or OCCAR.

Thus, in order to capture the variation in relative position across the elemental institutions of the European defense complex, in other words, to investigate where and why cooperation takes place, it is necessary to sharpen the focus while retaining a view of the complex as a whole (Fig. 1.1). Only then can we observe the competitors faced by every elemental institution and see that the relational authority that stems from an institution's actual use is, in fact, a relative concept and the collective outcome of member states' interaction in regime complexes. Whenever a specific institution is used, that choice implies the non-use of an equally mandated competitor. Broadening the perspective and sharpening the focus of the existing literature on the CSDP allows us to find an answer to why the EDA and PESCO demonstrated varying levels of authority relative to their competitors at different points in time. It is not sufficient to investigate the EU member states' diverging preferences for and against European integration. Rather we have to consider their institutional choices from a set of available alternatives (Jupille et al., 2013).

If the EDA and PESCO are understood as being subject to institutional competitors outside the European Union, including—but not limited to—NATO, the question of why European security and

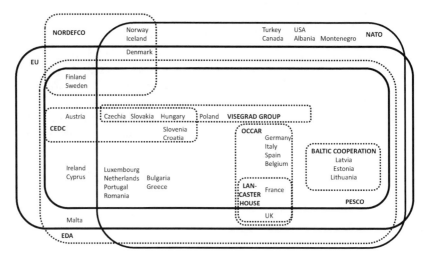

Fig. 1.1 The regime complex of European defense[3]

defense institutions demonstrate varying degrees of success in fulfilling their mandates—why, that is, they possess different levels of relational authority—offers a new perspective on the study of the EU's CSDP. It allows basic regime complexes to be delineated that consist of two or more institutions with overlapping mandates and "rival authority claims" (Alter & Raustiala, 2018, p. 332) to govern a specific issue area at different points in time. The EU member states have added new institutions to the landscape and removed others from the emerging complex. Therefore, using the lens of regime complexity and contested multilateralism to study the European defense policy complex contributes to an in-depth understanding of the interinstitutional dynamics at the level of the elemental institutions in the complex and enables us to observe differences in the distribution of authority between them as well.

---

[3] Cf. Fauré (2017). For simplicity's sake, only those frameworks that will be dealt with during the empirical analysis are included.

The Theoretical Argument in Brief

Institutions in regime complexes such as PESCO and NORDEFCO on the one hand and the EDA, the WEAG, and OCCAR on the other exercise varying degrees of authority in the issue areas in which they operate. While some institutions are regularly used by states and thus become focal points within a complex (Jupille et al., 2013, p. 27), others are neglected by their members and find themselves relegated to the margins. If such uneven patterns of use are perpetuated, different distributions of authority emerge. They range from instances in which one institution hierarchically subordinates its alternatives to instances in which elemental institutions co-exist in a non-hierarchical and uncoordinated relationship. My claim that regime complexes vary in their distribution of authority, which may (but does not necessarily) lead to hierarchical relationships between elemental institutions, adds to a small but growing strand in the regime complexity literature that emphasizes authority relations among institutions (Daßler, 2022; Faude & Fuss, 2020; Henning & Pratt, 2020; Pratt, 2018).

By regime complexes I specifically mean situations in which at least two institutions are mandated, and thus have the formal-legal authority (Lake, 2009), to operate in an issue area. Beyond the claim that "regime complexity is, at its core, about how diverse elemental institutions establish overlapping and (potentially) rival authority claims regarding international governance" (Alter & Raustiala, 2018, p. 332), I take regime complexes as the starting point of my research and inquire into the possible outcomes of the authority distributions that emerge in these complexes. I argue that the distribution of "relational authority" (Lake, 2009, pp. 28–33) across the elemental institutions in a regime complex can constitute different interinstitutional relationships. This book, therefore, engages with two theoretical questions: *What types of authority distribution can emerge in regime complexes, and which pathways lead to each particular type?*

Types of Interinstitutional Relations

Situations of contested multilateralism are the origin of regime complexity as I understand it. Dissatisfied coalitions of states that are unable to reform an institution from within engage in competitive regime creation or regime shifting to challenge the institutional status quo (Morse &

Keohane, 2014); a regime complex emerges when two elemental institutions with overlapping mandates govern the same issue area. Taking a regime complex defined in this way as a *starting point*, overlap in membership and resources can vary. This variation contributes to different distributions of authority between the elemental institutions within the complex. Overlaps in membership and resources constitute patterns of institutional use and can thus influence the amount of relational authority an institution has in an issue area. As overlap varies across regime complexes, the distribution of authority between the elemental institutions varies too. Authority can be distributed evenly or unevenly across institutions. Some complexes may thus be characterized by a center of authority, while others are fragmented. A regime complex can display hierarchical relationships between the institutions of which it consists. This is the case when an elemental institution becomes central, has the bulk of financial and political resources at its disposal, and is accepted by both single and multiple members. Based on these considerations, I develop a typology of the dependent variable, namely the authority distributions between the institutions of the complex.

Four types of relationships can emerge in a basic regime complex consisting of a pre-existing institution and its newly created institutional competitor. Elemental institutions with separate memberships and resources are typical of a *fragmented* relationship. There is no—formal or informal—hierarchy among the elemental institutions, as all the members are single members using the only institution to which they belong. If, by contrast, the two elemental institutions are *integrated*, they have identical membership and pooled resources, and authority is centralized in a formal hierarchical framework. Finally, there are two intermediate cases. In a situation where membership and resources overlap, relational authority over the issue area is distributed unevenly, making one institution focal while sidelining the other. There are single and dual members who are interested in coordinating the institutions in a way that makes their preferred venue the center of relational authority in the complex. Two semi-hierarchical (Keohane & Victor, 2011) types are possible. Either the original institution is sidelined, while the newly created alternative becomes focal (*marginalization*), or the originally contested institution is refocused, while its competitor withers (*resilience*).

Causal Pathways to Authority Distributions

When dissatisfied states engage in competitive regime creation to challenge an institutional status quo, this challenger coalition has an interest in turning its newly created alternative into the new center of authority, while the defenders of the original institution prefer the *status quo ante*. Accordingly, I argue that the dynamic interaction between challengers and defenders of the institutional status quo determines the subsequent distribution of authority between the two overlapping institutions. In line with Rational Choice Institutionalism (Axelrod, 1984; Hall & Taylor, 1996; Keohane, 1984; Koremenos et al., 2001), I present a state-centric theory of strategic interaction within regime complexes, specifying the conditions under which either integration, fragmentation, marginalization or resilience is to be expected.

In short, I argue that the particular type of authority distribution that emerges in a complex depends on the go-it-alone power (Gruber, 2000) and membership preference (Thompson & Verdier, 2014) of the dissatisfied challenger coalition. First, I predicate that different outcomes are the result of the varying influence state coalitions have on the overall distribution of resources among institutions (Colgan et al., 2012). This influence depends on the challenger coalition's go-it-alone power (Gruber, 2000), which determines its ability to present the defenders of the status quo with a credible threat of exclusion. This power helps to explain why defenders of the status quo end up accepting, and even trying to join, a new institution, despite its being detrimental to their utility. In other words, go-it-alone power is the condition that determines whether a newly created institutional competitor can become the new center of authority, the focal institution in the issue area—even if it goes against the original preferences of the defender states.

Second, I contend that the challengers' membership preference depends on the ratio between the costs of inclusion and exclusion (Thompson & Verdier, 2014; Williamson, 1985). When the costs of including additional members are high (e.g., when there are distributive concerns and a high risk of free riding), the challenger coalition will prefer an exclusive institution to an inclusive one. When the costs of inclusion are low and the network effects are strong (e.g., if the institution governs regulatory issues, such as standard setting), the challengers will prefer inclusive membership. Membership preference thus determines whether the challengers are willing to accept the defenders as members of the institutional competitor.

Triggered by the challenger's creation of a competitive regime, the combination of the challenger's ability to create a credible threat of exclusion and their membership preference will determine the pathway leading to one of the four distinct authority distributions between the institutions of a complex. The two conditions combined will account for whether the two entities have separate, identical, or overlapping membership and resources (see Table 1.1). What is more, when the two institutions overlap in membership and resources, the two conditions can explain which of the two fora will become focal.

Only challenger coalitions possessing the power to go it alone successfully turn their institutional alternative into a new center of authority. In other words, only if powerful coalitions engage in contestation will the outcome be integration or the marginalization of the original institution to the benefit of the competitor. This supports prior research on the effects of regime complexity: It seems to benefit the most powerful by offering them the ability to create and select their most preferred venue (Benvenisti & Downs, 2007; Drezner, 2009, 2013). Yet my framework offers a more nuanced approach. While state coalitions that lack go-it-alone power have difficulties creating a new center of authority, they still have the means to challenge the institutional status quo in a sustainable way and block cooperation they deem detrimental. This is the case when they have an exclusive membership preference. Institutional fragmentation as an outcome can be an improvement for less powerful states that have not profited from cooperation in the pre-existing institution.

My theoretical approach unpacks the dynamics enshrined in the interplay of states' power and preferences when struggling for the authority of their preferred institutions. This approach has two advantages. First,

Table 1.1 Theoretical framework

		Challengers' Membership Preference	
		Inclusive	*Exclusive*
Challengers create a Threat of Exclusion	Yes	Integration	Marginalization
	No	Resilience	Fragmentation

the framework widens the scope of the regime complexity literature by including and explaining the emergence of hierarchical and semi-hierarchical orders. Second, by specifying the pathways leading to the distinct authority distributions in regime complexes, the latter appear less complicated, less contingent, and thus more predictable than they used to be.

Analyzing the CSDP through the lens of contested multilateralism and regime complexity, I contribute not only to the scholarly literature on European security and defense cooperation but, as importantly, to the literature on regime complexes. Developing a framework for the interinstitutional relationships emerging in such complexes, I work toward reducing the intricacy connected with the complexity and making regularities visible.

The Empirical Findings in Brief

The empirical part of this book applies the theoretical framework to the regime complex of European defense cooperation and thereby tests its explanatory power. Combining a congruence analysis (Blatter & Haverland, 2012) with theory-testing causal process tracing (Beach & Pedersen, 2013) enables me to achieve a dual objective. Through causal process tracing, I can make within-case inferences to enhance the internal validity of the theoretical framework, while the congruence analysis allows me to control for alternative explanations and thus strengthen the framework's external validity. Applying the framework to both the EDA and PESCO to explain the variation in their development and their success in becoming the focal institution in their complex necessitates dividing their geneses into two cases each.

The four case studies thus consist of

1) The integration of the WEAG/WEAO structures into the EDA (1997–2004)
2) The marginalization of the EDA through OCCAR (2004–2012)
3) The fragmentation of European defense planning (2007–2016)
4) PESCO's resilience (2016–2018)

As the empirical analysis will demonstrate in detail, the two conditions—the presence or absence of the challengers' go-it-alone power on the one hand and their inclusive or exclusive membership preference on the other—can explain the different outcomes of authority relations and, thus, the relative positions of the EDA and PESCO in their respective complexes at different points in time.

Integration: The WEAG/WEAO and the EDA

The pathway to integrating the WEAG/WEAO into the EDA was laid down when a powerful coalition of six dissatisfied states found a way to develop the WEAO into a European armaments agency blocked and consequently decided to create an institutional alternative, the EDA. While the remaining EU member states, due to their relatively uncompetitive defense-industrial bases, preferred minimal cooperation within the pre-existing WEAG/WEAO structures, they finally joined the EDA as well. The powerful coalition's initiative and ability to create a credible threat of exclusion by demonstrating their ability to organize cooperation exclusively among themselves erased the non-cooperative status quo from the set of feasible alternatives. Consequently, for the defenders of the status quo, joining the EDA was better than being excluded from defense cooperation altogether.

Integration only occurs if the memberships of the contested and the competing institutions are close to identical, so that maintaining both institutions provides no benefit for any dual member. EDA's powerful proponents demonstrated an unequivocal preference for an inclusive EDA membership. They relinquished entry barriers, introduced a safeguard mechanism allowing the outsiders to vote down any prospective collaborative program, and promised the dissolution of the exclusive OCCAR and LoI frameworks in the medium term. Thus, the EDA's proponents made considerable concessions to convince the maximum number of states to join.

Both conditions together determined the outcome of the WEAG/WEAO defenders joining the EDA. Their willingness to join when faced with the alternative of being excluded and the incentives provided by the EDA's proponents convinced even the least competitive state to join and thus led to EDA's unanimous creation. As all eligible WEAG/WEAO member states became members of the EDA, keeping both institutions was inefficient. Thus, within months of EDA's inception in July 2004, both the WEAG and the WEAO were dissolved, and their tasks and resources were integrated into the EDA, which then was supposed to develop into the new center of authority in European defense cooperation.

Marginalization: The EDA and OCCAR

The EDA's subsequent marginalization through OCCAR was triggered by the same states that pushed the EDA's creation in the first place. This group was no longer willing to keep its promise to incorporate OCCAR into the EDA. This promise had been issued on the false premise that the powerful coalition would act in concert. Yet any attempt to scale up the EDA was torpedoed not only by the defenders of the original WEAO/WEAG but also by the United Kingdom. Dissatisfied with the functioning of the EDA and unable to induce reforms, the challenger coalition shifted its focus to OCCAR, which, as a result of its exclusive membership, was better suited to their needs.

As OCCAR members represented more than 80% of the EU's defense spending,[4] being out of OCCAR meant being excluded from the bulk of defense-industrial cooperation. States with a single EDA membership consequently attempted to join OCCAR as well. However, in view of the distributive implications of managing armaments contracts for national budgets, OCCAR members faced high costs from including additional members and preferred OCCAR to remain an exclusive club. Nevertheless, they were interested in the EDA's continued existence as a framework for identifying capability gaps and setting standards, and as a marketing platform. They therefore suggested an administrative arrangement between the two institutions that would formalize their coordination in a way that cemented OCCAR's focality on armaments cooperation. While this certainly went against the less powerful states' original preferences, they agreed to it. Cutting their losses and accepting OCCAR's primacy, as far as they were concerned, signified access to cooperation in armaments programs on the margins of the production chain instead of being sidelined altogether. Consequently, OCCAR emerged as the focal institution in the field of armaments cooperation, while the EDA was marginalized.

---

[4] Military Expenditure 2016, source: SIPRI Milex data 1949–2016, available at: https://www.sipri.org/databases/milex.

Fragmentation: PESCO and Regional Defense Cooperation

Analyzing the genesis of PESCO, a flexible institution allowing a coalition of the willing to engage in deeper cooperation in the realm of defense planning and military cooperation, shows that similar dynamics were at play. While some states actively supported it, others opposed the concept from the very start. PESCO could, on the one hand, have undermined NATO's primacy and have increased the dependency of less competitive states on the EU's major powers on the other. The need for defense cooperation increased in light of the Euro crisis, which put national defense budgets under strain. The opposing states prevented PESCO's activation and revived regional cooperation frameworks outside the EU or founded new ones to organize cooperation among like-minded and homogenous countries.

Given their negligible economic and military weight, these frameworks did not create a threat of exclusion to proponents of PESCO—joining these frameworks would not have offered a large potential for savings or enhanced capabilities. Nevertheless, the opposing states were able to sustain regional cooperation because their regional frameworks were backed by NATO security guarantees, which decreased the cost of non-agreement within the EU. They had an exclusive membership preference and no interest in admitting additional members to the institutions they created.

The sustainable blockage of PESCO forced its proponents to find alternative options for cooperation, given pressurized budgets. The result was several bi- and minilateral frameworks with overlapping mandates to organize joint military planning. None of these numerous frameworks had the potential to attract new members, and no state coalition was able to dictate the terms of coordination among the institutions in the defense-planning complex. This stalemate found expression in a persistent situation of fragmented authority: While the institutions overlapped in the mandate, they had separated memberships and resources and coexisted independently. No center of authority emerged, and institutional fragmentation was locked into a stable equilibrium.

Resilience: PESCO Withstanding Competition

PESCO's activation in 2017 was the result of two external shocks, Brexit and the election of Donald Trump, which both influenced the two key conditions, the power to go it alone and the membership preference. While none of the regional cooperation frameworks posed a threat of exclusion to PESCO's proponents, the UK's decision to leave the EU distorted the balance of power that had emerged between the Europeanist proponents and Atlanticist opponents of PESCO. Blocking PESCO became increasingly difficult for the remaining Atlanticists, as their veto power was undermined. The election of Donald Trump thus brought about a turnaround from fragmentation to resilience as far as PESCO was concerned. NATO's credibility suffered considerably, so PESCO's opponents could no longer rely on their exclusive regional cooperation frameworks. Their membership preference changed from exclusive to inclusive and regional cooperation lost its attractiveness.

This situation opened the window of opportunity that PESCO's proponents had been waiting for. They were able to pull the Atlanticists into participation in PESCO. Its Europeanist proponents proposed to establish a European defense core and thereby create a threat of exclusion themselves. While they could have set more ambitious entry criteria, they refrained from doing so, as Germany especially demonstrated a strong preference for inclusive membership. One after the other, the Atlanticists accepted PESCO's role as the focal institution in the complex. They did so against their original preferences, but lacked alternatives. Blocking PESCO was no longer an option, and staying outside would have been even worse for their defense industries and military capabilities than becoming members of an institution they had previously opposed.

This resulted in PESCO's formal activation in December. EU member states participating in PESCO shifted the bulk of their resources to the framework while neglecting PESCO's institutional competitors. This shift made PESCO the center of authority in European defense planning. A decade after its codification, PESCO finally proved resilient to contestation.

Confronting Alternative Explanations

While the four case studies demonstrate that the theoretical framework can account for the distinct authority relations in the CSDP, I have undertaken a congruence analysis to rule out bias in my approach. Contrasting my framework with two theoretical contenders is good practice that requires "the exclusion of rival explanations" (Gehring & Oberthür, 2009, p. 130) and considerably increases confidence in the external validity of the framework. The explanations I test derive from neorealism and neofunctionalism. Neorealism is the elephant in the room throughout this book. When discussing international security and defense in International Relations (IR), to unwittingly neglect geopolitics is inadvisable. NATO and the US hegemon are always looming in the background. Neofunctionalism is another serious challenger to the rationalist framework I advance, even though defense cooperation in the EU has been largely intergovernmental. Scholarship on the CSDP argues that the European Commission has had considerable influence on the development of this policy area (Blauberger & Weiss, 2013; Fiott, 2015; Weiss & Blauberger, 2015). Recently established supranational facilities, such as the European Defense Fund, also point in this direction (Haroche, 2019).

First, I examine neorealist theorizing of the CSDP, as exemplified by Dyson and Konstadinides (2013), Rosato (2011), Posen (2006), and Jones (2003), who build on a defensive reading of structural realism (Schweller, 1994; Waltz, 1979). This strand of theory expects progress or stagnation in European defense cooperation to depend on whether EU member states navigate the alliance security dilemma (Snyder, 1984)by engaging in bandwagoning or balancing behavior (Dyson & Konstadinides, 2013). "Balancing" involves creating independent EU military capabilities; "bandwagoning" means relying on NATO. An evaluation of the empirical evidence reveals that neorealism overemphasizes US power as the driving force behind EU institution-building, while underestimating intra-EU bargaining dynamics and more nuanced member state preferences for inclusive or exclusive cooperation. This approach, therefore, has difficulties in accounting for EU member states' varying institutional choices at the level of individual institutions beyond the EU–NATO dichotomy.

Second, I confront neofunctionalist expectations emerging from the key concepts of functional, political, and cultivated spillovers (Haas, 1961, 2004, 1958; Haroche, 2019; Niemann, 1998; Niemann & Schmittner, 2009; Stone Sweet & Sandholtz, 1997). Neofunctionalist theorizing would expect the EDA and PESCO to be established and regularly used if functional pressure for pooling and delegation was high and supranational actors incentivized the member states to do so. Discussing the evidence demonstrates that neofunctionalism overestimates supranational entrepreneurship and the importance of functional pressure while neglecting (intergovernmental bargaining) power. Hence, this theory struggles to explain instances of non-integration and interinstitutional contestation.

While the explanatory framework I present is not a synthesis of these two theoretical competitors, it is still commensurable with the insights provided by both. As such, while parsimonious, the explanatory power of my framework goes beyond both alternative explanations. Understanding the CSDP as a regime complex emerging from contestation and taking institutional alternatives beyond both the EU and NATO into account provides a convincing explanation for the variation observed. An institution's relative position in an emerging complex depends on its go-it-alone power and the membership preference of the challengers of the institutional status quo.

Summing up, to evaluate the success or failure of the CSDP in organizing European defense cooperation, it is advisable to analyze it based on its individual institutions, that is, to treat it as part of a regime complex. Only when one asks what mechanisms make one institution focal while others are neglected do the basic frictions between EU member states become visible. The analysis shows that differences in strategic cultures and the competitiveness of defense industries drive substantial preference divergence among EU member states, which leads in turn to battles for authority among their preferred institutions. The EDA and PESCO suffer from these conflicts and are thus ill-equipped to provide the structures for a well-functioning EDTIB. Consequently, it is not surprising that in 2022 even those Europeanist states that had a vital interest in European armaments cooperation and strong EU capabilities reflexively focused on NATO as the number one security institution.

Indeed, this book argues that to understand the present and future of European defense cooperation, it is necessary to examine its past. Analyzing and explaining EU member states' most important institutional choices in European defense and armaments cooperation over the last 25 years allows varying levels of institutional success and failure to be comprehended and contributes to our understanding of why the current weakness of European institutions is not contingent on the war in Ukraine. Instead, it appears that the decision in favor of NATO structures is endogenous to the problematic European integration process in defense cooperation.

Plan of the Book

The book has four parts. This first part has introduced the research problem. Part II now goes on to develop the explanatory framework: Chapter 2 discusses the scope conditions for both the conceptualization and the causal framework before developing a typology of authority distribution in regime complexes on the basis of its four manifestations: integration, marginalization, resilience, and fragmentation. Chapter 3 specifies the pathways to the individual authority relationships. It analyzes the role of power in contested multilateralism and proposes go-it-alone power as a key concept determining the collective outcomes of authority distribution. Additionally, it discusses the membership preferences of states that challenge the institutional status quo. Subsequently, it combines the two conditions to develop the theoretical pathways linking the emergence of a regime complex through contestation with the outcomes of authority distributions.

Part III comprises a brief chapter on the methodological approach (Chapter 4) and the empirical Chapters 5 to 8, which present the four causal-process-tracing case studies—the WEAG/WEAO integration into the EDA (Chapter 5), the EDA's marginalization through OCCAR (Chapter 6), the fragmentation of European defense planning (Chapter 7), and PESCO's resilience (Chapter 8). All four follow a similar pattern and demonstrate how the trigger, competitive regime creation, led to a particular authority relationship. The first section of each of these chapters is given over to demonstrating that the scope conditions and trigger were present, while the subsequent sections examine the causal pathway to the particular interinstitutional relationship. The second section examines the challenger's ability or inability to generate a credible threat of exclusion and its consequences; the third provides evidence of the causal force of its (in- or exclusive) membership preference; the final section shows how the respective combination of these two conditions caused the specific authority relationship.

Part IV of the book discusses the theoretical framework and empirical evidence in light of the two other theoretical contenders and the most recent developments in the European security and defense complex. In Chapter 9, I conduct a congruence analysis contrasting the explanatory power of the rational-choice institutionalist framework built around the power and preferences of both challengers and defenders of the institutional status quo with the alternative explanations provided by neorealism and neofunctionalism. Re-evaluating the evidence demonstrates that both neorealism and neofunctionalism add important insights to the empirical subject, but neither of them provides a convincing account of the development of the EDA's and PESCO's relative authority.

Finally, Chapter 10 brings all the threads together by summarizing the findings and pinning down their implications for the literature on regime complexity and European integration. It also revisits the most recent developments in the relationship between the EU and NATO and discusses how this book paves the way for future research on regime complexes beyond the EU and on the endogenous stability or otherwise of the four outcomes. In the same vein, the book ends with a look ahead to the future development of the EU's CSDP.

REFERENCES

Alter, K. J., & Meunier, S. (2009). The politics of international regime complexity. *Perspectives on Politics, 7*(01), 13–24. https://doi.org/10.1017/S1537592709090033

Alter, K. J., & Raustiala, K. (2018). The rise of international regime complexity. *Annual Review of Law and Social Science, 14*(1), 329–349. https://doi.org/10.1146/annurev-lawsocsci-101317-030830

Augustine, N. R. (1997). *Augustine's laws* (6th ed.). American Institute of Aeronautics and Astronautics.

Axelrod, R. M. (1984). *The evolution of cooperation*. Basic Books.

Beach, D., & Pedersen, R. B. (2013). *Process-tracing methods: Foundations and guidelines*. Ann Arbor, Mich.: University of Michigan Press. http://site.ebrary.com/lib/subhamburg/Doc?id=10658497

Benvenisti, E., & Downs, G. W. (2007). The emperor's new clothes: Political economy and the fragmentation of international law. *Stanford Law Review, 60*(2), 595–632.

Bickerton, C. J., Irondelle, B., & Menon, A. (2011). Security co-operation beyond the nation-state: The EU's common security and defence policy. *JCMS: Journal of Common Market Studies, 49*(1), 1–21. https://doi.org/10.1111/j.1468-5965.2010.02126.x

Biermann, F. (2022). The differentiation paradox of European Integration: Why going it alone produces suboptimal results. *JCMS: Journal of Common Market Studies*, Early view. https://doi.org/10.1111/jcms.13373

Biermann, F., Pattberg, P., van Asselt, H., & Zelli, F. (2009). The fragmentation of global governance architectures: A framework for analysis. *Global Environmental Politics, 9*(4), 14–40. https://doi.org/10.1162/glep.2009.9.4.14

Blatter, J., & Haverland, M. (2012). *Designing case studies: Explanatory approaches in small-N research.* Palgrave Macmillan.

Blauberger, M., & Weiss, M. (2013). 'If you can't beat me, join me! ' How the Commission pushed and pulled member states into legislating defence procurement. *Journal of European Public Policy, 20*(8), 1120–1138. https://doi.org/10.1080/13501763.2013.781783

Börzel, T. A. (2005). Mind the gap! European integration between level and scope. *Journal of European Public Policy, 12*(2), 217–236. https://doi.org/10.1080/13501760500043860

Britz, M. (2010). The role of marketization in the Europeanization of Defense Industry Policy. *Bulletin of Science, Technology & Society, 30*(3), 176–184. https://doi.org/10.1177/0270467610367492

Colgan, J. D., Keohane, R. O., & van de Graaf, T. (2012). Punctuated equilibrium in the energy regime complex. *The Review of International Organizations, 7*(2), 117–143. https://doi.org/10.1007/s11558-011-9130-9

Council Decision establishing Permanent Structured Cooperation (PESCO) and determining the list of Participating Member States, *Official Journal of the European Union* (2017).

Council of the European Union. (2018). *Council Decision establishing the list of projects to be developed under PESCO* (Legislative Acts and other Instruments No. 6393/18). http://data.consilium.europa.eu/doc/document/ST-6393-2018-INIT/en/pdf

Daßler, B. (2022). Good(s) for everyone? Policy area competition and institutional topologies in the regime complexes of tax avoidance and intellectual property. *Journal of International Relations and Development, 54*(3), 421. https://doi.org/10.1057/s41268-022-00267-x

Drezner, D. W. (2009). The power and peril of international regime complexity. *Perspectives on Politics, 7*(01), 65–70. https://doi.org/10.1017/S1537592709090100

Drezner, D. W. (2013). The tragedy of the global institutional commons. In J. Goldstein & M. Finnemore (Eds.), *Back to basics: State power in a contemporary world* (pp. 280–310). Oxford University Press. https://doi.org/10.1093/acprof:oso/9780199970087.003.0013

Dyson, T., & Konstadinides, T. (2013). *European defence cooperation in EU law and IR theory.* Palgrave Macmillan.

European Union. (2005). *Treaty establishing a constitution for Europe.* Office for Official Publ. of the Europ. Communities. http://europa.eu.int/constitution/index_en.htm

European Union. (2010). *Consolidated versions of the treaty on European Union and of the treaty on the functioning of the European Union: Charter of fundamental rights of the European Union.* Publications Office of the European

Union. http://publications.europa.eu/de/publication-detail/-/publication/ 3c32722f-0136-4d8f-a03e-bfaf70d16349

Faude, B., & Fuss, J. (2020). Coordination or conflict? The causes and consequences of institutional overlap in a disaggregated world order. *Global Constitutionalism, 9*(2), 268–289. https://doi.org/10.1017/S2045381719000376

Fauré, S. (2017). Mapping European defence policy after Brexit: NATO, OCCAR, CSDP, PESCO, etc. https://samuelbhfaure.com/2017/12/03/mapping-european-defence-policy-after-brexit-nato-occar-csdp-pesco-etc/

Fiott, D. (2015). The European Commission and the European Defence Agency: A case of rivalry? *JCMS: Journal of Common Market Studies, 53*(3), 542–557. https://doi.org/10.1111/jcms.12217

Fiott, D. (2018). Strategic autonomy: Towards 'European sovereignty' in defence. *European Union Institute for Security Studies* (12). https://www.jstor.org/stable/pdf/resrep21120.pdf

Gehring, T., & Faude, B. (2013). The dynamics of regime complexes: Microfoundations and systemic effects. *Global Governance, 19*, 119–130.

Gehring, T., & Faude, B. (2014). A theory of emerging order within institutional complexes: How competition among regulatory international institutions leads to institutional adaptation and division of labor. *The Review of International Organizations, 9*(4), 471–498. https://doi.org/10.1007/s11558-014-9197-1

Gehring, T., & Oberthür, S. (2009). The causal mechanisms of interaction between international institutions. *European Journal of International Relations, 15*(1), 125–156. https://doi.org/10.1177/1354066108100055

Genschel, P., & Jachtenfuchs, M. (Eds.). (2014). *Beyond the regulatory polity?* Oxford University Press.

Gholz, E., & Sapolsky, H. M. (2000). Restructuring the U.S. Defense Industry. *International Security, 24*(3), 5–51. https://doi.org/10.1162/016228899560220

Gruber, L. (2000). *Ruling the world: Power politics and the rise of supranational institutions.* Princeton University Press.

Haas, E. B. (1961). International Integration: The European and the Universal Process. *International Organization, 15*(03), 366. https://doi.org/10.1017/S0020818300002198

Haas, E. B. (2004 [1958]). *The uniting of Europe: Political, social, and economical forces: 1950–1957. Contemporary European politics and society.* University of Notre Dame Press.

Hall, P. A., & Taylor, R. C. R. (1996). Political science and the three new institutionalisms. *Political Studies, 44*(5), 936–957. https://doi.org/10.1111/j.1467-9248.1996.tb00343.x

Haroche, P. (2019). Supranationalism strikes back: A neofunctionalist account of the European Defence Fund. *Journal of European Public Policy, 14*(3), 1–20. https://doi.org/10.1080/13501763.2019.1609570

Hartley, K. (2011). Creating a European Defence Industrial Base. *Security Challenges, 7*(3), 95–111.

Henning, C. R., & Pratt, T. (2020). Hierarchy and differentiation in international regime complexes: A theoretical framework for comparative research. 13th Annual Conference on The Political Economy of International Organization. PEIO website: https://www.peio.me/wp-content/uploads/2020/01/PEIO13_paper_66.pdf

Hill, C. (1993). The capability-expectations gap, or conceptualizing Europe's international role. *JCMS: Journal of Common Market Studies, 31*(3), 305–328. https://doi.org/10.1111/j.1468-5965.1993.tb00466.x

Hofmann, S. C. (2009). Overlapping institutions in the realm of international security: The case of NATO and ESDP. *Perspectives on Politics, 7*(01), 45–52. https://doi.org/10.1017/S1537592709090070

Hofmann, S. C. (2011). Why institutional overlap matters: CSDP in the European Security Architecture. *JCMS: Journal of Common Market Studies, 49*(1), 101–120. https://doi.org/10.1111/j.1468-5965.2010.02131.x

Hofmann, S. C. (2018). The politics of overlapping organizations: Hostage-taking, forum-shopping and brokering. *Journal of European Public Policy, 13*, 1–23. https://doi.org/10.1080/13501763.2018.1512644

Hooghe, L., & Marks, G. (2015). Delegation and pooling in international organizations. *The Review of International Organizations, 10*(3), 305–328. https://doi.org/10.1007/s11558-014-9194-4

Howorth, J. (2004). The European Draft Constitutional Treaty and the Future of the European Defence Initiative: A Question of Flexibility. *European Foreign Affairs Review, 9*(4), 483–508. http://www.kluwerlawonline.com/document.php?id=EERR2004039

Hyde-Price, A. (2006). 'Normative' power Europe: A realist critique. *Journal of European Public Policy, 13*(2), 217–234. https://doi.org/10.1080/13501760500451634

Jones, S. G. (2003). The European Union and the security dilemma. *Security Studies, 12*(3), 114–156. https://doi.org/10.1080/09636410390443107

Jupille, J., Mattli, W., & Snidal, D. (2013). *Institutional choice and global commerce*. Cambridge University Press.

Keohane, R. O. (1984). *After hegemony: Cooperation and discord in the world political economy (1st Princeton)* (classic). Princeton University Press.

Keohane, R. O., & Victor, D. G. (2011). The regime complex for climate change. *Perspectives on Politics, 9*(01), 7–23. https://doi.org/10.1017/S1537592710004068

Koenig-Archibugi, M. (2004). Explaining Government Preferences for Institutional Change in EU Foreign and Security Policy. *International Organization, 58*(01), 137–174. https://doi.org/10.1017/S0020818304581055
Koremenos, B., Lipson, C., & Snidal, D. (2001). The rational design of international institutions. *International Organization, 55*(4), 761–799. https://doi.org/10.1162/002081801317193592
Lake, D. A. (2009). *Hierarchy in international relations. Cornell studies in political economy*. Cornell University Press.
Lake, D. A. (2010). Rightful rules: Authority, order, and the foundations of global governance. *International Studies Quarterly, 54*(3), 587–613. https://doi.org/10.1111/j.1468-2478.2010.00601.x
Le Monde. (2022). Vladimir Poutine marginalise les Européens. https://www.lemonde.fr/international/article/2022/01/07/face-a-vladimir-poutine-l-inquietude-des-europeens_6108494_3210.html
Leuffen, D., Rittberger, B., & Schimmelfennig, F. (2013). *Differentiated integration: Explaining variation in the European Union* (1. publ). The European Union series. Palgrave Macmillan.
Manners, I. (2002). Normative power Europe: A contradiction in terms? *JCMS: Journal of Common Market Studies, 40*(2), 235–258. https://doi.org/10.1111/1468-5965.00353
Mearsheimer, J. J. (2014). Why the Ukraine crisis is the West's fault: The liberal delusions that provoked Putin. *Foreign Affairs, 93*(5), 77–127.
Mearsheimer, J. J. (2018). *The great delusion: Liberal dreams and international realities*. Yale University Press.
Mölling, C. (2015). State of play of the implementation of EDA's pooling and sharing initiatives and its impact on the European defence industry. https://op.europa.eu/en/publication-detail/-/publication/5dfb4548-526d-4f33-be3d-ea7a1d4c4ce9/language-en
Moravcsik, A. (1993). Preferences and power in the European Community: A liberal intergovernmentalist approach. *JCMS: Journal of Common Market Studies, 31*(4), 473–524. https://doi.org/10.1111/j.1468-5965.1993.tb00477.x
Moravcsik, A. (1998). *The choice for Europe: Social purpose and state power from Messina to Maastricht. Cornell studies in political economy*. Cornell University Press.
Morse, J. C., & Keohane, R. O. (2014). Contested multilateralism. *The Review of International Organizations, 9*(4), 385–412. https://doi.org/10.1007/s11558-014-9188-2
Niemann, A. (1998). The PHARE programme and the concept of spillover: Neofunctionalism in the making. *Journal of European Public Policy, 5*(3), 428–446. https://doi.org/10.1080/135017698343901

Niemann, A., & Schmittner, P. C. (2009). Neofunctionalism. In A. Wiener & T. Diez (Eds.), *European integration theory* (2nd ed., pp. 45–66). Oxford University Press.

PESCO Member States. (2018). *Permanent Structured Cooperation (PESCO) updated list of PESCO projects.* https://www.consilium.europa.eu/media/37028/table-pesco-projects.pdf

Platteau, E. (2015). *Defence Data 2013.* https://issuu.com/europeandefenceagency/docs/eda_defence_data_2013_web/1?e=4763412/12106343

Politico. (2021). *Von der Leyen finds EU's soul—and its weakness—in State of Union address.* https://www.politico.eu/article/ursula-von-der-leyen-eu-soul-weakness-state-of-union-address/

Posen, B. R. (2006). European Union Security and Defense Policy: Response to unipolarity? *Security Studies, 15*(2), 149–186. https://doi.org/10.1080/09636410600829356

Pratt, T. (2018). Deference and hierarchy in international regime complexes. *International Organization, 72*(3), 561–590. https://doi.org/10.1017/S0020818318000164

Rasmussen, A. F. (2010). *Strategic concept for the defence and security of the members of the North Atlantic Treaty Organisation adopted by Heads of State and Government in Lisbon: Active engagement, modern defence.* https://www.nato.int/lisbon2010/strategic-concept-2010-eng.pdf

Raustiala, K., & Victor, D. G. (2004). The regime complex for plant genetic resources. *International Organization, 58*(2), 277–309. https://doi.org/10.2139/ssrn.441463

Reuters. (2017, June 10). *Germany, France drafting details of defense fund: German minister.* https://www.reuters.com/article/us-eu-defence-germany-france-idUSKBN1910H4

Rosato, S. (2011). Europe's troubles: Power politics and the state of the European project. *International Security, 35*(4), 45–86. https://doi.org/10.1162/ISEC_a_00035

Rynning, S. (2011). Realism and the common security and defence policy. *JCMS: Journal of Common Market Studies, 49*(1), 23–42. https://doi.org/10.1111/j.1468-5965.2010.02127.x

Salmon, T. C., & Shepherd, A. J. K. (2003). *Toward a European army: A military power in the making?* Rienner.

Schimmelfennig, F., Leuffen, D., & Rittberger, B. (2015). The European Union as a system of differentiated integration: Interdependence, politicization and differentiation. *Journal of European Public Policy, 22*(6), 764–782. https://doi.org/10.1080/13501763.2015.1020835

Schweller, R. L. (1994). Bandwagoning for profit: Bringing the revisionist state back in. *International Security, 19*(1), 72. https://doi.org/10.2307/2539149

Shepherd, A. J. K. (2015). EU military capability development and the EDA: Ideas, interests and institutions. In N. Karampekios & I. Oikonomou (Eds.), *Routledge studies in European security and strategy. The European Defence Agency: Arming Europe*. Routledge, Taylor & Francis Group.
SIPRI. (2022). Explainer: The proposed hike in German military spending. https://www.sipri.org/commentary/blog/2022/explainer-proposed-hike-german-military-spending
Snyder, G. H. (1984). The security dilemma in alliance politics. *World Politics, 36*(04), 461–495. https://doi.org/10.2307/2010183
Stone Sweet, A., & Sandholtz, W. (1997). European integration and supranational governance. *Journal of European Public Policy, 4*(3), 297–317. https://doi.org/10.1080/13501769780000011
Thompson, A., & Verdier, D. (2014). Multilateralism, bilateralism, and regime design. *International Studies Quarterly, 58*(1), 15–28. https://doi.org/10.1111/isqu.12100
Toje, A. (2008). The consensus expectations gap: Explaining Europe's Ineffective Foreign Policy. *Security Dialogue, 39*(1), 121–141. https://doi.org/10.1177/0967010607086826
Wagner, W. (2003). Why the EU's common foreign and security policy will remain intergovernmental: A rationalist institutional choice analysis of European crisis management policy. *Journal of European Public Policy, 10*(4), 576–595. https://doi.org/10.1080/1350176032000101262
Waltz, K. N. (1979). *Theory of international politics*. Addison-Wesley Pub. Co.
Weiss, M. (2011). *Transaction costs and security institutions of the state institutions: Unravelling the EDSP*. Palgrave Macmillan.
Weiss, M., & Biermann, F. (2018). Defence industrial cooperation. In H. Meijer & M. Wyss (Eds.), *The handbook of European defence policies and armed formces* (pp. 693–709). Oxford University Press.
Weiss, M., & Blauberger, M. (2015). Judicialized law-making and opportunistic enforcement: Explaining the EU's challenge of national defence offsets. *JCMS: Journal of Common Market Studies*, 1–19. https://doi.org/10.1111/jcms.12290
Williamson, O. E. (1985). *The economic institutions of capitalism: Firms, markets, relational contracting*. Free Press. http://www.loc.gov/catdir/bios/simon051/87011901.html

PART II

Concepts and Theory

CHAPTER 2

Authority Relations in Regime Complexes

This chapter will lay out the conceptual basis of the book by discussing the emergence and consequences of regime complexity and developing a typology of the authority distributions that can emerge in regime complexes. Institutions in regime complexes demonstrate varying degrees of authority in the issue area they govern. While states use some institutions regularly and thus make them *focal* within a complex (Jupille et al., 2013, p. 27), they neglect others, which find themselves relegated to the margins. If two institutions overlap in their mandates to govern an issue area, I assume that their use becomes a *relative concept*: When states do not wish to use a specific institution to tackle an issue, they shift their political and financial resources to an alternative forum rather than foregoing cooperation altogether (Morse & Keohane, 2014). Thus, if two or more institutions have mandates that cover the same issue area, the use of one often implies the non-use of the alternative. If such uneven patterns of use persist and states make one institution focal while neglecting others, this will lead to differences in the relative authority each institution possesses and thus constitutes a particular distribution of authority. These outcomes range from a set-up in which only one overarching institution remains, which hierarchically subsumes its alternatives, to regime complexes made up of elemental institutions that exist in a non-hierarchical relationship, so that no focal institution emerges. Thus,

© The Author(s), under exclusive license to Springer Nature   37
Switzerland AG 2023
F. Biermann, *The Battle for Authority in European Defence Cooperation*,
Palgrave Studies in European Union Politics,
https://doi.org/10.1007/978-3-031-30054-7_2

when we are interested in why specific institutions, such as the EDA or PESCO, became or did not become the center of authority in their respective regime complex, it is not enough to analyze them in isolation. Rather, we need to consider their alternatives and their respective positions in the complex. Only if we understand the possible outcomes of authority distribution are we able to analyze the emergence and direction of an informal, power-based hierarchy between institutions and thus explain why a specific international institution emerged as the center of authority in a complex.[1]

One central theoretical claim of this book is that regime complexes vary in the authority distributions between their constitutive institutions and can be characterized by (quasi-)hierarchical relationships. This represents a novel argument, which adds to a recent stream of regime complexity literature (Henning & Pratt, 2020; Pratt, 2018). Complementing existing arguments that an informal, "power-based hierarchy" in regime complexes can develop through deferral among international institutions (Pratt, 2018, p. 580), I present a state-centric line of argumentation. Ultimately, the relationships between, and the relative authority of, international institutions are crucially shaped by states' choices.

A regime complex is often defined as "an array of partially overlapping and *nonhierarchical* institutions governing a particular issue-area" (Raustiala & Victor, 2004, p. 279, *emphasis added*; see also, Alter & Raustiala, 2018). Reformulating this definition, I specify regime complexes as situations in which at least two institutions are mandated and thus have the formal-legal authority (Lake, 2009) to govern an issue area. Beyond the claim that "Regime complexity is, at its core, about how diverse elemental institutions establish overlapping and (potentially) rival authority claims regarding international governance" (Alter & Raustiala, 2018, p. 332), I am interested in the resulting authority distributions emerging in such complexes. While I concede that at the moment a regime complex is

---

[1] These introductory remarks should make one thing clear: While this book is motivated by the observation that some institutions are used more regularly than others, institutional use is not the dependent variable of interest. I treat patterns of institutional use, the distribution of financial and political resources, as a measurement of the institutions' relational authority in a complex. Thus, varying patterns of institutional use, together with variation in membership overlap, help measure the value of the dependent variable of interest: interinstitutional authority relations ranging from fragmentation via marginalization and resilience through to integration.

created, its constituent institutions are non-hierarchical in a "formal-legal" sense (Lake, 2009, pp. 24–28), I argue that the distribution of "relational authority" (Lake, 2009, pp. 28–33) between the elements of a regime complex can constitute different interinstitutional relationships that vary in the degree of hierarchy that they exhibit (Keohane & Victor, 2011; Pratt, 2018). In absence of a formal-legal hierarchy that may resolve rule conflict between overlapping institutions, states attempt to engage in power-based bargaining to establish informal hierarchical relationships—they attempt to make their preferred institution the center of authority. This means that when states add a new institution to a policy area already governed by a pre-existing one, they can shape different relationships between the two institutions. These relationships vary with respect to the distribution of authority between the institutions.

I demonstrate that when two institutions overlap in mandate as a result of institutional contestation (Morse & Keohane, 2014), their relationship can develop into four different configurations, which can be described along a gradual *hierarchy scale* that ranges from fragmentation to integration (cf. Johnson & Urpelainen, 2012; Keohane & Victor, 2011). At the one end, where we find very low levels of hierarchy among the institutions involved, the regime complex is *fragmented*. The institutions with overlapping mandates have separate memberships, thus each is used by a different coalition of states. In this instance, the use of one institution does not necessarily imply that another is not being used, since it may be being used simultaneously by a different state coalition. Institutional use is therefore unrelated, and none of the institutions becomes focal (i.e., develops into the center of authority) either in a formal or a relational sense. At the other end of the scale, we find extreme levels of hierarchy, with the two institutions being *integrated* into one. In this configuration, the two entities with overlapping mandates have identical memberships, and one institution incorporates the others, thereby becoming the sole forum for cooperation. Only one institution remains in control of the issue area—formal authority resides within the remaining institution, while the pre-existing institution is dissolved. Cases lying between fragmentation and integration are more ambiguous. They describe a semi-hierarchical relationship between two co-existing institutions with overlapping membership and uneven patterns of use. To develop a satisfactory answer to the question of *which* institution becomes focal and under what conditions, we have to account for two different institutional outcomes of such a situation: *marginalization* in which the new institution comes to be used regularly, and the pre-existing one loses authority over the issue area and *resilience* in which the pre-existing institution remains focal and the new institution hardly plays any role in the governance of the policy area.

This chapter has three sections. The first takes stock of the existing literature on regime complexes and contested multilateralism and discusses both the emergence and the effects of regime complexity. I locate my approach in the literature and specify important scope conditions for both the conceptualization of authority distributions and their subsequent explanation. The second develops a typology of the dependent variable, the distribution of authority within a regime complex in its four manifestations: integration, marginalization, resilience, and fragmentation. The third summarizes and paves the way for the explanatory framework presented in the subsequent chapter.

THE EMERGENCE AND CONSEQUENCES OF REGIME COMPLEXES

Both the conceptualization and the theoretical framework I propose build on a rationalist assumption that regime complexes emerge from contestation. This perspective has important implications for the theorized effects of complexity on interinstitutional relationships. These I do not analyze, however, in categories of competitive versus cooperative, as has been done in the bulk of the literature, but rather in terms of the institutions' relative positions within a complex. This section thus seeks to answer the following three questions: What is a regime complex? How do regime complexes emerge? And what are the effects of regime complexity? The answers to those three questions will allow me to develop a typology of authority distributions in the subsequent section.

What Is a Regime Complex?

International institutions are "explicit arrangements, negotiated among international actors, that prescribe, proscribe, and/or authorize behaviour" (Koremenos et al., 2001, p. 762). This definition includes intergovernmental organizations, as well as codified agreements among states, that regulate future behavior regardless of their legal status and subsumes both formal and informal intergovernmental organizations on condition that they have a declared membership, regular meetings, and explicitly shared expectations. It excludes decentralized cooperation with varying membership, which is built around tacit, unwritten understandings (Vabulas & Snidal, 2013, p. 198). The definition of international institutions I build on in this study is therefore more demanding than that of broader accounts that define institutions as "principles, norms, rules, and decision-making procedures around which actor expectations converge in a given issue-area" (Krasner, 1982, p. 185). The focus on codified rules, excluding norms and implicitly shared understandings, has an important pragmatic advantage. It facilitates the description of an international institution along three observable dimensions, its *membership*, *mandate*, and *resources* (Hofmann, 2009, p. 46).

The function of an international institution is to regulate states' behavior with regard to a set of cooperation or coordination problems as delineated by the institution's mandate. Its ability to fulfill its mandate depends on the (financial and political) resources at its disposal. On a domestic level, institutions are mostly hierarchically structured. Whenever two rules contradict one another, decision-making is referred to the next higher level. In an essentially anarchic international system, however, there are more possible solutions than problems. There is no overarching, fully integrated institutional setting with complete membership, an all-encompassing mandate, and generally acknowledged jurisdiction—"all global governance ... is fragmented to some degree" (Biermann et al., 2009, p. 17). This truism not only describes the international system as a whole but seems to hold for almost every individual issue area governed by an international institution as well. International institutions overlap—in terms of their mandates, memberships, and resources.

In 2004 Kal Raustiala and David Victor defined "regime complexes" as "an array of partially overlapping and nonhierarchical institutions governing a particular issue-area" (Raustiala & Victor, 2004, p. 279). They are "marked by the existence of several legal agreements that are created and maintained in distinct fora with participation of different sets of actors. The rules in these elemental regimes functionally overlap, yet there is no agreed upon hierarchy for resolving conflicts between rules" (Raustiala & Victor, 2004, p. 279). Karen Alter and Sophie Meunier broadened this definition by including "nested, partially overlapping, and parallel international regimes that are not hierarchically ordered" (Alter & Meunier, 2009, p. 13). Both definitions share two propositions: there is at least some degree of overlap between the institutions, and there is no hierarchy between the elements of a regime complex. I propose three refinements to these definitions.

First, institutions can overlap in mandate, membership, and resources. Hofmann (2009, 2011) suggests that regime complexity requires overlap in all three dimensions. Gehring and Faude (2014, p. 474) propose that dynamics of regime complexity arise when mandate and membership overlap. Finally, for Alter and Meunier, even "parallel international regimes" without overlap in any of those dimensions (Alter & Meunier, 2009, p. 15) can constitute a complex. *I argue, however, that overlap in one dimension, namely in the mandate, is a necessary condition for a regime complex.* Only if two (or more) different institutions are mandated to govern the same issue area and thus have "rival authority claims" (Alter & Raustiala, 2018, p. 332), do questions of membership overlap and resource distribution matter. Unless decisions taken in one institution generate some externalities at least for an issue governed by another institution, we cannot speak of complexity. If there was no overlap in the mandate, what was agreed in institution A would not matter to institution B. Overlap in membership and resources, contrariwise, are not necessary conditions: Even two institutions with completely separate memberships and resources can produce externalities for one another if they govern the same issue area. The same holds true for institutions with identical membership. If they govern the same issue area, they can generate incommensurable rule outcomes over time.

Second, I do not share the perspective that interinstitutional relations in regime complexes are, by definition, non-hierarchical. While I do not question the non-hierarchical character of the international legal system (Alter & Meunier, 2009, p. 15), I hold that regarding the "absence of hierarchy among institutions and rules [as] the key political feature of a regime complex" (Alter & Raustiala, 2018, p. 332) neglects an important reality of regime complexes. Some institutions have more authority than others—states refer to them more often than to their alternatives. As "the issue of hierarchy is intrinsic to authority" (Alter & Raustiala, 2018, p. 332; see also, Lake, 2009, pp. 17–19; MacDonald, 2018), it only makes sense to define regime complexes as non-hierarchical if the concept of hierarchy is built on a *formal-legal* understanding of authority (Lake, 2009, pp. 24–28). As David Lake has argued, however, there is a second conception of authority: relational authority results from "an exchange or bargain between ruler and ruled" (Lake, 2009, p. 28). What is more, "[w]here formal-legal conceptions of authority exclude the possibility of authority between states [and between institutions] by definition, relational authority permits and even encourages hierarchy" (Lake, 2009, p. 44). This relational authority (Lake, 2009, pp. 28–33) does not stem from legal status defining hierarchy as *legal* primacy but manifests as the rational outcome of states *negotiating* on which institution's rules to follow, which institution to provide with resources to grant authority to and of which institution to become a member. This form of authority amounts to a *recognized* claim to govern (Abbott et al., 2020) and "a political construct created and sustained through practice" (Lake, 2009, p. 20).[2] Thus, not only is hierarchy intrinsic to authority, but hierarchy itself is best understood as a stable authority relationship (MacDonald, 2018). If there is no formal mechanism to resolve jurisdictional conflict between institutions but states—through power-based negotiations (see, next chapter)—regularly agree to use one of the overlapping institutions as their preferred venue for cooperation while neglecting its alternatives, this implies that they grant it authority (Lake, 2010) while denying it to alternative venues. If this uneven pattern persists, the preferred institution becomes focal and has more authority than its alternatives in the issue area to be governed. This implies a certain degree of informal hierarchy between them—a semi-hierarchical relationship emerges independently of the formal-legal relationship (Pratt, 2018). Consequently, the degree of hierarchy in regime complexes can vary depending on how authority is distributed between the institutions that constitute a complex, (cf. Keohane & Victor, 2011, p. 8).

Finally, two institutions are enough to build a complex. While the term "array" (Raustiala & Victor, 2004, p. 279) does not specify the minimum number of institutions necessary to speak of a complex, Orsini et al. (2013), set the threshold at *three*, claiming that network effects can only arise when a third institution is added to the equation (Orsini et al., 2013). Focusing on states as the central actors, I argue that an issue area populated by two elemental institutions with overlapping mandates is enough to theorize the most important dynamics accounting for the ordering principles in a regime complex (cf. Gehring & Faude, 2014, p. 474).

---

[2] Thus, this conceptualization of both relational authority and the resulting informal, power-based hierarchy does not necessarily imply legitimacy in a Weberian sense.

In sum, I define a regime complex as a situation in which at least two institutions overlap in their mandate—and thus have rival authority claims—to govern an issue area. The degree of overlap in membership and resources can vary—they can be separate, identical (pooled), or actually overlapping. The same holds true for the potential hierarchy between the elemental institutions of the complex. Depending on how authority is distributed, the relationship between the institutions in the complex is a matter of degree and can range from non-hierarchical to semi-hierarchical to hierarchical.

How Do Regime Complexes Emerge?

The literature discusses two dominant explanations for the emergence of regime complexes. According to the functionalist account, complexity is the unintended consequence of states reacting to functional pressure or purposely creating regime complexes to challenge the institutional status quo (Gehring & Faude, 2014, p. 474). Here I focus on the latter perspective, centering member state contestation as the origin of competition between institutions with overlapping mandates.

The functional account states that increasing issue complexity requires increasingly complex institutional arrangements. Functional differentiation of institutional arrangements is seen as "a rational response to the increasing complexity of society" (Zürn & Faude, 2013, p. 120). A growing number of stakeholders and increasing interdependence among issues characterizes this complexity, which generates negative externalities across issue areas (Humrich, 2013; Zelli & van Asselt, 2013). In an attempt to accommodate these spillovers, states expand the mandates of given international institutions in a "desire to meet new regulatory demand" and thereby cause overlap (Gehring & Faude, 2014, p. 474). Moreover, growing numbers of stakeholders affected by regulation lead to greater divergence of interests (Snidal, 1994). States are therefore prompted to use "linkages across agreements ... that collectively are more attractive to various participants" (Alter & Meunier, 2009, p. 14), and then regime complexity results from this attempt to create new "legitimating frames" for cooperation (Muzaka, 2011, p. 770). While I acknowledge the applicability of the functionalist argument to some instances of regime complexity, this perspective only works under constraining scope conditions, such as the existence of spillovers across issues or the emergence of new regulatory challenges. Yet we often observe overlapping institutions governing a single stable issue: for example, the International Energy Agency and the International Renewable Energy Agency, which overlap in each having a mandate to govern the proliferation of renewable energy sources (van de Graaf, 2013).

I contribute to a second strand of the literature that attributes the emergence of regime complexes to the dynamics that arise from states contesting an existing institution (Benvenisti & Downs, 2007; Morse & Keohane, 2014; Schneider & Urpelainen, 2013). This perspective relies on the assumption that "distributional conflict … can increase regime complexity through institutional proliferation" (Schneider & Urpelainen, 2013, p. 14). States that are dissatisfied with an institution's (expected) outcomes or its design in terms of decision-making procedures or membership and find the way to internal reform blocked try either to transfer cooperation to an alternative institution or to create an institutional competitor (Helfer, 2009; Morse & Keohane, 2014). As states generally demonstrate a status quo bias (Jupille et al., 2013), they will use the institutions they have subscribed to as long as cooperation is satisfactory (Simon, 1957). If actors are satisfied with an institution, they will, in the absence of exogenous change, refrain from attempting to reform it and allow the status quo to persist (Colgan et al., 2012, p. 120). Only if some of the members are dissatisfied with the way the institution functions is any form of change likely to occur. This makes dissatisfaction a "necessary condition for innovation" (Colgan et al., 2012, p. 118). However, as institutions are generally "easier to maintain than to construct" (Keohane, 1984, p. 102), the first best option for dissatisfied states is to try to reform the institution from within in order to harvest prior investments (Jupille et al., 2013). Therefore, a second condition for competitive regime creation is needed: the impossibility of reform. Dissatisfied states will only decide to exit an institution and shift cooperation to another forum if voicing dissatisfaction and reforming the institution in question prove to be impossible (Hirschman, 1978; Jupille et al., 2013; van de Graaf, 2013). This is by no means a rare occurrence. As state preferences often diverge and reasons for dissatisfaction are ubiquitous, finding common grounds for reform is difficult. Veto players may block reform attempts (Tsebelis, 1995) or raise the costs of reform to a prohibitive level (Jupille et al., 2013). Especially in intergovernmental organizations that rely on unanimity, reform is hard to realize. The emergence of regime complexes thus depends on the formation of a coalition of dissatisfied states, which finds the way for internal reform blocked

(Colgan et al., 2012, p. 120) and consequently engages in competitive regime creation or regime shifting to challenge the institutional status quo (van de Graaf, 2013). The dissatisfied coalition challenges the institutional status quo by expanding the mandate of an existing alternative institution or creating a genuinely new one. The resulting situation where two institutions have overlapping mandates to govern the same issue area constitutes the birth of the regime complex.

What Are the Consequences of Regime Complexity?

We come now to the question of what the consequences of regime complexes are and why they matter. Regime complexes create both opportunities for and threats to international cooperation that are widely discussed in the literature. There are good reasons to assume that regime complexity both furthers cooperation and reinforces conflict. Therefore, I propose that, instead of asking whether regime complexity results in conflictive or cooperative behavior, we should ask instead about the kind of interinstitutional authority relations that emerge in regime complexes. These relationships represent opportunity spaces for both cooperative and conflictive behavior. Regime complexes are characterized by competition for resources and authority over a given issue area (Gehring & Faude, 2014, p. 475). An institution usually serves as the focal point for cooperation likewise in a given issue area (Jupille et al., 2013; Schelling, 1960). "Regime complexity inevitably increases the number of possible focal points, however, focal points should be rare" (Drezner, 2009, p. 66). If regime complexes arise from contestation, as argued above, this implies that states are likely to disagree on which institution should become the new focal point. Alter and Meunier argue that the effects of regime complexity are ambiguous and depend on the results of the competition.

> International regime complexity creates competition among institutions and actors. Competition can have negative effects – turf battles and a failure to coordinate efforts. Competition can also have positive effects – increasing total resources, spreading risk, allowing experimentation. (Alter & Meunier, 2009, p. 20)

Biermann et al. share this perspective, offering a typology of the configurations of fragmented governance architecture that range from cooperative to conflictive (Biermann et al., 2009, p. 19). Consequently, scholars interested in the consequences of regime complexity can be roughly divided into two camps—the first, more optimistic faction suggests that rising institutional density leads to efficient work-sharing arrangements and enhanced cooperation (Faude & Fuss, 2020; Gehring & Faude, 2013, 2014). The second has a more pessimistic take on the consequences of regime complexity, emphasizing its potential to foster inefficient competition for resources (Hofmann, 2009), turf battles, and possibilities for undermining agreements (Benvenisti & Downs, 2007; Drezner, 2009). Both perspectives are justified, which suggests that the cooperative—conflictive dichotomy embodies a conceptual problematic.

The optimistic account of regime complexity assumes a general tendency to "cooperative fragmentation" (Faude & Fuss, 2020; Zürn & Faude, 2013). Complexity increases states' room for maneuver when it comes to interpreting rules and selecting an adequate venue for cooperation and thus offers opportunities for "forum shopping" (Raustiala & Victor, 2004, p. 280). Therefore, systematic engagement in these activities on the part of states leads on to work sharing and the specialization of institutions (Gehring & Faude, 2013, pp. 124–125). If states regularly cooperate through institution A when confronted with problems of type A and through institution B when type B problems arise, this can induce enhanced productivity and effectiveness. Such regularities can either emerge tacitly or through negotiated agreements and result from mechanisms of normative or behavioral adjustment over time (Gehring & Faude, 2014; Gehring & Oberthür, 2009). States are assumed to prefer consistent institutional obligations. They consider the commitments entered into through institution A when negotiating new agreements in institution B (Gehring & Oberthür, 2009, p. 136). This underlying preference, together with states' wish to choose the most beneficial cooperation framework through forum shopping, constructs a mixed-motive situation whose long-term outcome is—centralized or decentralized—coordination across institutions (Gehring & Faude, 2014, p. 478). If the preference for consistency is strong enough, a regime complex could even generate positive feedback by creating incentives for imitation that develop into a "race to the top" (Keohane & Victor, 2011, p. 19).

The more pessimistic camp argues that regime complexity leads to conflictive fragmentation of institutional arrangements (Zelli & van Asselt, 2013), increased transaction costs for cooperation (Drezner, 2009), and wide inefficiencies as states engage in "chessboard politics"

(Hofmann, 2009). Benvenisti and Downs (2007), as well as Drezner (2009, 2013), argue that this development serves the most powerful and undermines both the scope and efficacy of institutional agreements. These theorized consequences of regime complexes largely depend on membership overlap, which is argued to benefit multiple members, that is, states with membership in more than one institution, in comparison to single members. Overlapping institutions reduce the cost for dual members that "abandon – or threaten to abandon – any given venue for a more sympathetic venue if their demands are not met" (Benvenisti & Downs, 2007, p. 597). Those perceptions of regime complexity rely on the view that states may have an interest in the "strategic inconsistency" of overlapping institutions (Raustiala & Victor, 2004, p. 301). Hofmann complements this view by demonstrating that single members can and do obstruct cooperation between elemental institutions by taking the relationship between two institutions hostage, in other words, vetoing decisions (Hofmann, 2018). Forum-shopping and hostage-taking are instruments at the disposal of both powerful and less powerful states (Fehl, 2016; Muzaka, 2011) that might lead to a conflictive and inefficient institutional landscape with weak links between elemental institutions and various veto points, inducing a "race to the bottom" (Keohane & Victor, 2011, p. 15).[3]

This ambiguity, I argue, is inherent in the existing literature's focus on complexity as an underspecified concept. Defined as a non-hierarchical array of overlapping institutions, a regime complex can reinforce or undermine pre-existing behavior in either direction. I will indirectly contribute to this debate but propose to go one step further and focus on the different outcomes of authority distributions that can emerge from regime complexes. Authority relations between the institutions

---

[3] To be fair, both camps reflect upon the possibility of both conflict and work sharing as potential consequences. Hofmann's account envisages brokering states having a vital interest in keeping both of the institutions in a complex functional (Hofmann, 2011). Elsewhere she even notes that if "a division of labor or hierarchy between the various institutions can be negotiated, this will most likely strengthen policies in the domain under consideration" (Hofmann, 2011, p. 106). Analogously, Gehring and Faude clarify that interinstitutional competition in regime complexes "may lead to open conflict and turf battles" (Gehring & Faude, 2013) and that "an emerging division of labor does neither exclude the power-based struggle of actors for their preferred institutional arrangement, nor ensure that the most effective forms of governance prevail within an institutional complex" (Gehring & Faude, 2014, p. 474). Thus, there is considerable ambiguity with respect to the outcomes of institutional complexes in terms of cooperation or conflict.

of a complex cannot simply be categorized under the cooperation–conflict dichotomy. Authority always implies "some element of consent" (Barnett & Finnemore, 2004, p. 28), which, however, does not imply that consent cannot be the result of a lost bargain. Focusing on regime complexes that result from contestation already implies that disagreement is at the root of complexity. The resulting authority distributions, however, again prestructure future behavior as they lock in an institutional configuration, which then either facilitates or complicates particular cooperative or conflictive strategies.

Reducing Complexity: A Typology of Authority Distributions

This section is devoted to developing a typology of interinstitutional relationships arising from regime complexes. It takes a regime complex, the result of competitive regime creation, as a starting point and asks which different authority distributions can be observed. The distribution of authority can be measured by means of two interrelated indicators—overlap in membership and overlap in financial and political resources, in other words, patterns of institutional use. Moreover, they display varying degrees of hierarchy. The first part briefly demonstrates how the typology builds on and further develops the conceptualization put forward by Keohane and Victor (2011). The second part demonstrates how overlap in membership and resources can be utilized as indicators for hierarchy. The final section presents the typology of interinstitutional relationships in regime complexes.

In line with Faude and Fuss (2020), Hofmann (2011), Gehring and Faude (2014), and Pratt (2018), I hold that a situation of contested multilateralism and rival authority can lead to work sharing and hierarchy. At the same time, I agree with Benvenisti and Downs (2007), Drezner (2009, 2013), and Zelli and van Asselt (2013) that a regime complex can also remain non-hierarchical and fragmented. Thus, the non-hierarchical character of a regime complex is not a defining attribute but an empirical phenomenon. While I acknowledge the non-hierarchical character of international law, it is not necessarily the case "that there is no way to definitively resolve questions about which rules, norms, or decision-making procedures take precedence" (Alter & Raustiala, 2018, p. 332). States can agree or disagree on various forms of authority distribution, and the relationship between two institutions can develop over time.

Membership overlap can persist or memberships separate out, resources can be equally or unequally distributed, and institutions can co-exist without further interconnections or become highly dependent on one another. In sum, taking the concept of relational authority as a basis, "[h]ierarchy is a dynamic, evolving relationship, not a static institution frozen at some prior moment of creation" (Lake, 2009, p. 36). Keohane and Victor (2011) suggest a scale of institutional outcomes ranging from integration to fragmentation and claim that regime complexes lie in between those two extremes:

> At one extreme are fully integrated institutions that impose regulation through comprehensive, hierarchical rules. At the other extreme are highly fragmented collections of institutions with no identifiable core and weak or nonexistent linkages between regime elements. In between is a wide range that includes nested (semi-hierarchical) regimes with identifiable cores and non-hierarchical but loosely coupled systems of institutions. What we are calling "regime complexes" are arrangements of the loosely coupled variety located somewhere in the middle of this continuum. (Keohane & Victor, 2011, p. 8)

While I share the view that regime complexes can be hierarchical or semi-hierarchical (i.e., hierarchical in a relational rather than a formal-legal sense), my perspective contrasts with the approach that defines regime complexity as an institutional *outcome* between fragmentation and integration. I consider regime complexes to be the *starting point*, which can develop varying authority distributions along a scale of hierarchy. This thought rests on the focus on regime complexes emerging from contested multilateralism. I posit that a regime complex develops against the foil of at least one pre-existing institution (Jupille et al., 2013, p. 25). Keohane and Victor's definition, by contrast, implicitly assumes that states have the possibility to shape the institutional outcome from scratch. In other words, while I take a similar scale, I measure a different outcome. Within a given regime complex, different types of interinstitutional authority structures can emerge and vary in the degree of hierarchy among their constituent institutions.

The relationship between two elemental institutions can develop into a full relational *and* formal hierarchy when the two institutions are integrated into one. It can also be completely non-hierarchical in both a formal-legal and a relational sense if they co-exist in an uncoordinated, fragmented way. Finally, it can be something in between, demonstrating relational, i.e., informal hierarchy, based on power-based bargains among states. I argue that there are two interrelated indicators that can measure the degree of hierarchy in the relationship between two institutions: overlap in membership and overlap in resources. This builds on the definitional discussion above. I hold that mandate overlap, that is, competition between two institutions over authority in a given issue area, is the only necessary condition for a regime complex. Overlap in membership or resources can vary across complexes. Membership overlap is a matter of degree. At one extreme, the two elemental institutions have clearly *separate memberships*. This can be the case either if membership overlap diminishes over time or if two or more institutional competitors with separate memberships are created and the original institution is shut down. Separate membership deprives the member states of an institution of the possibility of engaging in forum shopping or hostage-taking (Hofmann, 2018). What is more, unless states are members of both institutions (i.e., dual members) the theorized mechanisms of efficiency gains and institutional adjustment proposed by Faude and Fuss (2020) and Gehring and Oberthür (2009) cannot take place. "International institutions with completely separate memberships are not directly related to each other" (Gehring & Faude, 2014, p. 474). This impedes the evolution of hierarchy, that is to say, of a stable authority relationship. At the other end of the scale, the two institutions may have *identical memberships*. If all the members of the original institution become members of the institutional alternative, forum shopping is rendered impossible. If both institutions have a comparable mandate and rely on similar decision-making mechanisms, there are no advantages in maintaining both, and we would expect one institution to take over the regulatory functions of the other. If the pre-existing institution is shut down, this amounts to institutional replacement (Cottrell, 2016). Coordination between two institutions with identical membership is very high, as one institution is merged with the other. Between the two extreme cases of separate and identical memberships, there are institutions with *overlapping memberships*. In this case, some states are members of both elemental institutions (dual members), while others are single members. Coordination between the institutions depends on states' ability to develop informal specialization or even negotiate formal work-sharing agreements (Gehring & Faude, 2014; Hofmann, 2011). Yet, from the membership perspective alone, it is impossible to predict which institution will be used more regularly than the other, in other words, which institution will become focal and acquire greater authority in the issue area in question. I argue that considering a second measure—overlap in resources—will allow the degree and direction of hierarchy characteristic of the authority distribution arising in the complex to be measured.

An institution's influence on a given issue area depends on whether it regulates state behavior within that area. In other words, an institution's relational authority depends on whether states use it and whether they support it in fulfilling its mandate. This can be measured by looking at the resources fed into the institution. Resources have both a financial and a political component. Financial capital enables international organizations to live up to their mandate, acquire new projects, and expand their operating space. Comparing the financial resources of two institutions with overlapping mandates thus gives us a hint of their relative importance. Political capital is just as important, as it is the prerequisite for the assignment of financial assets. Whether state governments meet in one particular institutional setting, whether they go back to particular institutions for conflict resolution or to initiate cooperative projects rather than to others, determines the authority an institution can exert. If states' financial resources are limited, their use of one specific institution implies the non-use of another institution. If regularities emerge, if, that is, there are clear use patterns, these represent the distribution of the institutions' relative authority in the field. Like membership overlap, resource overlap is a matter of degree. Resources can be distributed evenly or unevenly across institutions, and a zero-sum logic may or may not apply to resource distribution, depending on the membership overlap. Again, there are two extreme and two intermediate cases, which are analogous to the different degrees of membership overlap. Take the case of *resource separation* first— each state focuses on only one of the two institutions in question. There is no forum shopping, as each state only uses one venue for cooperation. This situation occurs in regime complexes with clearly separate memberships. States do not need to apportion their resources across institutions, as they are all single members and only use the institution to which they belong. The second variation in the use pattern is *centralized distribution of resources*—the exclusive use of one institution, while the second is politically and financially neglected. All resources are diverted from one institution to the other, which implies a complete shift of authority. This is most likely to be the case when there are two institutions with identical memberships. In this situation, as I have mentioned before, there is not much sense in keeping both institutions alive. Consequently, "[w]e have little reason to expect that states will choose to devote scarce resources to formal organizations that will be superfluous" (Martin, 1992, p. 776). Finally, there are cases in between. States have the possibility to allocate the bulk of resources to one institution but keep the other as a body with institutional potential. The result is an *uneven use pattern*, in which one institution has more authority over an issue than another but both institutions persist. This is the case when membership overlaps, that is, both single and dual members exist. In line with the "strategic inconsistency" argument (Raustiala & Victor, 2004), multiple members benefit from having more than one institution at their disposal and prefer to use different institutions for different purposes. This leads to an uneven authority distribution across the institutions, leading to one institution becoming focal and having more authority in an issue area than the other.

The uneven distribution of resources is an indicator of differences in an institution's relative authority. An institution can become focal—states use it regularly, while they use its competitor only sporadically. This corresponds to the existence of a semi-hierarchical relationship regarding the relative authority states delegated to each institution in a given issue area. Thus, a situation where there are overlaps in mandate, membership, and resources is associated with differences in the distribution of authority. Hierarchy does not necessarily mean that the rules codified in one institution have primacy over those of its competitors, but that states regularly decide to follow the rules of one institution rather than those of its competitors and thus attribute it substantially more authority (Henning & Pratt, 2020; Lake, 2009, 2010; Pratt, 2018) in an issue area than the alternative. This semi-hierarchical intermediate configuration between integration and fragmentation, however, is indeterminate, as membership overlap is no longer directly related to the distribution of resources. Thus, the direction of the hierarchical relationship is ambiguous. There is no clear expectation as to which of the institutions will get the lion's share of resources. Therefore, we need to differentiate between two additional institutional configurations rather than one. If an institution B is added to an issue area governed by institution A, either B or A might become focal. What I call *marginalization* is what happens when the new institution B is used regularly and acquires relational authority, whereas the pre-existing institution A loses authority.

Contrarily, what I call *resilience* describes the outcome when the pre-existing institution A remains focal or becomes focal again, and the new institution B hardly plays any role in the governance of the policy area.

In sum, two dimensions, overlap in membership and overlap in resources, define the interinstitutional authority relation. Both dimensions combined constitute the possible distribution of authority between institutions with overlapping mandates. These authority distributions vary in the degree of hierarchy they exhibit in the regime complex and can be distinguished into four possible types that range from a fragmented, separate array of institutions to an integrated outcome in which both membership and resources are pooled in one institution. In between there are two outcomes, in which either of the two institutions with overlapping membership and resources can become focal. In these cases, membership overlap is no longer related to the distribution of resources, making it necessary to distinguish between marginalization and resilience in order to account for the direction of the hierarchical relationship. Building on this, the next paragraphs present a typology of the variations in interinstitutional authority relations, which categorizes the different outcomes of regime complexes consisting of two elemental institutions.

A Typology of Interinstitutional Relationships

Taking a regime complex consisting of two elemental institutions as a starting point, different interinstitutional relationships can emerge. Creating an additional venue in an issue area already governed by one institution can lead to considerable changes in the use patterns of the elemental institutions. When a new institution B is added to a field occupied by the pre-existing institution A, there are four interinstitutional relationships possible. Figure 2.1 depicts these: fragmentation and integration, and two intermediate outcomes, marginalization and resilience.

Integration: The interinstitutional relationship may develop into an instance of integration. Institutions A and B pool their relational and formal authority and their membership structure is identical. Institution B thus equals institution A in terms of membership and resources, and as elemental institutions, they merge into one. Potential interinstitutional conflict is resolved by integrating the overlapping mandates into one overarching framework, thus creating a coherent set of rules. Regime complexity is thereby abolished as only one institution remains in charge.

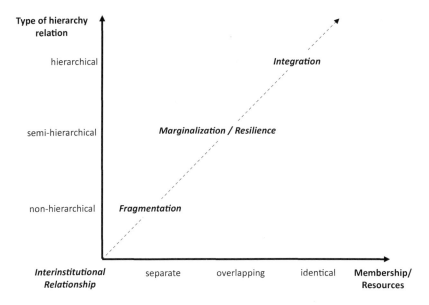

Fig. 2.1 Typology of interinstitutional authority relationships

This configuration comes closest to the concept of formal-legal *hierarchy*, as understood by Alter and Raustiala (2018) and Keohane and Victor (2011).

Fragmentation: Authority over an issue area can become fragmented. Institutions A and B both consist of single members and there is no membership overlap. States have no discretion as to which forum to use, as there is only one venue available to each of them. Resources are distributed separately to each venue, the use of one forum does not imply the non-use of the other, and states do not face trade-offs. Moreover, there is minimal coordination between the elemental institutions, even though there is overlap in the mandate and despite the potential externalities that decisions taken by members of institution A may have on members of institution B, and vice versa. Regime complexity is, therefore, high, and the relationship between the institutions is not formally regulated. Authority is distributed equally between the institutions, and neither of them becomes focal, so in this case authority distribution is non-hierarchical.

Marginalization and Resilience: In between integration and fragmentation sit the more ambiguous cases of marginalization and resilience. They differ from fragmentation insofar as their authority distributions are characterized by overlaps in membership and resources, which lead to interconnections and linkages between institutions. Through the overlap in resources, the use of one institution implies the non-use of the other. They also differ from integration, in that the two institutions co-exist, and neither is subsumed under the other. Relational authority is distributed unequally across the elemental institutions. States use one of them regularly and it becomes focal; they neglect the other in terms of resources. While there is no formal-legal hierarchy between the institutions, they co-exist in a semi-hierarchical relationship. Both have the formal mandate to govern an issue area, but one of them has more relational authority than the other. Thus, when states add an institution B to an issue area already governed by forum A, two distributions of authority are possible. Either institution B becomes focal and states sideline institution A, or institution A, which has been challenged by institution B, prevails as the focal institution. I call the first outcome *marginalization*. States create an institutional competitor B that overlaps in mandate, membership, and resources with the pre-existing institution A. They manage to shift the bulk of the total resources spent on cooperation over the issue regulated by the overlapping mandates to the new institution B while keeping the A only as an institutional potential. Institution B is used regularly while institution A loses resources and authority over the issue area in question. This can, but does not have to, lead to institution A's mandate being cut back (Abbott et al., 2013; Jupille et al., 2013), which would then add a formal-legal dimension to the relational authority of institution B. Institution B becomes the center of relational authority, while the pre-existing institution A is sidelined. I call the second outcome *resilience*. While institutional competitor B initially challenged original institution A, the latter remains focal or becomes so again. Once again, states create an institutional competitor B with a mandate, membership, and resources that overlap with those of a pre-existing institution A. Yet, though shifting cooperation to B may put A under stress, states, for whatever reason, decide to focus on it again. The original institution A is more regularly used and has comparatively greater authority in the issue area in question than its competitor. Analogously, institution B loses some of the resources and authority it initially acquired back to institution A.

Summary

This chapter had two central tasks: The first was to mark my approach off from the existing literature on regime complexity. I understand situations of contested multilateralism to be the origin of regime complexity. Dissatisfied coalitions of states, unable to reform an institution from within, engage in competitive regime creation or regime shifting to challenge the institutional status quo. Two elemental institutions with overlapping mandates to govern the same issue area then exist. Taking a regime complex of this kind as my starting point, I have demonstrated that overlap in membership and resources can vary, logically enabling different distributions of authority between the elemental institutions in a complex. Based on these considerations, my second task in this chapter was to develop a typology of the dependent variable, the type of authority relation between the institutions that make up a complex. Four types of authority distribution can emerge. Elemental institutions with separate memberships and resources characterize a *fragmented* distribution. If the two elemental institutions are *integrated*, they have identical memberships and pooled resources, and both relational and formal authority are centralized. Finally, there are two intermediate cases. In situations of membership and resource overlap, relational authority over the issue area is distributed unevenly, which makes one institution focal while sidelining the other. Either the original institution is sidelined, while the newly created alternative becomes focal (*marginalization*), or the original institution is reinforced, because the alternative is ineffective (*resilience*).

Although it has developed a useful typology, this chapter does raise further questions. Most obviously, a typology adds little value when the conditions under which we can expect each type to occur are not specified. What are the pathways that lead to the specific outcomes of interinstitutional authority relations? And how can we make use of this framework to explain the developments in the regime complex of European defense cooperation? The answer to this question, I argue, also contributes to the debate on the beneficiaries of regime complexity. While some scholars clearly state that complexity first and foremost serves the great powers (Benvenisti & Downs, 2007; Drezner, 2009), others point out that regime complexes also offer viable strategic options for lesser powers to assert themselves (Fehl, 2016; Hofmann, 2018). The answer I propose is, as so often in social sciences, "it depends." On what exactly, I will reveal in the next chapter.

REFERENCES

Abbott, K. W., Genschel, P., Snidal, D., & Zangl, B. (2020). Competence versus Control: The Governor's Dilemma. *Regulation and Governance, 14*(4), 619–636.

Abbott, K., Green, W., Jessica, F., & Keohane, R. O. (2013). Organizational ecology and organizational strategies in world politics. Discussion Paper 2013–57. Harvard Project on Climate Agreements.

Alter, K. J., & Meunier, S. (2009). The politics of international regime complexity. *Perspectives on Politics, 7*(01), 13–24. https://doi.org/10.1017/S1537592709090033

Alter, K. J., & Raustiala, K. (2018). The rise of international regime complexity. *Annual Review of Law and Social Science, 14*(1), 329–349. https://doi.org/10.1146/annurev-lawsocsci-101317-030830

Barnett, M. N., & Finnemore, M. (2004). *Rules for the world: International organizations in global politics.* Cornell University Press. http://www.jstor.org/stable/10.7591/j.ctt7z7mx

Benvenisti, E., & Downs, G. W. (2007). The emperor's new clothes: Political economy and the fragmentation of international law. *Stanford Law Review, 60*(2), 595–632.

Biermann, F., Pattberg, P., van Asselt, H., & Zelli, F. (2009). The fragmentation of global governance architectures: A framework for analysis. *Global Environmental Politics, 9*(4), 14–40. https://doi.org/10.1162/glep.2009.9.4.14

Colgan, J. D., Keohane, R. O., & van de Graaf, T. (2012). Punctuated equilibrium in the energy regime complex. *The Review of International Organizations, 7*(2), 117–143. https://doi.org/10.1007/s11558-011-9130-9

Cottrell, P. M. (2016). *The evolution and legitimacy of international security institutions.* Cambridge University Press. http://www.h-net.org/reviews/showrev.php?id=46936

Drezner, D. W. (2009). The power and peril of international regime complexity. *Perspectives on Politics, 7*(01), 65–70. https://doi.org/10.1017/S1537592709090100

Drezner, D. W. (2013). The tragedy of the global institutional commons. In J. Goldstein & M. Finnemore (Eds.), *Back to basics: State power in a contemporary world* (pp. 280–310). Oxford University Press. https://doi.org/10.1093/acprof:oso/9780199970087.003.0013

Faude, B., & Fuss, J. (2020). Coordination or conflict? The causes and consequences of institutional overlap in a disaggregated world order. *Global Constitutionalism, 9*(2), 268–289. https://doi.org/10.1017/S2045381719000376

Fehl, C. (2016). *Forum shopping from above and below: Power shifts and institutional choice in a stratified international society*. Paper prepared for the workshop on "Power Transitions and Institutional Change". Munich.

Gehring, T., & Faude, B. (2013). The dynamics of regime complexes: Microfoundations and systemic effects. *Global Governance, 19*, 119–130.

Gehring, T., & Faude, B. (2014). A theory of emerging order within institutional complexes: How competition among regulatory international institutions leads to institutional adaptation and division of labor. *The Review of International Organizations, 9*(4), 471–498. https://doi.org/10.1007/s11558-014-9197-1

Gehring, T., & Oberthür, S. (2009). The causal mechanisms of interaction between international institutions. *European Journal of International Relations, 15*(1), 125–156. https://doi.org/10.1177/1354066108100055

Helfer, L. R. (2009). Regime shifting in the international intellectual property system. *Perspectives on Politics, 7*(01), 39–44. https://doi.org/10.1017/S1537592709090069

Henning, C. R., & Pratt, T. (2020). *Hierarchy and differentiation in international regime complexes: A theoretical framework for comparative research*. 13th Annual Conference on The Political Economy of International Organization. PEIO website: https://www.peio.me/wp-content/uploads/2020/01/PEIO13_paper_66.pdf

Hirschman, A. O. (1978). Exit, voice, and the state. *World Politics, 31*(01), 90–107. https://doi.org/10.2307/2009968

Hofmann, S. C. (2009). Overlapping institutions in the realm of international security: The case of NATO and ESDP. *Perspectives on Politics, 7*(01), 45–52. https://doi.org/10.1017/S1537592709090070

Hofmann, S. C. (2018). The politics of overlapping organizations: Hostage-taking, forum-shopping and brokering. *Journal of European Public Policy, 13*, 1–23. https://doi.org/10.1080/13501763.2018.1512644

Hofmann, S. C. (2011). Why institutional overlap matters: CSDP in the European Security Architecture. *JCMS: Journal of Common Market Studies, 49*(1), 101–120. https://doi.org/10.1111/j.1468-5965.2010.02131.x

Humrich, C. (2013). Fragmented international governance of Arctic offshore oil: Governance challenges and institutional improvement. *Global Environmental Politics, 13*(3), 79–99. https://doi.org/10.1162/GLEP_a_00184

Johnson, T., & Urpelainen, J. (2012). A strategic theory of regime integration and separation. *International Organization, 66*(04), 645–677. https://doi.org/10.1017/S0020818312000264

Jupille, J., Mattli, W., & Snidal, D. (2013). *Institutional choice and global commerce*. Cambridge University Press.

Keohane, R. O. (1984). *After hegemony: Cooperation and discord in the world political economy* (1st Princeton classic ed.). Princeton University Press.

Keohane, R. O., & Victor, D. G. (2011). The regime complex for climate change. *Perspectives on Politics, 9*(01), 7–23. https://doi.org/10.1017/S1537592710004068

Koremenos, B., Lipson, C., & Snidal, D. (2001). The rational design of international institutions. *International Organization, 55*(4), 761–799. https://doi.org/10.1162/002081801317193592

Krasner, S. D. (1982). Structural causes and regime consequences: Regimes as intervening variables. *International Organization, 36*(2), 185–205.

Lake, D. A. (2009). *Hierarchy in international relations. Cornell studies in political economy.* Cornell University Press.

Lake, D. A. (2010). Rightful rules: Authority, order, and the foundations of global governance. *International Studies Quarterly, 54*(3), 587–613. https://doi.org/10.1111/j.1468-2478.2010.00601.x

MacDonald, P. K. (2018). Embedded authority: A relational network approach to hierarchy in world politics. *Review of International Studies, 44*(1), 128–150. https://doi.org/10.1017/S0260210517000213

Martin, L. L. (1992). Interests, power, and multilateralism. *International Organization, 46*(04), 765. https://doi.org/10.1017/S0020818300033245

Morse, J. C., & Keohane, R. O. (2014). Contested multilateralism. *The Review of International Organizations, 9*(4), 385–412. https://doi.org/10.1007/s11558-014-9188-2

Muzaka, V. (2011). Linkages, contests and overlaps in the global intellectual property rights regime. *European Journal of International Relations, 17*(4), 755–776. https://doi.org/10.1177/1354066110373560

Orsini, A., Morin, J.-F., & Young, O. R. (2013). Regime complexes: A buzz, a boom or a boost for global governance? *Global Governance, 19*(1), 27–39.

Pratt, T. (2018). Deference and hierarchy in international regime complexes. *International Organization, 72*(3), 561–590. https://doi.org/10.1017/S0020818318000164

Raustiala, K., & Victor, D. G. (2004). The regime complex for plant genetic resources. *International Organization, 58*(2), 277–309. https://doi.org/10.2139/ssrn.441463

Schelling, T. C. (1960). *The strategy of conflict.* Harvard University Press.

Schneider, C. J., & Urpelainen, J. (2013). Distributional conflict between powerful states and international treaty ratification 1. *International Studies Quarterly, 57*(1), 13–27. https://doi.org/10.1111/isqu.12024

Simon, H. A. (1957). *Models of man: Social and rational mathematical essays on rational human behavior in society setting.* Wiley.

Snidal, D. (1994). The politics of scope: Endogenous actors, heterogeneity and institutions. *Journal of Theoretical Politics, 6*(4), 449–472. https://doi.org/10.1177/0951692894006004003

Tsebelis, G. (1995). Decision making in political systems: Veto players in presidentialism, parliamentarism, multicameralism and multipartyism. *British Journal of Political Science, 25*(03), 289. https://doi.org/10.1017/S00071 23400007225

Vabulas, F., & Snidal, D. (2013). Organization without delegation: Informal intergovernmental organizations (IIGOs) and the spectrum of intergovernmental arrangements. *The Review of International Organizations, 8*(2), 193–220. https://doi.org/10.1007/s11558-012-9161-x

Van de Graaf, T. (2013). Fragmentation in global energy governance: Explaining the creation of IRENA. *Global Environmental Politics, 13*(3), 14–33. https://doi.org/10.1162/GLEP_a_00181

Zelli, F., & van Asselt, H. (2013). Introduction: The institutional fragmentation of global environmental governance: Causes, consequences, and responses. *Global Environmental Politics, 13*(3), 1–13. https://doi.org/10.1162/GLEP_a_00180

Zürn, M., & Faude, B. (2013). Commentary: On fragmentation, differentiation, and coordination. *Global Environmental Politics, 13*(3), 119–130. https://doi.org/10.1162/GLEP_a_00186

CHAPTER 3

Struggling for Authority in Regime Complexes

This chapter analyzes the conditions leading to the four types of authority relationships in regime complexes—*when do we expect to find integration, fragmentation, marginalization, or resilience?* I argue that the answer lies in the dynamic interaction between states challenging the institutional status quo and those defending it. Their respective bargaining power and membership preferences determine the distribution of authority between institutions with overlapping mandates. A dissatisfied challenger coalition that engages in competitive regime creation is trying to change the focal institution, while the remaining states are defending the institutional status quo. But attempts to create a new center of authority are not always successful. The international system encompasses fragmented complexes with no identifiable focal institution, as well as cases where a contested institution is resilient enough to retain relational authority over its competitor. Differing outcomes are the result of the varying degrees of influence that coalitions of states have on the overall distribution of resources among the elemental institutions (Colgan et al., 2012). This influence, I argue, depends on the challenger coalition's go-it-alone power (Gruber, 2000), which is what determines its ability to create a credible threat of exclusion for the defenders of the status quo and helps to explain why the defenders accept a new distribution of institutional authority that is detrimental to their utility. In other words, go-it-alone

© The Author(s), under exclusive license to Springer Nature Switzerland AG 2023
F. Biermann, *The Battle for Authority in European Defence Cooperation*, Palgrave Studies in European Union Politics, https://doi.org/10.1007/978-3-031-30054-7_3

power is the condition that determines whether a newly created institutional competitor can become the new focal institution within a given issue area even against the preferences of the defender states. The previous chapter showed that, when we are interested in the distribution of authority among the elemental institutions of a complex, the membership structure of a newly created institution matters. I will argue that the challengers' *membership preference* for either an inclusive or an exclusive institutional alternative depends on the "member surplus" involved (Thompson & Verdier, 2014), in other words, the cost incurred by the founders of an institution when they include further members in relation to the transaction costs they save by their inclusion (Williamson, 1985). When the member surplus is high (when faced, e.g., with a high risk of free riding or distributive concerns), the challenger coalition will prefer an exclusive institution to an inclusive one. Contrariwise, if transaction costs are high and the member surplus is low (e.g., if the institution governs regulatory issues, such as standard setting), challengers will prefer a broad membership (Thompson & Verdier, 2014, p. 16). Thus, the theoretical framework I present draws on rational choice institutionalism (RCI) (Hall & Taylor, 1996), conceptualizing states as unitary and goal-oriented actors with fixed and transitive preferences (Axelrod, 1984; Keohane, 1984). To facilitate cooperation under anarchy, states create institutions that resolve collective action problems (Hasenclever et al., 1997; Ostrom, 1990; Zürn, 1992) and serve as "focal points" for negotiation between themselves (Drezner, 2013, p. 282; Schelling, 1960).

The first section of this chapter theorizes the—endogenous or exogenous—sources of states' dissatisfaction with an institution and, thus, the rationale behind the creation of competitive regime complexes. I argue that states' dissatisfaction originates in their inability to profit from the level of cooperation enshrined in an institution and then show that dissatisfied states engage in, and can potentially benefit from, competitive regime creation independently of their relative power. Even for a relatively weak state coalition, it can be rational to contest an institution they cannot benefit from. Then I put forward go-it-alone power as a condition determining the collective outcomes of authority distribution. Only a coalition of challenger states that possesses go-it-alone power can successfully turn an institutional contender into the new focal institution. Subsequently, I introduce the second condition: the challengers' membership preference. States base their preferences for inclusive or exclusive cooperation on the ratio between the costs of inclusion and the costs of exclusion, that is, the membership surplus and transaction costs. Combining the two perspectives allows me to develop the theoretical pathways linking the emergence of a regime complex through contestation with the outcomes of authority relations. Four different pathways emerge, depending on the absence or presence of the two basic conditions, the challengers' ability to create a threat of exclusion and their membership preference. Each pathway leads to a distinct distribution pattern of institutional authority.

Sources of Dissatisfaction

States' dissatisfaction with an institution and inability to reform it have been established as the scope conditions for competitive regime creation, that is, the creation of a regime complex in which at least two institutions have overlapping authority claims. To be able to theorize the conditions leading to particular outcomes for authority distribution between the institutions in a complex, one has to examine the sources of this dissatisfaction. In general terms, I hold that states become dissatisfied when an institution—for reasons endogenous or exogenous to its design—fails to provide their preferred level of cooperation. State preferences are motivated by geopolitical and economic interests (Moravcsik, 1998, p. 26), which can be approximated by considering a state's positional characteristics (cf., for example, Biermann et al., 2019; Schimmelfennig, 2001). In economic terms, a state's preference for cooperation depends on the benefits it can expect from trade, mutual market liberalization, or common standards in a given issue area—the more competitive a state's industry, the more profitable is international cooperation (Keohane, 1984; Porter, 1990). In geopolitical terms, a state prefers deeper cooperation in a specific issue area if this is consistent with its strategic orientation and interest in national sovereignty, and does not produce any negative security externalities (Moravcsik, 1998, p. 26). While economic and security interests often point in the same direction, since economic growth enhances power, there may be contradictions between the geopolitical and economic dimensions, which is why both sources of underlying preferences need to be considered.

A state's benefits from cooperation, in either case, depend on its ability to profit from mutually agreed commitments. Importantly, however, institutional membership is not always beneficial—not even in absolute terms. The reduction of trade barriers, for example, might considerably damage a state's immature industry. The introduction of high environmental standards might have a similar effect if the domestic status quo is far below the proposed standard. Analogously, an agreement to renounce the use of one type of weaponry predominantly benefits states that can draw on a larger number of alternatives. Especially in defense cooperation, preferences for the joint procurement, development, or production of armaments not only depend on a state's industrial capabilities, they also directly interfere with its strategic interests. The relation between economic and security considerations is disputed in the literature. Some hold that the "key to cooperation or conflict in the armaments sector is the primacy of concentrated domestic interests over a diffuse national security interest" (Moravcsik, 1993a, p. 160); others, in the realist tradition, assume the opposite (Dyson & Konstadinides, 2013; Rynning, 2011) and emphasize the national security interest over industrial preferences. As different issue areas vary in their importance depending on a state's positional characteristics in both economic and geopolitical terms, determining preferences is a task that must be undertaken for each policy area individually—and empirically.[1]

States become dissatisfied with an institution if the level of cooperation it provides does not correspond (or no longer corresponds) to its ability to profit from it. An institution locks in a specific level and scope of cooperation depending on the bargaining power of its signatories (Moravcsik, 1993b; Pierson, 2016). When states are dissatisfied with the collective outcomes produced through an institution, they try to renegotiate the terms of cooperation. Dissatisfaction can have exogenous and endogenous causes. Exogenous causes are rooted in developments beyond the logic of the institution. They are external changes that influence a state's ability to profit from institutional membership. If the institution does not adapt to such changes, contested multilateralism is the consequence (Zangl et al., 2016). Examples of such exogenous causes are wars, economic crises, domestic changes, and power shifts (Daßler et al., 2018). Endogenous causes emanate from "engrained practices" within an institution (Morse & Keohane, 2014, p. 391), such as inefficient outcomes due to stalemates in decision-making or recurring non-compliance. Moreover, some of the

---

[1] In Chapter 4 I will work out each EU member state's preference for cooperating under the auspices of either the EU or NATO on the one hand and of either a liberalized or a protectionist regime on the other, on the basis of their strategic orientation and their defense industrial characteristics.

distributive consequences of an institution might not have been obvious at the time of its creation—either because new governance challenges emerged and the institutional mandate was gradually stretched (Raustiala & Victor, 2004) or because the institution produced unintended consequences for some of its members (Menon, 2011b; Pierson, 2000).

Depending on their ability to profit from cooperation, states will create and use an alternative institution that either deepens or weakens cooperation by comparison with the original one (Snidal, 1994). It is important to note that, in view of interdependence and functional pressure to cooperate, challengers of the status quo cannot simply decide to stop using an institution with which they are dissatisfied without having an alternative at their disposal. Consequently, depending on their positional characteristics, states create intuitional alternatives for two reasons. First, they may, as a result of their relative position, have an interest in closer cooperation and be dissatisfied with an institution's lack of ambition and wish to create additional space for cooperative yields. When the defenders of the status quo capture the focal institution and prevent reforms (van de Graaf, 2013), the challengers establish an alternative in order to move on independently. Second, challengers who do not profit from cooperation do not want an institution to unfold its full potential as the collective outcomes generated on the basis of unfavorable rules would be detrimental to their utility. So they block the original institution. Confronted with functional pressure to cooperate, however, they join with like-minded states to create an institutional competitor.

In sum, challenger coalitions create institutional alternatives when they are dissatisfied with the terms of cooperation enshrined in an institution. Dissatisfaction can have exogenous or endogenous causes. States profit from cooperation to varying degrees depending on their economic and geopolitical positions. Some are dissatisfied with the inefficiency of an institution and push for deepened cooperation in an institutional alternative. Others, by contrast, attempt to block unfavorable cooperation by exiting the institution. As unilateralism is not an option, however, even states that want to weaken cooperation need to create an institutional alternative.

Contestation and Power

Building on the argument that states can become dissatisfied with an institution either because they deem cooperation to produce no benefits or because they view the institution as too unambitious, this section discusses the role of power in regime complexes. Contrary to conventional wisdom (as represented by, e.g., Drezner, 2009, 2013 or Benvenisti & Downs, 2007), the creation of competitive regimes and, thus, regime complexity may be beneficial to both relatively powerful and relatively weak coalitions of states.

Institutions are representative of the power distribution among their members. They reflect the fact that some states "have had greater influence over time" (Pierson, 2016, p. 129) in shaping their mandate, membership, and resources. I extend this argument, which, I argue, applies not only to elemental institutions but also to entire regime complexes governing given issue areas. Under contested multilateralism, a coalition of dissatisfied challenger states is pitted against the defenders of an institution. The challengers create an alternative forum with the intention of shifting resources away from the original institution and creating new use patterns thus making their favored venue the new center of authority in the issue area. By contrast, the defenders prefer using the original institution and oppose change. The challengers are not always able to achieve their goal of creating a new focal point by marginalizing or integrating the original institution. When they fail, the outcomes tend to be either institutional fragmentation, where no focal institution emerges and institutions co-exist in an uncoordinated environment, or resilience, where the original venue survives contestation. I argue that the determinant of whether contestation leads to a new anchor point in a complex—whether through integration or marginalization—is the relative power of the challengers and defenders.

My notion of relative power has two dimensions, one direct and one indirect. Keohane and Victor suggest power should be viewed as a "function of both the impact of one's own decisions on others (which depends mainly on the size and economic output) and on favorable asymmetries in interdependence leading to better default (no-agreement) positions for the state" (Keohane & Victor, 2011, p. 8). Interdependence means that states cannot reach their governance goals alone (Keohane, 1984;

Krasner, 1982; Moravcsik, 1993b).[2] Variation in a state's exposure to interdependence constitutes the indirect dimension of power, while the impact of one state's decisions on others is the more direct dimension. Interdependence is asymmetric if some states, due to positional characteristics such as their geographical position and strategic culture or the size of their economy and military apparatus, are less dependent on cooperation than others. For example, states situated on the eastern borders of the EU are more likely, in view of the recent Russian attack on Ukraine, to have a greater need for safety and cooperation need than, say, Portugal or Luxembourg. Similarly, the United Kingdom, due to its special relationship with the United States and its possession of nuclear weapons, might be less dependent on European defense cooperation than Germany. The lower the cost of a state's non-agreement, the higher its bargaining power and the more likely it is that the outcome of negotiations will be closer to its preferences (Moravcsik, 1993b, 1998). The more direct dimension mentioned by Keohane and Victor refers to the impact a state's decisions have on others. States with larger markets and higher capabilities are more important to the functioning of an institution than others. If the United States left NATO, this would have a higher impact than if Albania did. States whose decisions have a direct impact on others are thus likely to have more influence in decision-making.

While power matters, both as a potential source of dissatisfaction (if power relations are no longer properly represented in the institutional design) and as a condition explaining institutional outcomes, I reject the conclusion that "weak actors" have no means of challenging the institutional status quo. Contrary to the view that regime complexity serves only the most powerful (Benvenisti & Downs, 2007), I argue that relatively less powerful states can also have considerable influence on the authority distribution in a complex for two reasons. First, weak states can build coalitions. The act of contestation through coalition building can work as "a strategy of enhancing the collective power" of states (Fehl, 2016, p. 2) by pooling material power and reducing dependence (Vabulas & Snidal, 2013). Through coalition building, weak states can create a critical mass

---

[2] In security and defense, EU member states are unable to tackle global challenges such as terrorism and humanitarian crises, or economic challenges such as exploding production costs for military capabilities unilaterally in light of their pressurized defense budgets (Augustine, 1997; Platteau, 2015).

and be successful in their undertaking to shift cooperation from one institution to another. Second, and more importantly, even if a challenger coalition is relatively weak in terms of direct influence on others, it may have low costs of non-agreement, allowing it to block the functioning of an institution. Hofmann describes a case in which a single state, Cyprus, was able to take the relationship between NATO and the EU hostage by threatening to block decision-making within the EU if cooperation with Turkey was intensified (Hofmann, 2011, 2018). Hence, in settings where decision-making relies on unanimity or requires a large majority in the contested institution, a relatively weak coalition of states might be unable to develop an institutional competitor they have created into the new focal institution (which would be their preferred outcome). Yet they might nonetheless be able to weaken cooperation by fragmenting institutionalized cooperation and the distribution of resources, blocking the original institution by means of their veto power.

These considerations do indeed suggest that "organizational proliferation can shift world politics from rule-based outcomes to power-based outcomes" (Drezner, 2013, p. 280). States compete to establish their favored forum as the center of authority. Yet weaker states intending to suppress cooperation might value institutional fragmentation with separate memberships and separate resources as an outcome more than powerful states. Regime complexity does not necessarily "marginalize … the role of weaker states, which do not enjoy the same leverage" (Benvenisti & Downs, 2007, p. 597) but can empower them to prevent cooperation from happening. This seemingly paradoxical theoretical finding has its origin in the two sources of power. A state coalition that is relatively weak in terms of direct influence on others and made up of countries with small economies and uncompetitive industries may well have low costs of non-agreement for that very reason. These states are unlikely to gain much from cooperation and thus might prefer a state of limited and fragmented coordination. While competitive regime creation by a weak coalition may not lead to the establishment of a new focal point, continuously blocking the contested forum "delegitimizes an institution, forcing concomitant change" (Morse & Keohane, 2014, p. 389). In sum, *the creation of regime complexes can serve as a worthwhile means of challenging the institutional status quo for both relatively powerful and relatively weak coalitions of states.*

In the next section, I introduce the notion of go-it-alone power, which combines both sources of power in a single concept, focusing on states' ability to create a credible threat of exclusion. Moreover, it puts the translation of power into action center stage. Go-it-alone power can explain why states that are satisfied with the institutional status quo could accept that a new institution of which they are not even a member becomes the new center of authority.

Condition I—Go-It-Alone Power

If we aim to determine the conditions under which to expect integration, marginalization, resilience, or fragmentation respectively, that is, the different distributions of authority among the elemental institutions of a complex, we need to theorize the conditions under which states agree to shift the bulk of financial and political resources to an institutional competitor. Under which conditions are dissatisfied challenger states successful in making their institutional alternative the new center of authority that is accepted by the defenders of the status quo? I argue that the success of state coalitions' attempts to alter the patterns of institutional use depends on their go-it-alone power (Gruber, 2000). If a coalition possesses the power to go it alone and can create a threat of exclusion to the defenders of the status quo, the latter states will try to join the institutional competitor and accept it as having the required relational authority to become the new focal institution. What is more, they will do so even if these institutional outcomes are detrimental to their utility in comparison to the status quo ante. Given diverging preferences, I thus understand the creation of regime complexity as a power-based renegotiation of cooperation. Powerful coalitions are successful in establishing a new center of authority, that is, an outcome of integration or marginalization. Less powerful coalitions can prevent institutionalized cooperation from happening, generating a situation of institutional fragmentation but are not able to create a new focal institution.

Lloyd Gruber (2000) observes that some states engage in institutionalized cooperation that puts them in a worse position than the non-cooperative status quo ante. Cooperation can generate winners and losers—not only in relative terms understanding cooperation as a zero-sum game but even in absolute terms (Gruber, 2000, p. 7). The reason states accept such arrangements

> is their fear of being left behind. What tips the balance for these participants – what motivates them to integrate their policies with those of the

winners – is not the prospect of mutual gain so much as the absence of any better alternative. Loath to exclude themselves from the regional and multilateral regimes appearing around them, the losers decide it is in their own interests to cooperate. But they do so despite, not because of, these regimes' utility consequences. (Gruber, 2000, p. 47)

States can induce other states to join institutional arrangements, which are detrimental to their utility compared to the status quo ante. They do not need to do so by means of coercive power, threatening negative consequences, but can reach their goal by moving ahead alone. In light of the challengers' demonstrated ability to go it alone, the defenders of the status quo have no alternative other than to grant the institution the right to rule as a result of a lost political struggle (Lake, 2009, p. 20). The non-cooperative status quo ante having been erased by the challengers' solo run, the options for the defenders are being sidelined or accepting the authority of the institution.

Take the following example (see Fig. 3.1). There are two groups of states, group A and group B. The states in group A want to establish a free-trade regime comprising all states and markets. Group B prefers a protectionist system with the ability to levy tariffs—its preferred outcome would be to establish free trade only in one specific sector where their industries are more mature. The states of group A now create a free-trade arrangement among themselves (SQ_1). This institution increases group A's utility compared to the status quo ante as it can benefit from enlarged sales markets, free movement of goods, and specialization. For group A, it would be irrational to return to the status quo ante (SQ_0), which thus has been erased from the set of feasible alternatives for group B (Gruber, 2000, p. 39). Group B can no longer prevent free trade from happening. Moreover, the existence of group A's free-trade regime decreases group B's utility as their products will be more expensive for the states of group A given a decreased world market price, and B's exports will consequently decrease. What is more, to protect their domestic industries, states of group B would have to further increase tariffs preventing their consumers from profiting from the lower world market prices. Consequently, the states of group B will now try to join the free-trade agreement in SQ_2. Doing so will increase their utility in comparison to SQ_1, as their consumers can now profit from free trade. Yet joining the free-trade agreement makes group B worse off in comparison to the non-cooperative status quo ante (SQ_0) as their uncompetitive industries will suffer and lose leverage, developing from price setters into price takers. The result is a situation in which group A has considerably improved its utility while the states of group B have suffered a loss by comparison with the non-cooperative starting point. The cooperative outcome is thus not situated on the Pareto frontier.

The dynamic of go-it-alone power sets in when some states are able to change the status quo on their own in a way that increases their own utility while decreasing the utility of others. This being the case, the concept of go-it-alone power is in line with Moravcsik's understanding that "the existence of opportunities to form attractive alternative coalitions (or deepen existing ones), while excluding other parties, strengthens the bargaining power of potential coalition members vis-à-vis those threatened with exclusion" (Moravcsik, 1993b, pp. 502–503). Importantly, however, go-it-alone power not only points to states strengthening their bargaining power in a way that helps the challengers reach an agreement on the Pareto frontier, which is closer to their optimum, but to

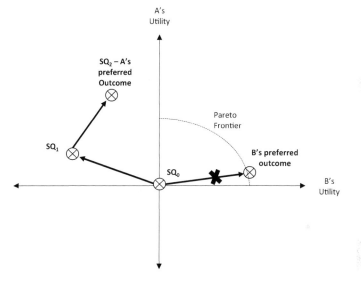

Fig. 3.1 Go-it-alone power[3]

[3] Cf. Gruber (2000, p. 39).

achieve institutional change *against* the preferences of the defenders by actually creating a *fait accompli*.

Simplified as a two-player game in Fig. 3.1 go-it-alone power unfolds its pulling force according to a "bandwagoning dynamic" (Gruber, 2000, p. 47, see also Biermann, 2022; van de Graaf, 2013, p. 21). If some states go it alone and create an institution while another group of states opposes this framework, the latter might diverge in their *degree* of opposition depending on the costs involved. Whenever the non-member state with the lowest compliance costs finds it beneficial to join the institution because the status quo ante is no longer available, this may generate additional negative externalities for those remaining outside (Gruber, 2000, p. 46). Hence, any joiner state increases the costs of staying outside for the next state in the ranking, which may now find joining the new institution to be beneficial.

Applying the concept to situations of contested multilateralism, a coalition of states possesses go-it-alone power when it can create an institutional arrangement that represents a credible threat of exclusion to its non-members. To exert its pulling force, go-it-alone power must not only have the ability to cooperate exclusively but also demonstrate that exclusion is detrimental to the outsiders as compared to the status quo ante. This pulling force is necessary if an institutional competitor is to become the new center of authority in the complex. Thus, only if the challengers of the institutional status quo possess go-it-alone power, in other words, are able to create a threat of exclusion that generates negative externalities for the non-members of the institution (cf. Johnson & Urpelainen, 2012) while improving their own utility as compared to the status quo, will the defenders try to join. Consequently, only if the defenders of the status quo accept the authority[4] of an institution and *want to join* it can the challengers renegotiate the terms of cooperation in a way that leads either to the integration or marginalization of the original institution to the benefit of its competitor.

---

[4] I understand recognition of the (relational) authority of an international institution as well as its hierarchical position relative to its competitor to be the outcome of negotiations (Lake, 2009, 2010) and thus refrain from engaging with broader conceptions, such as "reflexive authority" emphasizing the recognition of expertise (Zürn, 2017). Yet, authority always contains "some element of consent" (Barnett & Finnemore, 2004, p. 28) resulting from weighing the alternatives and thus is distinct from coercive power.

However, if the challengers lack go-it-alone power, the institutional competitor they create will not pose a credible threat of exclusion. Even so, dissatisfied challengers lacking the power to go it alone will be able to block cooperation in the contested institution and generate disutility for its defenders. Yet the act of competitive regime creation does not generate additional negative externalities. While the challengers can enhance their utility unilaterally by shifting cooperation away from the institution they are dissatisfied with, they do not generate a pulling force, as the utility of the defenders is not diminished through the establishment of the institutional competitor. Therefore, the defenders will not accept the institutional competitor as the new focal institution against their preferences. Building on this, two conjectures can thus be specified:

1. *When the challengers of the institutional status quo possess go-it-alone power, they can successfully shift authority from a contested to an alternative institution.*
2. *When the challengers of the institutional status quo do not possess go-it-alone power, they will be unable to shift authority from the contested to the alternative institution.*

In sum, the ability to go it alone determines whether the challengers of the institutional status quo can induce a shift of authority from the contested to the challenger institution. Nevertheless, the creation of an institutional alternative without go-it-alone power can still be consequential. It may result not only in the integration or marginalization of the contested institution but also in the fragmentation of a regime complex or the resilience, and even the further expansion, of the original institution. Before being able to spell out the four pathways to the different interinstitutional authority relations, it is necessary to theorize a second condition: the challengers' membership preference, which determines whether the defenders are *allowed* to join an institution, which presents them with a threat of exclusion.

Condition II—Membership Preference

Challenger coalitions' preference for either inclusive or exclusive membership is arrived at, according to my argument, on the basis of a trade-off between the member surplus and transaction costs, in other words, on the ratio between the cost of including and the cost of excluding additional member states. This preference will determine whether the outcome is characterized by membership overlap or by separate or identical membership structures within the two institutions. Club theory has a long tradition of pointing to the costs that arise from having too many members, which can, through congestion or crowding, endanger the functioning of an institution (Buchanan, 1965). Moreover, cooperation is typically easier in smaller groups as compliance is easier to monitor (Ostrom, 1990). The higher the number of members, the more likely preferences are to be heterogeneous and the more difficult it is to reach an agreement (Gehring & Oberthür, 2009, p. 139; Snidal, 1994). A high number of members with diverging preferences often merely makes for minimal consensus—especially under unanimity requirements (Moravcsik, 1993b, p. 501). Consequently, it seems obvious that states with a preference for deepened cooperation strive for an exclusive institution with a limited membership consisting of capable and ambitious participants. Yet this is only one side of the coin. Broad membership can provide considerable benefits to its members. If an institution provides a collective good, the more members that participate in its production, the cheaper it is for the individual state (Sandler & Tschirhart, 1997). Moreover, multilateral institutions serve to reduce transaction costs (Williamson, 1985). The more members an institution has, the more comprehensive its rules and the fewer parallel agreements need to be negotiated. The benefits of broad membership are most apparent when considering "technical standards, where actors have no incentive to defect" (Koremenos et al., 2001, p. 776), and each additional member reduces transaction costs. One good example here would be the agreement on interoperability requirements for machinery. Every additional adherent to the standard increases the benefits of those who already subscribe to it.

It is difficult for states to maximize the benefits connected with a large membership and those deriving from a broad spectrum of cooperation. Alexander Thompson and Daniel Verdier (2014) argue that the difficulties the founders of a new institution face when deciding on the admission of additional members are based on the trade-off between transaction costs and member surplus. This trade-off captures the inverse relation between the transaction costs saved by not having to negotiate an additional agreement with an outside state (cost of exclusion) and the cost the founders of an institution incur in incentivizing a new member to join and to securing its compliance with the agreed commitments (cost of inclusion). The member surplus comprises the losses the founder of a multilateral institution incurs when admitting additional members as compared to negotiating bilateral agreements with outside states. These losses, on the other hand, are benefits to new members that would have joined an institution with less of an incentive as compared to the state with the highest cost of compliance. I will provide an example:

Imagine a situation in which state A wants to found an institution to coordinate a reduction of 300 million tons of CO_2 per year. The institution will oblige every member to reduce its CO_2 emissions by 100 million tons per year. To persuade two additional states to join the agreement, the founder of the institution has to offer an incentive that will make it attractive for the state with the highest costs of compliance. State B is willing to join the agreement as it stands; state C, however, will only join if the commitment is reduced to 90 million tons per year. As "multilateralism in its pure form offers only one deal" (Thompson & Verdier, 2014, p. 16) to all members, the agreement will have to be settled at 90 million tons—leaving state B (who would have reduced 100 million tons if required) with a surplus of 10 million tons—a price that will now have to be paid by state A to reach the goal of a total reduction of 300 million tons. The institutionally agreed total reduction would amount to 270 million tons instead of 290 if A had created two separate bilateral institutions with B and C. To achieve its goal of 300 tons per year, state A will thus have to reduce its CO_2 emissions by 120 tons instead of only 110, so the member surplus works out at the cost of 10 million tons of CO_2 reduction—around 400 million Euros.[5] Admittedly, negotiating two agreements instead of only one will place an additional cost burden on the founder state as well. The costs of negotiating the agreements and enforcing them will be higher than those of establishing only one institution. Moreover, cooperating in separate regimes can cause negative spillovers, that is, externalities that negatively influence the effectiveness of institutional agreements (Johnson & Urpelainen, 2012). Even so, in this example, it is hardly imaginable that the cost of negotiating and maintaining two institutions would outweigh the member surplus, which is why state A would prefer two bilateral agreements over one multilateral deal.

---

[5] This is an imaginary number based on a McKinsey estimate to grasp the correct magnitude (cf. https://www.mckinsey.com/business-functions/sustainability-and-resource-productivity/our-insights/a-cost-curve-for-greenhouse-gas-reduction).

The two inversely running cost functions constitute the transaction cost–member surplus trade-off. A number of variables can determine the ratio between transaction costs and member surplus, in other words, the ratio between the costs of exclusion and of inclusion. First, regarding transaction cost, the costs of negotiating various bi- or minilateral frameworks for a founding coalition rise the more states are affected by a cooperation problem (Koremenos et al., 2001). Similarly, the broader the issue area governed by an institution, the more likely there are to be negative spillovers when cooperating through various separated frameworks (Johnson & Urpelainen, 2012). In other words, the broader the issue is and the greater the number of states affected, the higher the costs of exclusion will be. Second, the greater the distributive effects (in financial and security terms) produced by an institution, the higher the member surplus (Thompson & Verdier, 2014). Similarly, if the cleavage between states with competitive and those with uncompetitive industries is deep, for instance, where there is a high degree of preference heterogeneity (Snidal, 1994), the member surplus is high, as potential inducements for unwilling states to join will have to be considerable. Thus, the more distributive effects an institution has and the more heterogeneous the potential member states, the higher the costs of inclusion.

States try to navigate the trade-off between membership surplus and transaction costs. They try to include additional members only when the member surplus of taking on additional board members is lower than the transaction costs the founder states of the institution would incur when excluding them. Figure 3.2 depicts the founding states' utility function in relation to the number of outside states admitted to their institutional competitor. To the left of the utility maximum, the *member surplus is low* in relation to the *high transaction costs*. Thus, any additional member of the institution decreases the transaction cost disproportionally to the increase in the member surplus. In other words, with every additional member, the *founders' utility increases*. Consequently, the founders prefer an *inclusive institution* with a wide membership. To the right of the utility maximum, the *member surplus is higher* than the relatively *low transaction costs*. Therefore, including further members in the institution creates *disutility for the founding states*, as the cost of assuring their compliance outweighs the benefits in transaction cost savings. Hence, the founders prefer to cooperate among themselves in an *exclusive institution* and do not want to include any further members in their club. As I have argued elsewhere, optimizing this trade-off is very difficult in practice—especially under the auspices of the European Union, where states need to be treated equally (Biermann, 2022). Therefore, we might surmise that states have two (suboptimal) options available:

At a given point in time, the following two conjectures can be made about the design preferences of a coalition of states that have founded an institution:

1. *When the member surplus is low in relation to the transaction costs, the founding coalition prefers the newly created institution to be inclusive.*
2. *When the member surplus is high in relation to the transaction costs, the founding coalition prefers to cooperate through an exclusive institution.*

In sum, states, that are dissatisfied with the institutional status quo and find a way to reform blocked, try to create a new focal institution that serves their preferences better. The challengers' preference for an institutional alternative with an inclusive as opposed to an exclusive membership will depend on the member surplus–transaction cost trade-off, which is the ratio between the costs of including and those of excluding additional members. If the member surplus is low in relation to the transaction costs,

Fig. 3.2 Membership surplus—transaction cost trade-off

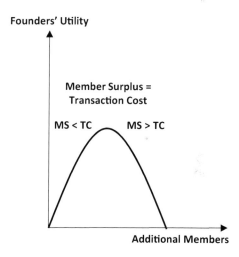

the challengers strive for an inclusive institutional competitor. If it is high, they will prefer to create an exclusive challenger institution alongside a marginalized inclusive one. The next section combines the two conditions, membership preference and go-it-alone power, to determine the distinct interinstitutional authority relations.

Explaining Authority Distributions

In this section, I connect challenger preferences for an inclusive or exclusive institutional competitor with their ability to change the focal institution, that is, their go-it-alone power. Combining the challengers' ability to generate a threat of exclusion with their membership preference allows us to specify the pathways leading to the four separate outcomes of authority distributions—integration, marginalization, fragmentation, and resilience—which will subsequently be subject to empirical examination.

Table 3.1 summarizes how the challenger's ability to create a credible threat of exclusion and its membership preference determine the authority distribution within a regime complex. While the member surplus–transaction cost trade-off determines the challenger coalition's preference for inclusive or exclusive membership in the institutional competitor, its go-it-alone power determines whether the challengers can issue a credible threat of exclusion and thus realize their preferred mode of coordination between the two institutions. The two conditions together account for whether the two entities will have separate, identical, or overlapping membership and resources. What is more, in cases where the two institutions are characterized by overlapping membership and resources, the two conditions can explain which of the two fora will have more authority in the area of overlap.

Table 3.1 Explanatory framework

		Challengers' membership preference	
		Inclusive	*Exclusive*
Challengers create a threat of exclusion	Yes	Integration	Marginalization
	No	Resilience	Fragmentation

Pathway to integration: I expect challenger states to integrate a contested institution's functions into a newly created alternative with identical membership when they can create a threat of exclusion and prefer inclusive membership. If challengers are dissatisfied with an institution but find the pathway to internal reform blocked, they will propose to create an institutional alternative. If they possess go-it-alone power, they will be able to improve their utility unilaterally while worsening the position of the defenders. Consequently, the defenders will fear being excluded and feel the urge to join the competing institution to prevent their being sidelined. There are two reasons why they may do so: either to get a piece of the cake distributed through the institution or to make sure that this cake is as small as possible by joining to prevent deeper cooperation from within. If the member surplus is low in relation to the transaction cost arising from non-coordination, that is, additional members will increase the benefits for the founding states, the challengers will have the ability to exclude the defenders but no interest in doing so. On the contrary, the creators of the new institution will have an actual interest in the defenders joining them and may even be willing to incentivize them to do so (Thompson & Verdier, 2014). Through the "bandwagoning" dynamic inherent in the concept of go-it-alone power, this will eventually lead to the new institution and the old having identical membership structures (Gruber, 2000, p. 47). Consequently, neither challengers nor defenders will be able to expect any further benefits, such as forum-shopping or hostage-taking (Hofmann, 2018), from maintaining both institutions (Martin, 1992). Therefore, the member states will centralize their resources and integrate the regulatory functions. Only one overarching and hierarchical institution will survive (Keohane & Victor, 2011).

Pathway to marginalization: I expect the marginalization of a contested institution to take place when the challengers of the institutional status quo possess go-it-alone power and prefer the institutional alternative to be exclusive. A coalition of challengers is dissatisfied with the institutional status quo. As internal reform is blocked, they create an institutional alternative to reorganize cooperation. As the challengers possess go-it-alone power, this unilateral move adversely affects the situation of the defenders while improving the challengers' utility. Marginalization is the outcome when challenger states have both the ability and the incentive to exclude defenders. A high member surplus, that is, a high cost of inclusion, will discourage the challengers from admitting further participants, especially if the institution has a distributive character and there is significant heterogeneity between the challengers and the defenders of the status quo (Thompson & Verdier, 2014). After setting up the competitive regime, the challenger states will have dual membership of both the contested and the new institution and be able to decide which they want to use. In light of the high member surplus, they would be expected to divert most of their resources to the exclusive institutional alternative. Consequently, the defenders fear that the contested institution will sink into insignificance. This allows the powerful challengers to arrange the interinstitutional relationship in the way that benefits them most and results in the new institution becoming focal while the original one loses authority in the area of mandate overlap. This will be successful since the defenders will accept the relational authority of the challenger institution in order to retain at least some influence for the original institution, which will lead to the latter's marginalization and the attribution of the bulk of relational authority to the exclusive venue. Eventually, the dual members will regularly use the new, exclusive institutional alternative and the defenders will accept the loss of authority of the original institution.

Pathway to fragmentation: Competitive regime creation is expected to result in fragmentation if the challengers do not possess go-it-alone power and prefer to cooperate in an exclusive institution. Once again, the challengers are dissatisfied with the institutional status quo. Fragmentation results if dissatisfied challengers lack the power to go it alone and create an institutional alternative because reforms are blocked. While the institutional competitor does not represent a threat of exclusion, the challenger's exclusive membership preference does allow it to divert its resources to the newly created institution while at the same time blocking the contested original institution. Not representing a threat of exclusion, the institutional alternative does not put any additional burden on the defenders. In other words, while the challengers are able to improve their own utility by exiting the inclusive institution, their creation of a competitive regime does not generate a pulling force for the defenders. Nonetheless, in light of functional pressure to uphold cooperation and because the challengers have blocked the contested institution, the defenders need to create a new forum themselves to re-establish the level of utility they had in the status quo ante. Without a credible threat of exclusion and in the absence of high transaction costs to stimulate inclusive cooperation, neither challengers nor defenders will be able to dictate the total resource distribution across the institutions. The challengers have no means of convincing the defenders to accept the focal position of their preferred venue. The consequence is a fragmented regime complex consisting of parallel elemental institutions with separate memberships and unrelated resources. Authority is divided across the institutions, and none of them becomes the center of authority.

Pathway to resilience: Finally, I expect resilience from the contested institution if the challengers are unable to create a threat of exclusion and prefer cooperation to be inclusive. When the challengers' competitive regime creation not only lacks a negative utility effect on the defender coalition—as in the case of fragmentation—but also causes disutility to the challengers themselves, the original institution will remain resilient. This situation may occur for two reasons. First, the challengers may underestimate the level of interdependence involved and the resulting need to cooperate with the defenders to reach their governance goals in which case their policy is likely to fail. Alternatively, external shocks, such as a deteriorating security environment, economic crises, or the loss of a coalition member through domestic changes, may increase interdependence, the cost of non-agreement, and thus the need to work together. In either case, the cost of inclusive cooperation will be reduced, and the cost of exclusion increased. With the challengers subject to this pressure to cooperate in an inclusive forum, the defenders of the original institution are now in the driver's seat and have the possibility of refocusing their preferred venue of cooperation. As the challengers have demonstrated their inability to go it alone, the defenders will now be able to dictate the terms of cooperation, thus improving their utility as compared to the status quo ante. If the defenders are able to generate a threat of exclusion themselves, this will lead to a situation in which the original institution is resilient and has more relational authority than the institutional competitor, which will be sidelined. Figure 3.3 summarizes all four causal pathways to the different outcomes of interinstitutional relationships.

SUMMARY

My task in this chapter was to identify the conditions leading to the different outcomes of interinstitutional relationships in a regime complex. When should we expect integration or fragmentation, and when do we observe marginalization or resilience? I have argued that the authority distribution between the elemental institutions of a complex depends on the dynamic interaction between the challengers and defenders of the institutional status quo. Finally, I theorized four pathways to distinct

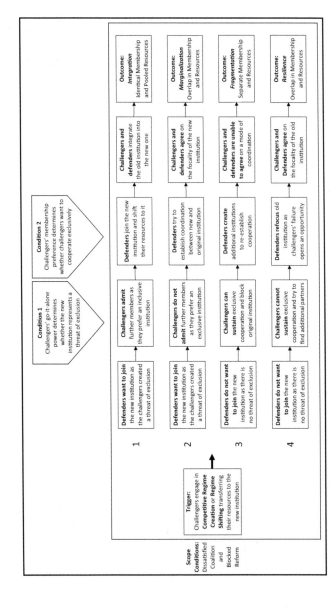

Fig. 3.3 Theoretical pathways to interinstitutional relationships in regime complexes

interinstitutional relationships. Figure 3.3 offers a schematic overview of these four pathways. All share the same scope conditions and trigger: first, a dissatisfied coalition of states with the goal of reforming an existing institution of which they are members; second, the impossibility, due to the existence of veto players (Tsebelis, 1995), of reform by internal means; finally, the challengers' engaging in competitive regime creation or regime shifting being the trigger to one of the four pathways. The challengers' go-it-alone power and their membership preference then determine which of the four pathways the process follows. If states possess go-it-alone power, their institutional alternative represents a credible threat of exclusion to the defenders of the status quo. Fearing to be left out, the defenders try to join the new institution. Whether the challenger states have an interest in admitting them depends on the ratio between member surplus and transaction cost. When the member surplus is low and transaction costs are relatively high, the challengers will have an interest in inclusive membership and accept the defenders into the new forum. In this case, the two institutions will end up with identical membership, and there will be no overlap. What is more, both challengers and defenders will allocate their resources only to the new institution as there are no extra benefits from maintaining both. The result will be the *integration* of the original institution's functions into the newly created alternative. When accepting new members is costly, the challengers will prefer to keep the new venue as an exclusive alternative to the pre-existing, inclusive institution. In this situation, the challengers will be dual members while the defenders are only members of the original institution, in other words, there will be membership overlap. As the challengers will shift their resources to the exclusive institution, this will have a detrimental effect on the defenders. The latter, consequently, will have an interest in coordinating activities between the two institutions to secure at least some influence on the issue area to be governed. Sectorial specialization, expanding the authority of the institutional competitor while limiting the influence of the original institution, is the result. The contested institution is *marginalized*. If the challengers lack go-it-alone power, the defenders will not fear being excluded and will not be urged to join the institution. Whether this leads to fragmentation or resilience depends on the challenger's membership preference, that is, their ability to sustain exclusive cooperation. If the member surplus is high and transaction costs are low, the challengers can sustain *exclusive* cooperation among themselves, which will enable them to block the original institution and shift their resources to the new forum. In this case, the defenders will no longer be able to use their preferred forum but need to create an alternative institution themselves to re-establish their original utility level. The challengers' lack of go-it-alone power, in combination with their preference for an exclusive forum, will lead to a quasi-symmetrical power distribution between challengers and defenders. *Fragmentation* of the institutional landscape will be the outcome. When transaction costs are high and membership surplus low, however, the challengers cannot sustain cooperation among themselves—they will prefer *inclusive* cooperation. This failure on the part of the challengers to create a credible outside option is tantamount to an ability on the defenders' part to refocus the original institution and generate a threat of exclusion themselves. The defenders are thus able to pull the challengers back to the original institution and they consequently agree to shift their resources back—the original institution is *resilient*.

The remainder of this book is devoted to demonstrating the explanatory value of the theorized explanatory framework and its respective pathways in the realm of European defense cooperation. I will first examine the four pathways individually by tracing the process connecting the trigger, competitive regime creation, with the respective outcomes of authority distribution. In a second step, I will conduct a congruence analysis contrasting the explanatory leverage of my framework with two alternative explanations, neorealism and neofunctionalism. At the beginning of the empirical part, I will briefly discuss the relevant actors in the case studies, the EU member states, and their (constant) preferences. EU member states can be divided into four groups according to their positional characteristics. The underlying preferences are subsequently used in the case studies to explain the sources of dissatisfaction and to derive the coalitions' membership preferences for specific institutions.

References

Augustine, N. R. (1997). *Augustine's laws* (6th ed.). American Institute of Aeronautics and Astronautics.

Axelrod, R. M. (1984). *The evolution of cooperation.* Basic Books.

Barnett, M. N., & Finnemore, M. (2004). *Rules for the world: International organizations in global politics.* Cornell University Press. http://www.jstor.org/stable/10.7591/j.ctt7z7mx

Benvenisti, E., & Downs, G. W. (2007). The emperor's new clothes: Political economy and the fragmentation of international law. *Stanford Law Review*, 60(2), 595–632.
Biermann, F. (2022). The differentiation paradox of European Integration: Why going it alone produces suboptimal results. *JCMS: Journal of Common Market Studies*, Early view. https://doi.org/10.1111/jcms.13373
Biermann, F., Guérin, N., Jagdhuber, S., Rittberger, B., & Weiss, M. (2019). Political (non-)reform in the euro crisis and the refugee crisis: A liberal intergovernmentalist explanation. *Journal of European Public Policy*, 26(2), 246–266. https://doi.org/10.1080/13501763.2017.1408670
Buchanan, J. M. (1965). An economic theory of clubs. *Economica*, 32(125), 1. https://doi.org/10.2307/2552442
Colgan, J. D., Keohane, R. O., & van de Graaf, T. (2012). Punctuated equilibrium in the energy regime complex. *The Review of International Organizations*, 7(2), 117–143. https://doi.org/10.1007/s11558-011-9130-9
Daßler, B., Kruck, A., & Zangl, B. (2018). Interactions between hard and soft power: The institutional adaptation of international intellectual property protection to global power shifts. *European Journal of International Relations*, 5(1). https://doi.org/10.1177/1354066118768871
Drezner, D. W. (2009). The power and peril of international regime complexity. *Perspectives on Politics*, 7(01), 65–70. https://doi.org/10.1017/S1537592709090100
Drezner, D. W. (2013). The tragedy of the global institutional commons. In J. Goldstein & M. Finnemore (Eds.), *Back to basics: State power in a contemporary world* (pp. 280–310). Oxford University Press. https://doi.org/10.1093/acprof:oso/9780199970087.003.0013
Dyson, T., & Konstadinides, T. (2013). *European defence cooperation in EU law and IR theory*. Palgrave Macmillan.
Fehl, C. (2016). *Forum shopping from above and below: Power shifts and institutional choice in a stratified international society*. Paper prepared for the workshop on "Power Transitions and Institutional Change". Munich.
Gehring, T., & Oberthür, S. (2009). The causal mechanisms of interaction between international institutions. *European Journal of International Relations*, 15(1), 125–156. https://doi.org/10.1177/1354066108100055
Gruber, L. (2000). *Ruling the world: Power politics and the rise of supranational institutions*. Princeton University Press.
Hall, P. A., & Taylor, R. C. R. (1996). Political science and the three new institutionalisms. *Political Studies*, 44(5), 936–957. https://doi.org/10.1111/j.1467-9248.1996.tb00343.x
Hasenclever, A., Mayer, P., & Rittberger, V. (1997). *Theories of international regimes. Cambridge studies in international relations* (Vol. 55). Cambridge University Press. https://doi.org/10.1017/CBO9780511521720

Hofmann, S. C. (2018). The politics of overlapping organizations: Hostage-taking, forum-shopping and brokering. *Journal of European Public Policy, 13*, 1–23. https://doi.org/10.1080/13501763.2018.1512644

Hofmann, S. C. (2011). Why institutional overlap matters: CSDP in the European Security Architecture. *JCMS: Journal of Common Market Studies, 49*(1), 101–120. https://doi.org/10.1111/j.1468-5965.2010.02131.x

Johnson, T., & Urpelainen, J. (2012). A strategic theory of regime integration and separation. *International Organization, 66*(04), 645–677. https://doi.org/10.1017/S0020818312000264

Keohane, R. O. (1984). *After hegemony: Cooperation and discord in the world political economy* (1st Princeton classic ed.). Princeton University Press

Keohane, R. O., & Victor, D. G. (2011). The regime complex for climate change. *Perspectives on Politics, 9*(01), 7–23. https://doi.org/10.1017/S1537592710004068

Koremenos, B., Lipson, C., & Snidal, D. (2001). The rational design of international institutions. *International Organization, 55*(4), 761–799. https://doi.org/10.1162/002081801317193592

Krasner, S. D. (1982). Structural causes and regime consequences: Regimes as intervening variables. *International Organization, 36*(2), 185–205.

Lake, D. A. (2009). *Hierarchy in international relations. Cornell studies in political economy*. Cornell University Press.

Lake, D. A. (2010). Rightful rules: Authority, order, and the foundations of global governance. *International Studies Quarterly, 54*(3), 587–613. https://doi.org/10.1111/j.1468-2478.2010.00601.x

Martin, L. L. (1992). Interests, power, and multilateralism. *International Organization, 46*(04), 765. https://doi.org/10.1017/S0020818300033245

Menon, A. (2011b). Power, institutions and the CSDP: The promise of institutionalist theory. *JCMS: Journal of Common Market Studies, 49*(1), 83–100. https://doi.org/10.1111/j.1468-5965.2010.02130.x

Moravcsik, A. (1993a). Armaments among allies: European weapons collaboration, 1975–1985. In H. K. Jacobson, P. B. Evans, & R. D. Putnam (Eds.), *Studies in international political economy* (vol. 25). *Double-edged diplomacy: International bargaining and domestic politics* (pp. 128–167). University of California Press.

Moravcsik, A. (1993b). Preferences and power in the European Community: A liberal intergovernmentalist approach. *JCMS: Journal of Common Market Studies, 31*(4), 473–524. https://doi.org/10.1111/j.1468-5965.1993.tb00477.x

Moravcsik, A. (1998). *The choice for Europe: Social purpose and state power from Messina to Maastricht. Cornell studies in political economy*. Cornell University Press.

Morse, J. C., & Keohane, R. O. (2014). Contested multilateralism. *The Review of International Organizations*, 9(4), 385–412. https://doi.org/10.1007/s11558-014-9188-2

Ostrom, E. (1990). *Governing the commons: The evolution of institutions for collective action*. Cambridge University Press.

Pierson, P. (2000). Increasing returns, path dependence, and the study of politics. *American Political Science Review*, 94(02), 251–267. https://doi.org/10.2307/2586011

Pierson, P. (2016). Power in historical institutionalism. In O. Fioretos, T. G. Falleti, & A. Sheingate (Eds.), *The Oxford handbook of historical institutionalism* (pp. 124–141). Oxford University Press.

Platteau, E. (2015). *Defence Data 2013*. https://issuu.com/europeandefenceagency/docs/eda_defence_data_2013_web/1?e=4763412/12106343

Porter, M. E. (1990). *The competitive advantage of nations*. Free Pr.

Raustiala, K., & Victor, D. G. (2004). The regime complex for plant genetic resources. *International Organization*, 58(2), 277–309. https://doi.org/10.2139/ssrn.441463

Rynning, S. (2011). Realism and the common security and defence policy. *JCMS: Journal of Common Market Studies*, 49(1), 23–42. https://doi.org/10.1111/j.1468-5965.2010.02127.x

Sandler, T., & Tschirhart, J. (1997). Club theory: Thirty years later. *Public Choice*, 93(3/4), 335–355. https://doi.org/10.1023/A:1017952723093

Schelling, T. C. (1960). *The strategy of conflict*. Harvard University Press.

Schimmelfennig, F. (2001). The community trap: Liberal norms, rhetorical action, and the Eastern enlargement of the European Union. *International Organization*, 55(1), 47–80. https://doi.org/10.1162/002081801551414

Snidal, D. (1994). The politics of scope: Endogenous actors, heterogeneity and institutions. *Journal of Theoretical Politics*, 6(4), 449–472. https://doi.org/10.1177/0951692894006004003

Thompson, A., & Verdier, D. (2014). Multilateralism, bilateralism, and regime design. *International Studies Quarterly*, 58(1), 15–28. https://doi.org/10.1111/isqu.12100

Tsebelis, G. (1995). Decision making in political systems: Veto players in presidentialism, parliamentarism, multicameralism and multipartyism. *British Journal of Political Science*, 25(03), 289. https://doi.org/10.1017/S000712340000722 5

Vabulas, F., & Snidal, D. (2013). Organization without delegation: Informal intergovernmental organizations (IIGOs) and the spectrum of intergovernmental arrangements. *The Review of International Organizations*, 8(2), 193–220. https://doi.org/10.1007/s11558-012-9161-x

Van de Graaf, T. (2013). Fragmentation in global energy governance: Explaining the creation of IRENA. *Global Environmental Politics, 13*(3), 14–33. https://doi.org/10.1162/GLEP_a_00181

Williamson, O. E. (1985). *The economic institutions of capitalism: Firms, markets, relational contracting*. Free Press. http://www.loc.gov/catdir/bios/simon051/87011901.html

Zangl, B., Heußner, F., Kruck, A., & Lanzendörfer, X. (2016). Imperfect adaptation: How the WTO and the IMF adjust to shifting power distributions among their members. *The Review of International Organizations, 11*(2), 171–196. https://doi.org/10.1007/s11558-016-9246-z

Zürn, M. (1992). *Interessen und Institutionen in der internationalen Politik: Grundlegung und Anwendungen des situationsstrukturellen Ansatzes*. VS Verlag für Sozialwissenschaften.

Zürn, M. (2017). From constitutional rule to loosely coupled spheres of liquid authority: A reflexive approach. *International Theory, 9*(2), 261–285. https://doi.org/10.1017/S1752971916000270

PART III

Explaining Authority Distributions in the European Defense Complex

CHAPTER 4

European Defense Cooperation and Member State Preferences

Before I engage with the first of the four process-tracing case studies, in this chapter, I briefly present my research strategy. I combine an x-centered theory testing causal process-tracing and a y-centered congruence analysis (see for example, Blatter & Haverland, 2012: ch. 5.3). Consequently, in the empirical part of this thesis, I first test the theorized pathways, which lead to the four outcomes of authority distribution in four separate case studies. Chapter 5 presents the integration of the WEAG/WEAO into the EDA; Chapter 6 the marginalization of the EDA through the exclusive OCCAR; in Chapter 7, I discuss the regional fragmentation of European defense cooperation through the blockade of the PESCO; and in Chapter 8, I analyze PESCO's resilience when it was activated in 2017. Building on the findings presented in the four case studies, in Chapter 9, I will engage in a congruence analysis. By contrasting the theoretical framework presented in Chapter 3 with alternative explanations rooted in both neorealism and neofunctionalism I will try to evaluate its explanatory power.

This chapter is divided into two parts. In the first, I will highlight the advantages of the two-step empirical analysis, justify my case selection, and present the data basis. In the second part, I describe the EU member states' underlying preferences in the realm of defense cooperation. Discussing member state preferences separately is helpful as they are

© The Author(s), under exclusive license to Springer Nature Switzerland AG 2023
F. Biermann, *The Battle for Authority in European Defence Cooperation*, Palgrave Studies in European Union Politics, https://doi.org/10.1007/978-3-031-30054-7_4

relatively stable across all four cases. Based on their preferences stemming from geopolitical and economic interests, I divide the EU member states into four groups.

Research Design and Case Selection

To analyze the four pathways to the outcomes of authority distribution in institutional complexes (Fig. 3.3), I conduct four theory-testing process-tracing case studies (Beach & Pedersen, 2013, p. 12, 2016; Checkel, 2006). I understand causal mechanisms "as relatively simple, parsimonious pathways" (Beach & Pedersen, 2013, p. 12) consisting of entities that engage in activities (Beach, 2016, p. 3; Beach & Pedersen, 2013, p. 39). In the pathways theorized, states create threats, react to them, and agree or disagree on interinstitutional arrangements. These "activities are the producers of change or what transmits causal forces" (Beach, 2016, p. 3). Successful theory-testing process-tracing provides for a high degree of confidence that the combination of conditions was present in each case and that they were a "necessary and/or sufficient cause of [the institutional outcome] in an individual case" (Beach & Pedersen, 2013, p. 27). The following empirical chapters thus demonstrate that, when a situation of contested multilateralism triggers a process of strategic interaction between a challenger and a defender coalition, the presence of a certain combination of the two theorized conditions—go-it-alone power and membership preference—leads to a specific outcome in terms of authority distribution. I cannot argue, however, that the pathway was the only cause producing the outcome. Consequently, when any of the four theorized pathways functions as expected in a case subject to empirical examination, this does not logically increase our confidence in the external validity of the overall framework. The insight provided by causal process-tracing may amount to no more—but also no less—than a high degree of plausibility that the pathways were present and unfolded as expected in each individual case (Beach & Pedersen, 2013, p. 11). In other words, theory-testing process-tracing alone does not allow for inferences beyond the cases studied. Moreover, the within-case focus of causal process-tracing implies difficulties in "cop[ing] with other potential causal conditions ... at the population level" (Beach & Pedersen, 2016, p. 17). Comparison with alternative explanations would, however, increase the external validity of the theoretical framework.

To overcome these limitations to generalizability, I complement the four case studies with a congruence analysis (Blatter & Haverland, 2012, ch. 4). A congruence analysis "stops short of any strong epistemological assumption that we can actually verify or falsify theories through empirical testing. Instead, it presupposes that we can use empirical information to judge the explanatory power of a theory in relative terms by comparing these actual observations with expectations that are deduced from this theory and with the expectations that we deduced from another theory" (Blatter & Haverland, 2012, p. 40). Congruence analysis is thus complementary to process-tracing, as it does not make any claims that evidence privileging one theory automatically rules out another, but is merely interested in its relative explanatory power. Moreover, pursuing the two different approaches one after the other is deemed "optimal" (Blatter & Haverland, 2012, p. 223) if the different epistemologies are kept separated. I will contrast my theoretical framework with two competing theories, neorealism and neofunctionalism. This comparison enhances the external validity of the theoretical framework and thus its potential applicability to instances of institutional complexes beyond the four cases analyzed in detail.

The first case study deals with the integration of the WEAO/WEAG into the EDA, which was then meant to be the EU's defense procurement and management agency. As a result of dissatisfaction with the WEAO, the EDA was formally established in 2004, and the WEAG/WEAO dissolved one year later when its functions were integrated into the EDA. The second case study covers the subsequent marginalization of EDA. As it proved unsatisfactory for a coalition of states, they shifted cooperation to the minilateral OCCAR. Consequently, in 2012, the EU member states signed an Administrative Arrangement (AA) cementing OCCAR's primacy in managing cooperative armaments projects—a task that was originally foreseen for the EDA. Third, I analyze the institutional fragmentation of European defense cooperation after the signature of the Lisbon Treaty, which included the possibility of PESCO in 2007. Within a short time of the Treaty's entry into force in 2009, several separate minilateral frameworks, such as Baltic, Nordic, and Central European Defense Cooperation, were revived or newly created, as states were reluctant to cooperate through PESCO. The final case study demonstrates that, when the dissatisfied challengers of PESCO proved unable to sustain exclusive cooperation in regional frameworks in 2017, PESCO's defenders were able to refocus the institution, which finally proved resilient to the pressure applied to it.

I have chosen these cases for three reasons. First, my case selection conforms to the selection criteria for causal process-tracing case studies. Theory-testing process-tracing should be conducted in typical cases, that is, cases where the trigger and the theorized conditions produce the expected outcome (Beach & Pedersen, 2016, p. 13). None of the four cases analyzed deviates in terms of its outcome or scope conditions. Therefore, we should be able to find the theorized pathways in all four case studies. The second reason relates to the scope of the theoretical framework. I chose cases according to the diverse case method, in order to demonstrate "maximum variance along relevant dimensions" (Seawright & Gerring, 2008, p. 300). I theorized four different outcomes of authority distribution, and each of the cases analyzed represents one of the four: integration, marginalization, resilience, or fragmentation. As I claim that combinations of the two conditions determining the four causal pathways can explain all four outcomes, it would not be sufficient to analyze any fewer than four cases. Third, the selection of four cases within the realm of European security and defense cooperation followed the "most similar method" (Seawright & Gerring, 2008, pp. 304–306), which has considerable advantages in eliminating rival explanations. Keeping the policy field, the social context of the EU, and the states involved constant while analyzing the very same institutions at different points in time, amounts to constructing a most similar systems design (Lijphart, 1971; Mill, 2010 [1843]). The case selection controls for possible intervening variables deriving from the specificities of different sectors or international organizations.

The case selection undoubtedly also puts certain constraints on the generalizability of the theoretical framework. Both causal process-tracing and congruence analysis are limited in their potential to generate generalizable claims. When intending to infer from small-n research designs, we should select "cases that are as representative as possible of the rest of a causally homogeneous population, enabling us to infer that the mechanism that worked in the studied cases should also be present in the rest of the population of causally similar cases" (Beach & Pedersen, 2016, p. 2). Selecting four cases in the realm of European security and defense might, therefore come at a price: The findings might not be easily generalizable to situations of contested multilateralism either in different policy areas or in settings beyond the EU. I would nevertheless argue that neither an exclusive selection of cases from the policy area of security nor a focus on frameworks under the auspices of the EU has a substantial negative impact on the generalizability of the framework.

The potential argument that cooperation in the realm of security is generally less likely than in other areas is mitigated by an increasing degree of interdependence, high functional pressure to cooperate in view of the changing character of conflict, high development costs, and pressures on defense budgets. Moreover, while states' sovereignty concerns are indeed paramount in security and defense matters (Mearsheimer, 1994; Toje, 2008), this does not mean that contested multilateralism works differently there from any other policy area. On the contrary, as the bargaining power of states is closely related to the size of their markets and their military capabilities, the defense sector might even be a typical case to demonstrate how state coalitions' relative power and diverging preferences shape the outcomes of authority distribution among international institutions.

Finally, while I take seriously the argument that the EU represents a special environment where social context plays an important role, potentially undermining the representativeness of the four cases for different regimes, I would hold that the EU's "specialness" actually increases the generalizability of the framework. Indeed, the EU context represents a hard case for power-based bargaining about institutional authority. High public attention (Hooghe & Marks, 2009), spillovers and integration dynamics (Haas, 2004 [1958]; Stone Sweet & Sandholtz, 1997), as well as the manifold possibilities for issue linkages, should make marginalization and fragmentation unlikely. If the theorized pathways can be identified within this rather unfavorable context, the likelihood that they will function in different contested regimes should be considerable. The two conditions theorized above are thus expected to have explanatory value for varying authority distributions in all regime complexes that have been created through a power-based renegotiation of cooperation.

Having discussed the methodological foundations of the research design, I will now briefly engage with the question of what kind of evidence needs to be advanced in the four case studies to demonstrate the presence of the theorized pathways. And in this connection, I will present the sources of my data. All four pathways are triggered when a challenger coalition that is dissatisfied with an existing institution and finds the internal pathway to reform blocked, creates or shifts cooperation to an institutional alternative. This implies a necessity to show, as a first step, that the instance of competitive regime creation/regime shifting to be analyzed was motivated by the challengers' dissatisfaction with an institution and that the two resulting institutions overlap in their mandate. In other words, I need first to demonstrate that the cases analyzed fall within the scope of my theoretical framework. Second, I have to establish the presence or absence of the challenger coalition's go-it-alone power. I do so, on the one hand, by engaging in an analysis of the relative interdependence of the challenger and defender coalitions and investigating whether the creation of the institutional alternative caused negative externalities for the defenders of the status quo. On the other hand, I examine whether the defenders intended to join the institutional alternative even though this was against their originally expressed preferences. This would allow the inference that it was indeed the pulling force of the challengers' go-it-alone power, erasing the status quo from the set of feasible options, which induced the defenders to try to join. Third, I investigate whether the challengers' membership preference for the institutional alternative was inclusive or exclusive and whether the challengers behaved accordingly, namely by admitting or excluding further members. On the one hand, when the institutional purpose is regulatory and the defenders' cost of compliance is low, the challengers are expected to prefer an inclusive venue. On the other, when the institution has significant distributive consequences, the challengers' membership preference is assumed to be exclusive. Fourth, depending on the presence and effects of the two theorized conditions, I collect evidence demonstrating the causal force they exercise to produce the respective outcomes.

To provide a convincing and uninterrupted chain of evidence for each of the four causal pathways and to visualize the "ultimately unobservable physical, social, or psychological processes through which agents with causal capacities operate" (George & Bennett, 2005, p. 137), I draw on a variety of data sources. The empirical case studies, therefore, rely on an extensive analysis of legal documents from the Council of the European Union, the European Commission, and Parliament, as well as official reports and press communications by those institutions for the relevant period—from 1997 to 2017. The 54 working documents of the European Convention Working Group VIII on "Defence" were another important source for identifying the positions of the states involved and tracing the bargaining processes that led to the establishment of the EDA and PESCO. In addition, I examined government documents, speeches, parliamentary debates, and interpellations from the EU's most powerful member states, Germany, France, Italy, and the United Kingdom (1997–2017), which were at the forefront of shaping the EU's CSDP. In addition, I drew on all publicly available official OCCAR and WEAG/WEAO documents, the joint communiqués by the Visegràd Group, and by Baltic, Central European, and Nordic Defense Cooperation for the same period. What is more, by analyzing newspaper articles (based on Nexis®, Factiva®, and Google keyword search) from every EU member state, I account for the individual national perspectives and validate the assumed national preferences. Moreover, I reviewed European outlets such as EURACTIV and *Politico* to collect process evidence without national bias. Statistical data concerning national defense spending, as well as institutional budgets, serve as an additional source for examining the relative power of the EU member states and resource distribution across institutions. Finally, 12 background interviews with members of the General Council Secretariat, the European External Action Service, NATO, and EU member state representatives were conducted to confirm the empirical findings from other sources. The combination of legal and economic primary data, as well as interviews and secondary sources in the form of policy papers and scientific and newspaper articles, allows for data to be triangulated and information gaps connected with a particular data source to be made good. While combining different kinds of data is certainly a quality criterion for process-tracing, it also runs the risk of selection bias. To address this potential shortcoming, the empirical chapters try to explicate any contradicting evidence that I came across in my research, and the congruence analysis discusses additional, potentially disconfirming evidence.

Member State Preferences on European Defense Cooperation

Before I start to analyze the first of the four cases, it is helpful to isolate the EU member states' underlying preferences with respect to defense cooperation and deal with them separately. As all four cases are to be found in the field of European defense cooperation, the basic preferences that apply in all of them can be conveniently discussed collectively ahead of the individual case studies. As it is generally difficult to observe true preferences directly, I derive them from the positional characteristics of each EU member state. This facilitates an understanding of the reasons why the challengers of the institutional status quo were dissatisfied, allows for a check on the plausibility of the preferences governments express, and permits me to judge their membership preference regarding the institutions they create.

The EU member states, which constitute the totality of the relevant actors in the four case studies,[1] have varying preferences regarding the scope of European defense cooperation. As I argued previously, state preferences are motivated by their basic geopolitical and economic interests (Moravcsik, 1998, p. 26), which can be calculated by considering their positional characteristics (Scharpf, 1997). The EU member states can, I argue, be sorted into four groups defined by the two intersecting dimensions along which they vary (see Table 4.1).[2] The first is their strategic orientation, favoring cooperation either through NATO (Atlanticists) or European defense arrangements (Europeanists). The second is their economic position. States can be characterized as having industries either at the lower (downstream) or at the upper (upstream) end of international defense-industrial supply chains (Bátora, 2009; Trybus, 2014).

The first divide between Atlanticists and Europeanists is widely acknowledged in the literature (Menon & Lipkin, 2003; Stahl et al., 2004; Wivel, 2005). Atlanticists are states that have a clear strategic orientation toward NATO as the focal framework for any questions relating to security and defense. For these states, European security primarily depends upon a good relationship with the United States. Europeanists, conversely, desire a stronger or even an autonomous role for the EU's CSDP. With the exception of the Netherlands, which is a traditionally Atlanticist state, the EU's founding members, together with Greece[3] and Spain (Menon & Lipkin, 2003, pp. 22, 27), are more strongly oriented toward independent European defense capabilities. Accordingly, the states

---

[1] Actions carried out by third country governments are treated as external shocks to the processes under examination.

[2] In the two EDA case studies the upstream/downstream divide features more prominently, while in the two PESCO cases the core conflict plays out between Europeanists and Atlanticists. Nonetheless, in all four case studies it will be necessary to consider both lines of conflict in order to understand the reasons for dissatisfaction and the make-up of the various challenger and defender coalitions.

[3] Greece is part of this group as it is skeptical of NATO due to its ongoing conflict with Turkey, which is also a NATO member (Hofmann, 2009, p. 48; Moustakis, 2003).

Table 4.1 EU member state positions regarding deepened European defense cooperation

		Political economy of defense	
		Upstream	Downstream
Strategic orientation	Atlanticist/ Neutral	Selective [United Kingdom, Sweden]	Reluctant [Austria, Bulgaria, Croatia, Czech Republic, Denmark, Estonia, Finland, Hungary, Ireland, Latvia, Lithuania, Malta, Netherlands, Poland, Portugal, Romania, Slovenia, Slovakia]
	Europeanist	Avant-Gardist [France, Germany, Italy, Spain]	Federalist [Cyprus, Belgium, Greece, Luxemburg]

that are the traditionally close allies of the United States, Denmark, Portugal, the Netherlands, and the United Kingdom (Menon & Lipkin, 2003, p. 27; Wijk, 2004), together with the Eastern and Central European states that joined the EU in 2004,[4] 2007,[5] and 2013[6] prefer the current EU–NATO relationship to remain intact and oppose any steps that might potentially undermine NATO's primacy (Asmus & Vondra, 2005; Král et al., 2008, p. 21; Valášek, 2005; Vukadinović, 2014).

Austria, Cyprus, Finland, Ireland, Malta, and Sweden are neutral states and thus difficult to characterize as either Atlanticist or Europeanist (Stahl et al., 2004, p. 418). Their governments find themselves caught up in a continuous struggle to legitimize their involvement in the EU's CSDP with their public (Devine, 2011). While Austria, Finland, Ireland, and Sweden have interpreted their military neutrality as being compatible with membership of the CSDP (Devine, 2011), Cyprus, due to its conflict with NATO member Turkey, can be seen to be part of the Europeanist camp, and Malta 'is but a drop in the ocean' in defense terms and consequently assumes a free-rider role (Fiott, 2015, p. 96). For the purposes of this book, I assume that the group of neutral states, excluding Cyprus, behaves similarly to the Atlanticist states, albeit for different reasons. They

---

[4] Czech Republic, Estonia, Hungary, Latvia, Lithuania, Poland, Slovakia, and Slovenia
[5] Bulgaria and Romania.
[6] Croatia.

find it difficult to agree to further European defense cooperation due to high domestic audience costs. In the subsequent chapters, the term "Atlanticists" thus comprises the neutral states as well.

The second divide between member states concerns the political economy of defense. I categorize the EU members as either upstream or downstream states. Downstream states' defense industries are characterized by comparatively low competitiveness and niche positioning, which leaves them with only minor work-shares at the margins of the supply chain. By contrast, upstream states have a comprehensive and competitive defense industry base with companies that serve for the most part as prime contractors (Mawdsley, 2015, p. 140; Moravcsik, 1993; Trybus, 2006, p. 677). While admittedly an approximation, this classification is in line with Trybus (2014), who differentiates the EU member states according to the size of their defense-industrial capabilities placing them in two groups, which match the downstream/upstream classification: states with significant defense-industrial capacities and states with limited or no capacities (Trybus, 2014, pp. 23–24).

The "big six," the UK, France, Germany, Italy, Spain, and Sweden,[7] make up the first group, while the second group consists of the remaining member states. In 2013 the big six accounted for "87% of European defence production. These countries also host the 20 European defence companies that are highest ranked in the top 100 defence companies in the world" (European Commission, 2013, p. 24). Moreover, in 2007 they were responsible for 78% of EU-27 defense spending (see Table 4.2), and in 2005 for "90% of the EU's industrial capabilities" (Commission of the European Communities, 2005, p. 2) were concentrated in them. In addition, most of the 2,500 small and medium-sized enterprises (SMEs) are located in these states (European Commission, 2018). In accordance with their relative positions, upstream states are assumed to have an interest in liberalized cooperation and reduced restrictions on trade and competition, whereas downstream states' national defense-industrial bases are too small to produce the full variety of armaments domestically, which is why they have to rely on off-the-shelf intergovernmental procurement (Bátora, 2009; Trybus, 2006) and therefore prefer defense cooperation to

---

[7] While Sweden ranked only ninth in defense spending in 2007, it possesses a large defense industry, which, due to its (past) policy of neutrality, it has always protected, so it thus belongs in the group of the big six arms producers (Commission of the European Communities, 2005, p. 2; Trybus, 2014, pp. 23–24).

retain protectionist properties, following political principles such as *juste retour*[8] or offset deals, where the exporter has to reinvest a share of the contract value in the importing country (Blauberger & Weiss, 2013; Weiss & Blauberger, 2015).

Four groups of states can be identified by combining those two dimensions. The first of the two Europeanist groups consists of the *avant-gardists*, France, Germany, Italy, and Spain. They prefer ambitious, far-reaching defense cooperation to achieve autonomous European capabilities. As they possess the bulk of the European defense industry, they have no genuine interest in including other member states' niche industries in the cooperation but prefer to rely on competition featuring their national champions instead. The second Europeanist group, the *federalists*, also favor independent European capabilities and military capacity. However, due to their lower defense-industrial capabilities, they prefer cooperation to be structured in such a way that states with niche industries are compensated for the costs of liberalization and get their share in armaments research, development, and production.

The Atlanticists are also divided into two groups. The first comprises the selective states and consists of the United Kingdom and Sweden. Because of their competitive defense industries, both accept multilateral defense cooperation à la carte, as long as it is not institutionalized within the EU structures. The United Kingdom deems multilateral cooperation in defense planning and procurement to be valuable so long as the use of capabilities is regulated under NATO auspices, such as the Berlin Plus agreement. To achieve maximum outcomes in European capabilities utilizable by NATO, cooperation is acceptable for the United Kingdom. Yet it rejects institutionalization of defense cooperation within the EU and thus potential competition with NATO. Similarly, Sweden has been in favor of case-by-case multilateral cooperation among the most capable states. Yet, due to its neutrality policy, Sweden has hitherto been skeptical of EU institutionalization, which has implications for its foreign policy autonomy. The second Atlanticist group comprises the reluctant states. Like the United Kingdom, they prefer NATO cooperation to CSDP cooperation. However, they also share similarities with the group of federalists, as they have an interest in protectionist defense cooperation to avoid further divergence in defense-industrial capabilities. A liberalized defense

---

[8] Principle of fair returns: The national work-shares in a cooperative project have to be proportional to the states' respective investments Trybus (2006, fn. 12).

Table 4.2 EU member states' defense expenditures 2004–2016 (US $m at 2015 constant prices)[9]

State	2004 Total defense spending	As % of EU 25 total (%)	2007 Total defense spending	As % of EU 27 total (%)	2010 Total defense spending	As % of EU 27 total (%)	2013 Total defense spending	As % of EU 28 total (%)	2016 Total defense spending	As % of EU 28 total (%)
UK	58.846	22.4	61.610	23.0	64.230	23.8	56.408	23.1	54.217	21.5
France	54.833	20.9	54.164	20.2	54.623	20.3	52.419	21.5	55.681	22.0
Germany	39.857	15.2	38.364	14.3	41.405	15.4	38.803	15.9	40.985	16.2
Italy	36.708	14.0	33.114	12.3	32.422	12.0	28.388	11.6	27.966	11.1
Spain	16.873	6.4	18.298	6.8	17.582	6.5	14.311	5.9	14.994	5.9
Netherlands	10.039	3.8	10.667	4.0	10.258	3.8	8.677	3.6	9.249	3.7
Poland	5.997	2.3	7.588	2.8	7.602	2.8	7.709	3.2	9.791	3.9
Greece	6.846	2.6	7.691	2.9	6.889	2.6	4.581	1.9	4.986	2.0
Sweden	5.394	2.1	5.520	2.1	5.210	1.9	5.031	2.1	5.344	2.1
Belgium	4.702	1.8	4.851	1.8	4.771	1.8	4.436	1.8	4.028	1.6
Portugal	3.964	1.5	3.907	1.5	4.230	1.6	3.954	1.6	3.750	1.5
Denmark	3.861	1.5	3.879	1.4	4.033	1.5	3.556	1.5	3.488	1.4
Finland	2.844	1.1	2.799	1.0	3.097	1.1	3.189	1.3	3.243	1.3
Austria	2.966	1.1	3.315	1.2	2.982	1.1	2.765	1.1	2.829	1.1
Czech Rep	2.687	1.0	2.618	1.0	2.086	0.8	1.669	0.7	1.923	0.8

[9] *Source* SIPRI Milex data 1949–2016.

4 EUROPEAN DEFENSE COOPERATION AND MEMBER STATE ... 105

State	2004 Total defense spending	2004 As % of EU 25 total (%)	2007 Total defense spending	2007 As % of EU 27 total (%)	2010 Total defense spending	2010 As % of EU 27 total (%)	2013 Total defense spending	2013 As % of EU 28 total (%)	2016 Total defense spending	2016 As % of EU 28 total (%)
Romania	2.095	/	2.190	0.8	1.890	0.7	2.047	0.8	2.816	1.1
Hungary	1.668	0.6	1.508	0.6	1.120	0.4	1.021	0.4	1.258	0.5
Ireland	1.133	0.4	1.147	0.4	1.118	0.4	998	0.4	993	0.4
Slovakia	1.087	0.4	1.208	0.5	1.036	0.4	805	0.3	1.036	0.4
Croatia	831	/	902	/	874	/	791	0.3	687	0.3
Bulgaria	894	/	1.054	0.4	798	0.3	740	0.3	756	0.3
Slovenia	549	0.2	645	0.2	685	0.3	422	0.2	405	0.2
Lithuania	344	0.1	453	0.2	294	0.1	294	0.1	634	0.3
Estonia	268	0.1	456	0.2	310	0.1	398	0.2	494	0.2
Cyprus	354	0.1	358	0.1	407	0.2	311	0.1	352	0.1
Latvia	311	0.1	496	0.2	234	0.1	239	0.1	406	0.2
Luxembourg	262	0.1	269	0.1	251	0.1	218	0.1	293	0.1
Malta	45	0.0	46	0.0	53	0.0	46	0.0	57	0.0
Total	262.438	100	268.215	100	269.616	100	244.226	100	252.661	100

market implies an increased dependence on large armament producers and the need to specialize further to be able to participate. This runs against sovereign states' interests. This group is the largest in terms of membership and faces the most in-group variation. The Netherlands and Poland had the relatively largest defense budgets, with 4% and 2.8% of total EU defense expenditures in 2007,[10] and together spent more than the other 12 group members combined (5.4%). Therefore, Poland and the Netherlands—like the other reluctant states—clearly emphasize the primacy of NATO, yet, they should be comparatively less reluctant toward defense cooperation as they would not suffer as much from liberalization as the other reluctant states.

Summing up this chapter, there are four groups of EU member states which diverge in their perspectives on whether and how European defense cooperation should be organized. While the Atlanticists reject any European institutions that endanger NATO's unqualified primacy in defending the EU member states, the Europeanists intend to develop independent EU defense capabilities to complement NATO. Both groups are divided with respect to their ability to profit from liberalization. While avant-gardist and selective states with their large defense industries have the ambition to cooperate according to market principles, federalist and reluctant states value cooperation based on political principles. They do so as they fear being left behind in their development of defense capabilities.

References

Asmus, R. D., & Vondra, A. (2005). The origins of Atlanticism in Central and Eastern Europe. *Cambridge Review of International Affairs, 18*(2), 203–216.
Bátora, J. (2009). European Defence Agency: A flashpoint of institutional logics. *West European Politics, 32*(6), 1075–1098.
Beach, D. (2016). It's all about mechanisms—What process-tracing case studies should be tracing. *New Political Economy, 21*(5), 463–472.
Beach, D., & Pedersen, R. B. (2013). *Process-tracing methods: Foundations and guidelines* [und]. University of Michigan Press.
Beach, D., & Pedersen, R. B. (2016). Selecting appropriate cases when tracing causal mechanisms. *Sociological Methods & Research, 47*(4), 837–871.

---

[10] Military Expenditure 2016, source: SIPRI Milex data 1949–2016, available at: https://www.sipri.org/databases/milex.

Blatter, J., & Haverland, M. (2012). *Designing case studies: Explanatory approaches in small-N research* [eng]. Research methods series. Palgrave Macmillan.
Blauberger, M., & Weiss, M. (2013). 'If you can't beat me, join me!: ' How the commission pushed and pulled member states into legislating defence procurement. *Journal of European Public Policy*, 20(8), 1120–1138.
Checkel, J. T. (2006). Tracing causal mechanisms. *International Studies Review*, 8(2), 362–370.
Commission of the European Communities. (2005). *Communication from the commission to the council and the European Parliament on the results of the consultation launched by the Green Paper on Defence Procurement and on the future commission initiatives*. Brussels. COM(2005) 626 final. http://www.europarl.europa.eu/RegData/docs_autres_institutions/commission_europeenne/com/2005/0626/COM_COM%282005%290626_EN.pdf.
Devine, K. (2011). Neutrality and the development of the European Union's common security and defence policy. *Cooperation and Conflict*, 46(3), 334–369.
de Wijk, R. (2004). Transatlantic relations: A view from the Netherlands. *International Journal: Canada's Journal of Global Policy Analysis*, 59(1), 167–186.
European Commission. (2013). *Commission staff working document on defence accompanying the document communication towards a more competitive and efficient defence and security sector COM(2013) 542 final*. SWD(2013) 279 final.
European Commission. (2018, December 1). *Defence industries: The importance of EU defence industries*. https://ec.europa.eu/growth/sectors/defence_en.
Fiott, D. (2015). The European Commission and the European Defence Agency: A case of rivalry? *JCMS: Journal of Common Market Studies*, 53(3), 542–557. https://doi.org/10.1111/jcms.12217
George, A. L., & Bennett, A. (2005). *Case studies and theory development in the social sciences* [eng]. BCSIA studies in international security. The MIT Press.
Haas, E. B. (2004 [1958]). *The uniting of Europe: Political, social, and economical forces : 1950–1957* [eng]. Contemporary European politics and society. University of Notre Dame Press.
Hofmann, S. C. (2009). Overlapping institutions in the realm of international security: The case of NATO and ESDP. *Perspectives on Politics*, 7(1), 45–52.
Hooghe, L., & Marks, G. (2009). A postfunctionalist theory of European integration: From permissive consensus to constraining dissensus. *British Journal of Political Science*, 39(01), 1–23.
Král, D., Řiháčková, V., & Weiss, T. (2008). *Views on American foreign policy: The atlanticism of political parties in Central and Eastern Europe*. EUROPEUM Institute for European Policy.

Lijphart, A. (1971). Comparative politics and the comparative method. *American Political Science Review, 65*(03), 682–693.
Mawdsley, J. (2015). France, the UK and the EDA. In N. Karampekios & I. Oikonomou (Ed.), *The European Defence Agency: Arming Europe. Routledge studies in European security and strategy* (pp. 139–154). Routledge, Taylor & Francis Group.
Mearsheimer, J. J. (1994). The false promise of international institutions. *International Security, 19*(3), 5.
Menon, A., & Lipkin, J. (2003). *European attitudes towards transatlantic relations 2000–2003: An analytical survey: Survey prepared for the informal meeting of EU Foreign Ministers, Rodhes and Kastellorizo, May 2 - May 3, 2003.* Groupement D'Études et de Recherches Notre Europe. Research and European Issues, 26.
Mill, J. S. (2010 [1843]). *A system of logic, ratiocinative and inductive* [English]. Nabu Press.
Moravcsik, A. (1993). Armaments among allies: European weapons collaboration, 1975–1985. In H. K. Jacobson, P. B. Evans & R. D. Putnam (Eds.), *Double-edged diplomacy: International bargaining and domestic politics* [eng]. Vol. 25 of *Studies in international political economy* (pp. 128–167). University of California Press.
Moravcsik, A. (1998). *The choice for Europe: Social purpose and state power from Messina to Maastricht* [eng]. *Cornell studies in political economy.* Cornell University Press.
Moustakis, F. 2003. *The Greek-Turkish relationship and NATO* [eng]. Routledge.
Scharpf, F. W. 1997. *Games real actors play: Actor-centered institutionalism in policy research. Theoretical lenses on public policy.* Westview Press.
Seawright, J., & Gerring, J. (2008). Case selection techniques in case study research. *Political Research Quarterly, 61*(2), 294–308.
Stahl, B., Boekle, H., Nadoll, J., & Jóhannesdóttir, A. (2004). Understanding the Atlanticist-Europeanist divide in the CFSP: Comparing Denmark, France, Germany and the Netherlands. *European Foreign Affairs Review, 9*(3), 417–441.
Stone Sweet, A., & Sandholtz, W. (1997). European integration and supranational governance. *Journal of European Public Policy, 4*(3), 297–317.
Toje, A. (2008). The consensus expectations gap: Explaining Europe's ineffective foreign policy. *Security Dialogue, 39*(1), 121–141.
Trybus, M. (2006). The new European Defence Agency: A contribution to a common European security and defence policy and a challenge to the community acquis? *Common Market Law Review, 43,* 667–703.
Trybus, M. (2014). *Buying defence and security in Europe: The EU defence and security procurement directive in context.* Cambridge University Press.

Valášek, T. (2005). New EU members in Europe's security policy. *Cambridge Review of International Affairs*, *18*(2), 217–228.
Vukadinović, L. Č. (2014). The Croatian view on the EU Common Security and Defence Policy (CSDP). *Austria Institut für Europa- und Sicherheitspolitik* (1).
Weiss, M., & Blauberger, M. (2015). Judicialized law-making and opportunistic enforcement: Explaining the EU's challenge of national defence offsets. *JCMS: Journal of Common Market Studies*, 1–19.
Wivel, A. (2005). The security challenge of small EU member states: Interests, identity and the development of the EU as a security actor. *JCMS: Journal of Common Market Studies*, *43*(2), 393–412.

CHAPTER 5

Integrating the WEAO into the EDA: Toward a European Armaments Agency?

This chapter is dedicated to an analysis of the pathway leading to the integration of the Western European Armaments Group (WEAG) and its subsidiary body, the Western European Armaments Organization (WEAO), into the European Defense Agency (EDA). In 2004 EU member states created the EDA, which overlapped with the pre-existing WEAG/WEAO mandate. With its functions and resources having been transferred to the EDA, the WEAG/WEAO was dissolved shortly after, and the EDA became the new center of authority for European armaments cooperation. In 1997, members of the WEAG[1] created the WEAO, which started out as an organization to facilitate cooperative Research & Technology (R&T) projects (Schilde, 2017, p. 167), and developed into a European armaments agency organizing joint research, development, and procurement (Council of Western European Union, 2003, para. 2; Trybus, 2014, p. 234). Yet no progress was achieved in the realm of armaments cooperation, and the WEAO did not develop into anything more than the WEAG's defense "research cell" (Mawdsley, 2003, p. 20; Trybus,

[1] In 1997, WEAG membership consisted of Belgium, Denmark, France, Germany, Greece, Italy, Luxembourg, the Netherlands, Norway, Portugal, Spain, Turkey and the United Kingdom—in 2000 Austria, the Czech Republic, Finland, Hungary, Poland, and Sweden were granted full membership.

© The Author(s), under exclusive license to Springer Nature Switzerland AG 2023
F. Biermann, *The Battle for Authority in European Defence Cooperation*, Palgrave Studies in European Union Politics, https://doi.org/10.1007/978-3-031-30054-7_5

2014, p. 234). In 2003, in reaction to a stalemate in armaments cooperation, dissatisfied upstream states proposed the creation of the EDA, which was then established by a Council Joint Action in 2004.[2] Subsequently, all EU member states that were members of the WEAG/WEAO, except Denmark joined the EDA.[3] Eventually, the EU member states integrated the WEAG/WEAO's functions into the EDA and dissolved the former institutions in 2005 and 2006, respectively.

This chapter demonstrates that the process that led to the incorporation of the WEAG/WEAO's functions into the EDA unfolded along the pathway to integration as theorized in Chapter 3. This pathway is depicted in Fig. 5.1. I will demonstrate that a coalition of dissatisfied states found the way to reforming the WEAG/WEAO as a European armaments agency blocked and therefore decided to create the EDA. As they could credibly threaten to exclude the defenders of the status quo and their membership preference was inclusive, the defenders of the status quo joined the EDA as they feared being left behind. Having shifted all resources to the EDA, no member state could expect benefits from maintaining the WEAG/WEAO, which was therefore dissolved and deprived of both its relational and formal-legal authority.

This chapter is structured in five sections. The first establishes that the scope conditions and the trigger for the pathway were present. It demonstrates that a coalition of upstream states was dissatisfied with the limited scope of cooperation within the WEAG/WEAO and tried to reform the institution. As the inclusion of armaments cooperation into the WEAG/WEAO's mandate proved impossible due to its defenders', that is, the downstream states', resistance, the idea emerged of creating an alternative institution, the EDA, within the context of the EU. Section "The Threat of Exclusion: "There Will Be Peer Pressure"" and "Membership preference: Welcome to the Club!" describe the causal force of the two conditions, the upstream states' ability to create a credible threat of exclusion (section "The Threat of Exclusion: "There Will Be Peer Pressure"")

---

[2] Council Joint Action 2004/570/CFSP—now replaced by Council Decision CFSP 2015/1835.

[3] Denmark opted out of all security- and defense-related policies after the unsuccessful attempt to ratify the Maastricht Treaty in 1992 and is thus domestically restrained from participation. Turkey and Norway were not and are not members of the EU and thus have never been eligible for membership of the EDA.

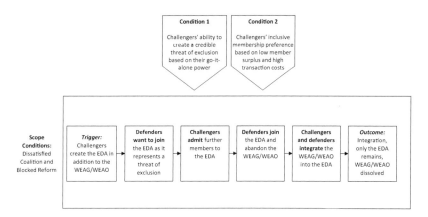

Fig. 5.1 Process leading to the integration of the WEAG/WEAO into the EDA

and their preference for inclusive cooperation (section "Membership preference: Welcome to the Club!"), which led the downstream states to join the EDA. The fourth demonstrates how the EU member states pooled their resources in the EDA and integrated the WEAG/WEAO's functions into the new forum. Consequently, the abandoned institution was formally dissolved. The final section summarizes the findings.

Stagnation in Armaments Cooperation

The declaration on the WEU annexed to the Maastricht Treaty of 1992 highlights the EU member states' objective of "enhanced cooperation in the field of armaments with the aim of creating a European armaments agency" ("Treaty on European Union," 1992, p. 245, para. 5). Such an agency, "in the longer term," was to become a part of the "common defense policy within the European Union" ("Treaty on European Union," 1992, p. 242). In 1993, shortly after the Maastricht Treaty came into force, the WEU created the WEAG[4] (Trybus, 2006, p. 671). The WEAG can thus be understood as a first cautious step toward the creation of a European armaments agency organizing joint armament

---

[4] The WEAG arose from the Independent European Program Group (IEPG), a European armaments cooperation forum, founded by the European NATO members in 1976 (Mawdsley, 2003, p. 19).

development and procurement projects (Eisenhut, 2010) as part of a European pillar within NATO. It was organized into three panels: (I) Cooperative Equipment Programs, (II) Research & Technology, and (III) Cooperation Procedures and Economic Matters.

Cooperation in the realm of armaments programs was an economic imperative in light of system duplication and excess capacity, interoperability problems, uncompetitive industries, and capability shortfalls (Hill, 1993). Only interaction between all three panels promised to relieve these inefficiencies. However, only panel II, R&T, was ever truly operable, while progress was achieved neither in the realm of collaborative armaments production and procurement nor in the development of common standards regarding the foundations of the EDEM (Eisenhut, 2010, pp. 63–66).

In 1997 the WEAG members consequently decided to create the WEAO as a subsidiary body. It was intended to

> assist in promoting and enhancing European armaments cooperation, strengthening the European defence technology base and creating a European defence equipment market, in accordance with policies agreed by the WEAG. (Council of Western European Union, 2003, para. 6)

As the first European body in the realm of armaments that had legal personality (Western European Union, 2000) and was thus able to conclude contracts independently, the WEAO was designated by Andries Schlieper, chairman of the WEAG Group of National Experts, as the "precursor of the future European Armaments Agency" (Sanfourche, 1999). The functions listed in WEAO's founding charter underline this intention. Next to "defense research and technology activities," it was tasked with the "procurement of defence equipment" and the "management of assets and facilities" (Council of Western European Union, 2003, para. 7). While the founding charter laid the ground for WEAO's transformation into a veritable European armaments agency, however, it was de facto "tasked only with cooperative research on armaments technologies," as the WEAG defense ministers noted (Western European Union, 1997, para. 39). In the very same declaration, the ministers pointed to the fact that it was still too early to turn the WEAO into a full-fledged armaments agency—this could only be achieved "as soon as all appropriate conditions are met" (Western European Union, 1997, para. 39).

Dissatisfaction: The Principle of "juste retour"

The most important of these "appropriate conditions" was the resolution of a deep-rooted conflict between the upstream states on the one side and the downstream states on the other. A problematic feature, the principle of *juste retour*, characterized European armaments cooperation. This principle suggested a "fair industrial return of a state's investment. As a result, national industrial policy criteria determined the distribution of work share rather than quality and price" (Weiss & Biermann, 2018, p. 706). The principle of *juste retour* was based on the idea that each state should maintain its own defense-industrial base, that is, the ability to produce each type of armament system independently (Hartley, 2008, 2011). Giving up this principle and organizing armaments cooperation according to market criteria—within the EDEM—would imply that the most competitive arms producers would get the largest production shares.

While perfect competition would bring into being a large number of highly specialized producers, the liberalization of the oligopolistic European defense market—in light of relatively few but very large contracts—would contribute to the creation of a limited number of national champions. Consequently, while the group of competitive upstream states, both selective and avant-gardist, had a strong interest in abolishing the principle of *juste retour*, the downstream states opposed this. Given the relative uncompetitiveness of the latter's defense firms, abandoning *juste retour* in the armaments sector and allowing competitive tendering would make them the losers from defense consolidation and competitively organized armaments procurement and production (Mawdsley, 2008). What is more, the prospect of establishing an EDEM fueled the downstream states' fear that they would be forced to buy "expensive and inferior European products when they can buy from the inexpensive and competitive US American defence industries" (Trybus, 2006, p. 677).

During their Erfurt meeting in 1997, the WEAG defense ministers agreed "a plan, including a timetable, should be developed to guide further steps" required to turn the WEAO into a European armaments agency (Western European Union, 1997, para. 39). One year later, in 1998, they praised and discussed this "Masterplan" and "welcomed the establishment of a group of national experts" working toward a political consensus regarding the WEAG members' stance toward the *juste retour* principle (Western European Union, 1998). This process was supposed to pave the way for a decision on the agency in 2001 (Schmitt, 2003).

Yet the efforts to work toward establishing a European armaments agency did not progress beyond formal commitments. The WEAG ministers formally "endorsed the concept of an evolutionary process towards a European armaments agency" (Western European Union, 2002, para. 4). At the same time, however, they cautioned that its establishment should be postponed until "all appropriate conditions are met, and political consensus is reached" (Western European Union, 2002, para. 4) and dissolved the national experts' group, which put an end to attempts to find consensus within the WEAG/WEAO (Deutscher Bundestag, 2003, p. 3; Eisenhut, 2010, p. 67; Schmitt, 2003, p. 22). In other words, hardly any progress in terms of developing the WEAO into an armaments agency was achieved between 1997 and 2002.

This was unsatisfactory for the upstream states, who were striving for closer cooperation in the realm of armaments and intended to create the conditions for the EDEM. Especially in view of the fresh impetus that the 1998 Franco–British St. Malo declaration had given to European security and defense,[5] asking for the incorporation of the WEU into the EU, the WEAG/WEAO's inertia was unbearable for the upstream states. The first scope condition, dissatisfaction, was present and, as we shall see in the next section, motivated several unsuccessful reform attempts.

Reform Attempts Blocked—OCCAR and the LoI

Besides trying to reform the WEAG/WEAO directly through (re)negotiations, the upstream states aimed to support their intra-institutional reform attempts indirectly. Creating *faits accomplis* by means of ad hoc cooperation in OCCAR and the Letter of Intent framework agreement (LoI), they intended to put pressure on the downstream states to move ahead with the incremental development of the WEAO into a European armaments agency—yet these efforts remained unsuccessful.

In 1998, Germany, France, the United Kingdom, and Italy signed a convention creating OCCAR (Convention on the Establishment of the Organisation for Joint Armament Cooperation [Organisation Conjointe de Cooperation en Matière d'ARmement]—OCCAR, 1998), which received legal personality as an international organization in 2001 and was joined by Belgium and Spain in 2003 and 2005, respectively. OCCAR's

---

[5] France and the UK bridged the differences between the Atlanticist and the Europeanist camp within the upstream states.

tasks were to award and manage collaborative defense procurement contracts while replacing the principle of *juste retour* with the *global balance* principle, allowing for more flexibility and competitive tendering. Instead of dividing work-shares evenly for each individual project, the *global balance* principle sought to balance work-shares across all OCCAR projects (Heuninckx, 2017, p. 185).

OCCAR was not intended as an institutional competitor to the WEAO but "as a practical step towards the creation of a European Armaments Agency" (Convention on the Establishment of the Organisation for Joint Armament Cooperation [Organisation Conjointe de Cooperation en Matière d'ARmement]—OCCAR, 1998). As such, it was not an exclusive forum but "open to other European nations" who took part in at least one collaborative project (UK Ministry of Defence, 2001, p. 35). The rationale behind creating OCCAR was straightforward. Making OCCAR, with its principle of global balance, an "*organe subsidiaire*" of the WEU would allow the upstream states to move ahead with the development of the WEAG's Panel I, defense equipment procurement. Thus, the upstream states intended to introduce liberal market principles to the WEAG/WEAO through the backdoor (Guillaume, 1998, p. 287). Yet as OCCAR, at the time, was not a serious contender for the role played by the WEU institutions, this attempt was unsuccessful. French Defence Minister Alain Richard explained to the French Senate his doubts about OCCAR's effectiveness in the absence of its integration into the broader context of a joint procurement strategy in 2000:

> Let us be frank. Our different countries, notwithstanding OCCAR, will continue to choose their own defence procurement programs. If a country takes the sovereign decision in a parliamentary framework to reduce its defence budget, then this will mean reviewing contracts which have already been placed. (cited in, Mawdsley, 2010, p. 13)

As with the attempts to move ahead with Panel I through OCCAR, the upstream states tried to speed up the process in WEAG's Panel III, cooperation procedures and economic matters. To this end, in 1998 the upstream states signed the LoI and in 2000 a framework agreement to "create the political and legal framework necessary to facilitate industrial restructuring to promote a more competitive and robust European Defence Technological and Industrial Base (EDTIB)" (UK Ministry of

Defence, 2012). The LoI's main functions were to guarantee the security of supply and the easy transfer of necessary production parts for the armaments industry across the signatory states, as well as to harmonize military requirements and cooperation on technical interoperability (Eisenhut, 2010, p. 78; France, Germany, Italy, Spain, Sweden, United Kingdom, 2000). While the upstream states intended to move ahead with the creation of the necessary preconditions for the EDTIB, the LoI's intergovernmental method "prove[d] to be extremely time-consuming and cumbersome" (Schmitt, 2003, p. 29). Thus, as it was obvious shortly after its signature that the framework agreement would "not lead to a permanent institutional structure" (Schmitt, 2003, p. 28), it was not capable of putting enough pressure on the downstream states to accept internal WEAG/WEAO reforms.

Through creating OCCAR and the LoI, the upstream states intended to push for reform of the WEAG/WEAO to endorse the abolition of *juste retour*, necessary to develop the WEAO into a veritable European armaments agency (Schilde, 2017, p. 171)—yet this attempt was only partially successful. In 2001, the members of the WEAG signed a Memorandum of Understanding (MoU) entitled "European Understandings for Research Organisation, Programmes and Activities" (EUROPA MOU) (Western European Armaments Group, 2003). It provided for the possibility of organizing R&T programs within the WEAO in accordance with a "variable geometry approach" (Jordan & Williams, 2007, p. 68) where work-shares would be negotiated on a case-by-case basis. Thus, EUROPA MOU ended the automatic and strict application of the *juste retour* principle in the realm of R&T (Eisenhut, 2010, p. 66).

However, no comparable process could be achieved in the realm of armaments cooperation, and the OCCAR members' ambition to incorporate the organization into the WEU was thwarted by the downstream states (Mörth, 2005, p. 107), whose undivided support was required due to the unanimity requirement for all decisions taken within the WEU (Council of Western European Union, 2003, para. 18). Greece and Belgium especially, two states with nascent (i.e., ambitious but uncompetitive) defense industries, opposed the end of *juste retour* in armaments cooperation (Mawdsley, 2003, p. 18). Thus, the way to further intra-institutional development of the WEAG/WEAO toward a European armaments agency was barred, as a compromise between the "bigger producing states' need for reform and the smaller producing countries' need to protect" was not in sight (Mawdsley, 2008, p. 371). "The WEAG geometry was deemed too complex at the time, and one of the problems we identified was that it lacked the support of real decision-making structures," said Christine Roger, the former French ambassador to the PSC (cited in, EDA, 2019).

In sum, then, the second scope condition required by the pathway, the dissatisfied challenger coalition's inability to achieve internal reform, was present. First, the WEAG/WEAO was unable to provide the expected benefits of an open EDEM based on efficiency and competition, which is why it lost the upstream states' support. Second, while the upstream states tried to push for a reform of these structures, these attempts were unsuccessful. Attempts to increase reform pressure by creating additional structures were countered by the downstream states. The intra-institutional way to reform was blocked. Therefore, as demonstrated in the next section, the upstream states gave up their undertaking to reform the WEAG/WEAO from within and redirected their focus to the creation of an institutional alternative to overcome disagreement with the downstream states. This triggered the pathway to the WEAG/WEAO's integration into the EDA.

The Trigger: The Franco-British Initiative at Le Touquet

Confronted with stalemate within the WEAG/WEAO structures and the unsuccessful attempts to incrementally reform the WEAO into a European armaments agency, the upstream states decided to move on to new pastures. The Franco-British declaration, elaborated at the Le Touquet summit in February 2003, for the first time officially asked for the creation of an additional EU agency, triggering a process that culminated in the establishment of the EDA in 2004 and consequently led to the integration of the WEAG/WEAO into the newly created agency.

Being a selective state, the United Kingdom "historically ... has opposed an armaments agency on the grounds that it could all too easily have become a sort of benefit to industry without regard to proper defence needs" (House of Lords, 2005a, para. 5) and feared that an EU armaments agency could prejudice its ability to cooperate bilaterally with the United States. This is exemplified by the United Kingdom's largest defense company, BAe Systems, which generated the bulk of its returns on the US market (Hartley, 2012) and had just refocused its corporate strategy toward further investments in the United States (Oshri et al., 2009, p. 200). As a result, from a UK perspective, an armaments agency ought not be directed toward creating a "fortress Europe" and establishing a protectionist regime that would discourage the United States from further cooperation with UK-based companies (House of Commons, 2004).

Against the background of the stagnation in armaments cooperation and an inability to reform the WEAG/WEAO structures, however, the idea of creating an EU agency resurfaced in the autumn of 2002. Delegates from all current and prospective EU member states discussed the future European constitution during the European Convention. Working Group VIII on European defense came up with the proposal for a European armaments agency under the aegis of the EU. Led by Michel Barnier, the French Commissioner at the time, the Working Group issued its final report on 16 December 2002 asking for an agency that "would incorporate, with a European label, closer forms of cooperation which already exist in the armaments field between certain Member States (OCCAR, LoI)" (European Convention, 2002a, para. 64). This was possible as the United Kingdom was able to achieve an agreement with the three most powerful avant-gardists, Germany, France, and Italy, to create "an agency, the primary focus of which would be the improvement of defence capabilities rather than armaments collaboration" (House of Lords, 2005a, para. 8). Since it was focused on capabilities rather than armaments, the United Kingdom could be confident that the new agency would not be a "Trojan horse" to undermine NATO primacy (House of Commons, 2004) or an obstacle to UK–US industrial relations. This was the necessary precondition for the United Kingdom to move ahead with the proposal, as Sarah Beaver, British Director General for International Security Policy, confirmed,

> It was thinking in government by ministers that said, 'We have not supported this. We do not want an armaments-driven agency in Europe, but what we do need in Europe is a sustained, steady focus on the improvement of defence capabilities'. If we could harness that as the primary focus of the Agency—and if you look at the mission statement, that is what it is—then that might be, or would be, a worthwhile enterprise. (House of Lords, 2005c, Q49)

Though the avant-gardists Germany and France had continued to propose a European Armaments Agency "based on OCCAR ... which could be progressively enlarged" (France and Germany, 2003, p. 23) in January

2003, the Franco-British Le Touquet summit can be interpreted as having marked the birth of the EDA. The crosscutting upstream coalition represented by France and the United Kingdom declared on 4 February 2003 that

> an intergovernmental defence capabilities development and acquisition agency could be established in the EU... . The objective of the agency would therefore be to promote a comprehensive approach to capability development across all EU nations. (United Kingdom and France, 2003, p. 38)

This agency, according to the Franco-British suggestions, should accomplish what had been impossible in the WEAG/WEAO. It should enshrine the principles institutionalized through OCCAR to manage cooperative armaments programs based on efficiency criteria and to strengthen "an internationally-competitive defence industrial and technological base, drawing on procedures identified in the Letter of Intent Framework Agreement" (United Kingdom and France, 2003, p. 39). Moreover, mandated with "efficient procurement," the "coordination of defence research and technology," and the "harmonization of military requirements" (United Kingdom and France, 2003, p. 39), the suggested agency would take over the tasks of all three panels that made up the WEAG.

The Franco-British proposal, building on the work of the European Convention, was thus to create an institution from scratch that would have considerable overlap in its mandate with the pre-existing WEAG/ WEAO structures but would serve the upstream states' underlying preferences better. The downstream states preferred the status quo, as this would allow them to stick to the principle of *juste retour* and to protect their—limited—shares in the European armaments production chains on the one hand and their freedom to pick and choose off-the-shelf products from US companies without running the risk of being caught in a Fortress Europe. Nonetheless, by the end of 2006, the WEAG/WEAO was dissolved, and the EDA had integrated its functions. All former EU members of the WEAG (except Denmark) and all ten new member states that had joined the EU in 2004 were part of the EDA, even though this ran against their status quo preference for politically steered rather than liberalized defense cooperation. The next two sections demonstrate that the outcome of integrating the WEAG/WEAO into the EDA was caused by the upstream states' go-it-alone power and their preference for the EDA's inclusive membership design.

The Threat of Exclusion: "There Will Be Peer Pressure"

This section shows that, due to the powerful upstream states' ability to create a credible threat of exclusion, the status-quo-oriented downstream states tried to join the EDA against their preference for cooperation within the WEAG/WEAO. Without the upstream states' demonstrated ability to go it alone, however, it would not have been possible to create a European Defence Agency directed toward a "competitive European defence equipment market" (Council of the European Union, para. 3). To be left out of European armaments' cooperation was deemed worse by the downstream states than becoming members of an institution whose purpose in establishing a competitive EDEM was disadvantageous to them compared with the status quo ante.

In 2002 the WEAG Council decided to terminate the efforts to develop the WEAO into a full-fledged armaments agency. The reason was that political consensus between the upstream and downstream states had proven impossible (Western European Union, 2002, para. 4). The downstream states' hostility to the abolition of the *juste retour* principle and the opening of the EDEM was also reflected in the discussions on the establishment of a European armaments agency, which took place in the autumn of 2002 in the European Convention Working Group VIII on defense. Nick Witney, the first Chief Executive of the EDA, summarized the core conflict during the discussions:

> some of the things we might want to do may look threatening from the point of view of relatively small countries. For example, a more open market: if we could snap our fingers and achieve it, I guess that is fine for people with strong defence industries. I guess it is fine for people without defence industries at all. If I were sitting in the middle with a rather weak defence industry, which was still rather important for jobs, then I would be worried about what the Agency was after. (House of Lords, 2005b, p. 54)

In other words, a European armaments agency would not have been to the advantage of quite a large group of downstream states, which consequently preferred the status quo. John Gormley, Irish delegate to the European Convention, stated that the pre-existing framework allowing for non-institutionalized ad-hoc cooperation "is the way the situation should remain" (Gormley, 2002, p. 5). Similarly, "Romania, as a candidate country, has a direct interest in continuing and deepening the WEAG type of Cooperation" (Maior, 2002, p. 3).

While the downstream states, due to their underlying preferences, agreed that their first best solution to maintain the status quo, they also made clear that, if there was to be an agency eventually, the EU member states should "not restrict the participation to only a group of countries" (Hübner, 2002, p. 7), as a Polish delegate put it. As a Slovenian official accordingly declared, "states willing to participate in EU's security system should not be blocked by defence criteria solely. Willingness to participate should be the primary criteria for admission [sic]" (Gaber and Slavko, 2002, p. 3). Yet, if the downstream states' preference was not to further integrate armaments cooperation, why did they want to participate in the EDA eventually?

Taking the genesis of the EDA after the Franco-British Le Touquet Summit into account, it becomes evident that the upstream states, who had already cooperated through the LoI and OCCAR, were the driving force and soon demonstrated unity vis-à-vis the reluctant states. Less than three weeks after France and the United Kingdom had taken up the idea of a new armaments agency within the EU framework, the United Kingdom and Italy reiterated the suggestion. They proposed to establish "a European defence capabilities and acquisition agency which would incorporate, at the appropriate time, existing bodies such as WEAG/WEAO, OCCAR, and LOI" and to "work together towards the progressive opening of defence markets" (United Kingdom and Italy, 2003, p. 42). With Italy joining the Franco-British tandem, three out of Europe's four largest arms producers had already signaled their interest in creating an EU agency.

The last of the four OCCAR founding members, Germany, followed suit two months later at the Tervuren summit. This summit also marks the moment at which the downstream states started joining the quest for an EU agency. The upstream states managed to get some of the federalist downstream states on board when on 21 April 2003, France and

Germany, together with Luxemburg and Belgium, declared their goal of creating an EU agency that would serve

> to increase the European military capabilities and strengthen the interoperability as well as the cooperation between the armed forces of the member states. The Agency will help to create a favourable environment for a competitive European defence industry (Germany, France, Luxembourg, Belgium, 2003, p. 77)

As the upstream states now also had two federalists on board, it seemed likely that a critical mass for agreeing to the establishment of a European armaments agency would be reached. After Belgium had joined the coalition of upstream states, Greece, which also fell into the abovementioned category of states "sitting in the middle" and thus was one of those that needed to "specialis[e] in particular fields ... rather than trying to do everything not very well" (BBC News, 2003), was convinced as well. Referring to the Tervuren summit, the then Greek President-in-Office of the Council, George Papandreou, stated one week later, "Many useful ideas have emerged, and they should be considered" (Greek Presidency, 2003). Consequently, under the Greek presidency, the June European Council in Thessaloniki mandated the "Council to undertake the necessary actions towards creating, in the course of 2004, an intergovernmental agency in the field of defence capabilities development, research, acquisition and armaments" (European Council, 2003, para. 65).

Why should Belgium and Greece be among the first states to embrace an EU agency, which would put their ambitious but limited defense industries under pressure? While market liberalization might be especially harmful for these states, the potential damage caused by being excluded from armaments cooperation was worse. Through the creation of OCCAR and its subsequent management of large-scale armament projects, such as the Airbus A400M, the upstream states had credibly shown that they were able to exclude the smaller EU member states. In May 2003 OCCAR signed a deal for over 180 A400M carrier aircraft (worth around 2 billion) with Airbus Military (EADS, 2003, p. 30), which further emphasized the seriousness of the OCCAR founders. Belgium, which was a co-signatory of the A400M deal, even became a member of OCCAR in 2003, accepting the principle of global balance in place of *juste retour*. The ambitious but not yet competitive states held that "the four members of OCCAR should not take all the good projects to OCCAR, and leave all of the Western European Armaments Group nations struggling on the crumbs falling off the table" (House of Commons, 1999, question 56). It was announced, however, that future armaments cooperation would take place within the EDA, as it was going to incorporate OCCAR "in due course" (European Convention, 2002b, para. 65), so staying outside of the new agency would mean not even getting the crumbs anymore.

Importantly, not all of the future members of the EDA were participants in the Thessaloniki European Council, as the Eastern enlargement was only scheduled for the subsequent year. While the EU-15 in 2003 recognized "the importance of the challenges created by the accession of new Member States for the overall European defence industry on which the EU attaches a great importance" (Council of the European Union, 2003b), they nonetheless proceeded with the establishment process, leaving the new EU members with a take-it-or-leave-it choice. Nick Witney, reflecting on the principles of the EDA, summarized the rationale behind the upstream states' strategy:

> I think we just have to learn not to be afraid of variable geometry and doing some things at four, eight or at 23 rather than 24. There will be peer pressure. It seems an observable fact that people hate to be left out. (House of Lords, 2005b, Q192)

The strategy worked. With the upstream, as well as a growing number of downstream, states supporting the establishment, the plan had gained critical momentum, and in 2004 all former WEAG/WEAO members except Denmark and Turkey, and all ten new EU member states became members of the EDA. The downstream states did so despite their concern that the EDA's role "would seem to be subordinated to the interests of the OCCAR states, in other words, the big Western European armaments-producing countries" (Assembly of Western European Union, 2004, p. xxv). Their hope was that "the Agency will play a useful role for the small and medium-sized states that do not possess the full range of capabilities" (Assembly of Western European Union, 2004, para. 6) and enable them to get a share of the cake. As far as the downstream states were concerned, it was important "to ensure that there [was] synergy as far upstream in the process as possible" (Assembly of Western European Union, 2004, para. 6). The pressure to participate was so strong that

Malta, one of the neutral member states, even risked domestic resistance. For Malta, "being part of the agency goes against our constitution," Mifsud Bonnici, former Maltese Prime Minister, claimed (Times of Malta, 2004). Yet this inconsistency did not prevent the Maltese government from joining the EDA.

Their reservations notwithstanding, the downstream states, that is, the defenders of the status quo, decided to join the EDA, which was created on 12 July 2004 through a unanimous Council Joint Action (Council of the European Union). The dissatisfied upstream states' ability to go it alone erased the status quo ante from the set of feasible alternatives, which impelled the downstream states to join. But why did the upstream states strive for an inclusive and rather unambitious setup for the EDA when they might have continued the exclusive collaboration among themselves or set the entry bar high enough to include only the most ambitious downstream states? The next section demonstrates why it was that the upstream states preferred inclusive cooperation over ambition and therefore refrained from suggesting entry criteria that would have deterred the downstream states, and even designed EDA's decision-making mechanism in a way that made concessions to the most reluctant states.

MEMBERSHIP PREFERENCE: WELCOME TO THE CLUB!

While I have demonstrated that the downstream states, faced with a credible threat of exclusion, had to adjust their strategy and tried to join the suggested EDA against their preference for non-cooperation, this section analyzes the upstream states' membership preference for the newly established institutional competitor. The theoretical pathway leads one to expect that integration will only be the outcome if the challengers, in this case, the upstream states, prefer inclusive cooperation because of the ratio between the transaction costs incurred by exclusion and the member surplus arising from inclusion. The upstream states should have demonstrated a preference for inclusive membership based on rational cost-benefit arguments. Evidence for this preference can be found throughout the EDA's genesis. The upstream states' preference for inclusion is most visible in their willingness to *incentivize* the downstream states to join. First, they renounced the possibility of introducing any preconditions, binding criteria, or commitments for future EDA members. Second, and even more intriguingly, they committed to incorporating the exclusive LoI and OCCAR frameworks into the

EDA and introduced safeguards accommodating the downstream states' fear of being sidelined within the new institution. Both instances allow the conclusion that the upstream states' expected losses from exclusion were high enough to encourage them to compensate defense-industrial laggards.

When the upstream states proposed the establishment of the EDA, they had to decide on the ideal membership structure to reach their goals. The EDA's goals can be largely divided into three categories: (1) regulatory measures furthering a competitive EDEM, (2) collaborative R&T as well as the definition of common standards and criteria for interoperability, (3) the identification of capability gaps and joint procurement and management of large-scale armaments programs to close them (cf. Council of the European Union, para. 5). The latter task, armaments cooperation, came with considerable distributive consequences, that is to say, that the division of work-shares, specialization, and the commitment to stick to agreed procurement contracts might have had a direct impact on national defense technological and industrial bases (DTIBs) and thus on both the national economy and national security. From the perspective of the competitive upstream states, therefore, the member surplus incurred by admitting additional states to an armaments program was high. Contrariwise, however, issues such as regulation, standardization, and collaborative R&T were connected with considerable transaction costs. The more states participate, the lower these costs become—which is why the upstream states should have had an interest in including as many of the downstream states as possible.

In view of these contradictory aspects woven into the EDA's mandate, it is no surprise that initially, during the 2002 discussions of Working Group VIII on defense in the realm of the European Convention, the upstream states' membership preference was not entirely clear. Gisela Stuart, the British representative, demanded

> Membership would depend on the ability of individual member states to meet agreed criteria. This would ensure co-operation that can deliver real results on EU capability goals. (Stuart, 2002, p. 5)

Emphasizing capability development, the initial British perspective was to stick to an exclusive circle of members that fulfilled the requirements and possessed the ability to "meet agreed criteria" (Stuart, 2002, p. 5) to cooperate according to liberal trade principles. Yet, considering the agency's broad focus that included research and technology as well as regulation and standard setting, the then British defense secretary, John Reid, said the United Kingdom would welcome "any mechanism that persuades, encourages, cajoles others to spend money on research and development" (BBC News, 2006). Thus, in working group VIII's final report, it was clearly stated that

> all Member States which so wished could participate in the Agency, the composition of which would not be linked to other, limited forms of defence cooperation. (European Convention, 2002a, para. 65)

While the Finnish Working Group representative, Kimmo Kiljunen, claimed it to be "only natural to make defence material cooperation open and accessible to all Member States, and thus the proposal for a new defence material agency found approval" (Kiljunen, 2004, p. 89), this perspective was too short-sighted. The upstream states' renunciation of ambitious entry criteria was rather the outcome of rational cost-benefit calculations. As far as those states were concerned, including as many EU members as possible in the definition of common standards and requirements allowed them to enlarge their sales markets and overcome the non-cooperative environment manifested in the deficient WEAO/WEAG. In 2004, then UK Secretary of State for Defence, Geoffrey Hoon, clarified the upstream states' ambition to create the EDA as an integrated and inclusive framework within the European Union as follows:

> [T]here is too much fragmentation. It remains a barrier to achieving the improvement in capability that we want. We expect the agency to make these embryonic co-operative frameworks a coherent whole under one roof and to spread their best practice across Europe. (House of Commons, 2004, col. 5)

In a nutshell, the upstream states preferred the EDA to be as inclusive as possible to increase its effectiveness as an R&T incubator and a forum for standard setting and regulation. However, one core conflict remained— not only between the upstream and downstream states but also among the upstream states themselves. How should the member states cope with the potential core business—the coordination and management of armaments procurement and the management of cooperative programs?

After the Thessaloniki European Council's call for the establishment of the agency in June 2003, the Committee of the Permanent Representatives (COREPER), a Council body at ambassador level, established an "Ad hoc Group to prepare the creation of the intergovernmental agency" (Committee of Permanent Representatives, 2003, p. 208) and thus to resolve the remaining issues regarding the functioning of the EDA. Recalling the downstream states' fear that they would need to fight for the "crumbs falling off the table" (House of Commons, 1999, question 56), the upstream states made additional concessions to convince as many states as possible to join. These concessions allowed the upstream states' inclusive membership preference to be observed indirectly.

The upstream states made two major concessions, which can only be explained by their desire to include as many downstream states in the EDA as possible to economize transaction costs. The first had to do with the future dissolution of the exclusive armaments cooperation fora, the LoI and OCCAR. Building on the Ad hoc Group's proposals, the November Council of 2003, agreed to "establish close working relations with relevant elements ... such as L.o.I, OCCAR, and WEAG/WEAO ... with a view to incorporat[ing] them or assimilat[ing] their principles and practices in due course, as appropriate" (Council of the European Union, 2003a, p. 265). This statement shows that this offer goes back to an upstream state initiative rather than having been a specific request by the downstream states. It thus evidences the former's inclusive membership preference. During the Convention Working Group negotiations in 2002, France had already emphasized that the EDA "would incorporate, with a European label, closer forms of cooperation conducted which already exist in the armaments field between among certain Member States (in the framework of OCCAR and L.o.I.)" (France and Germany, 2002, p. 18).

The second concession is connected to the internal design and decision-making structures of the EDA. The agency's design reflected the attempt to achieve a "balance between inclusiveness on the one hand and flexibility on the other" (Georgopoulos, 2015, p. 121). The upstream states tried to eliminate the weaknesses of both WEAG/WEAO and OCCAR. Inefficient decision-making hampered the former, while the latter excluded the downstream states (Mawdsley, 2003). The outcome was a dual structure allowing for two different kinds of collaborative projects. "Category A" projects are inclusive by default, and any member state unwilling to participate needs to opt out of them (Council of the European Union, Art. 20). By contrast, "category B" projects can be proposed by at least one member state to be conducted within the auspices of the agency. Every member state with the wish to participate can notify this intention and will be accepted (Council of the European Union, Art. 21).

At first sight, these provisions seem to be the logical consequence of the upstream states' attempt to get the best of both worlds. An inclusive institutional setup for those aspects in which the membership surplus is low and the transaction costs connected with exclusion are high on the one hand (category A) and a flexible, exclusive branch for those projects that have considerable distributive consequences (category B). Yet, interestingly, the Ad-hoc group came up with an additional provision, which can only be explained in light of the upstream states' preference for an inclusive membership. The creation of both new category A and B projects is conditional on the Steering Board's approval. The EDA's steering board is composed of one representative of each member state and decides by a reinforced qualified majority as regulated in Art. 31(2) TEU (former Art. 23) (Council of the European Union, Art. 9 [2]). This mechanism is a safeguard to prevent the downstream states from being sidelined within the EDA (Eisenhut, 2010, pp. 291–292; Interviews #3 and #4). It is not possible for the upstream states to engage in an exclusive EDA project against the will of the downstream states.

The division of the EDA's work into category A and B projects certainly reflects the upstream states' attempt to design the agency in a way that reflected the transaction cost–membership surplus trade-off. Flexible category B projects combined with inclusive category A projects would have meant squaring the circle. Yet, to ensure that even the least competitive downstream state would join the EDA, the upstream states decided on inclusiveness over ambition and offered considerable concessions. No binding entry criteria, the promise to incorporate not only the WEAG/WEAO but also OCCAR and the LoI into the new agency, and finally, the introduction of the Steering Board safeguard are clear expressions of the upstream states' preference for an inclusive membership.

INTEGRATION OF THE WEAG/WEAO INTO THE EDA

On 12 July 2004, the Council unanimously[6] adopted the Joint Action 2004/551/CFSP to create the EDA. What is more, all signatories of the Joint Action also decided to notify their participation in the newly created agency. With the exception of Denmark and the two non-EU members Turkey and Norway, all former members of the WEAG/WEAO participated in the EDA. As the Joint Action's provisions allowed for close relationships with non-EU members (Council of the European Union, Art. 23 (1), 25 [6]), neither the upstream nor the downstream states had any incentive to maintain both institutions. The WEAG/WEAO's creeping political orphaning (Keohane, 2004) was manifest in its members' agreement to shift cooperation to the EDA and led to its dissolution in 2005. Likewise, during the following year, the WEAO's activities were incorporated into the EDA, and it was dissolved in 2006. The WEAG/WEAO were integrated into the ambit of the EU's CSDP.

When two institutions with overlapping mandates co-governing an issue area have identical membership, it is unlikely to be beneficial for their members to maintain both, but we would expect that they pool the institutions' resources in one of them. As has been mentioned, however, the two non-EU WEAG members, Turkey and Norway, were not eligible to become full members of the EDA. Thus, there might have been an incentive to keep the WEAG/WEAO structure alive to facilitate cooperation with these states. In 2003, when the negotiations on the EDA were already ongoing, the WEU assembly alluded to the potential difficulties connected with Norway's and Turkey's exclusion from the EDA:

> Third countries are not represented on the Steering Board or in the other political and military structures of the ESDP. They therefore cannot be involved upstream in the definition of the programmes that they might be invited to join in the best of cases. The issue at stake here is … participation in the decision-making process, from the identification of requirements through to the implementation phase. (Western European Union, 2004, p. 21)

This issue was resolved in the agency's preparation phase. The text of the Council Joint Action guarantees that the "non-EU WEAG members shall

---

[6] With the exception of Denmark, which due to its general opt-out is not bound by decisions in the realm of the CSDP.

be provided with the fullest possible transparency" (Council of the European Union, 25 [6]) by establishing a consultative committee that keeps associated partner states informed throughout the whole project cycle. Thus, while the situation certainly worsened for Turkey and Norway as they lost their ability to participate in the formal decision-making process, the EDA members would not forgo any benefits from transferring their resources from the WEAG/WEAO into the newly created EU agency.

Consequently, the WEAG defense ministers worked on shifting their political and financial resources toward the new agency. Transferring the tasks of Panel I (defense procurement) and Panel III (procedures and economic matters) to the EDA was not a challenging task and did not meet resistance, as they were largely defunct. In the period 2003/2004, there had been one single WEAG meeting at the ministerial level, and the first meeting on 22 November 2004 was to be the last at the same time. In their conclusions, the WEAG defense ministers made clear that they saw no further benefits connected with maintaining the WEAG:

> In view of the establishment of this European Defence Agency ... the Ministers recognised that ... there is no longer a need for activities in the framework of the WEAG. ... The Ministers tasked their National Armaments Directors (NADs) to ... close WEAG no later than 30 June 2005. (Western European Armaments Group, 2005)

On 2 March 2005, the WEAG's Panels I and III were closed by the NADs (Western European Armaments Group, 2005), and the WEAG itself was dissolved on 23 May 2005.

Panel II, R&T, with its executive organ, the WEAO, lasted for another year. The reason for this, however, was not political disagreement but rather technical requirements related to the EDA's inception. The WEAO was managing a number of contracts, which the EDA was not yet prepared to incorporate in terms of personnel, facilities, and structures. On 22 May 2005, the EDA's Steering Board agreed to take over the WEAG/WEAO's Research and Technology activities when "additional resources should be available to EDA to handle transferred contracts" (EDA, 2005; 2006, p. 85).[7] There was no disagreement on the transfer of resources and tasks from the WEAO to the EDA. Finally, on 31

---

[7] This took more time than expected, as the conflict over the EDA's strategic direction resurfaced within the group of the upstream states, specifically between avant-gardist

August 2006, the WEAO was dissolved, and its mandate, membership, and resources were integrated into the EDA.

Summary

This chapter has demonstrated the presence of the theorized causal pathway leading to the integration of the WEAG/WEAO into the EDA. When a coalition of dissatisfied upstream states found the pathway to internal reform blocked, namely, that it was not possible to develop the WEAO into a European armaments agency, they decided to create an institutional alternative, the EDA. The theoretical framework expects that, if the institutional competitor represents a threat of exclusion to the defenders of the original institution, the latter will try to join the former against their original preferences. And in fact, although the downstream states preferred minimum cooperation within the WEAG/WEAO structures, this was no longer feasible when the upstream states proposed to create the EDA. The upstream states' initiative and their ability to create a credible threat of exclusion by demonstrating their ability to organize cooperation exclusively among themselves through OCCAR and the LoI erased the non-cooperative status quo from the set of feasible alternatives. Consequently, for the downstream states, it was better to join the EDA than be excluded from defense cooperation altogether.

Moreover, the theorized pathway hypothesizes that integration will only occur if the membership structures of the contested and the competing institutions are close to identical and there is no benefit for any dual member from maintaining both institutions. This would only be the case if the relatively powerful upstream states actively sought to make the EDA's membership as inclusive as possible, otherwise, they could have excluded additional members by means of high entry criteria or decision-making mechanisms that were designed to deter them. As expected, the empirical analysis showed that the upstream states demonstrated an unequivocal preference for inclusive EDA membership. They relinquished any sort of barriers to entry, introduced a safeguarding mechanism that would allow downstream states to vote down any prospective collaborative program with a blocking minority, and suggested the dissolution of the exclusive OCCAR and LoI frameworks in the medium term.

France and selective UK, in the course of the negotiations on the EDA's budget (Jordan & Williams, 2007).

Taken together, the upstream states made considerable concessions to convince a maximum number of downstream states to join.

Together these two conditions determined an outcome in which all former WEAG members joined the EDA. The downstream states' willingness to join when faced with the alternative of being excluded and the upstream states' preparedness to offer incentives to convince even the least competitive state to join led to a unanimous Council Joint Action. As all former WEAG/WEAO member states except Turkey, Norway, and Denmark became members of the EDA, keeping both institutions became inefficient. Within months of the EDA's inception in July 2004, the WEAG was dissolved in May 2005, and the WEAO followed one year later in August 2006. Their tasks and resources were formally integrated into the EDA, which then was supposed to develop into the new center of legal and relational authority in European defense cooperation.

The next case study starts out where this one ended—with the creation of the EDA. Although the EDA was intended to develop into the new anchor point for European armaments cooperation, incorporating existing minilateral frameworks such as OCCAR, this goal was not accomplished. The EDA never gained a foothold in its designated core business, armaments cooperation and collaborative procurement, and was marginalized by the upstream states, which quickly shifted their cooperative efforts back to OCCAR.

References

Assembly of Western European Union. (2004). *The interparliamentary European security and defence assembly: The European Defence Agency—Reply to the annual report of the council.* Document A/1856.

BBC News. (2003, February 5). *UK and France boost defence ties.* http://news.bbc.co.uk/1/hi/world/europe/2726111.stm.

BBC News. (2006). *EU keen on defence research fund.* http://news.bbc.co.uk/2/hi/europe/4781548.stm (December 13, 2018).

Committee of Permanent Representatives. (2003). Armaments agency [Brussels, 4 September 2003]. In A. Missiroli (Ed.), *From Copenhagen to Brussels European defence: Core documents, Volume IV.* Vol. 67 of *Chaillot Papers* (pp. 208–210). Institute for Security Studies European Union.

Council of the European Union. Council Joint Action 2004/551/CFSP of 12 July 2004 on the establishment of the European Defence Agency. *Official Journal of the European Union* 2004 (L 245/17).

Council of the European Union. (2003a). *General affairs and external relations council* [17 November 2003]: Council conclusions. In A. Missiroli (Ed.), *From Copenhagen to Brussels European defence: Core documents, Volume IV*. Vol. 67 of *Chaillot Papers* (pp. 256–268). Institute for Security Studies European Union.

Council of the European Union. (2003b). *2518th council meeting: External relations*. Brussels. Press Release, C/03/166.

Council of Western European Union. (2003). WEAO Charter [1997]. In B. Schmitt (Ed.), *European armaments cooperation: Core documents*. Vol. 59 of *Chaillot Papers* (pp. 11–22).

Deutscher Bundestag. (2003). *Unterrichtung durch die Bundesregierung: Bericht der Bundesregierung über die Tätigkeit der Westeuropäischen Union für die Zeit vom 1. Januar bis 31. Dezember 2002*. Drucksache 15/1485.

EADS. (2003). *To new levels: Corporate presentation 2003*.

EDA. (2005). *Latest news: European Defence Agency steering board agrees transfer of WEAG/WEAO activities to EDA*. Brussels.

EDA. (2006). European Defence Agency steering board agrees transfer of WEAG/WEAO activities to EDA: 22 April 2005. In *EU security and defence: Core documents 2005*. 6th ed. *Chaillot Papers* (pp. 85–89).

EDA. (2019). *15 years of working together: The birth of an agency*. https://www.eda.europa.eu/Aboutus/our-history/the-birth-of-an-agency (March 27, 2019).

Eisenhut, D. (2010). *Europäische Rüstungskooperation: Zwischen Binnenmarkt und zwischenstaatlicher Zusammenarbeit* [ger] (1st ed.). Vol. 59 of *Augsburger Rechtsstudien*. Univ., Diss.--Augsburg, 2009. Baden-Baden: Nomos Verl.-Ges.

European Convention. (2002a). *Final report of Working Group VIII—Defence* (461st ed.). Brussels. WG VIII 22. https://web.archive.org/web/200706092 35907/http://register.consilium.eu.int/pdf/en/02/cv00/00461en2.pdf.

European Convention. (2002b). *Rapport du Président du Groupe de travail VIII "Défense" à la Convention: Rapport final du Groupe de travail VIII "Défense"*. CONV 461/02. https://www.cvce.eu/en/obj/final_report_of_ working_group_viii_defence_16_december_2002-en-71dbaa92-ac9e-4556-a639-3c7665fd0812.html.

European Council. (2003). *Presidency conclusions*. Brussels. 11638/03.

France, and Germany. (2002). *Working document 36—WG VIII: Franco-German comments on the preliminary draft final report of Working Group VIII "Defence"* (WD 022). http://european-convention.europa.eu/docs/wd8/5925.pdf.

France, and Germany. (2003). Franco-German summit—40th anniversary of the Elysée Treaty: Declaration by the Franco-German Defence and Security

Council [22 January 2003]. In A. Missiroli (Ed.), *From Copenhagen to Brussels European defence: Core documents, Volume IV*. Vol. 67 of *Chaillot Papers* (pp. 22–26). Institute for Security Studies European Union.
France, Germany, Italy, Spain, Sweden, United Kingdom. (2000). *Framework agreement concerning measures to facilitate the restructuring and operation of the European defence industry*. Farnborough. Treaty series, 33 (2001). https://assets.publishing.service.gov.uk/government/uploads/system/uploads/attachment_data/file/518178/TS0033_2001.pdf.
Gaber, and Slavko. (2002). *Working document 32—WG VIII: Comments on the preliminary draft final report of Working Group VIII "Defence"*. http://european-convention.europa.eu/docs/wd8/5881.pdf.
Georgopoulos, A. (2015). The EDA and EU defence procurement integration. In N. Karampekios & I. Oikonomou (Eds.), *The European Defence Agency: Arming Europe. Routledge studies in European security and strategy* (pp. 118–136). Routledge, Taylor & Francis Group.
Germany, France, Luxembourg, Belgium. (2003). European defence meeting—'Tervuren' [29 April 2003]: Meeting of the Heads of State and Government on European Defence. In A. Missiroli (Ed.), *From Copenhagen to Brussels European defence: Core documents, Volume IV*. Vol. 67 of *Chaillot Papers* (pp. 76–80). Institute for Security Studies European Union.
Gormley, J. (2002). *Working document 40—WG VIII: Comments by Mr John Gormley on the preliminary draft final report of Working Group VIII "Defence" (WD 022)*.
Greek Presidency. (2003). *Informal general affairs and external relations council (Gymnich), May 2–3: Press statement*. http://www.eu2003.gr//en/articles/2003/5/3/2662/ (May 4, 2019).
Guillaume, M. (1998). L'Organisation conjointe de coopération en matière d'armement. *Annuaire français de droit international, 44*(1), 283–297. http://www.persee.fr/docAsPDF/afdi_0066-3085_1998_num_44_1_3514.pdf.
Hartley, K. (2008). Collaboration and European defence industrial policy. *Defence and Peace Economics, 19*(4), 303–315. Accessed June 2, 2016.
Hartley, K. (2011). Creating a European defence industrial base. *Security Challenges, 7*(3), 95–111.
Hartley, K. (2012). Company survey series I: BAE systems PLC. *Defence and Peace Economics, 23*(4), 331–342.
Heuninckx, B. (Ed.). (2017). *The law of collaborative defence procurement in the European Union* [eng]. Cambridge University Press.
Hill, C. (1993). The capability-expectations gap, or conceptualizing Europe's international role. *JCMS: Journal of Common Market Studies, 31*(3), 305–328.
House of Commons. (1999). *Defence—Minutes of evidence: Taken before the defence committee*. Publications on the internet—Defence Committee

Publications, Session 1999–2000. https://publications.parliament.uk/pa/cm199900/cmselect/cmdfence/69/9111001.htm.
House of Commons. (2004). *Establishing a European Defence Agency: European Standing Committee B.*
House of Lords. (2005a). *European Union Committee Ninth Report of Session 2004–05: European Defence Agency—Report with evidence.* European Union, HL Paper 76. https://publications.parliament.uk/pa/ld200405/ldselect/ldeucom/76/7605.htm.
House of Lords. (2005b). Examination of witness: Mr. Nick Witney chief executive, European Defence Agency (17 January 2005). In *European Union Committee Ninth Report of Session 2004–05: European Defence Agency—Report with evidence.* European Union.
House of Lords. (2005c). Minutes of evidence taken before the select committee on the European Union (Sub-Committee C): 10 June 2004. In *European Union Committee Ninth Report of Session 2004–05: European Defence Agency—Report with evidence.* European Union.
Hübner, D. (2002). *Working document 25—WG VIII: Improving the functioning and effectiveness of ESDP in the service of CFSP.* http://european-convention.europa.eu/docs/wd8/5518.pdf.
Interview #3: EDA representative, 12 December 2017 in Brussels.
Interview #4: EDA representative, 12 December 2017 in Brussels.
Jordan, G., & Williams, T. (2007). Hope deferred? *The RUSI Journal, 152*(3), 66–71.
Keohane, D. (2004). *Europe's new defence agency.* London. Policy Brief. http://www.cer.eu/sites/default/files/publications/attachments/pdf/2012/policy brief_defence_agency-5618.pdf.
Kiljunen, K. (2004). *The EU constitution: A Finn at the convention.* Publications of the Parliamentary Office, 01. https://www.eduskunta.fi/FI/tietoaedusku nnasta/julkaisut/Documents/ekj_1+2004.pdf.
Maior, L. (2002). *Working document 45—WG VIII: Note by Mr Liviu Maior.* Trans. European Convention.
Mawdsley, J. (2003). *The European Union and defense industrial policy* (Paper 31). https://www.bicc.de/uploads/tx_bicctools/paper31.pdf.
Mawdsley, J. (2008). European Union armaments policy: Options for small states? *European Security, 17*(2–3), 367–385.
Mawdsley, J. (2010). Arms, agencies, and accountability: The case of OCCAR. *European Security, 12*(3–4), 95–111.
Mörth, U. (2005). *Organizing European cooperation: The case of armaments.* Rowman & Littlefield.
OCCAR. (1998). *Convention on the establishment of the organisation for joint armament cooperation (Organisation Conjointe de Cooperation en Matière d'ARmement)—OCCAR: OCCAR convention.* Farnborough.

Oshri, I., Kotlarsky, J., & Willcocks, L. (2009). *The handbook of global outsourcing and offshoring* [eng]. Palgrave Macmillan.

Sanfourche, J.-P. (1999). The WEAG and the future European armaments agency: Interview with major general Andries Schlieper. *Air & Space Europe*, *1*(3), 6–9.

Schilde, K. (2017). *The political economy of European security*. Cambridge University Press.

Schmitt, B. (2003). *The European Union and armaments: Getting a bigger bang for the Euro*. https://www.iss.europa.eu/sites/default/files/EUISSFiles/cp063e.pdf.

Stuart, G. (2002). *Working document 23—WG VIII*. http://european-convention.europa.eu/docs/wd8/5452.pdf.

Times of Malta. (2004, July 19). European Defence Agency membership "could be in violation of constitution".

Treaty on European Union. (1992). *Treaty on European Union* [eng]. Office for Official Publ. of the Europ. Communities.

Trybus, M. (2006). The new European Defence Agency: A contribution to a common European security and defence policy and a challenge to the community acquis? *Common Market Law Review*, *43*, 667–703.

Trybus, M. (2014). *Buying defence and security in Europe: The EU defence and security procurement directive in context*. Cambridge University Press.

UK Ministry of Defence. (2001). *Maximising the benefits of defence equipment co-operation (HC 300 2000–2001)—Full report (665 KB): Report by the comptroller and auditor general*. London. Session 2000–2001, HC 300. Accessed December 6, 2018.

UK Ministry of Defence. (2012, August 4). *Letter of intent: Restructuring the European defence industry: Overview of the work of the Letter of Intent (LoI) group*. https://www.gov.uk/guidance/letter-of-intent-restructuring-the-european-defence-industry.

United Kingdom, and France. (2003). Declaration on strengthening European cooperation in security and defence [4 February 2003]: Le Touquet. In A. Missiroli (Ed.), *From Copenhagen to Brussels European defence: Core documents, Volume IV*. Vol. 67 of *Chaillot Papers* (pp. 36–39). Institute for Security Studies European Union.

United Kingdom, and Italy. (2003). Declaration defence and security [31 February 2003]. In A. Missiroli (Ed.), *From Copenhagen to Brussels European defence: Core documents, Volume IV*. Vol. 67 of *Chaillot Papers* (pp. 40–45). Institute for Security Studies European Union.

Weiss, Moritz, and Felix Biermann. (2018). Defence industrial cooperation. In H. Meijer & M. Wyss (Eds.), *The handbook of European defence policies and armed formces* [eng] (pp. 693–709). Oxford University Press.

Western European Armaments Group. (2003). EUROPA MoU [2001]. In B. Schmitt (Ed.), *European armaments cooperation: Core documents*. Vol. 59 of *Chaillot Papers* (pp. 95–107).
Western European Armaments Group. (2005). *Information on the Spring 2004 meeting of the WEAG national armaments directors: Dublin, 26 February 2004*. http://www.weu.int/weag/whatsnew.htm.
Western European Union. (1997). *Erfurt Declaration*. http://www.weu.int/weag/.
Western European Union. (1998). *Rome Declaration*. http://www.weu.int/weag/.
Western European Union. (2000). *WEU Today*. Brussels. http://www.weu.int/.
Western European Union. (2002). *Rome Declaration*. http://www.weu.int/weag/Rome_Declaration.pdf.
Western European Union. (2004). *Assembly of Western European Union—The interparliamentary European security and defence assembly: The European Defence Agency—Reply to the annual report of the council*. Paris. A/1856. http://stopwapenhandel.org/sites/stopwapenhandel.org/files/imported/projecten/Europa/EDA/WEU_on_EDA.pdf.

CHAPTER 6

The Marginalization of the EDA: False Premises, False Promises?

The purpose of this chapter is to analyze the process that led to the marginalization of the EDA through OCCAR. When the EU member states created the EDA in 2004, its mandate to enhance and manage joint armaments projects and procurement programs overlapped with OCCAR's. While the initial plan was to establish the EDA as the new focal point for European armaments cooperation and eventually to integrate OCCAR, OCCAR survived. What is more, the upstream states shifted cooperation in the realm of armaments back to it and suppressed the EDA's development in this field. The Administrative Arrangement (AA) between OCCAR and the EDA, signed in 2012, cemented the EDA's marginalization.

The EU member states allocated the bulk of political and financial resources in the field of armaments cooperation to OCCAR and thus "marginalised the agency, instead of using its full mandate" (Mölling, 2015, p. 6). When it came to the supreme discipline of organizing Europe's hard power, that is, its armaments cooperation and joint procurement, the EDA remained in the passenger's seat. The EU member states consistently organized large armaments cooperation programs, such as the transport aircraft A400M and the more recent undertaking to develop a fifth-generation Future Combat Air System (FCAS) or a European drone, outside the EDA. OCCAR manages these programs.

© The Author(s), under exclusive license to Springer Nature Switzerland AG 2023
F. Biermann, *The Battle for Authority in European Defence Cooperation*, Palgrave Studies in European Union Politics, https://doi.org/10.1007/978-3-031-30054-7_6

Comparing their respective budgets makes EDA's marginalization for the benefit of OCCAR apparent. While the EDA has managed a total project value of around €1 billion since its inception in 2004 (EDA, 2011, p. 44), OCCAR's budget for 2017 alone was €3.77 billion (OCCAR-EA, 2016, p. 51). With ca. €176 million in 2017 (EDA, 2011, p. 44; 2016a), the EDA's budget amounted to about 5% of OCCAR's. Moreover, the 2012 AA ascribes "complementary" roles to the two institutions in the management of cooperative armaments projects (EDA & OCCAR, 2012, para 3.2.1). This means that their overlap in mandate has finally been disentangled. While the EDA is involved in the identification of capability gaps, standardization, and co-financing R&T, the real business—awarding contracts, coordinating production, negotiating procurement guarantees, organizing the financing, etc.—is being managed by OCCAR. Thus, OCCAR became the focal institution in armaments cooperation while the EDA was marginalized.

This chapter demonstrates that the AA formalizing the EDA's marginalization in 2012 was an outcome of the process theorized in Chapter 3 (and visualized for this case in Fig. 6.1) and is structured in five sections. The first shows that the process was triggered by a coalition of dissatisfied upstream states shifting cooperation back to OCCAR when they found the way to internal reform blocked. The blockade on reform was partly rooted in a long-smoldering and newly inflamed conflict within the group of upstream states, namely between the selective UK, which was set on a limited role for EDA, and avant-gardist France, which had plans to develop the EDA into a full-fledged supranational armaments agency. Moreover, the ongoing conflict between upstream and downstream states around liberal practices in cooperation led to paralysis in the EDA. The second section demonstrates that, based on the upstream states' power to go it alone, shifting to OCCAR represented a credible threat of exclusion to the downstream states. The third shows that downstream states' attempts to join the organization were halted by their upstream counterparts, which preferred to keep cooperation exclusive in an area with enormous distributive implications. The penultimate section provides evidence that, when the downstream states were confronted with the upstream states' go-it-alone power and their exclusive membership preference for OCCAR, the only way they could prevent themselves from being sidelined was to agree to formalize the relationship between the EDA as a marketplace for ideas and OCCAR as the contract-awarding

6 THE MARGINALIZATION OF THE EDA: FALSE PREMISES ...   143

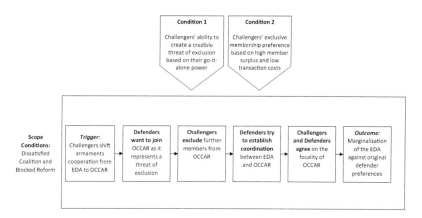

Fig. 6.1 Process leading to the EDA's Marginalization through OCCAR

institution in an AA. The final section concludes by summarizing the findings.

This section demonstrates that the present case study falls within the scope of the theoretical argument presented in Chapter 3. The process leading to the EDA's marginalization was triggered by a dissatisfied challenger coalition of powerful avant-gardist states that shifted cooperation to OCCAR. As they found the way to developing the EDA into a European armaments cooperation and procurement agency blocked by both the downstream states and the United Kingdom, they set out to divert their resources away from the EDA and toward OCCAR, a framework with an overlapping membership and mandate.

The EDA was intended to cope with four main tasks after its inception in 2004: the enhancement of European defense capabilities, the development of a competitive EDEM, improved effectiveness of R&T in the defense sector, and the promotion of European armaments cooperation (Council of the European Union, Art. 3). To fulfill all four tasks efficiently, the EDA was initially supposed to consolidate and replace the various multilateral frameworks for armaments cooperation outside the EU (Council of the European Union, Art. 25(2); Trybus, 2006). Yet, while the WEAG/WEAO and their functions in the realm of the EDEM, R&T cooperation, and capabilities development were successfully transferred to the EDA in 2005 and 2006 (see Chapter 5), OCCAR, which organized armaments cooperation, survived.

When the Council established the EDA in 2004, it did so on the basis that it would incorporate OCCAR "in due course" (Council of the European Union, Art. 25(2)). Commentators were sure that projects "such as the British-German-Italian-Spanish 'Eurofighter/Typhoon' would be conducted by the EDA" (Trybus, 2006, p. 692). During their Council meeting on 17 November 2003, the EU member states agreed on a two-stage process for setting up the new defense agency. During the EDA's initial phase in 2004, it was supposed to establish working relations "for the management of collaborative projects through OCCAR" (Council of the European Union, 2003, para. 6.2). As soon as it was "fully operational," however, EDA was to "incorporate or assimilate the principles and practices" of OCCAR (Council of the European Union, 2003, para. 6.3). This, however, did not happen—when the EDA's steering board agreed to incorporate the WEAG/WEAO in April 2005 (EDA, 2006), there was no longer any mention of similar actions with regard to OCCAR.

Why was OCCAR not incorporated into the EDA to create an integrated, competitive, and specialized defense equipment market relying on joint armaments development and procurement? Even though the OCCAR members themselves laid the foundation for a step toward integrative European armaments cooperation within the EDA, they were the ones who eventually brought about its marginalization. The reason for this was their dissatisfaction and their inability to overcome internal resistance.

Dissatisfaction: Spirits That They've Summoned, Their Commands Ignore[1]

To understand the reasons why the upstream states triggered a process leading to the EDA's marginalization, it is necessary to consider two core conflicts that were already going on during EDA's establishment phase. The first divided the upstream group, separating the avant-gardist from the selective states along the Europeanist/Atlanticist fault line. The second revolved around the question of how potential armaments cooperation and joint procurement projects should be structured and pitted the upstream against the downstream states. As a result, the EDA was never

---

[1] The reference here is to J. W. von Goethe's poem, *The Sorcerer's Apprentice*.

able to really get going—either in the realm of armaments cooperation or in enhancing capability development.

The first conflict between the selectives and the avant-gardists is best exemplified by the differences between the United Kingdom, which emphasized the primacy of NATO, and France, which preferred strong and independent European security and defense cooperation. While the British were in favor of an EDA that focused on capability development, such as joint training, without interfering with national procurement decisions, the French advocated for a genuine armaments agency (EDA, 2014, p. 20). The United Kingdom feared that moving away from NATO toward a strong European defense industry base with preferential treatment given to the European single market could lead to their exclusion from contracts in the United States (Trybus, 2006, p. 672). France's markets for defense sales, by contrast, are traditionally situated on the African continent and among emergent states, such as India (Weiss, 2019), making them less vulnerable to adverse US reactions. Accordingly, when "the United Kingdom proposal for an agency, the primary focus of which would be the improvement of defence capabilities rather than armaments collaboration, gained support in the Convention" (House of Lords, 2005a, point 8), the French continued to push for a predominant armaments role (EDA, 2014, p. 20).

The outcome was neither an *armaments* agency nor a *capabilities* agency but a *defense* agency, whose "job was to demonstrate that the Agency was able to do both, and moreover by doing both it could succeed better in each," Nick Witney explained (EDA, 2014, p. 20). Yet this constellation turned out to be an "unhappy compromise" (Jordan & Williams, 2007). Progress was hard to achieve during the EDA's first months, as the United Kingdom interpreted any further step toward strengthening the EDA's position as creating a "Trojan horse" for NATO (House of Commons, 2004). Therefore, it was not until December 2005, almost 18 months after its creation, that the EDA was awarded its first minor R&T contract (EDA, 2018).

However, this divide alone cannot explain the upstream states' overall dissatisfaction with the EDA. Providing the possibility for 'category B' projects, in which a group of willing member states could move ahead and engage in joint procurement projects, there would have been the option to proceed without the United Kingdom. Nor does it explain why even the United Kingdom, which favored a limited mandate for the EDA, held that "the Agency lacks structure and orientation" (House of Commons,

2008, para. 43). The reason for this dissatisfaction lies in two flaws in the EDA's decision-making process, which, once again, pitted upstream against downstream states.

First, the EDA's Steering Board, composed of one representative from each member state (Council Decision (CFSP) 2015/1835 of 12 October 2015 defining the statute, seat, and operational rules of the European Defence Agency (recast), 2015), had the discretion to decide whether to launch a collaborative project. This gave smaller member states the power to stop any project from happening whenever they "feel they have been locked out" (Trybus, 2006, p. 702). Moreover, and equally important, as soon as member states signaled their interest, they were allowed into a program and were thus able to influence the process of specifying the requirements (Interview #3). This de facto undermined the formal flexibility introduced with category B projects. The upstream states themselves had introduced this feature as a concession to the downstream states; they now lamented the consequences. Second, while the Steering Board's decision-making relied on qualified majority voting (QMV), "the QMV has never been utilised and unanimity became the rule" (Mauro & Thoma, 2016, p. 20). The reason for this might have been the emergency break included in the QMV decision-making process. Article 9 (3) of the Council Decision (CFSP) 2015/1835 states that "a vote shall not be taken" if a member of the steering board for "important and stated reasons of national security" intends to oppose a decision. With the effectiveness of QMV undermined (Eisenhut, 2010; Trybus, 2006, p. 682) and in order to live up to its role as an EU entity trying to work toward convergence (Interview #3), there was a preference for initiating category A projects that included all the members of the EDA (Jordan & Williams, 2007, p. 68).

These two flaws led to a situation in which the downstream states, "those whose contribution to [the CSDP] is slight or negligible – often, perversely, [are] those most ready to hijack meetings in pursuit of some narrow national concern" (Witney, 2008, p. 25). What is more, as a result of levering out QMV, the avant-gardist upstream states lacked the ability to establish armaments programs within the EDA that were undesired by the United Kingdom. "In short, the EDA ... inherited the same problems the WEAO had" (Mawdsley, 2008, p. 379). The German ministry of defense (MoD) complained about the EDA's poorly harmonized financial planning, the lengthy definition of joint requirements, and the contradictory industrial interests of potential partner states (BMVg, 2016, p. 42).

In a similar vein, Admiral Christian Pénillard stated in consultation with the French defense committee:

> The true difficulty is to convince member states to cooperate, as they often argue along the logic of *juste retour* to further their national interest. ... Twenty-four states take part in the Agency. One of the difficulties is that there are also twenty-four different perceptions, twenty-four cultures, twenty-four economic and strategic situations. (Assemblée Nationale, 2006, 133–134, author's translation)

As a group, the avant-gardist states were dissatisfied with the EDA's inability to fulfill its mandate, both because the mandate as such was contested by the United Kingdom and because the decision-making process did not allow them to move ahead independently of the downstream states. A possible way out of this stalemate would have been early reform of the EDA, allowing for more flexibility and differentiation. Yet the internal way to reform proved to be blocked.

Reform Blockade: Resistance on All Fronts

The downstream states, as well as the Atlanticist United Kingdom, unequivocally demonstrated that they would not accept any substantial reform of the EDA. The intra-institutional pathway to reform was blocked, as political consensus was attainable neither between the avant-gardists and the United Kingdom nor between upstream and downstream states. It was thus impossible to adjust any dimension of the institution. Try as they might to adjust the agency's resources, membership, or mandate, there was resistance on all fronts. Three instances illustrate this situation.

First, when the avant-gardists tried to increase the EDA's budget and personnel to enhance its effectiveness and capacity to handle new projects, the United Kingdom continuously blocked their efforts (Jordan & Williams, 2007). Even when the amounts of money involved were very limited, the United Kingdom went into opposition. French Defense Minister Michele Alliot-Marie pointedly summarized the stalemate on the EDA's budget in 2006:

Haggling over €1 million for an agency which will be decisive in providing us with the resources and research means to prepare the future EU defence – that seemed to me a bit of a joke. (EUobserver, 2006)

The United Kingdom was unwilling to allow the EDA personnel and money enough to turn it into an armaments agency and signaled that it considered it a "waste of money" (O'Donnell, 2011, p. 3). Consequently, the EDA's general budget stagnated at a very low level. From €19.9 million in 2005, it increased slightly to €21.5 million in 2007, only to decrease again to €20.8 million in 2008 (EDA, 2008, p. 4). Similarly, the operational budget invested in actual projects, though demonstrating a positive trend from 2.4 to 3.8 to 4.4 million Euros (EDA, 2008, p. 4), was only marginal in a sector where, for example, one Eurofighter jet cost €62.5 million (News.at).

Second, the downstream countries held on tightly to the principle of *juste retour* and did not accept its abandonment in the realm of armaments cooperation since it was vital to their markets (Vestel, 1995, p. 45). The new EU member states that joined after 2004 in particular feared that their defense industries could not stand European competition. Poland, for example, voiced strong concerns against a single European arms production market (SIPRI, 2008, p. 274). The Polish ministry of foreign affairs described one of its core tasks as the "protection of the interests of the Polish industry in international forums" (Ministry of Foreign Affairs of the Republic of Poland, 2012). This position of the downstream states did not change over the years. Even in 2014, the Visegràd states, the Czech Republic, Hungary, Poland, and Slovakia (V4), were still voicing their concern that their region might be "turning into a mere market for global defence companies" (V4, 2014, pp. 1–2). Moreover, in June 2017, Jiří Hynek, the President of the Czech Defence and Security Industry Association, stated: "We want to protect our industry, and we wish to invite other countries, such as Austria, Slovakia or Slovenia to join forces to counterbalance pressures of large corporations" (IDET, 2017).

Third, when the EDA was founded, the OCCAR members had a strong interest in including their NATO partner, Turkey. A witness in the United Kingdom's House of Commons stated, "Turkey's exclusion from membership of the EDA, despite its membership of NATO and the EDA's predecessor body, OCCAR, was a major weakness of the Agency ... and is deeply regrettable" (House of Commons, 2008, para. 245–6). Subsequent pushes to negotiate Turkey's admission as an associate member of the EDA remained unsuccessful, however. Both Cyprus and Greece derailed any efforts in this direction (Karampekios, 2015), leaving the upstream states aggrieved.

In sum, both the downstream states and the United Kingdom, albeit for different reasons, blocked any attempt to establish the EDA as a forum for European armaments collaboration. While the United Kingdom was especially pre-occupied with NATO primacy, the prevention of duplication, and securing its US market access, for the downstream states, a "buy-European" defense industry policy would be a double jeopardy. Liberalizing the EDEM would push them further toward the margins of the international production chain while, if they managed to participate in a tender, they would be obliged to buy inferior but more expensive goods rather than importing US systems. In view of the strong opposition to further development of the EDA, the avant-gardists needed to consider their external institutional options.

The Trigger: Avant-Gardist Resignation

Soon after the EDA's inception in 2004, it was foreseeable that the agency would not be easily able to develop into a European armaments agency as desired by the avant-gardist states. It is difficult, however, to determine the specific event that triggered the process that eventually led to the EDA's marginalization. The shift from the EDA to OCCAR started in 2005, when the creation of new projects within the OCCAR rather than a transfer of ongoing projects to the EDA undermined the former's incorporation into the latter. The shift of financial resources toward OCCAR is also well documented in the budgetary development of the two institutions. Finally, France officially renounced its original intention to integrate OCCAR into the EDA in 2008 when it suggested negotiating an AA making OCCAR the executive branch of the EDA and was followed by the other OCCAR members.

While the EU member states transferred the R&T contracts, which were handled by the WEAO to the EDA until August 2006, and had initially planned to do the same with the OCCAR projects (Trybus, 2006, p. 692; Interviews #6 and #7), these plans were abandoned after 2004. What is more, the avant-gardist states not only decided against a transfer of ongoing programs away from OCCAR but even agreed to conduct new programs within it. Eight out of the thirteen currently ongoing armaments procurement programs managed by OCCAR started after 2004.

Moreover, in the relevant period between the EDA's foundation in 2004 until the signature of the AA in 2012, the three major programs that had been integrated into OCCAR (the FREMM frigate, the ESSOR radio system, and the MUSIS imaging system)[2] were concluded without the United Kingdom's participation and went back to French–Italian initiatives. This further supports the hypothesis that the shift back was, in part, stimulated by the possibility of cooperating without the consent of either the downstream states or the United Kingdom.

OCCAR's increased importance in this period is exemplified by the development of its operational budget. Figure 6.2 shows how, starting from 2004, OCCAR's operational budget increased considerably and had more than quadrupled by 2008. This development can be explained by the overflowing costs of ongoing OCCAR projects on the one hand[3] and by intensified cooperation within the OCCAR framework on the other. It should be noted that the EDA budget too increased during the same period—yet the numbers were of a completely different order of magnitude, for example, a nine million EDA budget compared to a budget of around four *billion* for OCCAR in 2010, and covered R&T projects and feasibility studies rather than armaments programs.

This very clear-cut preference for OCCAR as the setting for armaments cooperation demonstrated by the avant-gardist states finally peaked in 2008. The French Council Presidency proposed to establish formal relations between the two institutions under which the EDA would facilitate "the use of OCCAR for the management of programmes resulting from its own preparatory work" (Council of the European Union, 2008, Annex I). Renouncing its ambition to turn the EDA into a veritable armaments agency in light of the ongoing conflict with the United Kingdom and the downstream states, France adjusted its position. OCCAR would manage all future armaments programs (Teissier & Rohan, 2011, p. 17) by becoming the "favoured partner of the EDA" (Council of the European Union, 2008, Annex I), while the latter would, it was suggested, be downsized to conduct "preparatory work" (Council of the European Union, 2008, Annex I) instead of actually getting involved in joint development or procurement programs.

---

[2] See the overview provided by OCCAR, available at: http://www.occar.int/our-work-programmes.

[3] Especially the problematic A400M transport aircraft, see Weiss and Heinkelmann-Wild (2020).

6 THE MARGINALIZATION OF THE EDA: FALSE PREMISES ... 151

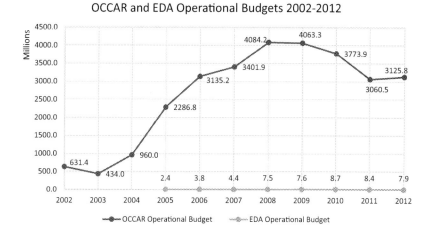

Fig. 6.2 OCCAR and EDA - operational budgets 2002–2012[4]

The avant-gardist regime's shifting to OCCAR, which culminated in the call for the AA, triggered the process leading to the EDA's marginalization. While the Council supported the general aim of coordinating the two overlapping institutions in 2008, it took until 2012 to sign the AA that formalized the EDA's sidelined position in the complex. I argue that the avant-gardists' shift from EDA back to OCCAR confronted the downstream states with a threat of exclusion. This threat and the upstream states' willingness to exclude them from armaments cooperation compelled the downstream states to accept OCCAR's primacy. Yet it took some time before even the most skeptical states, namely Greece and Cyprus, joined the cause and accepted that coordinating with OCCAR was their only chance of keeping the door to armaments contracts open.

The Threat of Exclusion—The Avant-Garde Goes It Alone

This section demonstrates that the upstream states' demonstrated ability to organize armaments cooperation among themselves led the downstream states to try to join OCCAR against their original preferences.

---

[4] EDA (2008, 2011, 2012, 2013), OCCAR numbers are not publicly available and were received from the German MoD in e-mail correspondence.

Being excluded from armaments cooperation altogether was worse for them than accepting the principles enshrined in the OCCAR convention. This is in line with the theoretical framework, which expects the defenders of the institutional status quo to try to join the institutional competitor if the challengers are able to create a credible threat of exclusion.

As demonstrated in Chapter 5, it was in the downstream states' interest not to liberalize the EDEM too quickly and to give up established protectionist principles such as *juste retour*, as this would have crowded out their limited defense industries. In 2004, in other words, the downstream states preferred armaments cooperation to take place within the EDA, which, due to its decision-making mechanisms, allowed them to co-determine which projects would be pursued and on what principles work-shares would be distributed. The incorporation of OCCAR into the EDA was generally in their interest, therefore. During the Convention, Poland, for example, stated, "initiatives such as OCCAR ... should become part of the network under the European Agency auspices" and that the EDA should serve as "an umbrella organisation for different multinational projects" (The Netherlands, 2002, p. 8). In a similar vein, the Czech MoD stated in 2004, "[i]t is an interest of the Czech Republic ... to start negotiations on the accession or cooperation with these organisations and their integration to EDA" (Ministry of Defence of the Czech Republic, 2004).

Joining OCCAR without integrating it into the EDA, by contrast, was considered detrimental by these states as every member would have to accept the principle of *global balance* and the preferential treatment of "equipment in whose development it has participated within OCCAR" (Convention on the Establishment of the Organisation for Joint Armament Cooperation (Organisation Conjointe de Cooperation en Matière d'ARmement)—OCCAR, 2001). The latter provision was particularly unattractive to the downstream states, which would only get minor shares in the work and would still be obliged to buy European instead of being free to choose from the world market.

Consequently, when OCCAR received legal personality in 2001, and the prospect was that this framework would first be incorporated into the WEU structures and later integrated into the EDA, there was no enthusiasm for joining it among the downstream states. Only the Netherlands and Belgium, which were participants in cooperative projects transferred to OCCAR, applied for membership.[5] In 2003, Belgium signed a contract to buy seven A400M aircraft and became an OCCAR member to participate in the aircraft's production through its aircraft construction and maintenance company Flabel rather than simply procuring it ready-made. The Netherlands, which participated in the Boxer tank program managed by OCCAR, however, decided that it was of no benefit to their overall industrial policy to join OCCAR and potentially be pressurized by the "big guys" (Steketee, 2001). Thus, only one downstream state, Belgium, joined the organization, despite its openness at that point in time (Taylor, 2003).

After 2004, however, when it became clear that the upstream states intended neither to fulfill their promise to incorporate OCCAR into the EDA nor to continue OCCAR and the LoI "with 15 and later 25 member states" (The Netherlands, 2002, p. 5), this changed. The six OCCAR member states' demonstrated an ability to cooperate within an exclusive constellation, such as in the A400M program, the Tiger helicopter, or the HOT/MILAN anti-tank missile system, which, together with the prospect of the increased importance of the framework, created incentives for the downstream states to join. As has been demonstrated, the cake distributed via OCCAR was of considerable size, with an operational budget reaching 4 billion in 2008, while the total value of the EDA projects amounted to some 7.5 million. Confronted with the OCCAR members' demonstrated ability to go it alone, Finland, Poland, and Sweden signaled their interest in joining OCCAR in 2008 when the ESSOR radio program was integrated (Bailes & Guðmundsson, 2009). This coincided with the French proposal to negotiate the AA between the EDA and OCCAR, signaling the end of the downstream states' hopes for OCCAR integration into the EDA. Yet none of these states became an OCCAR member, they all merely participated in one project, like the Netherlands and Turkey, which had joined the A400M project in 2003 (House of Commons, 2012).

In light of the upstream states' shift back to OCCAR, the downstream states showed an increased interest in the institution, yet none of them actually became a member. This, however, was not due to any lack of willingness on the part of the downstream states, which felt excluded from

---

[5] The accession of Spain, an upstream state, into the organization's structures was not surprising, as in CASA it possessed a competitive aerospace company, which intended to secure a share in the A400M program.

armaments cooperation. The reason was that the OCCAR members had a vital interest in keeping the framework as exclusive as possible and were not ready to make concessions toward potential new members.

Membership Preference—Six Is Company, Seven's a Crowd

While the upstream states preferred inclusive membership for the EDA, it was an entirely different matter with OCCAR. This section will show that due both to the existence of the inclusive EDA and the problematic distributive effects of armaments cooperation, the upstream states preferred exclusive membership and consequently erected high entry barriers for the downstream states, which resulted in their exclusion from OCCAR.

The 1998 OCCAR convention signed by the "big four," France, Germany, Italy, and the United Kingdom, generally allowed for the accession of new members. But, in contrast to the EDA, which could be joined by any EU member state without requiring any further approval, the OCCAR founders secured for themselves the discretion to decide whether or not to permit new members. The Board of Supervisors (BoS) has to vote on the admission of any state that notifies its desire to become a member (Convention on the Establishment of the Organisation for Joint Armament Cooperation (Organisation Conjointe de Cooperation en Matière d'ARmement)—OCCAR, 2001). Every founding state has a veto in the BoS, but this is not the case for new members (Convention on the Establishment of the Organisation for Joint Armament Cooperation (Organisation Conjointe de Cooperation en Matière d'ARmement)— OCCAR, 2001). Hence, as any "European State which wishes to become a Member State *may be invited* by the BoS to accede to this Convention" (Convention on the Establishment of the Organisation for Joint Armament Cooperation (Organisation Conjointe de Cooperation en Matière d'ARmement)—OCCAR, 2001, *emphasis added*) interested states are not automatically admitted. In addition, opposing founding states cannot be outvoted on such a decision. The institution is dominated by its founders.

The rationale behind OCCAR's creation is economic. The preamble to the Convention starts with the founders' "Wish ... to increase their armaments cooperation to improve efficiency and reduce costs" (Convention on the Establishment of the Organisation for Joint Armament Cooperation (Organisation Conjointe de Cooperation en Matière d'ARmement)—OCCAR, 2001). Consequently, the decision on whether or not to accept an interested state into OCCAR is based on economic principles. A new member must be involved in one collaborative equipment program with at least one OCCAR partner (Taylor, 2003, p. 28) and needs to accept "all the provisions of" the Convention (Convention on the Establishment of the Organisation for Joint Armament Cooperation (Organisation Conjointe de Cooperation en Matière d'ARmement)— OCCAR, 2001). The economic relevance of new member states is evaluated by the existing members and will have direct consequences on their influence within the organization:

> Any new Member State in OCCAR will have an appropriate number of voting rights as decided by the existing Member States. (OCCAR, 2001)

Every member can be assigned a number of votes between one and nine, while the founders hold ten votes each. With Spain being assigned eight and Belgium five votes (Sartori et al., 2018), it becomes evident that within OCCAR there is no room for political goodwill.

Taking into account that armaments cooperation and joint procurement is an issue area with considerable distributive consequences that has both economic and security implications (national job markets, the national defense technological and industrial base), for the upstream states, it is only rational for them to accept states that can make a considerable contribution to the efficiency of the programs. This implies that, first, the procured numbers have to be relatively high and, second, that the relevant companies in the interested states have to be competitive. Thus, within armaments cooperation, that is, collaborative development projects, the member surplus to accommodate uncompetitive states is high. Every additional member state that claims a share in production but orders the product only in small numbers, decreases the efficiency of the production process while not compensating for this loss by economies of scale, which undermines the very rationale for cooperation (Mawdsley, 2013; Interview #6). Consequently, considering OCCAR's demanding preconditions, any downstream state that wants to participate in an OCCAR project has to make painful concessions (Interview #3). In addition, not only is the member surplus in armaments cooperation high, but the accession negotiations themselves represent an additional hurdle to the inclusion of further member states. As there are no general terms for membership, the accession process "would be time-consuming and complex for every member-state to join OCCAR"

(Keohane, 2002, p. 27), which further discourages OCCAR members from inviting additional members.

What, counterfactually, might have incentivized the OCCAR members to open up their membership? A collaborative armaments program has three pillars: specification and agreement on requirements; R&T, and development; production and procurement. While the last step, production and procurement, in other words, contract management, is conducted by OCCAR and has direct distributive consequences and a high member surplus, the first two pillars are connected with high transaction costs for non-cooperation. First, states that play no part in the specification of military requirements, are less likely to actually procure the final product; second, any additional funds invested in basic and applied R&T increase its effectiveness. From the upstream states' perspective, it would thus make sense to include as many states as possible in these processes to increase the potential market size for their products. This was the rationale behind the EDA's inclusive design (see Chapter 5).

Yet as the EDA existed and was operational in precisely these areas, it would have been detrimental for the upstream states to open up OCCAR's membership, which is why they "were tough in resisting demands for smaller states to join" (Bailes & Guðmundsson, 2009, p. 8). In light of the blockade against reform of the EDA, the second-best option for the dissatisfied avant-gardist states was to maintain an inclusive EDA for R&T as well as for the definition of requirements, standardization, and interoperability, in short, as a *capabilities agency* alongside an exclusive OCCAR for the core business, an *armaments agency*.

This option was the United Kingdom's preferred outcome from the outset. The United Kingdom accepted the incorporation of the WEAG/WEAO (House of Lords, 2005b, para. 11) as well as the economic and security principles enshrined in the LoI framework agreement (House of Lords, 2005b, para. 13) into the EDA. But the UK government held the view that the EDA and OCCAR "complement one another" (House of Lords, 2005b, para. 12). When the avant-gardist states recognized that the EDA was not the appropriate structure to conduct minilateral projects, the UK suggested formalizing this complementary relationship between the two institutions as a way of securing the largest possible sales market with the smallest possible influence from downstream states.

In sum, the upstream states preferred an exclusive OCCAR membership for two reasons. First, the structure of armaments cooperation was characterized by serious distributional consequences, which led to a high member surplus being incurred when additional states were accepted. Second, the very existence of the EDA, which organized related issues, standardization, interoperability, R&T, and the definition of requirements, all of which are connected with high transaction costs for non-cooperation, reduced the pressure to open OCCAR's membership. So OCCAR remained a closed club, only allowing associated program participation. Consequently—in the absence of any formal coordination mechanism—the EDA and OCCAR had overlapping mandates, membership, and resources in 2008. The next section demonstrates how the upstream states' go-it-alone power and their preference for exclusive membership led to the signing of the AA, which formalized the EDA's marginalization in the realm of armaments cooperation.

Formalizing Marginalization: The Administrative Arrangement

This section demonstrates that despite the upstream states' ability and willingness to exclude the downstream states from armaments cooperation, the former had an interest in the co-existence of both OCCAR and the EDA. They made no efforts to close the EDA down again, as it provided substantial benefits for them. The upstream states intended to make OCCAR the center of relational authority for armaments cooperation, equipped it with the bulk of available resources, and were even able to formalize its central position in armaments cooperation against the resistance of the most reluctant downstream states. The latter finally gave in and accepted OCCAR's primacy to avoid being sidelined completely and to secure at least a place on the margins of the European armaments production chain.

The OCCAR members had no interest in dissolving the EDA as they recognized that exploiting the internal markets of the downstream states would only be possible if they offered them some say in the definition of requirements and some part in the division of work-share in R&T. Yet it was also clear that the upstream states were no longer willing to incorporate OCCAR into the EDA but intended to secure the independence of both institutions. The unregulated status quo, with OCCAR and the EDA both mandated to manage armaments programs and working relations between the two not officially established, was inefficient. Consequently, France, during its 2008 Council presidency, pushed for a formalization of their relationship. The final report on the development of the European defense industry submitted to French Premier Minister Francois Fillon stated,

> a more formal rapprochement of OCCAR and the EDA is desirable and should be one of the projects of the French Council presidency ... in order to make OCCAR the natural vessel for the programs generated in the agency's armaments branch. (Fromion, 2008, 18, author's translation)

France was aware of the inefficiencies and thus deemed it necessary to "avoid unnecessary overlapping of effort and expertise" and to achieve "reduced administrative costs and shorter lead times between the definition of requirements and the production of the corresponding capabilities" (Council of the European Union, 2008, Annex I, pp. 21–22). This general demand was supported by all EU member states, which included it as an Annex to the Council conclusions on CSDP in November 2008. While the exact terms of coordination were still to be negotiated, the member states thus agreed that the EDA and OCCAR were to conclude an AA "*at the earliest opportunity*" (Council of the European Union, 2008, Annex I, pp. 22, italics in the original).

The upstream states had a clear conception of what the future relationship between the two institutions should look like. OCCAR was to become the "executive branch" of the EDA—limiting the latter's functions to identifying capability gaps and conducting research projects (Ministère de la Défense, 2009). The EDA was to be used to identify capability gaps, while the armaments cooperation to close these gaps would be conducted within OCCAR (Interview #7). While the EDA had its own budget and personnel and was allowed to conclude contracts with third parties, it would be obliged to draw on OCCAR when it came to the staging of concrete projects (BITS, 2004, p. 46). Thus, OCCAR would not only manage projects agreed upon among its own members but also projects agreed upon within the EDA structures. This signified a further shift of resources to the OCCAR framework that could have otherwise been spent within the EDA. This was rational from the upstream states' perspective, as it would allow them to collect funds via the EDA, an inclusive forum, and then distribute the resources via the more exclusive OCCAR framework. Especially in light of the limited funds available at this time—the crisis was at its height—broadening the buyers' base for the systems developed in OCCAR by keeping the downstream states engaged in the definition phase in the EDA would be beneficial (Deutscher Bundestag, 2010, p. 5).

Yet the upstream states' wish to conclude the AA quickly did not materialize. While *prima facie* an administrative act, the negotiations on the arrangement went on for almost four years. The reason is that some downstream states were initially resistant to accepting a solution formalizing the EDA's marginalization in armaments procurement and still preferred the EDA to be the focal institution (Barrasa Martín, 2010). In a hearing before the Italian Senate, OCCAR director Nazzareno Cardinali stated that the formal accord between the two institutions was hard to achieve because the EDA opposed it (Senato della Repubblica, 2007, p. 17). In addition, Cyprus and Greece had reservations concerning the transfer of classified information between the two institutions, as Turkey participated in OCCAR projects (Hoeffler, 2012, p. 444; Zandee, 2017, p. 4). Greek and Cypriot resistance had already prevented a direct association agreement between the EDA and Turkey in the aftermath of the agency's creation.

In light of the upstream states' demonstrated ability and willingness to exclude additional members and the downstream states' "determination not to be kept outside any defence markets integration process" (Vestel, 1995, p. 45), the latter had an interest in having at least indirect access to large-scale armaments programs. From this perspective, that is, in view of their exclusion from OCCAR, the downstream states had an interest in formalizing the relationship between the two institutions as well—to secure for themselves the possibility of participating in OCCAR projects. In recognition of this interest, the OCCAR members made the successful negotiation of the AA a precondition for third states to have simplified access to their programs. Without the AA, a third state would need to obtain individual approval to participate from OCCAR's executive administration—a process that took 18 to 24 months (Kolín, 2010). The AA, by contrast, would involve a generalized procedure transferring EDA projects to OCCAR and ensuring third-state participation.

In 2011 the upstream states used the renegotiation of the EDA's "statute, seat and operational rules" (Council Decision 2011/411/CFSP defining the statute, seat and operational rules of the European Defence Agency and repealing Joint Action 2004/551/CFSP, 2011) to further increase the pressure on the downstream states. In the updated version, the original reference to OCCAR's "assimilation or incorporation" (Council of the European Union, recital 8) was deleted (Council

Decision 2011/411/CFSP defining the statute, seat, and operational rules of the European Defence Agency and repealing Joint Action 2004/551/CFSP, 2011) and any hopes of OCCAR's incorporation were buried. Shortly thereafter, a breakthrough in the negotiations for the AA were achieved. In addition, Greek and Cypriot resistance was overcome when the AA was made separate from a Security Arrangement that was to be negotiated at a later stage to settle the issue of information sharing with OCCAR participating states, such as Turkey.[6]

On 6 June 2012, the OCCAR BoS agreed on the draft AA, and the Council did so on 10 July, paving the way for the arrangement to be signed on 27 July 2012. The punch line of the AA was that all EU member states "recognise that EDA and OCCAR are organisations independent from each other and take into account their respective decision making autonomy" (EDA, 2012, recital c) and that OCCAR will be a "privileged partner" of the EDA (EDA, 2012, Art. 3.3.2). While this outcome was sold as beneficial to the downstream states, as the "EDA will derive benefit from the programme management knowledge of OCCAR, in particular on behalf of pMS [participating member states in the EDA] which are not OCCAR members (EDA & OCCAR, 2012, recital h), it cemented the EDA's marginalization in the realm of armaments cooperation.

This arrangement formalized the mode of coordination between the two institutions, which Nick Witney, former chief executive of the EDA, had described as "where we finish is roughly where OCCAR starts in terms of procurement" (House of Lords, 2005a, para. 34). The AA brought to an end the ongoing talk by OCCAR non-members such as the Netherlands of merging OCCAR and the EDA to bring armaments cooperation under EU control (Interview #6). It entailed the selection of OCCAR as the first-choice institution for armaments cooperation while the EDA was merely to serve as a market place to discuss capability gaps (Trybus, 2014, p. 220; Interview #6). From the perspective of the upstream states, this was the best possible outcome, at least given the disagreement between the Europeanists and Atlanticists. They remained firmly in the driver's seat when it came to dividing the work-shares within OCCAR, while the EDA served as an opportunity to attract new countries to join the programs once the OCCAR members had shown their interest

---

[6] This agreement was concluded two years later, on 8 December 2014 (EDA, 2014).

in pursuing them (Interview #4). The downstream states, by contrast, had to accept OCCAR as the institutional focal point in European armaments cooperation against their original preferences.

SUMMARY

This chapter has demonstrated that the group of powerful avant-gardist states, originally firm proponents of the EDA, worked toward the marginalization of the institution. They were no longer willing to keep their promise to incorporate OCCAR into the EDA structure but shifted cooperation to the exclusive forum. The reason for this was that the promise had been made based on the false premise that the upstream states would act in concert. Yet any avant-gardist attempt to scale up the EDA was torpedoed not only by the downstream states but also by the United Kingdom. Dissatisfied with the functioning of the EDA and unable to bring about reforms, the avant-gardists shifted their focus to OCCAR, which, due to its exclusive membership, was better adapted to their needs.

As the six OCCAR members represented more than 80% of the EU's defense spending,[7] being out of OCCAR meant being excluded from any defense-industrial cooperation, as far as the downstream states were concerned. Therefore, after 2005 downstream states such as Finland or Poland attempted to join the framework. In light of the distributive implications of managing armaments contracts to fit national budgets, however, OCCAR's members preferred it to remain an exclusive club. Even Sweden, an upstream state with a relatively competitive defense industry, was denied membership.

Even so, the group of upstream states had an interest in the continuous existence of the EDA as a framework for identifying capability gaps, standard setting, and getting the downstream states interested in procuring new European armament systems. France therefore suggested the negotiation of an AA between the two institutions, which would formalize their coordination in a way that cemented OCCAR's focality in armaments cooperation and marginalized the EDA. While this went against the downstream states' original preferences, in light of the upstream states' demonstrated willingness and ability to exclude them from OCCAR,

---

[7] Military Expenditure 2016, source: SIPRI Milex data 1949–2016, available at: https://www.sipri.org/databases/milex.

they agreed. Cutting their losses and accepting OCCAR's primacy meant having third-state access to armaments programs and getting workshares at the margins of the production chain instead of being sidelined completely. Consequently, OCCAR emerged as the center of relational authority in the field of armaments cooperation, while the EDA plays hardly any role in conducting such projects.

A more recent example of the EDA's marginalized role is the MALE RPAS drone project. While the EDA was responsible for the definition of its mostly regulatory requirements, Germany, France, Spain, and Italy launched a €65 million definition phase within OCCAR in 2015. The capability gap was identified within the EDA, but the specification of requirements was conducted through informal talks among the four upstream states (Interview #6). Consequently, instead of being involved, the EDA had no other choice than to "congratulate OCCAR, the four contributing Member States and the companies involved" (EDA, 2016b).

Having analyzed two cases in which the dissatisfied challenger coalition possessed the power to go it alone and was able to create a credible threat of exclusion, which was decisive for their ability to shape the distribution of authority between the competing institutions, the cases I now move on to are different. The following chapter examines another CSDP flagship project, PESCO. Despite the creation of PESCO as a body with institutional potential in 2007, it lay dormant until 2017. I will show that dissatisfied state coalitions were able to suppress PESCO by creating a series of competing regional frameworks. Due to their creators' lack of go-it-alone power, none of these frameworks became focal, however, and the institutional outcome was the fragmentation of European defense planning.

References

Assemblée Nationale. (2006). *Rapport D'Information: Déposé en application de l'article 145 du Règlement Par la Commission des Finances, de l'Économie Générale et du Plan en conclusion des travaux de la Mission d'évaluation et de contrôle (MEC) sur les programmes d'armement: l'exemple du véhicule blindé de combat d'infanterie* (No. N° 3254). http://www.assemblee-nationale.fr/12/pdf/rap-info/i3254.pdf

Bailes, A., & Guðmundsson, Jón Ágúst. (2009). *The European Defence Agency (EDA) and Defence Industrial Cooperation: Implications and*

options for Iceland. https://dokumen.tips/documents/the-european-defence-agency-eda-and-web-view-the-norwegian-precedent-25.html?page=1
Barrasa Martín, J. I. (2010). Cooperation in armaments. In Ministerio de Defensa de Espana (Ed.), *European Defence Agency: Past, present & future* (pp. 125–172). CESEDEN, Ministerio de Defensa; Isdefe.
BITS. (2004). *Querschnitt 2004*. Berlin.
BMVg. (2016). *4. Bericht des Bundesministeriums der Verteidigung zu Rüstungsangelegenheiten: Teil 1*. Berlin. https://www.bmvg.de/resource/blob/15378/fa614131fc4c41ea34509e756fa8d96c/b-07-01-02-download-4-ruestungsbericht-data.pdf
Deutscher Bundestag. (2010). *Antwort der Bundesregierung auf die Kleine Anfrage der Abgeordneten Paul Schäfer (Köln), Jan van Aken, Christine Buchholz, weiterer Abgeordneter und der Fraktion DIE LINKE: Aufklärung über den Stand der Rüstungskooperation Deutschlands auf europäischer Ebene* (No. Drucksache 17/3937). http://dip21.bundestag.de/dip21/btd/17/039/1703937.pdf
Convention on the Establishment of the Organisation for Joint Armament Cooperation (Organisation Conjointe de Cooperation en Matière d'ARmement) - OCCAR, *JORF* 4468 (2001).
Council Decision (CFSP) 2015/1835 of 12 October 2015 defining the statute, seat and operational rules of the European Defence Agency (recast), *Official Journal of the European Union* (2015).
Council Decision 2011/411/CFSP defining the statute, seat and operational rules of the European Defence Agency and repealing Joint Action 2004/551/CFSP, 16 *Official Journal of the European Union* (2011).
Council of the European Union. (2003). *2541st Council meeting: External relations* (Press Release No. C/03/321). Brussels.
Council of the European Union. (2008). *Council Conclusions on the ESDP* (No. 15465/08). Brussels. http://register.consilium.europa.eu/doc/srv?l=EN&f=ST%2015465%202008%20INIT
EDA. (2006). European Defence Agency steering board agrees transfer of WEAG/WEAO activities to EDA: 22 April 2005. In *EU security and defence: Core documents 2005* (Chaillot Papers No. 87, pp. 85–89).
EDA. (2008). *2007 Financial Report*. European Defence Agency website: https://eda.europa.eu/docs/finance-documents/2007-financial-report.pdf?sfvrsn=0
EDA. (2011). *Defence Data 2010*. Brussels. European Defence Agency website: https://www.eda.europa.eu/docs/eda-publications/defence_data_2010
EDA (European Defence Agency). (2012, July 27). *Latest News: EDA & OCCAR build links, seeking efficiencies through cooperation* [Press release]. Brussels. https://www.eda.europa.eu/info-hub/press-centre/latest-news/2012/07/27/eda-occar-build-links-seeking-efficiencies-through-cooperation

EDA. (2013). *2012 Financial Report*. European Defence Agency website: https://www.eda.europa.eu/docs/default-source/documents/2012-financial-report.pdf

EDA. (2014). *10 years of working together*. Brussels.

EDA. (2016a). *2017 Budget*. https://www.eda.europa.eu/docs/default-source/finance-documents/eda-budget-2017-with-staff-establishment-plan.pdf

EDA. (2016b, September 28). *Latest News: European MALE RPAS Definition Study contract awarded* [Press release]. https://www.eda.europa.eu/info-hub/press-centre/latest-news/2016/09/28/european-male-rpas-definition-study-contract-awarded

EDA. (2018). 15 years of working together. https://www.eda.europa.eu/Aboutus/our-history/15-years

EDA, & OCCAR. (2012). *Administrative Arrangement between the EDA and OCCAR concerning the establishment of their cooperation*. https://www.eda.europa.eu/docs/default-source/documents/aa---eda---occar-27-07-12.pdf

Eisenhut, D. (2010). *Europäische Rüstungskooperation: Zwischen Binnenmarkt und zwischenstaatlicher Zusammenarbeit*. Univ., Diss.--Augsburg, 2009 (1. Aufl.). *Augsburger Rechtsstudien* (vol. 59). Nomos Verl.-Ges.

EUobserver. (2006, November 14). UK under French fire over defence. https://euobserver.com/news/22849

Fromion, Y. (2008). *Les moyens de développer et de structurer une industrie européenne de défense: Rapport final confié par Monsieur François Fillon*. https://www.ladocumentationfrancaise.fr/var/storage/rapports-publics/084000456.pdf

Hoeffler, C. (2012). European armament co-operation and the renewal of industrial policy motives. *Journal of European Public Policy, 19*(3), 435–451. https://doi.org/10.1080/13501763.2011.640803

House of Commons. (2004). *Establishing a European Defence Agency: European Standing Committee B*.

House of Lords. (2005a). *European Union Committee Ninth Report of Session 2004–05: European Defence Agency—Report with Evidence* (European Union No. HL Paper 76). https://publications.parliament.uk/pa/ld200405/ldselect/ldeucom/76/7605.htm

House of Lords. (2005b). *European Union—Government Responses: 9th Report— The European Defence Agency*. https://publications.parliament.uk/pa/ld200607/ldselect/ldeucom/38/38we06.htm

House of Commons (2008). *Defence—Ninth Report*. https://publications.parliament.uk/pa/cm200708/cmselect/cmdfence/111/11102.htm

House of Commons. (2012). *European Scrutiny Committee—Tenth Report: European Defence Agency and the OCCAR*. https://publications.parliament.uk/pa/cm201213/cmselect/cmeuleg/86-x/86x02.htm

IDET. (2017). *Security Fairs: Final Report*. http://www.bvv.cz/_sys_/FileStorage/download/6/5813/final-report-idet-pyros-iset-2017.pdf
Interview #3: EDA representative, 12 December 2017 in Brussels.
Interview #4: EDA representative, 12 December 2017 in Brussels.
Interview #6: OCCAR representative, 15 December 2017 in Bonn.
Interview #7: OCCAR representative, 15 December 2017 in Bonn.
Jordan, G., & Williams, T. (2007). Hope deferred? *The RUSI Journal, 152*(3), 66–71. https://doi.org/10.1080/03071840701470889
Karampekios, N. (2015). Understanding Greece's policy in the European Defence Agency: Between national interest and domestic politics. *Southeast European and Black Sea Studies, 15*(1), 37–52. https://doi.org/10.1080/14683857.2015.1007750
Keohane, D. (2002). *The EU and armaments co-operation* (Centre for European Reform - Working Paper).
Kolín, V. (2010). *April*). Defence and strategy. Advance online publication. https://doi.org/10.3849/1802-7199.10.2010.01.021-044
Mauro, F., & Thoma, K. (2016). *The future of EU defence research*. European Union, Directorate-General for External Policies, Policy Department.
Mawdsley, J. (2013). The A400M Project: From Flagship Project to warning for European Defence Cooperation. *Defence Studies, 13*(1), 14–32. https://doi.org/10.1080/14702436.2013.774961
Mawdsley, J. (2008). European Union Armaments Policy: Options for small states? *European Security, 17*(2–3), 367–385. https://doi.org/10.1080/09662830802525923
Ministère de la Défense. (2009). *M. Marc Dolez - Question Écrite: Union européenne - fonctionnement - présidence française perspectives* (Journal Officiel - 13ème législature No. QE 28821). http://questions.assemblee-nationale.fr/q13/13-28821QE.htm
Ministry of Defence of the Czech Republic. (2004). *Národní strategie vyzbrojování: National armaments strategy* (1. vyd). Praha: Ministerstvo obrany České republiky - Agentura vojenských informací a služeb.
Ministry of Foreign Affairs of the Republic of Poland. (2012). Cooperation of defence industries. https://www.msz.gov.pl/en/foreign_policy/security_policy/defence_industries/
Mölling, C. (2015). State of play of the implementation of EDA's pooling and sharing initiatives and its impact on the European defence industry. https://op.europa.eu/en/publication-detail/-/publication/5dfb4548-526d-4f33-be3d-ea7a1d4c4ce9/language-en
OCCAR-EA. (2016). *OCCAR Business Plan 2017*. Bonn. http://www.occar.int/media/raw/OCCAR_Business_Plan_2017_External.pdf

O'Donnell, C. M. (2011). *Britain and France should not give up on EU defence co-operation* (Policy Brief). London. http://www.cer.eu/sites/default/files/publications/attachments/pdf/2011/pb_csdp_24oct11-3907.pdf

Sartori, P., Marrone, A., & Nones, M. (2018). *Looking through the fog of Brexit: Scenarios and implications for the European Defence Industry* (DOCUMENTI IAI No. 18). https://www.iai.it/sites/default/files/iai1816.pdf

Senato della Repubblica. (2007). *4a Commissione Permanente (Difesa): Indagine Conoscitiva Sullo Stato Attuale e Sulle Prospettive Dell'Industria Della Difesa e Sulla Cooperazione in Materia di Armamenti* (Giunte e Commissioni No. 68a seduta). http://www.senato.it/documenti/repository/commissioni/stenografici/15/comm04/04a-20070529-IC-0431.pdf

SIPRI. (2008). *Armaments, disarmament and international security 2008*. Oxford University Press. https://books.google.de/books?id=EAyQ9KCJE2gC

Steketee, M. (2001, January 13). 'Defensie negeert alternatief voor nieuw pantservoertuig'. https://www.nrc.nl/nieuws/2001/01/13/defensie-negeert-alternatief-voor-nieuw-pantservoertuig-7525823-a535462

Taylor, C. (2003). *UK Defence Procurement Policy* (RESEARCH PAPER No. 03/78).

Teissier, G., & Rohan, J. de (Eds.) (2011, September). *9 ème Université d'été de la Commission de la Défense nationale et des Forces armées de l'Assemblée nationale et de la Commission des Affaires étrangères, de la Défense et des Foces armées du Sénat: Etat-industries: de l'urgent opérations aux grands systèmes de Défense*. http://testleni2.site.exhibis.net/Data/ElFinder/s4/UD/universit%C3%A9s/actes_mars_ix.pdf

The Netherlands. (2002, December 4). Working Document 28—WG VIII: Dutch comments on the preliminary draft final report of Working Group VIII "Defence" (WD 022). http://european-convention.europa.eu/docs/wd8/5837.pdf

Trybus, M. (2006). The New European Defence Agency: A contribution to a common European Security and defence policy and a challenge to the community acquis? *Common Market Law Review, 43*, 667–703.

Trybus, M. (2014). *Buying defence and security in Europe: The EU defence and security procurement directive in context*. Cambridge University Press.

V4. (2014). *Long term vision of the Visegrad Countries on deepening their defence cooperation*. Visegrad. Visegrad Group website: www.visegradgroup.eu/calendar/2014-03-14-ltv

Vestel, P. (1995). *Defence markets and industries in Europe: time for political decisions?*

Weiss, M. (2019). State vs. market in India: How (not) to integrate foreign contractors in the domestic defense-industrial sector. *Comparative Strategy, 37*(4), 286–298. https://doi.org/10.1080/01495933.2018.1497323

Weiss, M., & Heinkelmann-Wild, T. (2020). Disarmed principals? Institutional resilience and the non-enforcement of delegation. *European Political Science Review*, *12*(4), 409–425. https://doi.org/10.1017/S1755773920000181

Witney, N. (2008). *Re-energising Europe's security and defence policy. Policy paper*: European Council on Foreign Relations.

Zandee, D. (2017). *Developing European defence capabilities: Bringing order into disorder* (Clingendael Report). https://www.clingendael.org/sites/default/files/2017-10/Developing_European_Defence_Capabilities.pdf

CHAPTER 7

The Fragmentation of European Defense Planning: PESCO's Deep Sleep

This chapter is devoted to analyzing the process that led to the fragmentation of European defense planning. The Treaty of Lisbon, signed in 2007, established the EU's CSDP, a provisional highlight in a process that began with the 1999 Franco-British St. Malo declaration and the 2001 Treaty of Nice that established the CSDP's predecessor, the European Security and Defence policy. One major pillar of the CSDP was the possibility of Permanent Structured Cooperation. This framework had the potential to revolutionize the EU's defense planning, military, and armaments cooperation by establishing an overarching "defence Euro-zone" (European Convention, 2002), a system of differentiated integration allowing a coalition of the willing to take further steps toward defense integration.

PESCO was expected to be the framework within which future cooperation in the definition of military requirements, interoperability, capability development, and the organization and maintenance of multinational military forces, such as the EU Battlegroups, would be subsumed (Articles 42 and 46, Protocol 10, TEU). Yet EU member states did not activate PESCO after the Lisbon Treaty came into force in 2009, instead they created a series of bi- and minilateral regional cooperation frameworks, such as the Visegràd Group and Nordic, Baltic, and Central European Defense Cooperation. These smaller frameworks existed outside EU structures and without any coordinating mechanism among them. No

© The Author(s), under exclusive license to Springer Nature Switzerland AG 2023
F. Biermann, *The Battle for Authority in European Defence Cooperation*, Palgrave Studies in European Union Politics, https://doi.org/10.1007/978-3-031-30054-7_7

169

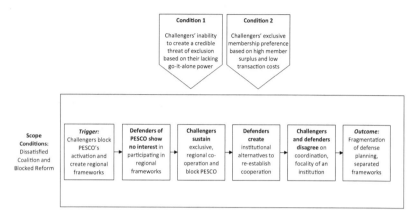

Fig. 7.1 Process Leading to the fragmentation of European defense planning

focal institution emerged, and any cooperation and work sharing between these institutions, if it occurred at all, was incidental. Paradoxically, the EU member states' agreement to establish the possibility of PESCO had induced the further fragmentation of European defense policy.

I argue that this development can be explained within the confines of the theoretical framework, set out in Chapter 3, and the pathway to fragmentation, as visualized in Fig. 7.1.

PESCO was first proposed during the European Convention negotiations and was contested from the outset. Both the selective and reluctant states, the Atlanticist challengers, were skeptical of the idea, as they feared the duplication and undermining of NATO on the one hand and negative defense-industrial implications comparable to those in the EDA case. Though they eventually agreed to establish PESCO as a body with future institutional potential, they did not intend to use it. In fact, the selective and reluctant states engaged in competitive regime creation to prevent PESCO from ever happening.

The newly established frameworks directed at strengthening regional cooperation, however, did not create a threat of exclusion to the avant-gardists, and none of them attracted additional members from beyond regional frontiers. They were not powerful enough to go it alone. Yet, they did not actually have to as they could rely on their powerful NATO partner on the other side of the Atlantic and thus preferred an exclusive membership. They were both willing and able to block PESCO and had no interest in a broader cooperation framework. As the Atlanticist states with their regional frameworks had blocked further integration in defense, this left the Europeanist defenders, both the avant-gardists and the federalists, worse off. They had no other option than to look for alternatives to establish at least some degree of cooperation.

Consequently, the Europeanists created institutional alternatives of their own, trying to convince at least some of PESCO's opponents to take part in deeper cooperation. Yet, after Germany was able to convince selective Sweden to co-sponsor the Ghent Initiative in November 2010, and the EU defense ministers subsequently agreed on the concept of "Pooling & Sharing" (Csiki & Németh, 2013, p. 13), it brought a temporary end to any attempts to establish a focal institution in the realm of defense planning. "Pooling and Sharing" was a "PESCO light," a non-binding "commitment" to look into efficiency potentials. Fragmentation and a persistent state of "muddling through" (Coelmont, 2017) were the consequences. This state of fragmentation, the uncoordinated co-existence of separate institutions, overlapping in mandate but separate membership and resources, lasted until 2015 and would have lasted even longer had not a series of external shocks occurred.

This chapter is structured as follows. The first part demonstrates that a broad coalition of member states was dissatisfied with the creation of PESCO from the outset but decided to agree to its incorporation in the 2007 Lisbon Treaty without intending to use it. Moreover, it shows that, even though functional pressure to activate PESCO increased in 2009/10, dissatisfied challenger coalitions engaged in competitive regime creation, which triggered the process that led to fragmentation. In line with theoretical expectations, the second section demonstrates that none of the established regional frameworks represented a credible threat of exclusion to the proponents of PESCO, which is why they provoked hardly any reaction. I then provide evidence in the third part to show that, while the challenger coalitions did not have go-it-alone power, they were able to prevent PESCO from happening—they had no interest in inclusive European cooperation, preferring their minilateral settings. The avant-gardists responded to this situation by creating bi- and minilateral frameworks themselves, as I show in the fourth part. One of the strongest proponents of PESCO, France, even engaged in undermining the very idea of a "European" defense. The result was the co-existence of uncoordinated institutions with separate membership and resources, a situation enshrined by the German–Swedish Ghent initiative. The fifth section summarizes.

BURIED ALIVE

This section engages with the scope conditions in this case, dissatisfaction and inability to agree, in order to demonstrate that PESCO's suppression and the fragmentation of European defense planning were part of the theoretical argument's universe of cases. I demonstrate, first, that PESCO was contested from the outset. When the EU member states first discussed it at the European Convention Working Group negotiations, insurmountable differences arose between the Europeanist states on the one hand and the Atlanticist and neutral states on the other. Despite these differences, the EU member states agreed on including PESCO in the Lisbon Treaty as a potential future institution. Second, I show that the first attempts to activate PESCO by a Belgian–Spanish initiative were blocked by the Atlanticist coalition despite increased functional pressure to intensify cooperation. Third and finally, in light of this functional pressure, the states dissatisfied with PESCO engaged in the creation of regional cooperative fora to prevent its activation. Having created PESCO as a body with institutional potential, the EU member.

The EU member states formally agreed to PESCO in articles 42 and 46 of the Treaty on European Union (TEU) signed in Lisbon in 2007. Article 42 reads,

> Those Member States whose military capabilities fulfil higher criteria and which have made more binding commitments to one another in this area with a view to the most demanding missions shall establish permanent structured cooperation within the Union framework. (European Union, 2010, Art. 42(6))

These "higher criteria" were spelled out in Protocol No.10, annexed to the Treaty. Article 1 of the Protocol states that PESCO should be open to any EU member state that undertakes to intensify capability development, increase national participation in multinational forces, participate in the main European equipment programs, and in the activity of the EDA. Moreover, it requires the participating member states to contribute to the European Battlegroup concept, which is a rotating standing multinational army, a rapid reaction force that should be able to carry out peace-building and peacekeeping missions under a CSDP mandate as specified in the *Petersberg Tasks* (now Article 43, TEU) within 30 days.

Article 2 of the Protocol then specifies PESCO's goals. It states that those EU member states participating in PESCO should work toward achieving a higher level of defense investment expenditure, convergence with respect to their defense apparatus, improved availability, interoperability, flexibility and deployability of forces, equalization of capability shortfalls (without prejudice to NATO), and appropriate participation in major joint or European equipment programs.

While PESCO's criteria and goals seem *prima facie* both understandable and reasonable, on closer examination, they reveal considerable shortcomings. The criteria are not operationalized—there is no reference to how they are to be measured. Indeed, when the Lisbon Treaty was signed, the Battlegroup concept was already operational (Barcikowska, 2013, p. 2), and all EU member states except Denmark were members of the EDA. Thus, every EU member state except Denmark was already eligible to participate without further specification, so the relevance of the entry criteria is doubtful. In other words, when the EU member states included PESCO in the Lisbon Treaty, it was no more (but also no less) than a possibility that would allow a group of willing member states to take steps toward more integration in defense planning under EU auspices. The reason for this watered-down and abstract formulation, I argue, lies in PESCO's conflictual genesis. The Atlanticists, both selective and reluctant states, opposed PESCO from the beginning.

Contested from the Outset

When PESCO was debated first in the context of the European Convention, there was considerable skepticism among both the reluctant and the selective states. The result of this cumbersome negotiation process was that Europeanists watered down the formulation of the treaty provisions on PESCO to get the Atlanticists on board. The latter agreed that PESCO should be included in the Lisbon Treaty yet had no intention of allowing it to become a reality.

PESCO "was born amid considerable controversy" (Howorth, 2004, p. 5). In December 2002 Working Group VIII on Defense published its final report to the European Convention which included the idea of making the concept of "enhanced cooperation," introduced by the Treaty of Nice in 2001, applicable to "matters having military or defence implications" (Treaty of Nice, Amending the Treaty on European Union, the Treaties Establishing the European Communities and Certain Related Acts, 2000). The new Constitutional Treaty should "provide for a form of closer cooperation between Member States, open to all Member States wishing to carry out the most demanding tasks and fulfilling the requirements for such a commitment to be credible" (European Convention, 2002, para. 54, emphasis omitted). The proposal to create a "defence Euro-zone" (European Convention, 2002, para. 54) found its way into the final report of the Working Group against considerable resistance from the Convention members (Howorth, 2004, p. 5). The concept was included in the 2003 Draft Constitutional Treaty under its new name, "permanent structured cooperation" (European Union, 2005, Art. III-312) even though representatives from Poland, Latvia, Slovenia, Sweden, Finland, the Netherlands, and the United Kingdom repeatedly voiced their concerns during the Working Group negotiations.

These reservations centered around two main issues. The "reluctant" states, EU member states with smaller defense industries and military capacities, and either Atlanticist or neutral strategic orientation feared that the criteria for joining the PESCO framework would be too high for them and would thus lead to their exclusion. Finland suggested PESCO should be "carried out by the maximum number of Member States possible" (Kiljunen, 2002, p. 6). In a similar vein, Slovenia argued, "[w]illingness to participate, should be the primary criteria for admission [*sic*]" (France & Germany, 2002, p. 3). Latvia's critique went even further, drawing a picture of the "defence 'Euro zone' [which] could draw a clear division line between EU member states being part of 'defence union' and those being outside. That would not foster cooperation, mutual trust, and solidarity among member states. De facto that would lead to creation of two-level memberships within the EU" (Piks & Rihards, 2002, p. 2). While Poland recognized differences in willingness and capabilities among the EU member states and therefore a need for "some flexibility," in its view "the use of constructive abstention or the general possibility of opting out" (The Netherlands, 2002, p. 3) would be sufficient to overcome the stalemate in decision-making. Finnish Foreign Minister Erkki Tuomioja summarized the reluctant states' position when he stated, a smaller group has to act as a vanguard without trying or even wanting to involve the Union as a whole. It is difficult to understand how splitting the Union serves to strengthen Europe's global standing. Suspicious minds may well wonder whether the proposal has less to do with defence than with the ambition of a core group of countries to retain a role as guardians of the true European faith - a faith that the 10 countries joining next year are perceived to threaten. (Tuomioja, 2003, p. 424)

The second concern voiced by the Convention representatives was that deepened European armaments cooperation could imply either duplication or, even worse, shifting the focus away from NATO structures. This reservation had already been raised during the Working Group negotiations by the prospective Eastern and Central European EU members that would be joining in 2004 as well as by the traditionally Atlanticist Netherlands that "welcome[d] the idea of enhanced co-operation in the field of defence—other than military operations" (The Netherlands, 2002, p. 4). For different reasons, the selective state Sweden, possessing a comparatively competitive defense-industrial base, seconded this view holding that the convergence criteria included in PESCO were "completely unacceptable" (The Netherlands, 2002, p. 4) with respect to its neutrality. The United Kingdom was a special case. In principle in favor of a stronger European commitment to increased defense capabilities and recognizing that such an enhancement would be best achieved by the most capable cooperating on a voluntary basis (United Kingdom, 2003), with the experience of the Iraq War behind it, the United Kingdom developed into the most PESCO-skeptical member state (Howorth, 2004, p. 5). Doubtful about the political conviction of both France and Germany in view of their lack of support for the United States, the United Kingdom feared that PESCO (governed by means of QMV) would have the potential to bypass the unanimity requirement for military operations and would therefore undermine NATO supremacy (Eisenhut, 2010, p. 268). "The UK is therefore against proposals which would fundamentally alter the balance achieved at Nice, especially any which would imply competition, rather than complementarity, with NATO" (United Kingdom, 2003, p. 207). The United Kingdom thus developed into the protecting power of all those EU member states fearing the exclusive character and the sidelining potential of PESCO.

Despite these two areas of conflict, the fear of exclusion and the role of NATO, PESCO found its way into the Lisbon Treaty. There are two reasons for this. On the one hand, France, Germany, Italy, and Spain, its avant-gardist proponents, were well aware that the prospect of PESCO without the United Kingdom, one of the, if not *the* most powerful EU member state in terms of military capabilities, would undermine its rationale of creating a more capable EU defense. Therefore, all references which could be interpreted as enabling EU military operations decided by a coalition of the willing were erased from the text of the Protocol (Howorth, 2004, p. 7), and PESCO maintained an exclusive focus on collective defense capability development.

On the other hand, the Atlanticist and neutral state coalition had nothing to lose by agreeing to the inclusion of PESCO in the Lisbon Treaty. As the criteria to join PESCO remained fuzzy and general, the crucial decisions on the operationalization of the commitments had still to be taken (Biscop, 2008, p. 5). Moreover, the activation of PESCO through regular QMV[1] could be prevented relatively easily in light of their strong coalition. Nothing was agreed until everything had been agreed—therefore, it was no longer worth opposing PESCO. On the contrary, maintaining PESCO as a potential for future cooperation in defense planning while having the prospect of being able to prevent any undesired developments that could undermine NATO was the best strategy not only for the United Kingdom but also for like-minded states. In sum, the creation of PESCO was highly contested, but even the most dissatisfied member states agreed to its inclusion in the Lisbon Treaty—without the intention of using it in the near future.

Blocking PESCO

The reluctance of the dissatisfied challenger coalition to activate PESCO was most visible over the period between 2007 and the first half of 2010. While the Europeanist states tried to push PESCO onto the political agenda, both selective and reluctant states continuously blocked these attempts. In the light of increasing functional pressure to cooperate, induced by the financial and fiscal crisis of 2008, their opposition frayed somewhat but did not fall apart.

In 2008 France made the activation of PESCO one of its top political priorities in preparation for its Council presidency. The French proposal

---

[1] 55% of the votes of the participating member states representing 65% of the population, see (European Union, 2010, Art 238(3a)).

was to establish a "60,000 strong intervention force" under the PESCO framework built around a core group consisting of the United Kingdom, France, Germany, Spain, Italy, and Poland, (Taylor, 2008; *The* Guardian, 2008). Knowing that their proposals, which also included the establishment of a permanent operational headquarters for military missions, would be met with resistance from the Atlanticists, France linked its suggestion with a guarantee to reintegrate their military structures into NATO in 2009, which was intended to appease critical voices from the United Kingdom and the United States, the French hope being to develop NATO and the CSDP in parallel (Taylor, 2008, pp. 3–4; van Eekelen & Kurpas, 2008, p. 14).

Despite this subtle approach, the French proposal, circulated informally, failed. It was fundamentally opposed by the United Kingdom. Geoffrey Van Orden, a Conservative MEP, warned, "[t]his will end in tears" (*The Guardian*, 2008). The United Kingdom's skepticism was shared by the new EU members from Central and Eastern Europe, "who were more concerned with collective defence than with the new tasks of peace enforcement and stabilization" and thus "feared a weakening of NATO" (van Eekelen & Kurpas, 2008, p. 2). Confronted with the first Irish "No" to the Lisbon Treaty, the French priorities had to be rearranged, and the activation of PESCO was not included in the official French work program for their Council presidency (France, 2008).

When the financial crisis turned into the Euro crisis in 2010, functional pressure to cooperate in defense matters increased. National budgets came under enormous pressure and led EU member states to recognize the need to cooperate in the capital-intense defense sector. Indeed, the savings potential was obvious. In 2010, only 23.4% of European defense procurement and 12.7% of Research and Technology spending was cooperative (EDA, 2011, 14, 16). The remainder of these expenditures were invested on a purely national basis, leading to system duplications, lack of interoperability, and inefficient production processes. In view of the exorbitant cost of armaments development and production (Hartley, 2008; Jones, 2007), losses through lack of cooperation were estimated at up to 100 billion euros per annum (European Commission, 2016).

PESCO offered a way out of this misery. In line with this perspective, two Europeanists, Spain and Belgium, took over the initiative. During the first half of 2010, Spain organized a first exploratory seminar on PESCO. In parallel, Belgium, in preparation for its upcoming presidency, issued a position paper on PESCO, which was subscribed to by the two other members of the prospective trio-presidency, Hungary and Poland (Andries, 2011). In this position paper, they stated that it would be

> in the EU's best interest to involve as many interested Member States as possible in this institutionalized defence cooperation. PESCO should not be limited to a core group of a small number of countries. PESCO should, from a BE-HU-PL perspective, rather be inclusive. A two-speed European defence needs to be avoided. (Belgium, Hungary, & Poland, 2010, p. 2)[2]

Building on this plea, the Belgian presidency then organized two further seminars mapping out the possibilities for activating PESCO (Biscop & Coelmont, 2012, p. 77). The outcome of these three seminars was more than limited: "a different reading of the outdated protocol texts, the binding character of the criteria to be defined, fear of a two-speed CSDP and an aversion to an additional institutional bureaucratic framework" (Andries, 2011) led to "an unbreachable wall" of member states' concerns (Biscop, 2017, p. 3). Aptly, Liam Fox, then prospective UK defense minister, not only made clear that Britain was not ready to go one step further but even threatened with a step back, putting the British engagement in the EDA into question.

> Fortunately, from a defence point of view, many of the elements found in the Treaty are either meaningless or voluntary. Consequently, we will reconsider such provisions as Permanent Structured Cooperation and the European Defence Agency closely if we form the next Government, to determine if we see any value in Britain's participation. (Fox, 2010, p. 2)

Consequently, at an informal meeting in Bruges later that year, the European defense ministers decided not to proceed with the activation of PESCO (EPRS, 2016, p. 4). The selective and the reluctant challenger states had demonstrated their resistance toward activating PESCO, which they deemed detrimental. The two scope conditions for the theoretical pathway to fragmentation were present: First, the Atlanticist challengers were dissatisfied with the framework. Second, as reforming PESCO would not have alleviated their concerns about the potential negative effects of

---

[2] The Belgian perspective as a federalist member state with an ambitious but limited defense industry is understandable. For Poland and Hungary, however, this plea for PESCO takes issue with their traditionally Atlanticist orientation and is an indicator for the severity of the external shock represented by the financial crisis.

EU cooperation on NATO, reform was impossible, which is why they blocked the institution. However, as demonstrated in the next section, the coalition of resisters crumbled under the pressure of the financial crisis' as demonstrated by the Polish and Hungarian signatures under Belgium's call for PESCO, they had to take additional measures and engaged in the creation of competing institutions.

Minilateral Regional Cooperation

The years 2009 and 2010 were characterized by a veritable flood of competitive regime creation and regime shifting outside the EU. In response to the high functional pressure to cooperate and fueled by fear of the disadvantages of accepting PESCO, which was considered unable to take the perspectives of the member states with niche industries into account (Németh, 2014), the "reluctant" states created a series of regional defense cooperation frameworks. These frameworks fulfilled a dual role: They were created as a relief from the high functional pressure and as a demonstration of unwillingness to accept PESCO under any circumstances.

First, Denmark, Finland, Iceland, Norway, and Sweden created NORDEFCO in 2009 (Denmark, Finland, Iceland, Norway, & Sweden, 2009). The reasons for this cooperation certainly reached beyond dissatisfaction with PESCO and included, inter alia, the possibility of incorporating non-EU members and, for Denmark, of participating without violating its defense opt-out. Yet the two neutral EU member states, Sweden and Finland, were undoubtedly prompted to invest in this regional framework by anticipation of the looming PESCO. A report on the defense prospects of the Nordic countries from Jens Stoltenberg, then Norway's defense minister, clearly reads that way:

> The alternative to cooperation could be a situation where small and medium-sized countries lose their ability to maintain a credible defence. The result could be a Europe where only countries like France, Russia, the UK and Germany have their own modern defence forces. Looking 15 to 20 years down the road, none of the Nordic countries will be able to maintain their armed forces at their current size and quality without closer Nordic cooperation. (Stoltenberg, 2009, p. 28)

Thus, PESCO was not perceived as an alternative. Only two options were considered: The Nordic states could cooperate either regionally or not at all. By implication, this meant that the creation of NORDEFCO in 2009, the subsequent signing of the Nordic General Security Agreement, and the actual establishment of the structures for cooperation in 2010 render a furthered engagement in PESCO superfluous from a Swedish–Finnish perspective.

Second, the CEDC was created by Austria, Croatia, the Czech Republic, Hungary, Slovakia, and Slovenia in 2010. Based on a rationale similar to that of the NORDEFCO countries, the CEDC countries agreed on 26 October 2010 that none of its members could sustain the entire range of military capability for crisis and peace operations (Bundesministerium Landesverteidigung Österreich, 2010). Thus, declining an EU-wide solution, their reaction was to rely on a common geographic location and common political and economic interests to find areas of cooperation that would generate win–win situations (Bundesministerium Landesverteidigung Österreich, 2010). Slovenia's then Defence Minister Ljubica Jelusic said,

> One cannot deny the fact that one of the most useful platforms for sharing lessons learned, knowledge, expertise and experiences from the process of Euro-Atlantic integration and defence reforms is through regional cooperation initiatives. (Jelusic, 2010)

Focusing on "the development of security and defence capabilities and the coordination of defence policy and planning issues" (Müller, 2016, p. 24), the CEDC did exactly what PESCO was supposed to do. Again, as in the case of NORDEFCO, regional cooperation allowed the membership overlap between NATO and EU members and non-members to be bridged. Croatia was not yet part of the EU (joining in 2013), Austria is not a NATO member: the regional approach in a smaller group of like-minded states was more suitable for overcoming the divisions that run deep through the EU membership (Németh, 2012).

Third, both the Visegràd Group (Poland, Hungary, the Czech Republic, and Slovakia) and the Baltic states reinvigorated their regional defense cooperation (Németh, 2014). The Baltic Defence Cooperation, still citing the Lisbon Treaty's provisions as a viable tool "for the reinforcement of the European Union Common Security and Defence

Policy" (Baltic Defence Cooperation, 2010, para. 9) at their ministerial meeting in May 2010, made no further references to the EU or the CSDP at the end of the year. On the contrary, the Baltic defense ministers "reiterated the need for further strengthening of defence cooperation among the three Baltic and five Nordic countries addressing common regional and global security interests and challenges" (Baltic Defence Cooperation, 2010, para. 7). The Visegràd Group's perspective was more ambivalent. In the first half of 2010, the Slovak presidency stressed the group's cautious support for PESCO and stated that the V4 countries would continue to take part "in exchanges of views on Permanent Structured Cooperation" (Slovakia, 2010). What is more, in 2011, the V4 decided to establish a joint EU Battlegroup, a criterion for participation in PESCO and at the same time an expression of the elevation of regional defense cooperation to a new level (Csiki & Németh, 2013, p. 15). While the Baltics set up their framework as a competitor to PESCO in 2010, the Visegràd countries' defense cooperation would still have been commensurable with a prospective strengthening of European defense.

In sum, the group of reluctant states, like the other EU members, was confronted with functional pressure to cooperate in defense matters. Yet their general skepticism about PESCO—which, they feared, would imply a break with NATO, on the one hand, and a loss of their sovereignty when it came to EU military missions, defense planning, and procurement, on the other—led them to create regional cooperation fora outside the EU whose mandates overlapped with PESCO yet which remained exclusive, regionally restricted institutions.

Sustaining Minilateralism

Recalling the theoretical argument presented in Chapter 3, a challenger coalition that lacks go-it-alone power and is thus unable to induce defenders of the status quo to join its newly created institutional competitor, may nonetheless be subject only to low non-agreement costs. If their positional characteristics translate into a preference for non-cooperation, this enables them to block the functioning of an institution that would be detrimental to them. To put it another way, a relatively weak coalition of states might be unable to develop an institutional competitor it has created into the new focal institution, but may still be able to undermine cooperation by fragmenting its institutionalized form and altering the distribution of resources by blocking the institution they are dissatisfied with. I argue that this is precisely what can be observed when one looks into the reluctant states' establishment of the four regional cooperation frameworks. In this section, I will demonstrate that none of the four challenger coalitions possessed the power to create a credible threat of exclusion for the avant-gardist proponents of PESCO, then, in the following section, show that they were still able to sustain minilateral cooperation on the basis of their exclusive membership preference.

Considering that in 2010 NORDEFCO (despite having two non-EU members on board[3]) was responsible for only 6.5 percent of the EU's total defense spending, the CEDC 3.2 percent, the Visegràd Group 4.4 percent, and the Baltic defense cooperation 0.3 percent, it is clear that none of these frameworks represented a threat of exclusion to the avant-gardist group (Fig. 7.2). The latter (Italy, Spain, France, and Germany) accounted for 54.1 percent. Non-participation in these institutions would not make any of the avant-gardists worse off, and they could have profited more from cooperating among themselves.

Consequently, an extensive analysis of French, Italian, German, and Spanish newspapers and governmental documents[4] did not deliver any results in terms of references by government officials to one or other of these frameworks—either in a positive nor in a negative way. Government officials seemingly did not feel the need to take a stance on their establishment. This is in line with the theoretical expectations: These frameworks did not generate a threat of exclusion. What is more, they did not even attract much attention.

Nevertheless, even though the establishment of regional frameworks did not represent a threat of exclusion, there was interest in Germany in observing more closely what the others were doing. When the Defense Ministers of NORDEFCO and Baltic Defence Cooperation met to sound out the possibilities for closer collaboration among themselves in

---

[3] The percentages do not amount to 100%, as Iceland, Norway, and Croatia were not part of the EU-27 in 2010, which served as the basis for the calculation.

[4] The analysis was conducted via the meta searches Factiva®, Nexis®, and via Google search. Moreover, the archives of the *Süddeutsche Zeitung* and *der Spiegel* (Germany), the *Corriere della Sera* (Italy), *El País* (Spain), and *Le Figaro* (France) as well as all publicly available parliamentary documents were searched for mentions of one of the four regional defense cooperation frameworks between 2009 and 2011.

2010 DEFENCE EXPENDITURE PER GROUP AS % OF TOTAL EU-27 SPENDING

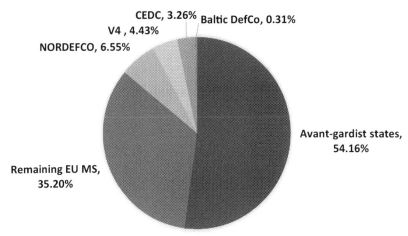

Fig. 7.2 2010 Defense expenditure per group as percentage of total EU-27 defense spending[5]

November 2010, Germany's Secretary of State for Defense was present at the meeting (M2 PressWIRE, 2010). This, however, cannot be traced to a threat of exclusion but rather to the strategic importance of the North Sea area (German News Informations Services, 2010). This assessment is also supported by the fact that Germany was the only country to send a state secretary to a ministerial meeting. Altogether, when the reluctant states engaged in competitive regime creation, this did not prompt any attempts to join on the part of the avant-gardist states.

Yet, while the reluctant states themselves lacked the power to go it alone, they were willing to keep cooperation exclusive and minimal. There are two interrelated reasons for this. First, they could rely on NATO, which considerably decreased their cost of non-agreement within the EU; second, opening up their regional cooperation frameworks beyond like-minded states, that is, entering a broader scheme of cooperation, would imply considerable losses in terms of strategic autonomy.

[5] Source: SIPRI Milex data 1949–2016, own compilation.

First, in 2010 in parallel to the reluctant states' creation or revival of regional cooperation, NATO defense ministers prepared a new strategic concept, which underlined both the United States' engagement and the European states' focus on NATO as the primary security institution in Europe (Rasmussen, 2010). From the perspective of the reluctant states, most of all those on the EU's eastern borders, NATO made PESCO redundant, especially when considering the generally stable security situation in 2009/2010.

Today, the Euro-Atlantic area is at peace and the threat of a conventional attack against NATO territory is low. That is an historic success for the policies of robust defence, Euro-Atlantic integration and active partnership that have guided NATO for more than half a century. (Rasmussen, 2010, para. 7)

The possibility of relying on NATO considerably decreased the cost of non-agreement in terms of security benefits for PESCO's opponents.

Second, recalling that the reluctant states created the competing institutions on the back of the financial crisis and their pressurized defense budgets, their preference was for an exclusive membership. Engaging in bi- and minilateral cooperation outside the EU treaties offered the reluctant states substantial advantages over the activation of PESCO. First, as they themselves had niche defense industries and comparatively small military capacities, regional cooperation allowed specialization within a framework of like-minded states. Specialization within a larger group, for example, at the European level, would have implied being subject to greater divergence in foreign policy goals and thus less strategic autonomy as to the use of their capabilities (Koenig-Archibugi, 2004). PESCO would have led to an increase in EU military capabilities, which could potentially have further increased the smaller member states' dependence on the bigger ones (Wivel, 2005, p. 402). A bottom-up regional approach characterized by ad-hoc cooperation was, for both the neutral and the reluctant states, preferable to institutionalized cooperation under CSDP. Thus, while every additional state joining their regional cooperation would have increased the members' saving potential through specialization, it would also have led to considerable losses in terms of the integrity and decision-making with regard to the use of their national defense-industrial base. Cooperating with states with a more competitive defense industry would be detrimental to them. V4 defense cooperation was built on the rationale of being

> involved as actively as possible preventing our region from turning into a mere market for global defence companies .... While deepening our cooperation, we should also build on ongoing projects and identify and develop niche capabilities where we have recognized competences. (V4, 2014, pp. 1–2)

This argument is in line with Vivien Pertusot's general observation that it is "appealing neither to larger countries nor to smaller ones to become bedfellows in cooperation where inequalities would likely be acute" (Pertusot, p. 20). It is easier for states to cooperate with similar partners as this decreases the member surplus incurred when accepting additional participants. The more homogenous the group, the more beneficial cooperation is.

Summing up, in light of the financial crisis and tightened defense budgets, there was a need to intensify defense cooperation. Specialization in military capabilities, joint procurement, and multinational forces were all necessary to sustain national security and defense. The reluctant states had two possibilities—either to agree to PESCO and join the Europeanist coalition or to go it alone and cooperate on a regional level. The first option would serve their security interest better, while the second option was better in terms of economic and autonomy benefits. As the security situation was stable and the United States a reliable partner, the costs of not intensifying EU cooperation were low. This is why the reluctant states were able to sustain their minilateral cooperation despite their lack of go-it-alone power, making regional cooperation "not a passing phenomenon" (Pertusot, 2015, p. 101).

However, given that the reluctant states engaged in competitive regime creation without go-it-alone power, the question still stands as to why the Europeanist states, the proponents of PESCO, did not try to move ahead on their own. The next section demonstrates that the most important reason for this was the continuous British resistance to further integration in the realm of European defense.

The Europeanist Reaction

This section shows that the blockade of PESCO decreased the Europeanists' utility. Consequently, they had to look out for alternative possibilities for establishing a level of cooperation that would allow them to sustain their military capabilities under crisis-induced budgetary constraints. Three developments exemplify this—the minilateral European Aircraft Transport Command (EATC), the Franco-British Lancaster House Treaties, and the German–Swedish Ghent Initiative, which were all agreed upon in the last quarter of 2010.

As it became foreseeable that PESCO was unlikely to be activated on account of the reluctant states' competitive regime creation and regime shifting to regional platforms, the Europeanists had to find new ways among themselves to alleviate budgetary pressures. As a first step, France and Germany, together with federalist Belgium and the Netherlands, inaugurated the EATC on 01 September 2010 as a joint command center operating the participants' military air transport assets (EATC, 2017). This single command allowed its members to pool their air transport capabilities and organize joint training (EATC, 2017)—in short, it allowed cost savings. In line with the theoretical expectations, during the next few years, federalist Luxembourg (2012) and the two further avant-gardist states, Spain and Italy (2014), joined the EATC as well. While creating a platform like EATC within the EU was not possible without the support of the other member states, the established platform was reconcilable with PESCO and could have been subsumed under its structures and thus become part of the EU framework at a later stage.

While the Europeanists might still have hoped for a change in the British position and thus a majority for PESCO in September 2010, this hope was destroyed on 2 November when France abandoned the cause. Due to its disillusionment with the CSDP's lack of development, France joined forces with the most outspoken opponent of PESCO, the United Kingdom, and signed the Lancaster House Treaties on bilateral defense cooperation (Menon, 2011). Both agreed on an unprecedented level of cooperation stretching from the alignment of their respective procurement policies and decisions on reciprocal defense market access (United Kingdom & France, 2011, Art. 7, 8) to a "Combined Joint Expeditionary Force" and "co-operation at a new joint facility of … nuclear warheads" (UK Prime Minister's Office, 2010).

This agreement, made in the context of the austerity imperative derived from the Euro crisis, was pragmatic, as it meant cooperation despite conflicting views over CSDP vs. NATO primacy. Indeed, for the United Kingdom, the conclusion of the Lancaster House Treaties was a success beyond pragmatism. It cemented the suppression of PESCO by demonstrating that EU member states could cooperate without further EU-level institutionalization, as was evident, since neither the treaty nor the agreements signed under its auspices contained an "agenda for a Europeanisation of the bilateral initiatives" (Von Ondaraza, 2011, pp. 324 325).

Some observers interpreted the Lancaster House Treaties as a reversal of the St. Malo summit that had laid the foundations for the creation of the CSDP (Biscop & Coelmont, 2012, p. 83). Fueled by disillusionment with the stalemate over PESCO, "[t]he Union's leading military powers seem increasingly to doubt the utility of an EU policy that was largely their own creation" (Menon, 2011, p. 88). Thus, the Treaties represented a further turning away from Europeanization of security and defense and, as such, a competitor institution for PESCO that, as Nick Witney, former Chief Executive of the EDA, put it, "suck[ed] the oxygen out of the air for wider EU cooperation" (defenceWeb, 2010).

The Franco-British treaty clearly furthered the fragmentation of European defense cooperation and displeased the remaining avant-gardist states. Robert Hochbaum, a member of the German parliament's defense policy committee, cautiously stated that it was "a bit unfortunate the British and the French are doing it without us" and "it's always harder to get involved when two states go on ahead than when joint talks are held from the outset" (Brunnstrom, 2010). In sum, little, if any, impetus for PESCO was left in November 2010.

At the end of 2010, the Europeanists were left to fear the insignificance of the CSDP in general and were pressurized to identify alternative possibilities for cost-sharing and specialization in light of the crisis. They needed to find ways to cope with the increased functional pressure for cooperation themselves without contributing to further fragmentation—this was when they came up with the concept of "Pooling & Sharing" as proposed by the German–Swedish Ghent Initiative (Csiki & Németh, 2013, p. 13).

Building on the outcome of a meeting in Ghent, Germany, and Sweden presented a "Food for Thought" paper on 10 November 2010.

This paper was a direct reaction to the most recent proliferation of bi- and minilateral cooperation frameworks. It stated,

> There are great profits to be made by finding ways of sharing expenses and burdens. This has already been proved by existing bilateral, regional and European cooperation. (Germany & Sweden, 2010, p. 1)

Germany and Sweden proposed to create a coherent frame around the regional initiatives. While claiming that they intended to "profit from the momentum" of increasing defense cooperation, they cautiously avoided any mention of PESCO and proposed the creation of yet another "new initiative" (Germany & Sweden, 2010, p. 1). To reach consensus in the Council, the Ghent Initiative did not include any binding commitments, made no reference to PESCO, and thus represented no more than a "buzzword, another euphemism for muddling through" (Coelmont, 2017), considerably "downgrading" the Europeanists ambitions (Chappell & Petrov, 2012) and further paving the way toward fragmentation.

By the end of 2010, European defense planning was a rag-rug of island solutions consisting of bi- and minilateral agreements loosely tied together by the Ghent Initiative. The latter, however, was a mere subjunctive, which "*would* form the basis for Member States" (Council of the European Union, 2010, para. 5, emphasis added) to consider coordination between the frameworks if they *were* willing to do so. This situation of parallel institutions with the same mandate—joint organization of defense planning—by characterized by separate membership[6] and resources, persisted. The reason, as discussed before, was that the challenger coalitions of reluctant states had neither the power to generate a credible threat of exclusion nor the incentive to join a broader framework themselves.

Fragmentation—The Least Common Security and Defense Policy

This section demonstrates that, while the dissatisfied challenger coalitions were successful in blocking PESCO by creating bi- and minilateral institutions outside the EU, the consequence was a stalemate between the

---

[6] With the exception of the Czech Republic, Hungary and Slovakia, which were members of both the V4 and the CEDC

Atlanticists and the Europeanists. Neither PESCO's challengers nor its defenders possessed the power to go it alone. The latter tried to put PESCO back on the agenda in 2010, 2012, and 2013; the selective and reluctant states countered these attempts. Fragmentation characterized interinstitutional relationships in the regime complex of defense planning.

Even if the Europeanist coalition had possessed go-it-alone power, their hands would have been tied, and open contestation would not have been an option. First, both the avant-gardists and the federalists preferred cooperation within the EU framework. Creating an additional minilateral institution outside the treaties would run contrary to this fundamental preference. Second, given the Atlanticist resistance to PESCO, the qualified majority necessary to establish it was unachievable. The United Kingdom needed eight other states to block any such proposal (Consilium, 2018). Given that there were 21 states in the Atlanticist camp, the outlook for the Europeanists in any crucial vote was worse than disadvantageous. Consequently, the Europeanists' attempts to put PESCO back on the agenda consistently failed.

After presenting the "Food for Thought" paper and the concept of Pooling & Sharing to the other EU member states, which met general acceptance due to its non-binding character, the German government tried to go one step further and push for PESCO once again. Shortly before the Council meeting on 9 December 2010, Germany's ministers of foreign affairs and defense convinced their colleagues in the two other members of the so-called Weimar Triangle, Poland, and France, to co-sponsor a letter to the EU's then High Representative for Foreign Affairs and Security Policy (HR), Catherine Ashton. The latter stated that PESCO "may be a useful tool to achieve progress in reinforcing European capabilities" (M. Alliot-Marie et al., personal communication, December 6, 2010, p. 2) and was directed at achieving a reference to PESCO in the Council Conclusions.

Thanks to this initiative, three days later, on 9 December 2010, the Council concluded that the "possibilities for the use of Permanent Structured Cooperation shall be explored" (Council of the European Union, 2010, para. 12). While, at first sight, this might seem like a success for the Europeanists, they actually found themselves in a situation resembling but essentially worse than that of 2007. PESCO's activation was further out of reach than ever, as the reluctant states were already cooperating regionally and the United Kingdom had signed the cooperation agreement with France. Given all that, together with the Ghent Initiative, which was "welcomed" by the Council (Council of the European Union, 2010, para. 5), PESCO's opponents no longer saw the need to engage in any further institutionalized EU framework. The minilateral institutions founded enabled them to mitigate the functional pressure to cooperate.

This situation proved stable. Despite further Europeanist attempts to convince the Atlanticists to activate PESCO, the latter were able to preserve the fragmented status quo. The Libyan crisis of 2011 is a case in point. Even though it once again demonstrated Europe's inability to act autonomously and revealed the shortcomings of joint decision-making on foreign policy, it also showed that the EU could rely on NATO. The humanitarian EU operation *EUFOR Libya* remained a purely "symbolic gesture" (Koenig, 2012, p. 22), with military actions being carried out by NATO only. While the Europeanists were disappointed with the EU's inability to act independently (Koenig, 2012, p. 27; Menon, 2011), the Atlanticists emphasized NATO's effectiveness, claiming that the operation "Unified Protector" was "one of the most successful operations NATO has conducted" (Sir David Richards, UK Chief of Defence Staff, as cited in *The Telegraph*, 2011).

With this experience in mind, it is not surprising that the 2012 "Westerwelle Report," subscribed to by the Europeanist states as well as Austria, Denmark, and Poland, petered out with no impact. The report claimed that the European "defence policy should have more ambitious goals which go beyond 'pooling and sharing' ..., in particular the establishment of Permanent Structured Cooperation should be implemented" (Future of Europe Group, 2012, p. 6). As the Atlanticists could rely on NATO, the benefits of further EU cooperation remained low. Consequently, it took more than a year for the CSDP to come back on the political agenda.

The heads of state and government's December 2013 meeting ended with the first European Council Conclusions on security and defense since the entry into force of the Lisbon Treaty in 2009. They called for "a strong commitment to the further development of a credible and effective CSDP, in accordance with the Lisbon Treaty and the opportunities it offers" (European Council, 2013, para. 2). Yet, while the European Council welcomed "cooperative approaches whereby willing Member States or groups of Member States develop capabilities based on common standards" (European Council, 2013, para. 10), it did not take an explicit stand on the form of such cooperation and whether it should take place within the EU framework or simply as continued regional cooperation. While the Europeanist interpretation was clearly EU-related and a step toward finally moving forward with PESCO, in the press conference following the European Council meeting, British Prime Minister David Cameron left no doubt about the opposite British position:

> Co-operation between nation states, yes. EU assets and EU headquarters, no. And I have made sure this is clear in the conclusions that we've agreed today. 8 more references to member states, 5 more references to NATO. And we have removed references to Europe's armed forces; to an EU pooled acquisition mechanism for new capabilities, and to EU assets and fleets. (Cameron, 2013)

This statement and the prior developments imply that the prospects for PESCO as an institutionalized EU-level capabilities development mechanism were bleak. With the reluctant states already cooperating bi- and minilaterally and the United Kingdom fundamentally opposing any further steps in this direction, there was no room for maneuver for the Europeanists to promote PESCO. Fragmentation even increased. In 2015 Bulgaria, Croatia, Hungary, and Slovenia signed a Letter of Intent to cooperate on training, modernization, procurement, and potentially even integrated multinational military units (Marrone et al., 2016, p. 21).

In sum, as neither Europeanists nor Atlanticists possessed the power to go it alone, fragmentation was the stable outcome. None of the two coalitions could move. While resources were pooled within regional minilateral institutions, there was no sharing beyond them. Thus, in line with the theoretical framework, the challengers' lack of go-it-alone power and their exclusive membership preference led to an outcome of institutional fragmentation, a myriad institutions with separate membership and resources.

Summary

This chapter has analyzed the process leading to the fragmentation of the European defense policy regime into bi- and minilateral, mostly regional, cooperation frameworks. While the Europeanist states supported PESCO, a flexible institution allowing a coalition of the willing to engage in deeper cooperation in the realm of defense planning and military cooperation, a coalition of Atlanticist states opposed this concept from the very start. First, the United Kingdom, generally in favor of enhanced international cooperation in defense planning and procurement to support NATO, fundamentally opposed the idea of further EU integration in the defense sector. Second, the reluctant states shared the view that NATO was the primary security institution in Europe and that any potential undermining or duplication should be avoided. Moreover, due to their relatively small defense industries, they were also skeptical believing that cooperation with the "big six" would pressure them into specialization, inability to maintain a national DTIB, and, finally, even stronger dependency.

In light of the financial crisis, which put national defense budgets under strain, the need for defense cooperation increased. To prevent PESCO's activation, which would have alleviated the pressure, the reluctant states revived or founded regional cooperation frameworks to organize cooperation among like-minded and homogenous countries, which allowed meeting on eye level. These frameworks, due to the latter's sheer economic and military weight, did not create a threat of exclusion to the Europeanists—joining these frameworks would not have offered a large potential for savings or enhanced capabilities. Yet the reluctant states were able to sustain regional cooperation because they enjoyed credible security backing from NATO and, thanks to their exclusive membership preference, the cost to them of non-agreement within the EU framework was low.

The sustainable blockade of PESCO forced the Europeanists to find alternative options for cooperation. France, one of PESCO's strongest proponents, sealed an agreement on bilateral defense cooperation with PESCO's greatest antagonist, the United Kingdom. When it became evident to the remaining Europeanists, especially Germany, that the outlook for PESCO had darkened, they attempted to introduce EU cooperation informally. The Ghent Initiative, with the concept of pooling and sharing, was an attempt to pave the way for PESCO without binding commitments. From the reluctant states' perspective, this further decreased the need for an institutionalized PESCO.

None of the numerous frameworks had the potential to attract new members, and no state coalition was able to dictate the terms of coordination among the institutions of the defense-planning complex. This stalemate found expression in a persistent situation of fragmented authority: While the institutions overlapped in the mandate, they had separate memberships and resources and co-existed independently of one another. The institutional fragmentation was locked into a stable equilibrium.

Throughout the period from 2010 until 2015, observers agreed that a change in this situation was not in sight. The prospects for PESCO were not rosy. Given that "the very preferences of the EU member states are unlikely to be easily altered" (van Langenhove & Maes, 2012) "it seems that the concept might not be operationalised" (Chappell & Petrov, 2012, p. 64) so it was "unlikely to be formally activated any time soon" (Biscop et al., 2015, p. 7). Fragmentation in European defense cooperation seemed to be the past, present, and future as

> Longstanding obstacles block further integration, such as differences between member states in threat perceptions and strategic cultures, divergences in intentions and preferences and, in some cases, lack of mutual trust and solidarity. (Centre for European Policy Studies, 2015, p. 1)

Against all the odds, however, the Council of the European Union formally established PESCO only two years later, on 11 December 2017. The next and final case study builds on the developments presented in this chapter but extends the period of analysis to the end of 2017. Two external shocks, the election of Donald Trump as President of the United States as well as the British vote to leave the EU in 2016, distorted the balanced distribution of power between the Europeanist proponents and the Atlanticist opponents of PESCO and altered the membership preference of the reluctant states. Given the challengers' lack of go-it-alone power, and the eventual change in membership preference, the Europeanists, whose relative power increased through Brexit, were able to bring PESCO back into focus, which finally resulted in the institution's becoming resilient to the reluctant states' competitive regime creation.

REFERENCES

Alliot-Marie, M., Westerwelle, G., Sikorski, R., Juppé, A., Guttenberg, K.-T. zu, & Klich, B. (2010, December 6). CSDP.

Andries, J. (2011). The 2010 Belgian EU Presidency and CSDP. *Egmont Security Policy Brief* (21). http://aei.pitt.edu/32038/1/SPB21-J.Andries-Belgian-EU-Presidency-CSDP.pdf

Baltic Defence Cooperation. (2010). *Joint Communiqué of the Ministerial Committee*. Tartu. http://www.kaitseministeerium.ee/sites/default/files/sis ulehed/balti_kaitsekoostoo/2010-12-17_jc_3b_defmin_tartu.pdf

Barcikowska, A. (2013). *EU Battlegroups—ready to go?* (Brief Issue No. 40). http://www.iss.europa.eu/uploads/media/Brief_40_EU_Battlegroups.pdf

Belgium, Hungary, & Poland. (2010). *Position Paper by Belgium, Hungary and Poland on Permanent Structured Cooperation*. http://ddata.over-blog.com/xxxyyy/0/50/29/09/Docs-Textes/CoopStructPsdcPap-BeHuPl1006b.pdf

Biscop, S. (2008). *Permanent structured cooperation and the future of ESDP* (Egmont Papers No. 20).
Biscop, S. (2017). *Oratio pro PESCO* (Egmont Paper No. 91). Brussels. http://www.egmontinstitute.be/content/uploads/2017/01/ep91.pdf?type=pdf
Biscop, S., & Coelmont, J. (2012). *Europe, strategy and armed forces: The making of a distinctive power*. Routledge.
Biscop, S., Coelmont, J., Drent, M., & Zandee, D. (2015). *European strategy, European defence, and the CSDP* (Clingendael Report). https://www.clingendael.org/sites/default/files/pdfs/European%20Strategy,%20European%20Defence%20and%20the%20CSDP.pdf
Brunnstrom, D. (2010, November 3). Analysis—Anglo-French defence deal could hurt Brussels goals. https://uk.reuters.com/article/uk-europe-defence/analysis-anglo-french-defence-deal-could-hurt-brussels-goals-idUKTRE6A251S20101103
Bundesministerium Landesverteidigung Österreich. (2010, November 9). Konferenz für mehr regionale Kooperation in Zentraleuropa. http://www.bundesheer.at/cms/artikel.php?ID=5362
Cameron, D. (2013, December 20). European Council December 2013: David Cameron's press conference. https://www.gov.uk/government/speeches/european-council-december-2013-david-camerons-press-conference
Centre for European Policy Studies. (2015). *More Union European defence: Report of a CEPS Task Force*. Centre for European Policy Studies.
Chappell, L., & Petrov, P. (2012). The European defence agency and permanent structured cooperation: Are we heading towards another missed opportunity? *Defence Studies, 12*(1), 44–66. https://doi.org/10.1080/14702436.2012.683973
Coelmont, J. (2017). With PESCO brought to life, will European defence live happily ever after? *Egmont Security Policy Brief* (90). http://aei.pitt.edu/88540/1/SPB90.pdf
Consilium. (2018). Voting calculator. http://www.consilium.europa.eu/en/council-eu/voting-system/voting-calculator/
Council of the European Union. (2010). *Council Conclusions on Military Capability Development: 3055th Foreign Affairs (Defence) Council meeting*. https://www.consilium.europa.eu/uedocs/cms_data/docs/pressdata/en/esdp/118348.pdf
Csiki, T., & Németh, B. (2013). Perspectives of Central European Multinational Defence Cooperation: A new Model? In M. Majer & R. Ondrejcsák (Eds.), *Panorama of Global Security Environment 2013* (pp. 11–24). Bratislava.
DefenceWeb. (2010, November 4). Anglo-French defence deal could hurt Brussels goals. https://www.defenceweb.co.za/industry/industry-industry/anglo-french-defence-deal-could-hurt-brussels-goals/

Denmark, Finland, Iceland, Norway, & Sweden. (2009). *Memorandum of understanding on Nordic Defence Cooperation.* Retrieved from https://www.nor defco.org/the-basics-aboutnordefco
EATC. (2017). The member nations. https://eatc-mil.com/en/who-we-are/the-member-nations
EDA. (2011). *Defence Data 2010.* Brussels. European Defence Agency website: https://www.eda.europa.eu/docs/eda-publications/defence_data_2010
Eisenhut, D. (2010). *Europäische Rüstungskooperation: Zwischen Binnenmarkt und zwischenstaatlicher Zusammenarbeit.* Univ., Diss.--Augsburg, 2009 (1. Aufl.). *Augsburger Rechtsstudien* (vol. 59). Nomos Verl.-Ges.
EPRS. (2016). *Implementation of the Lisbon Treaty provisions on the Common Security and Defence Policy (CSDP)* (European Council Briefing). www.europarl.europa.eu/RegData/etudes/BRIE/2016/573285/EPRS_BRI(2016)573285_EN.pdf
European Commission. (2016). *European defence action plan: Towards a European Defence Fund.* Brussels. http://europa.eu/rapid/press-release_IP-16-4088_en.htm
European Convention. (2002). *Final report of Working Group VIII - Defence* (No. WG VIII 22). Brussels. https://web.archive.org/web/200706092 35907/http://register.consilium.eu.int/pdf/en/02/cv00/00461en2.pdf
European Council. (2013). *European Council meeting (19/20 December 2013)—Conclusions* (No. EUCO 217/13). Brussels. http://data.consilium.europa. eu/doc/document/ST-217-2013-INIT/en/pdf
European Union. (2005). *Treaty establishing a constitution for Europe.* Office for Official Publ. of the Europ. Communities. http://europa.eu.int/constitut ion/index_en.htm
European Union. (2010). *Consolidated versions of the treaty on European Union and of the treaty on the functioning of the European Union: Charter of fundamental rights of the European Union.* Publications Office of the European Union. http://publications.europa.eu/de/publication-detail/-/publication/ 3c32722f-0136-4d8f-a03e-bfaf70d16349
Fox, L. (2010). *The Armed Forces, NATO and the EU: What should the UK's role be?* London. POLITEIA website: http://www.politeia.co.uk/wp-content/Politeia%20Documents/2010/March%20-%20The%20Armed%20F orces%2C%20NATO%20and%20the%20EU/%27The%20Armed%20Forces% 27%20March%202010.pdf
France, & Germany. (2002). *Working Document 36—WG VIII: Franco-German comments on the preliminary draft final report of Working Group VIII "Defence"* (WD 022). http://european-convention.europa.eu/docs/wd8/ 5925.pdf
France. (2008). *French Presidency of the Council of the European Union: Work Programme: Europe taking action to meet today's challenges.* archive-ue2008. fr/webdav/site/PFUE/shared/ProgrammePFUE/Programme_EN.pdf

Future of Europe Group. (2012). *Final Report of the Future of Europe Group: Of the Foreign Ministers of Austria, Belgium, Denmark, France, Italy, Germany, Luxembourg, the Netherlands, Poland, Portugal and Spain*. http://www.cer.eu/sites/default/files/westerwelle_report_sept12.pdf

German News Informations Services. (2010, November 15). Militarizing the Arctic. https://www.german-foreign-policy.com/en/news/detail/5078/

Germany, & Sweden. (2010). *Pooling and sharing, German-Swedish initiative: European Imperative Intensifying Military Cooperation in Europe—"Ghent Initiative"*. Berlin and Stockholm. http://www.europarl.europa.eu/meetdocs/2009_2014/documents/sede/dv/sede260511deseinitiative_/sede260511deseinitiative_en.pdf

Hartley, K. (2008). Collaboration and European Defence Industrial Policy. *Defence and Peace Economics*, 19(4), 303–315. https://doi.org/10.1080/10242690802221585

Howorth, J. (2004). The European Draft Constitutional Treaty and the Future of the European Defence Initiative: A Question of Flexibility. *European Foreign Affairs Review*, 9(4), 483–508. http://www.kluwerlawonline.com/document.php?id=EERR2004039

Jelusic, L. (2010). Regional security and defence cooperation in South East Europe. https://www.rcc.int/articles/31/regional-security-and-defence-cooperation-in-south-east-europe-by-ljubica-jelusic-minister-of-defence-of-slovenia

Jones, S. G. (2007). *The rise of European security cooperation*. Cambridge University Press.

Kiljunen, K. (2002). *Working Document 30—WG VIII: Comments on the preliminary draft final report of Working Group VIII "Defence" (WD 022)*. http://european-convention.europa.eu/docs/wd8/5859.pdf

Koenig, N. (2012). The EU and the Libyan Crisis—In quest of coherence? *The International Spectator*, 46(4), 11–30. https://doi.org/10.1080/03932729.2011.628089

Koenig-Archibugi, M. (2004). Explaining Government Preferences for Institutional Change in EU Foreign and Security Policy. *International Organization*, 58(01), 137–174. https://doi.org/10.1017/S0020818304581055

M2 PressWIRE. (2010, November 15). Desire for broad cooperation in the North.

Marrone, A., De France Olivier, & Fattibene, D. (2016). *Defence budgets and cooperation in Europe: Developments, trends and drivers*. Istituto Affari Internatzionali website: http://www.iai.it/sites/default/files/pma_report.pdf

Menon, A. (2011). European Defence Policy from Lisbon to Libya. *Survival*, 53(3), 75–90. https://doi.org/10.1080/00396338.2011.586191

Müller, P. (2016). Europeanization and regional cooperation initiatives: Austria's participation in the Salzburg Forum and in Central European Defence Cooperation. *Österreichische Zeitschrift für Politikwissenschaft, 45*(2), 23. https://doi.org/10.15203/ozp.1102.vol45iss2

Németh, B. (2012). How to bridge the 'three islands': The future of European military co-operation. https://kclpure.kcl.ac.uk/portal/files/11764177/Nemeth_How_to_bridge_the_three_islands_The_future_of_European_military_co_operation.pdf

Németh, B. (2014, April 16). Why don't Europeans Use NATO and the EU? http://www.css.ethz.ch/en/services/digital-library/articles/article.html/178665/pdf

Pertusot, V. (2015). European defence: Minilateralism is not the enemy. In D. Fiott (Ed.), *Egmont Paper* (vol. 79). *The Common Security and Defence Policy: National Perspectives* (pp. 101–104).

Piks, & Rihards. (2002). *Working Document 29—WG VIII: Comments to the preliminary draft final report of Working Group VIII "Defence"*. http://european-convention.europa.eu/docs/wd8/5848.pdf

Rasmussen, A. F. (2010). *Strategic concept for the defence and security of the members of the North Atlantic Treaty Organisation adopted by Heads of State and Government in Lisbon: Active engagement, modern defence*. https://www.nato.int/lisbon2010/strategic-concept-2010-eng.pdf

Slovakia. (2010). Program of the Slovak Presidency of the Visegrad Group July 2010–June 2011: Efficient Visegrad—Continuity, coehsion, solidarity, awareness. http://www.visegradgroup.eu/documents/presidency-programs/2010-2011-slovak-110412

Stoltenberg, T. (2009). *Nordic Cooperation on Foreign and Security Policy: Proposals presented to the extraordinary meeting of Nordic foreign ministers in Oslo on 9 February 2009*. Oslo. https://www.regjeringen.no/globalassets/upload/ud/vedlegg/nordicreport.pdf

Taylor, C. (2008). *Priorities for ESDP during the French Presidency of the EU* (No. SN/IA/4807).

The Guardian. (2008, June 7). European HQ heads Sarkozy plan for greater military integration. https://www.theguardian.com/world/2008/jun/07/eu.france

The Netherlands. (2002, December 4). Working Document 28—WG VIII: Dutch comments on the preliminary draft final report of Working Group VIII "Defence" (WD 022). http://european-convention.europa.eu/docs/wd8/5837.pdf

The Telegraph. (2011, October 24). David Cameron's statement on the European Council: In full. https://www.telegraph.co.uk/news/worldnews/europe/eu/8846553/David-Camerons-statement-on-the-European-Council-in-full.html

Treaty of Nice, Amending the Treaty on European Union, the Treaties Establishing the European Communities and Certain Related Acts, *Official Journal C 80 of 10 March 2001; 2001/C 80/01* (2000).

Tuomioja, E. (2003). 'Europe needs to work as a whole on defence': Article by Erkki Tuomioja, Finnish Foreign Minister [*The Financial Times*, 28 October 2003]. In A. Missiroli (Ed.), *Chaillot Papers* (vol. 67). *From Copenhagen to Brussels European defence: Core documents* (vol. IV, pp. 424–425). Institute for Security Studies European Union.

UK Prime Minister's Office. (2010, December 2). UK–France summit 2010 declaration on defence and security co-operation. https://www.gov.uk/government/news/uk-france-summit-2010-declaration-on-defence-and-security-co-operation

United Kingdom, & France. (2011). *Treaty between the United Kingdom of Great Britain and Northern Ireland and the French Republic for defence and security co-operation: London, 2 November 2010. Treaty series: no. 36 (2011)*. Stationery Office.

United Kingdom. (2003). British non-paper: "Food for thought". In A. Missiroli (Ed.), *Chaillot Papers* (vol. 67). *From Copenhagen to Brussels European defence: Core documents* (vol. IV, pp. 204–207). Institute for Security Studies European Union.

V4. (2014). *Long term vision of the Visegrad Countries on deepening their defence cooperation*. Visegrad. Visegrad Group website: www.visegradgroup.eu/calendar/2014-03-14-ltv

Van Eekelen, W. F., & Kurpas, S. (2008). *The evolution of flexible integration in European defence policy: Is permanent structured cooperation a leap forward for the common security and defence policy? CEPS working document* (vol. 296). CEPS.

Van Langenhove, L., & Maes, L. (2012). The role of the EU in peace and security. https://unu.edu/publications/articles/the-role-of-the-eu-in-peace-and-security.html

Von Ondaraza, N. von (2011). Common security and defence policy: Bilateral vs. structured cooperation? Flexible cooperation in and outside the EU framework as a tool for advancing European capabilities. In E. Fabry (Ed.), *Think Global—Act European (TGAE): The contribution of 16 European Think Tanks to the Polish, Danish and Cypriot Trio Presidency of the European Union* (pp. 322–326). Notre Europe.

Wivel, A. (2005). The security challenge of small EU member states: Interests, identity and the development of the EU as a security actor. *JCMS: Journal of Common Market Studies, 43*(2), 393–412. https://doi.org/10.1111/j.0021-9886.2005.00561.x

CHAPTER 8

PESCO's resilience: Jumpstarting the bandwagon

This chapter builds on the previous case study of the fragmentation of European defense planning. While fragmentation was the stable institutional outcome of the Atlanticists' creation of a regime that competed with PESCO until 2015, only two years later, in December 2017, the Council formally established PESCO with the participation of 25 out of 28 EU member states[1]—a result that previously seemed impossible. I argue that the equilibrium of fragmented defense planning was distorted by two external shocks: the British vote to leave the European Union on 23 June 2016 and the election of NATO-skeptic Donald Trump as US President on 9 November that year.

In line with rationalist theorizing, external shocks may punctuate an achieved equilibrium outcome of authority distribution across institutions (Colgan et al., 2012). As theorized in Chapter 3, an external shock has the potential to directly affect the functional pressure to cooperate by raising the cost of non-cooperation. Moreover, it indirectly increases pressure to cooperate by influencing the go-it-alone power of a state coalition. Both effects can result in an exclusive institution's no longer being able to provide the collective good it previously offered without the help of

---

[1] The three EU member states that did not participate in PESCO, were the United Kingdom, Denmark, and Malta.

© The Author(s), under exclusive license to Springer Nature Switzerland AG 2023
F. Biermann, *The Battle for Authority in European Defence Cooperation*, Palgrave Studies in European Union Politics, https://doi.org/10.1007/978-3-031-30054-7_8

199

additional states. The same effect might be generated if coalitions of states fell apart. If a state, due to a change in domestic preferences, decided not to support the resistance against an institution any longer or to exit an exclusive challenger institution (Moravcsik, 1997), this might overturn the "inherited distribution of power" locked in the regime complex (Pierson, 2016, p. 129).

I provide evidence that the two external shocks previously mentioned had precisely these effects. The British decision to leave the European Union weakened the Atlanticist coalition and its ability to block PESCO considerably; moreover, the election of Donald Trump, who overtly undermined the credibility of US engagement in NATO, increased the costs of non-cooperation in the realm of joint European defense planning and thus altered the reluctant states' membership preference from exclusive to inclusive. Therefore, extending the period of analysis examined in Chapter 7 (2004–2015) until the end of 2017, to include the time following the external shocks, allows me to analyze the pathway to resilience—the fourth and final outcome of authority distribution in institutional complexes.

In the following sections, I will demonstrate that the theorized pathway leading to resilience was present and operated as expected and depicted in Fig. 8.1. Although the process was triggered by the Atlanticist states engaging in competitive regime creation in the years 2009 and 2010, to avoid repetitions my analysis will recommence in May 2015, when the British Houses of Parliament passed the bill allowing for a Brexit referendum. The first section thus demonstrates that in 2015 the preferences of both the Europeanist and the Atlanticist coalitions were still diametrically opposed. As soon as Brexit became a theoretical possibility in 2015, the Europeanists tried but failed to get PESCO back on the agenda. The Atlanticist coalition stood firm and continued to block any attempt to make PESCO the focal institution in European defense. The second section shows the weakening effect of Brexit on the Atlanticist coalition. The reluctant states and Sweden could no longer rely on the United Kingdom as their most powerful ally, which considerably undermined their ability to prevent the Europeanist coalition from establishing PESCO among themselves. In other words, while the challengers were without go-it-alone power from the outset, they now in addition lost their veto power. Third, I show that the election of an outspoken NATO-skeptic, Donald Trump, as the 45th US President dramatically altered

8 PESCO'S RESILIENCE: JUMPSTARTING THE BANDWAGON 201

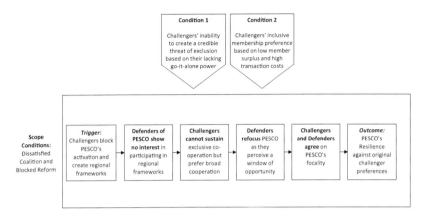

Fig. 8.1 Process leading to PESCO's resilience in light of competitive regime creation

the reluctant states' membership preference. If they had preferred exclusive, regional cooperation backed by the NATO promise of collective defense before, they now reoriented toward the European Union as a security provider. The fourth section unveils how the Europeanists were able to exploit this window of opportunity. Given the reluctant states' lack of go-it-alone power and their current preference for inclusive membership, the Europeanists were able to convince one state after the other to accept PESCO as the new center of relational authority. This process progressed analogously to the pathway leading to the integration of the EDA. Following the Atlanticists' unsuccessful attempt to organize defense cooperation among themselves, the Europeanists were now able to create a credible threat of exclusion. Consequently, there followed a veritable cascade of reluctant states deciding to join PESCO. This resulted in the formal activation of PESCO with 25 members in December 2017 and the decision on a first package of projects in March 2018. In accordance with theoretical expectations, the EU member states participating in PESCO shifted the bulk of their resources to that framework and thereby acknowledged its authority over the regional cooperation frameworks, which they thereby pushed to the margins. The final section summarizes the argument.

Taking Stock: Europeanist Dreams and Atlanticist Reality

This section briefly delineates the interim phase after the European Council meeting on 20 December 2013 that was a nail in the coffin of PESCO and cemented fragmentation before the Brexit vote and the election of Donald Trump. This is necessary to underline the argument that it was only the co-occurrence of Brexit, which overturned the power balance between Europeanists and Atlanticists, and the election of Donald Trump, which altered the reluctant states' membership preference, that was able to pave the way for PESCO's restoration, which then played out along the lines of the theorized pathway. Neither the renegotiation of the terms of British EU membership in light of the prospective Brexit referendum nor the worsened security situation after the Russian Annexation of Crimea in 2014 could alter the Atlanticist coalition's stance regarding closer EU defense cooperation. Although the Europeanists anticipated a window of opportunity to put PESCO back on the agenda, the Atlanticist opposition did not crumble.

On 27 May 2015, when the British Houses of Parliament passed a bill allowing a referendum on UK's EU membership, Brexit, for the first time, became a possibility. In light of the rise of the Eurosceptic populist UKIP party, in 2013, UK's Premier Minister David Cameron announced his intention to renegotiate the terms of the British EU membership and then present the sealed deal to the voters. For the Europeanists, especially for Germany, anticipation of a British negotiation of a retreat from an "ever-closer Union," as stated in the preamble to the Treaties, was an opportunity to ask the United Kingdom to give way to further integration in European defense. Reportedly, German Chancellor Angela Merkel tried to tie the envisaged exemptions in the realms of migration, financial and fiscal policy, and budgetary contributions to a British defense opt-out to overcome its resistance (*The Telegraph*, 2011). This could either follow the Danish precedent, a general defense opt-out, or amount solely to non-participation in PESCO. When the final deal between the EU-27 and the United Kingdom was crafted, however, no such conditionality was included in the final European Council conclusions. Instead, the conclusions merely "recalled" that the "Treaties ... contain also specific provisions whereby some Member States are entitled not to take part in or are exempted from the … decisions having defence implications" (European Council, 2016, p. 9). Yet why could the Europeanists not achieve a tit-for-tat with Britain? The reason lies in the Atlanticist alliance, which moved even closer together after experiencing deteriorating relations with Russia. In 2014 the Russian Federation unlawfully annexed the Ukrainian Crimea, a move that startled the EU's Eastern member states. The first reaction of the Baltic States and Poland, EU member states sharing a border with Russia, was not to strengthen the EU's CSDP. Rather, the four states eagerly called for the stationing of additional NATO troops on their territory (*The Telegraph*, 2014). While NATO was cautious in stationing permanent troops on the Russian border, the United Kingdom was at the forefront of deploying soldiers, materiel for military exercises, and air policing in the border areas (NATO, 2014; UK Foreign and Commonwealth Office & UK Ministry of Defence, 2014). Moreover, hosting the 2014 NATO summit in Cardiff, the United Kingdom was in a good position to renew the Atlanticist coalition across the EU member states by backing NATO's Eastern members. Prime Minister Cameron wrote in a letter to all NATO member states,

> We should agree how we can sustain a robust presence in Eastern Europe, consistent with the NATO Russia Founding Act, to make clear to Russia that neither NATO nor its members will be intimidated. (Cameron, 2014)

This strategy seems to have been successful. In December 2015, with the European Council to negotiate the EU–UK deal drawing closer, Polish Foreign Minister Waszczykowski declared that Poland would consider supporting the UK position if the latter were willing to further strengthen its military presence on NATO's Eastern flank: "Britain could offer something to Poland in terms of international security" (Reuters, 2016a). Three weeks later, the United Kingdom confirmed it would send around 1,000 personnel to NATO exercises taking place in Poland (UK Ministry of Defence, 2016). On 5 February 2016, two weeks before the European Council meeting, Prime Minister Cameron visited Poland and, together with his Polish counterpart, Beata Szydlo, announced the beginning of a new "strategic partnership" (*The Guardian*, 2016a). Cameron stated that the United Kingdom and Poland "want to make sure that [the] two countries' cooperation is as close as possible. We want to see a full strategic partnership in the EU and in NATO ... to secure NATO's eastern flank" (EUobserver, 2016a).

Thus, the Atlanticist coalition was stable, and fragmentation persisted. A new distribution of authority was unfeasible as long as the group of reluctant states could still count on the United Kingdom and NATO, which, despite an increasingly threatening security situation from the East, continued to impede any Europeanist initiatives to establish PESCO.

Leaving Them Alone—The Atlanticist Coalition After Brexit

This changed rapidly after 23 June 2016, the day of the British referendum, which some see as the "date for the (re)birth of European defence" (Mauro & Santopinto, 2017, p. 11). However, when Britain voted to leave the European Union, this had no direct influence on the preferences of the group of reluctant states. They retained an exclusive membership preference and could still rely on their NATO-backed regional cooperation frameworks. Yet, as I will show, Brexit did have an important effect. The loss of the United Kingdom implied a weakening of the Atlanticist coalition and undermined their ability to block attempts to activate PESCO. The bargaining power of the Europeanists relative to the Atlanticists increased. The former were still unable to go it alone without the support of at least some of the reluctant Atlanticists. Thus, Brexit made PESCO's resilience more likely, but, in light of the reluctant states' exclusive membership preference, it was not yet sufficient to allow the Europeanists to refocus their preferred venue.

The prospect of the United Kingdom leaving the European Union changed the power balance between Atlanticists and Europeanists. The EU member states could activate PESCO by QMV, and thus would be able to do so when 55% of the member states representing 65% of the population voted for it (European Union, 2010, Art. 16). While a successful vote required a minimum of 15 member states even after Brexit (the Europeanist coalition consisted of seven states), British non-participation nonetheless increased the requirements to block a proposal. As the United Kingdom accounted for nearly 13% of the EU's total population, it would have been able to form a blocking minority with eight other reluctant states. After the Brexit vote, eleven Atlanticists would need to stand firmly together to block the establishment of PESCO (Consilium, 2018). Even more importantly, the United Kingdom served as the protective power of the Atlanticists in decision-making on European defense, due both to its military capabilities and its relative importance as the third largest net contributor to the EU's budget (European Commission, 2017a). Without the United Kingdom, blocking PESCO against the wishes of the powerful Europeanists was likely to have negative consequences in terms of linking defense to budgetary negotiations. Hence, the Brexit vote had considerable repercussions for the Atlanticists with respect to their ability to prevent further defense integration.

Nevertheless, the Atlanticists' unwillingness to activate PESCO remained unaffected. When the EU High Representative, Federica Mogherini, who was tasked with presenting the EU's new Global Strategy, mentioned in June 2016 that the EU's CSDP should be developed "making full use of the Lisbon Treaty's potential" (EEAS, 2016, p. 11), and thus indirectly pointed to the potential benefits of PESCO in the post-Brexit era, this set alarm bells ringing in the reluctant states. In anticipation of the PESCO debate re-emerging, the V4 heads of government issued a joint statement in July 2016, warning that

> [o]ne of the worst conclusions that Member States may draw from Brexit is dividing the EU in small clubs. This could fuel the fragmentation of the EU. ... To prevent possible fragmentation the EU needs to refocus on proposals with tangible benefits for our citizens where agreement can be reached, while refraining from wasting energy on proposals that divide Member States. (V4, 2016, p. 1)

While this statement seems almost cynical in light of the ongoing fragmentation of European defense cooperation, it clarifies the reluctant states' position of continuing to stand together to prevent PESCO from happening.

Unimpressed, the avant-gardists nevertheless tried to climb through the window of opportunity created by Brexit for the first time only a few weeks later. Published on 12 September 2016, a German–French non-paper specifically drew a connection between the United Kingdom leaving the Union and the opportunity to establish PESCO:

> On the basis of the UK's decision to leave the European Union, it is now our goal to move forward at 27. We suggest the development of a precise roadmap for the renewal of a transparent and integrative CSDP of the

27 – open to all member states. ... Participation in PESCO is voluntary, inclusive, and open to all EU members. Once decided, clear goals and standards and a binding commitment will be created. Therefore, PESCO can enable real progress in CSDP. (Germany & France, 2016, p. 2, author's translation)

Four days after the Franco-German non-paper had been circulated, the European heads of state and government, except for the United Kingdom, held an informal meeting in Bratislava, which was perceived as a summit to "set an agenda for the coming months," according to Angela Merkel (Politico, 2016a). In light of the divergent views on how to realize further defense cooperation, reactions to the Franco-German proposal on the activation of PESCO were cautious. The final Bratislava document only vaguely suggested that the upcoming December European Council should "decide ... on how to make better use of the options in the Treaties, especially as regards capabilities" (EU27, 2016).

Thus, there was no direct reference to PESCO yet again. While the avant-gardists applauded the prospect of moving forward in defense cooperation, most notably Italy, which voiced demands for a "Schengen for Defence" (Politico, 2016b), the Atlanticist coalition remained skeptical. After the Bratislava summit, the V4 heads of government stated that they welcomed enhanced practical CSDP cooperation in general but were wary of duplications with NATO (V4, 2016). Similarly, the Baltic States made clear that they would not accept any EU military structures as the Baltics "cannot afford to overlap NATO" (*The Baltic Times*, 2016).

The Baltic States and Poland, as well as neutral states such as Sweden and Austria, feared that the French, German, and Italian proposals were working toward the establishment of the EU's strategic autonomy from NATO. Especially the proposal for a permanent EU military headquarters (Germany & France, 2016, p. 2), which was interpreted as a step toward a European army, was strongly opposed (*The Times*, 2016). Thus, even though the Brexit vote, reshuffling the power constellation between Atlanticists and Europeanists, opened a window of opportunity for the Europeanists to refocus on PESCO, the preferences of the two coalitions remained stable.

Confronted with weakened but continuing resistance, the avant-gardists could not yet agree on the best strategy to convince at least the four Atlanticist states necessary to allow for the activation of PESCO[2] France and Germany largely disagreed on the level of ambition that should be pursued: whether they should try to cooperate in an exclusive circle, asking only for the Atlanticists' approval, or rather try to design PESCO to be as inclusive as possible. Consequently, the Franco-German non-paper did not include any reference to the criteria and commitments which member states would have to fulfill to join the framework. In principle open to every willing member state, "willingness" would depend on the ambition of the entry criteria and thus on how the five commitments stated in Article 2 of the Protocol on PESCO were operationalized.[3]

While the French vision of PESCO had always been one of an exclusive and ambitious circle of the most capable member states—French president Hollande stated that he was "in favor of a differentiated Europe" (Hollande, 2016, *author's translation*), the German position was more cautious. Germany shared the French view that the Brexit vote constituted a window of opportunity to further defense integration. Yet Brexit also demonstrated the fragility of the European project. Consequently, immediately after the Brexit vote, the then German Chancellor Angela Merkel warned of new fractions between EU member states and emphasized the necessity to move ahead "together," which "means always: all 27—the Euro-states together with the non-Euro-states, the small countries with the larger, the old member states with the newer" (Deutscher Bundestag, 2016, *author's translation*). In relation to PESCO, Merkel stated that differentiated integration had to be "inviting not exclusive" (Deutscher Bundestag, 2017a). Thus, while Germany was "generally open to multiple speeds, it is keen to avoid new dividing lines along the boundaries of a Euro defence core" (Koenig & Walter-Franke, 2017, p. 12; Interview #1).

These disagreements on the membership preference within the Europeanist coalition provided additional—albeit indirect—evidence that the window of opportunity was not open wide enough yet. As long as there

---

[2] Importantly, formally voting for the activation of PESCO in the Council did not imply participation.

[3] Art. 2 of Protocol No. 10 annexed to the Lisbon Treaty asked the participants in PESCO to strive to achieve a higher level of defense investment expenditure, convergence with respect to their defense apparatus, improved availability, interoperability, flexibility and deployability of forces, making good on capability shortfalls (without prejudice to NATO), and appropriate participation in major joint or European equipment programs.

was no hope that the avant-gardists could motivate enough member states to either participate in or at least tolerate PESCO, finding a common position proved difficult. While France's strategy was confrontational, trying to create a threat of exclusion for the Atlanticists to achieve PESCO's focality, the German route was directed at accommodating the fear of being economically sidelined affecting both the federalist and the reluctant states. In September 2016 it was still unforeseeable whether and which of these two options would be successful. Indeed, the theoretical expectation would be that, all things being equal, and in view of the reluctant states' preference for exclusive and regional defense cooperation, neither would succeed. As the Atlanticists did not possess go-it-alone power and the ability to create a credible threat of exclusion even before Brexit, a further weakening of these coalitions alone, given their persistent preference for exclusive membership, would not have led to an outcome in which PESCO proved resilient.

THE EUROPEANIST TRUMP CARD—A NEW NEED FOR EUROPEAN DEFENSE

However, all things did not remain equal. On 8 November 2016, Donald Trump was elected President of the United States. This section demonstrates that this election was a shock for NATO's credibility as a security provider in Europe and thus altered the ratio between the transaction cost of non-cooperation and the member surplus as far as the reluctant states were concerned. As a result, their membership preference changed from exclusive to inclusive. The states on the EU's eastern border in particular felt a new need for European security and defense cooperation. This development widened the avant-gardists' room for maneuver and allowed them to find a consensus between PESCO's ambition and inclusiveness, since they would no longer need to offer excessive concessions to convince the reluctant states to join.

Having declared during his election campaign that he held NATO to be "obsolete," outdated in its focus on Russia, and not prepared to tackle the right problems (*The New York Times*, 2016), Donald Trump's election drastically increased uncertainty for the states on Europe's eastern flank. What was even more serious, Trump openly questioned the absolute character of the NATO solidarity clause, "They say: 'What would happen if Russia or somebody attacks?' I said: 'I don't know; have they paid?'" (The Guardian, 2016b). Without an unconditional US commitment to support future operations, however, the credibility of the Atlanticist EU member states' regional cooperation frameworks decreased considerably. Exclusive minilateral cooperation was no longer attractive as the transaction costs of European non-cooperation increased for the Atlanticists.

The V4, the CEDC, and Baltic Defence Cooperation had no plan B to make sure that adequate military capabilities would be generated, present, and deployable on the European continent. Consequently, the first reactions to Trump's electoral victory were anxious and reflected the fear that NATO would no longer operate as a shield against the Russian Federation. Ojars Eriks Kalnis, then chair of the Latvian parliament's foreign affairs committee, stated that, as Trump was "the first presidential candidate to question Nato and Nato commitments ... we are facing a great deal of uncertainty. For Latvia, for Europe, we have no idea what to expect in terms of foreign policy" (*The Financial Times*, 2016). In a similar vein, Lithuanian Foreign Minister Linas Linkevicius thought it important that the United States should not "repeat the mistakes of the past" (Spiegel Online, 2016), that is, neglect developments on Europe's eastern border. What is more, the representatives from the V4 and Baltic Defence Cooperation even feared that Trump "could hit upon the idea of bringing about a bipolar world again, and in that world we are merely a playing card" (Spiegel Online, 2016). Sandra Kalniete, a Latvian Member of the European Parliament, sums up the perspective of the reluctant states when stating that, through Brexit and Trump, "the two pillars of our security are weakened" (*The Financial Times*, 2016).

Even for NORDEFCO, whose EU members Finland and Sweden were not aligned with NATO, the combination of Brexit and Trump's election created a feeling of insecurity and an impetus to turn their gaze toward the CSDP. Swedish Foreign minister Margot Wallstrom, referencing Trump's comments on NATO, said, "Clearly it is a message for all of us to see how we can increase and improve our coordination" (Reuters, 2016b). Thus, as the two external shocks made exclusive regional cooperation unsustainable, the Atlanticist states shifted their focus to the CSDP while simultaneously trying to convince the United States to ensure "credible deterrence by continuing persistent presence of the United States' forces and pre-positioning" (Reuters, 2016c) in light of the perceived incalculable Russian threat (*BBC News*, 2016).

As inconvenient and insecure as the outlook for NATO cooperation was in November 2016, the avant-gardists were presented with a unique opportunity to try to convince the Atlanticist states to move on with PESCO. Moreover, as NATO no longer served as a security backup, the avant-gardists could hope to overcome the skepticism concerning PESCO's negative consequences for the downstream states. The avant-gardists were well aware of the Atlanticists' fears. Then German Foreign minister Frank-Walter Steinmeier confirmed, "I know from numerous conversations with our European neighbors how irritated they are with these dismissive remarks about NATO and NATO partners" (Time.com, 2016). The then German Defense Minister Ursula von der Leyen was even more straightforward, stating:

> Europe needs common political will for more security policy relevance. The outcome of the election in America could provide an additional impetus. … The Brexit decision and the election in the United States have set a new course. (EUobserver, 2016b)

The combination of Brexit, which weakened the Atlanticist coalition considerably by removing the most powerful opponent of European defense integration, and the election of Donald Trump decreased the credibility of the regional institutional alternatives to PESCO beyond the European Union framework and prompted the Atlanticist challenger coalition to give up its general resistance to PESCO. Indeed, barely one week after Trump's election, the EU's defense ministers explicitly referred to PESCO in an official document for the first time since the inauguration of the Lisbon Treaty. This reference is interesting beyond evidencing a shift of attention toward the CSDP and the window of opportunity this presented for PESCO. It bears witness to the emergence of a compromise between French ambition and the German preference for inclusiveness. On 14 November 2016, the Foreign Affairs Council agreed,

> to also explore the potential of an inclusive Permanent Structured Cooperation (PESCO), including a modular approach as regards concrete projects and initiatives, subject to the willingness of Member States to undertake concrete commitments. It invites the High Representative to provide elements and options for further reflection as soon as possible. (Council of the European Union, 2016, para. 17)

The principles of having an "inclusive" framework with a "modular approach" were not part of the original provisions in the Treaty Protocol (De France et al., 2017, p. 5) and represented an innovation implying a two-tier governance of PESCO. This would make possible a number of ambitious projects within the framework in which not all PESCO members would have to take part, thus accommodating the French vision. With the general criteria for participation set to allow every willing member state to take part in PESCO, the proposal also took account of the German fear of further divisions. No state would be excluded for lacking capacity. In other words, two-tier governance was an attempt to accommodate the inconsistent membership preferences of PESCO's main proponents. Allowing states with marginal military and defense-industrial capabilities to join the overall framework while still intending to move forward with more ambitious projects in smaller groups resembled the institutional set-up of the EDA as discussed in Chapters 5 and 6.

Despite this compromise, however, the Council was unable to agree on a clear deadline for the HR to operationalize the proposed modular two-tier PESCO. The downstream states, both federalist and reluctant, would only accept PESCO's focality for European defense cooperation if the avant-gardists were able to create a credible threat of exclusion themselves. This incremental process was fully in line with the theoretical concept of go-it-alone power: Only when the first downstream states signaled their intention to participate and made PESCO's functioning realistic did the bandwagoning effect start and the others follow, as staying outside an activated PESCO would have been worse.

PESCO's Resilience—Awakened by the Bandwagon

This section demonstrates that, in the absence of the United Kingdom and in view of decreased NATO credibility, the reluctant states were no longer able to resist the activation of PESCO (see, Biermann, 2022). As the reluctant had changed their membership preference from exclusive to inclusive, the avant-gardists were now in a position to go it alone themselves and dictate the terms of cooperation. Confronted with pressure from the avant-gardists, the reluctant states signaled their willingness not only to allow PESCO but also to participate in it against their original preferences. This process followed the "bandwagoning dynamic" (Gruber, 2000, p. 47) as theorized in Chapter 3—with many additional states intending to participate in PESCO and thus leave the Atlanticist coalition, staying outside PESCO became costlier for the outsiders. In the end, 25 out of the 27 remaining EU member states signed up for PESCO and agreed to make it the focal institution in European defense planning. Though PESCO's membership overlapped with the various regional frameworks, the bulk of resources was transferred to the former, and projects originally conducted in regional frameworks were now continued within the PESCO framework.

The next formal stage in the process of activating PESCO, which was initiated in November 2016, was the Foreign Affairs Council meeting on 6 March 2017. In the run-up to the meeting, the reluctant states voiced their concerns that the avant-gardists might try to create a European defense core among themselves. They feared that this move would lead to their exclusion. In an attempt to discourage an ambitious and exclusive PESCO of this kind, Jaroslaw Kaczyński, the head of Poland's ruling PiS party cautioned that it would lead to the "breakdown, and in fact the liquidation, of the European Union in its current sense" (*The Guardian*, 2017). In a similar vein, the heads of government of the V4 issued a joint statement on 2 March 2017 "The EU's unity is of vital importance and should always be the starting point of our approach. Reaching consensus is indispensable" (V4, 2017a). These pre-emptive warnings are comprehensible in light of the Treaty provisions regarding PESCO. Article 46(3) of the Treaty on European Union called for a qualified majority of the *already participating member states* for a new member to be admitted to the club. Participation from the outset was thus important for every potentially interested state.

The reluctant states' fears were well-grounded. Aware of the window of opportunity and the weakened state of the Atlanticist coalition, the avant-gardists engaged in active lobbying and explicitly tried to set up a threat of exclusion to realize PESCO. On 6 March, the day of the Council meeting, the heads of state and government of Germany, France, Italy, and Spain met at Versailles for a mini-summit. At this venue, then French President François Hollande countered the V4 statement by clarifying, "Unity is not uniformity" (Deutsche Welle, 2017). German Chancellor Angela Merkel made the point even more explicitly: "A multispeed Europe is necessary; otherwise we are blocked. ... We must have the courage to accept that some countries can move forward a little more quickly than others" (Deutsche Welle, 2017). The avant-gardists put enough pressure on the reluctant states by voicing these threats of exclusion that the Council "agree[d] on the need to continue work on an inclusive Permanent Structured Cooperation (PESCO) based on a modular approach" (General Secretariat of the Council, 2017, para. 6).

While no *fait accompli* was created in the Council (which was not in the interest of Germany either, which preferred as inclusive a PESCO as possible), the Versailles summit was perceived as voicing threats of exclusion, reaping negative reactions from the reluctant states. "The Versailles summit does not look so good if you come from one of the small member states," György Schöpflin, Hungarian Member of the European Parliament, stated (Euractiv, 2017). Bulgaria's then Deputy Prime Minister Denitsa Zlateva, reporting the attitude of Bulgaria, Romania, and Croatia, explained why: "We declare ourselves against the creation of the so-called core of Europe and the rest, the periphery" (Balkan Insight, 2017). Petr Drulak, the Czech Republic's ambassador to France, expressed a more nuanced perspective on the Versailles Group's statement. He deemed it "important for countries to have informal debates … [b]ut any initiatives that come out of them must be open and other member states must be able to influence them" (Euractiv, 2017). The Estonian ambassador to France, Alar Streimann, also seconded this perspective and recalled that Estonia had "always wanted a united Europe" (Euractiv, 2017). This collection of perspectives clearly demonstrates that the threat of exclusion created by the avant-gardists took effect. The fear of being sidelined led the reluctant states to consider their participation in PESCO against their original preferences for regional cooperation. While not having PESCO at all was their preferred outcome, this was no longer a viable option in light of the external shocks. Therefore, being a member of a less ambitious PESCO was better than being excluded from defense cooperation altogether.

This calculus became even more acute when Estonia, which was to hold the Council presidency in the second half of 2017, became the first of the reluctant states to back PESCO publicly. On 3 May 2017, Prime Minister Jüri Ratas made public that "Estonia today decided that should PESCO materialize, Estonia definitely wishes to be a part of that cooperation" (ERR News, 2017). In addition, the avant-gardists further increased the pressure when the four heads of state and government reiterated their case for a multispeed Europe, in which "some countries will go faster than others" (Merkel) and "different levels of integration" (Gentiloni) should be allowed (Politico, 2017a), only about two weeks before the next scheduled Council meeting on 23 June 2017.

Considering the crumbling of Atlanticist resistance and the maintenance of the threat of exclusion, it is no surprise that the formal process in the Council reached its preliminary peak in June. After "exploring" in November and "continuing the work" in March, the Council now

> agree[d] on the need to launch an inclusive and ambitious Permanent Structured Cooperation (PESCO). A common list of criteria and binding commitments … will be drawn up by Member States within three months, with a precise timetable and specific assessment mechanisms, in order to enable Member States which are in a position to do so to notify their intentions to participate without delay. (European Council, 2017)

While this was a breakthrough regarding PESCO's activation, it was still unclear how many states would finally participate in the framework. This question crucially depended on the specific entry criteria and commitments. As the theorized pathway predicts, the avant-gardists, especially Germany and France, remained firmly in the driver's seat in setting the terms of cooperation through PESCO. On 13 July 2017, the two states came up with a proposal for the operationalization of the criteria and commitments (Conseil franco-allemand de défense et de sécurité, 2017), which was backed by Italy and Spain and—most notably—Belgium, the Czech Republic, Finland, and the Netherlands only one week later (France, Germany, Spain, & Italy, 2017). As one observer stated, "this group represents different geographical … profiles, as well as NATO and non-NATO member states" (Billon-Galland, & Quencez, 2017, p. 3). Even more strikingly, from the perspective of the theorized pathway, there was one representative from the group of the federalists (Belgium), one from NORDEFCO (Finland), one from the Visegràd Group and the CEDC (Czech Republic), as well as one of the states with the strongest Atlanticist orientation, the Netherlands. This constellation had a dual function: First, it was a test of how far the commitments agreed on were acceptable for member states with different strategic cultures and foreign policy priorities, while second, it sent a message to the other member states organized in regional cooperation. Signaling the further crumbling of resistance, the reluctant states' risk of being excluded increased. Every further member state joining PESCO made it costlier for others to stay outside. The bandwagon had been jumpstarted, thus fueling the rush of joining member states (Interview #2).

The veritable cascade of states signaling their willingness to join PESCO was certainly encouraged by the inclusive nature of the agreed criteria and commitments. Germany's inclusive membership preference had gained acceptance among the avant-gardists. The commitments described in the proposal were deliberately vague. Provisions did not, for instance, specify the date by which the few quantified commitments, namely the 2% defense-spending goal and defense investment expenditure of 20% of total defense spending (France et al., 2017, Art. III (1, 4)) were to be reached. Instead, the provisions left the decision to the member states' discretion, emphasizing the "voluntary nature" (Art. III (8)) of most commitments. With the "binding" commitments being not so binding after all and in view of the threat of being left behind, one after the other, the reluctant states thus decided to participate.

A few days after the communication of the proposed criteria, Sweden (Altinget, 2017), Bulgaria, Hungary, and Latvia signaled their readiness to join PESCO (Mauro & Santopinto, 2017, 46, 48, 50). Greece, together with Finland, Belgium, Italy, and Germany, even proposed that concrete projects be conducted under the PESCO umbrella (Deutscher Bundestag, 2017b). Luxembourg published its intention to join in July (Ministère des Affaires étrangères et européennes de Luxembourg, 2017). After that, it took only a few more weeks, until 7 September 2017, for the next two EU member states, Slovakia and Austria, to declare their intention to join PESCO (Die Presse, 2017; Permanent Representation of the Slovak Republic to the EU, 2017). Lithuania followed suit one day later (Ministry of National Defence Republic of Lithuania, 2017). The PESCO bandwagon continued with Romania and Croatia declaring their interest in joining on 17 October 2017 (Business Review, 2017; Jutarnji List, 2017) and Cyprus and Slovenia on 8 and 10 November 2017, respectively (Cyprus Mail, 2017; Vidmajer, 2017).

While this cascade is evidence of the reluctant states' rationale for joining PESCO being primarily to prevent exclusion and against their original preferences, this becomes most obvious in the Polish case. Poland only decided to join the framework at the last minute, three days before the formal Council notification on 13 November 2017 (V4, 2017b). It did so very reluctantly, as it still had many doubts concerning the framework. Consequently, the Polish foreign and defense ministers Witold Waszczykowski and Antoni Macierewicz formally attached to their accession notification a letter to HR Mogherini. The letter raised three concerns; the unclear relationship between PESCO and NATO, the fear that capability specialization would mean a loss of independence for some member states, and the risk of neglecting the eastern flank (Waszczykowski & Macierewicz, personal communication, November 17,

2017). Yet, as advised by a Polish foreign policy think tank, the need to avoid a "defence core" which would likely leave "countries such as Poland on the margins of defence industry cooperation in Europe" (Terlikowski, 2016) was stronger. Joining PESCO was the second-best option as it allowed for some control over the shape of the framework, whereas not taking part meant assuming a bystander position. The first best option, the "legal and political *status quo* ... to allow states to deploy legal loopholes in EU law to continue using offsets as tools of national security, industrial, and innovation policies" (Terlikowski, 2016) had been erased from the set of feasible alternatives.

Thus, on 13 November 2017, 23 member states[4] notified the Council of their intention to establish PESCO (PESCO Member States, 2017). The wording of the notification was almost congruent with the July proposal by France, Germany, Spain, and Italy (France et al., 2017). Except for one article referring to cooperation in the realm of cyber defense (PESCO Member States, 2017, Art. II (11)), no substantial changes had been made, and both Atlanticists and federalists accepted the avant-gardist terms of the agreement. On 11 December 2017, the Council was supposed to take the final decision on the establishment of PESCO—four weeks, in which Portugal and Ireland once more attested the functioning of the theorized pathway.

Unlike those of most member states, the Portuguese and Irish governments had to deal with considerable domestic resistance to the PESCO plans—Ireland because of its deeply anchored neutrality (*The Irish Times*, 2018) and Portugal because the government had to rely on the opposition as the governing coalition comprised a left-wing party that categorically ruled out any further defense commitments (Politico, 2017b). Despite these hurdles, both governments decided to subscribe to PESCO. Irish Minister of State for Defense, Paul Kehoe, countered opposition concerns by reminding them that "Sweden and Austria, which have neutrality policies similar to ours, have already signed up to Pesco [sic]" (TheJournal.ie, 2017). Portuguese Foreign Minister Augusto Santos Silva emphasized that it was important for Portugal "to be part of PESCO, and from the start" (Politico, 2017b). Thus, confronted with the threat of exclusion, the respective governments were willing to confront considerable domestic resistance.

---

[4] The missing member states were the United Kingdom, Denmark, Portugal, Ireland, and Malta.

When the Council decided on the formal activation of PESCO, 25 member states thus participated (Council of the European Union, 2017, Art. 2). The exceptions were Denmark, for whom, due to its defense opt-out, PESCO was never a consideration, the United Kingdom, which was set on leaving the EU, and Malta, which was still undecided and took a "wait-and-see" approach considering joining at a later stage (*Malta Today*, 2017).

Confronted with two mutually reinforcing external shocks, the Atlanticist coalition fell apart, and regional cooperation was no longer attractive. Thus, the avant-gardist coalition was able to shift the focus back to PESCO and, by creating a credible threat of exclusion, incentivize even the most skeptical EU member states to join. The outcome was a situation where there was considerable membership overlap between PESCO and the various bi- and minilateral cooperation frameworks. PESCO's resilience to competitive regime creation and emergence as the focal institution is furthermore evident in the distribution of resources among the institutions in question. In March 2018, the Council agreed on a list of 17 projects to be conducted under PESCO (Council of the European Union, 2018) and added another 17 projects in November 2018 (Council Decision (CFSP) 2018/1797 of 19 November 2018 amending and updating Decision (CFSP) 2018/340 establishing the list of projects to be developed under PESCO, 2018). Examining the totality of the 34 PESCO projects and their participants (PESCO Member States, 2018); see also 8.1, two aspects attract special attention.

First, PESCO became the focal institution in cooperative defense planning as the member states transferred the bulk of their defense-planning resources from bi- and minilateral frameworks to it. Supported by the European Defense Fund and an annual budget of €5.5 billion (European Commission, 2017b) proposed by the European Commission to incentivize collaborative R&T projects under PESCO, groups of member states, which would previously have cooperated regionally and outside the European Union, now conduct their programs under PESCO. Examples such as the "Integrated Unmanned Ground System," which was proposed by Estonia, Latvia, and Finland (Defense News, 2018) or the "Cyber Rapid Response Teams and Mutual Assistance in Cyber Security," which was initiated by Lithuania, are evidence that member states have seized the opportunities provided by PESCO. In other words, the Atlanticists and the federalists have not only participated formally but have also actually transferred resources to PESCO, which previously would have been spent regionally. PESCO not only functions as an umbrella covering regionally structured cooperation. There is not one out of the 34 current projects whose membership is limited to the members of one of PESCO's institutional competitors (see Table 8.1). This implies that the dual members (i.e., reluctant states that are members both of PESCO and of a regional cooperation framework) have de facto accepted PESCO as the new center of relational authority, opening up new formats for cooperation beyond regional confines.

Second, not only were the avant-gardists able to make PESCO the focal institution for European defense cooperation, they also managed to dictate the terms of cooperation and exercise control over most of the projects. Germany, France, Italy, and Spain are the lead nations in 21 out of the total 34 PESCO projects (Table 8.1). However, like the Atlanticists, they not only cooperate among themselves in these projects but are able to attract resources from dual member states. The avant-gardists opened up projects that have minimal distributive consequences and thus a low member surplus, such as the Network of Logistic Hubs in Europe (13 participants), the Military Mobility Project (24), or the European Union Training Mission Competence Centre (14). At the same time, they kept membership minimal and exclusive for projects involving armaments cooperation with high monetary and defense-industrial implications, such as the MALE RPAS Eurodrone (5) or the Tiger Mark III helicopter (3). This, once again, is in line with the theoretical expectations. As the Atlanticists had unsuccessfully attempted to go it alone, the avant-gardists were now able to dictate the terms of cooperation, improving their utility in line with their membership preference.

Summary

A decade after its inclusion in the Treaty of Lisbon, PESCO finally emerged as the focal institution in European defense cooperation, thus paving the way for a European Defense Union. After it had been subject to considerable contestation from varying challenger coalitions consisting of different Atlanticist states, which created competing bi- and minilateral, mostly regional cooperation frameworks outside the EU, in December 2017, 25 out of 28 EU member states decided to participate in PESCO and to shift their financial and political capital to the new framework. I have demonstrated that PESCO's resilience in European defense cooperation was a result of two external shocks, Brexit and the election of

Table 8.1 PESCO-Projects, Lead nations (L), and Participants (P)[5]

Project:	AUT	BEL	BGR	CYP	CRO	CZE	EE	ESP	FIN	FRA	GER	GRE	HUN	IR	IT	LTU	LVA	LUX	NLD	POL	PRT	ROU	SI	SVK	SWE
European Medical Command															P				P			P		P	P
European Secure Software-defined Radio		P						P	L	P					P			P	P						
Network of logistic Hubs in Europe and support to Operations		P		P	P	P		P			L	P	P		P				P				P	P	
Military Mobility	P	P		P	P	P	P	P	P	P	P	P	P	P	P	P	P	L	P	P	P	P	P	P	P
European Union Training Mission Competence Centre	P	P						P	L	P					P				P			P		P	P
European Training Certification Centre for European Armies															P						L				
Energy Operational Function		P						P	L	P					P										

(continued)

[5] Cf. PESCO Member States (2018), see also https://pesco.europa.eu.

Table 8.1 (continued)

Project:	AUT	BEL	BGR	CYP	CRO	CZE	EE	ESP	FIN	FRA	GER	GRE	HUN	IR	IT	LITU	LVA	LUX	NLD	POL	PRT	ROU	SI	SVK	SWE
Deployable Military Disaster Relief Capability Package	P			P		P			P						P L						P				
Maritime (Semi-) Autonomous Systems for Mine Countermeasures		L									P				P P				P		P P				
Harbour & Maritime Surveillance and Protection											P				P L										P
Upgrade of Maritime Surveillance			P P	P				P			L				P P										
Cyber Threats and Incident Response Information Sharing Platform	P			P		P			L P		L P				P P P						P				
Cyber Rapid Response Teams and Mutual Assist. in Cyber Security					P		P P P									L			P						P

Project:	AUT	BEL	BGR	CYP	CRO	CZE	EE	ESP	FIN	FRA	GER	GRE	HUN	IR	IT	LTU	LVA	LUX	NLD	POL	PRT	ROU	SI	SVK	SWE
Strategic Command and Control System								L		P					P					P					
Armoured Infantry Fighting Vehicle												P			L										P
Indirect Fire Support																									L
EUFOR Crisis Response Operation Core		P						P		P L					P										
Joint EU Intelligence School		P										L			P										
EU Test and Evaluation Centres								P		L															P L
Helicopter Hot and High Training												L			P					P					
Integrated Unmanned Ground System	P					P L	P P		P					P			P			P P					
EU Beyond Line of Sight Land Battlefield Missile System		P						L																	

(continued)

Table 8.1 (continued)

Project:	AUT	BEL	BGR	CYP	CRO	CZE	EE	ESP	FIN	FRA	GER	GRE	HUN	IR	IT	LTU	LVA	LUX	NLD	POL	PRT	ROU	SI	SVK	SWE
Deployable Modular Underwater Intervention Capability Package		L							P		P														
MALE RPAS						P	P		P	L	P				P										
European Arrack Helicopters						P			L	P															
TIGER Mark III																									
Counter Unmanned Aerial System						P					P					L									
European High Atmosphere Airship Platform											L					L									
Command Post (CP) for Small Joint Operations for SJO				P								L													
Electronic Warfare Capability and Interoperability Programme						L							P												
Co-basing		P				P	P		L	P								P							

Project:	AUT	BEL	BGR	CYP	CRO	CZE	EE	ESP	FIN	FRA	GER	GRE	HUN	IR	IT	LTU	LVA	LUX	NLD	POL	PRT	ROU	SI	SVK	SWE
Geo-meteorological and Oceanographic Support											P									P					
Chemical, Biological, Radiological and Nuclear Surveillance	L			P						P					P							P			
EU Radio Navigation Solution	P							P			L	P			P										
European Military Space Surveillance Awareness Network											P				L										
Total Project Participations	5	10	4	9	6	8	3	16	4	17	14	13	5	7	22	2	2	2	9	3	9	7	6	3	4
Total Serving as Leadnation	1	1	1	0	0	1	1	1	0	7	6	5	0	0	7	1	0	0	1	0	0	0	1	0	1

Donald Trump, which influenced the two key conditions, the power to go it alone and the membership preference.

The UK's decision to leave the European Union distorted the balance of power that had emerged between the Europeanist proponents and Atlanticist opponents of PESCO. Blocking PESCO became increasingly difficult for the remaining Atlanticists, since their veto power was undermined. The election of Donald Trump represented the turnaround point away from fragmentation and toward PESCO's resilience. As NATO's credibility suffered considerably, the reluctant states could no longer rely on their exclusive regional cooperation frameworks. Without credible NATO guarantees, their focus shifted to Europe as their membership preference changed from exclusive to inclusive.

This situation opened the window of opportunity the avant-gardists had been waiting for. Actively lobbying, creating a threat of exclusion, and proposing to move ahead by establishing a European defense core, the avant-gardists were able to push the Atlanticists to not only allow but also to participate in PESCO. While the avant-gardists could have set more ambitious entry criteria, they refrained from doing so as Germany especially demonstrated a preference for inclusive membership fearing further divisions would lead to the EU drifting apart. Consequently, a cascade of Atlanticist states decided to accept PESCO's role as the focal institution in the complex. They did so against their original preferences as they lacked alternatives. Blocking PESCO was no longer an available option, and staying outside would have been even worse for their defense industry and military capabilities than becoming a member of an institution they had previously rejected.

This resulted in the formal activation of PESCO with 25 members in December 2017 and the decision to conduct a total of 34 projects within the framework between March and November 2018. Thus, the EU member states participating in PESCO, both single and dual members, shifted the bulk of their resources to the framework while neglecting PESCO's institutional competitors. This made PESCO the center of authority in European defense planning. With a great deal of help from both sides of the Atlantic, one decade after its codification, PESCO proved resilient to contestation.

REFERENCES

Altinget. (2017, June 23). Sverige går med i europeiskt försvarssamarbete. https://www.altinget.se/sakerhet/artikel/sverige-gaar-med-i-europeiskt-forsvarssamarbete

Balkan Insight. (2017, March 2). Balkan EU States Reject a 'Multi-Speed' Union. http://www.balkaninsight.com/en/article/balkan-member-states-reject-a-multi-speed-eu-03-02-2017

BBC News. (2016, November 18). Baltic warning of Russian test for Nato. https://www.bbc.com/news/world-europe-38014997

Biermann, F. (2022). The differentiation paradox of European Integration: Why going it alone produces suboptimal results. *JCMS: Journal of Common Market Studies*, Early view. https://doi.org/10.1111/jcms.13373

Billon-Galland, Alice, & Quencez, M. (2017). *Can France and Germany make PESCO work as a process toward EU defence* (Security and Defense Policy Program - Policy Brief No. 33). Washington DC.

Business Review. (2017, October 17). Romania to join EU's defence initiative PESCO. http://business-review.eu/news/romania-to-join-eus-defence-initiative-pesco-150010

Cameron, D. (2014, August 2). PM writes to NATO leaders ahead of NATO Summit Wales 2014. https://www.gov.uk/government/news/pm-writes-to-nato-leaders-ahead-of-nato-summit-wales-2014

Colgan, J. D., Keohane, R. O., & van de Graaf, T. (2012). Punctuated equilibrium in the energy regime complex. *The Review of International Organizations*, 7(2), 117–143. https://doi.org/10.1007/s11558-011-9130-9

Conseil franco-allemand de défense et de sécurité. (2017, July 13). Relevé de Conclusions. https://www.france-allemagne.fr/IMG/pdf/fiche-cfads.pdf

Consilium. (2018). Voting calculator. http://www.consilium.europa.eu/en/council-eu/voting-system/voting-calculator/

Council Decision (CFSP) 2018/1797 of 19 November 2018 amending and updating Decision (CFSP) 2018/340 establishing the list of projects to be developed under PESCO, *Official Journal of the European Union* (2018).

Council of the European Union. (2016). *Council conclusions on implementing the EU Global Strategy in the area of Security and Defence* (No. 14149/16). http://www.consilium.europa.eu/media/22459/eugs-conclusions-st14149en16.pdf

Council of the European Union. (2017, December 11). *Defence cooperation: Council establishes Permanent Structured Cooperation (PESCO), with 25 member states participating*. Press release 765/17 [Press release]. http://www.consilium.europa.eu/en/press/press-releases/2017/12/11/defence-cooperation-pesco-25-member-states-participating/

Council of the European Union. (2018). *Council Decision establishing the list of projects to be developed under PESCO* (Legislative Acts and other Instruments No. 6393/18). http://data.consilium.europa.eu/doc/document/ST-6393-2018-INIT/en/pdf

Cyprus Mail. (2017, November 8). Cyprus move a step closer to being part of an integrated European defence policy. https://cyprus-mail.com/2017/11/08/cyprus-move-step-closer-part-integrated-european-defence-policy/

De France, O., Major, C., & Sartori Paola. (2017). *How to make PESCO a Success?* (Policy paper No. 21). Armament Industry European Research Group (ARES) website: http://www.iris-france.org/wp-content/uploads/2017/09/Ares-21-Policy-Paper-Sept-2017.pdf

Defense News. (2018, August 2). These Baltic nations could build Europe's next ground drone. https://www.defensenews.com/global/europe/2018/08/02/these-baltic-nations-could-build-europes-next-ground-drone/

Deutsche Welle. (2017, March 6). Merkel backs idea of 'multispeed Europe' at Versailles meet. https://www.dw.com/en/merkel-backs-idea-of-multispeed-europe-at-versailles-meet/a-37833273

Deutscher Bundestag. (2016, June 28). *Protocol Session 181, 18.* Legislature: Government Statement by Dr. Angela Merkel. https://dip.bundestag.de/plenarprotokoll/protokoll-der-181-sitzung-des-18-deutschen-bundestages/827

Deutscher Bundestag. (2017a, March 9). *Protocol Session 221, 18.* Legislature: Government Statement by Dr. Angela Merkel. https://dserver.bundestag.de/btp/18/18221.pdf

Deutscher Bundestag. (2017b). *Sachstand: Aktuelle Fortschritte bei der europäischen Zusammenarbeit in ausgewählten Bereichen der Sicherheits- und Verteidigungspolitik* (No. WD 2–3000–069/17). Berlin. https://www.bundestag.de/resource/blob/525944/69cccfc49df56f4bf594e1d90b6c2760/WD-2-069-17-pdf-data.pdf

Die Presse. (2017, September 7). Doskozil: Österreich beteiligt sich an EU-Militärzusammenarbeit. https://diepresse.com/home/ausland/eu/5281471/Doskozil_Oesterreich-beteiligt-sich-an-EUMilitaerzusammenarbeit

EEAS. (2016). *Shared vision, common action: A stronger Europe: A global strategy for the European Union's Foreign and Security Policy.* Brussels. European External Action Service (EEAS) website: https://eeas.europa.eu/sites/eeas/files/eugs_review_web_0.pdf

ERR News. (2017, May 3). Estonia joins EU defense cooperation initiative. https://news.err.ee/593552/estonia-joins-eu-defense-cooperation-initiative

EU 27. (2016). *The Bratislava Declaration.* Bratislava. The Bratislava Summit of 27 Member States website: http://www.consilium.europa.eu/media/21250/160916-bratislava-declaration-and-roadmapen16.pdf

EUobserver. (2016a, February 5). Poland 'satisfied' with UK demands in EU referendum talks. https://euobserver.com/political/132158

EUobserver. (2016b, November 11). Germany: Trump victory to spur EU military union. https://euobserver.com/foreign/135877
Euractiv. (2017, March 8). Two-speed Europe highlights East-West divide. https://www.euractiv.com/section/future-eu/news/two-speed-europe-hig hlights-east-west-divide/
European Commission. (2017a). EU expenditure and revenue 2014–2020. http://ec.europa.eu/budget/figures/interactive/index_en.cfm
European Commission. (2017b, June 7). A European Defence Fund: €5.5 billion per year to boost Europe's defence capabilities. http://europa.eu/rapid/press-release_IP-17-1508_en.htm
European Council. (2016). *European Council meeting (18 and 19 February 2016)—Conclusions* (No. EUCO 1/16). Brussels. http://www.consilium.eur opa.eu/media/21787/0216-euco-conclusions.pdf
European Council. (2017). *European Council meeting (22 and 23 June 2017)—Conclusions* (No. EUCO 8/17). http://www.consilium.europa.eu/en/press/press-releases/2017/06/23-euco-conclusions/
European Union. (2010). *Consolidated versions of the treaty on European Union and of the treaty on the functioning of the European Union: Charter of fundamental rights of the European Union*. Publications Office of the European Union. http://publications.europa.eu/de/publication-detail/-/publication/3c32722f-0136-4d8f-a03e-bfaf70d16349
France, Germany, Spain, & Italy. (2017). *Permanent Structured Cooperation (PESCO): FR/DE/ES/IT Proposals on the necessary commitments and elements for an inclusive and ambitious PESCO Supported by BE, CZ, FI and NL*. Paris, Berlin, Madrid, Rome. http://club.bruxelles2.eu/wp-content/upl oads/2017/08/principescommuns-pesco-propfrallespita@ue170721.pdf
Germany, & France. (2016). *Erneuerung der GSVP—hin zu einer umfassenden, realistischen und glaubwürdigen Verteidigung in der EU: Deutsch-französische Verteidigungsinitiative zur Erneuerung der Gemeinsamen Sicherheits- und Verteidigungspolitik (GSVP)*. https://augengeradeaus.net/wp-content/upl oads/2016/09/20160909_DEU_FRA_EU-Verteidigung.pdf
Gruber, L. (2000). *Ruling the world: Power politics and the rise of supranational institutions*. Princeton University Press.
Hollande, F. (2016, February 19). Conférence de presse de François Hollande à l'issue du Conseil européen. https://ue.delegfrance.org/oui-je-suis-pour-une-europe#III-Conference-de-presse-de-Francois-Hollande-a-l-issue-du-Con seil-europeen-nbsp
Interview #1: Representative of the General Council Secretariat, 30 November 2017 (Munich, via phone).
Jutarnji List. (2017, October 17). Pejčinović Burić za zadržavanje nadzora nad migracijskim rutama. https://www.jutarnji.hr/vijesti/hrvatska/pejcin ovic-buric-za-zadrzavanje-nadzora-nad-migracijskim-rutama/6658404/

Koenig, N., & Walter-Franke, M. (2017). *France and Germany: Spearheading a European Security and Defence Union?* (Policy paper No. 202). Berlin.

Malta Today. (2017, December 15). Malta to 'wait and see' before deciding on PESCO defence pact, Muscat says. https://www.maltatoday.com.mt/news/europe/83085/malta_to_wait_and_see_before_deciding_on_pesco_defence_pact_muscat_says#.WsDXUZdpG71

Mauro, F., & Santopinto, F. (2017). *Permanent Structured Cooperation: National Perspectives and State of Play.*

Ministère des Affaires étrangères et européennes de Luxembourg. (2017). *Lignes directrices de la défense luxembourgeoise à l'horizon 2025 et au-delà.* https://defense.gouvernement.lu/dam-assets/la-defense/lignes-dir ectrices-de-la-defense-luxembourgeoise-a-l-horizon-2025-et-au-dela.pdf

Ministry of National Defence Republic of Lithuania. (2017, September 8). Lithuania proposes for EU members to establish a military Schengen and to tighten cyber defence cooperation. https://kam.lt/en/news_1098/cur rent_issues/lithuania_proposes_for_eu_members_to_establish_a_military_sche ngen_and_to_tighten_cyber_defence_cooperation.html

Moravcsik, A. (1997). Taking preferences seriously: A liberal theory of international politics. *International Organization, 51*(4), 513–553. https://doi.org/10.1162/002081897550447

NATO. (2014, April 29). Allies enhance NATO air-policing duties in Baltic States, Poland, Romania. https://www.nato.int/cps/ic/natohq/news_109354.htm

Permanent Representation of the Slovak Republic to the EU. (2017, September 7). Ivan Korčok of MFEA SR attends an informal meeting of EU diplomacy heads in Tallinn. https://www.mzv.sk/web/szbrusel-en/news/-/asset_pub lisher/olsKsIdtEfpB/content/statny-tajomnik-mzvaez-sr-ivan-korcok-na-nef ormalnom-stretnuti-sefov-diplomacie-krajin-eu-v-tallinne/10182

PESCO Member States. (2017). *Notification on Permanent Structured Cooperation (PESCO) to the Council and to the High Representative of the Union for Foreign Affairs and Security Policy.* https://www.consilium.europa.eu/media/31511/171113-pesco-notification.pdf

PESCO Member States. (2018). *Permanent Structured Cooperation (PESCO) updated list of PESCO projects.* https://www.consilium.europa.eu/media/37028/table-pesco-projects.pdf

Pierson, P. (2016). Power in historical institutionalism. In O. Fioretos, T. G. Falleti, & A. Sheingate (Eds.), *The Oxford handbook of historical institutionalism* (pp. 124–141). Oxford University Press.

Politico. (2016a, August 25). Angela Merkel: Brexit won't dominate Bratislava summit. https://www.politico.eu/article/angela-merkel-brexit-wont-dom inate-bratislava-summit-european-union-priorities-agenda-estonia/

Politico. (2016b, September 15). EU needs 'Schengen for defense'. https://www.politico.eu/article/italian-foreign-minister-eu-needs-schengen-for-def ense-paolo-gentiloni-islamic-state-migrants-security/

Politico. (2017a, June 3). In Versailles, EU's big 4 back multispeed Europe. https://www.politico.eu/article/in-versailles-eus-big-4-back-multi-speed-europe-italy-france-germany-spain/

Politico. (2017b, November 11). EU defense pact tests Portugal's left-wing government alliance. https://www.politico.eu/article/eu-defense-pact-tests-portugals-left-wing-government-alliance/

Reuters. (2016a, January 3). Exclusive: Poland wants Britain's help over NATO troops in Brexit talks. https://www.reuters.com/article/us-britain-eu-poland-idUSKBN0UH0IE20160103

Reuters. (2016b, November 14). Europeans agree defense plan after campaign swipes by Trump. https://www.reuters.com/article/us-eu-defence/europeans-agree-defense-plan-after-campaign-swipes-by-trump-idUSKBN1391HH

Reuters. (2016c, December 14). Baltic states urge strong U.S. defense commitment to region. https://www.reuters.com/article/us-baltic-security-usa-trump/baltic-states-urge-strong-u-s-defense-commitment-to-region-idUSKB N14321O

Spiegel Online. (2016, November 16). 'Extreme and unprecedented uncertainty': NATO prepares for Trump Presidency. http://www.spiegel.de/international/world/worry-grows-over-trump-threat-to-european-security-a-1121536.html

Terlikowski, M. (2016). Defence policy in the European Union: Multi-speed security? https://www.pism.pl/publications/bulletin/no-74-924

The Baltic Times. (2016, September 16). Lithuanian president attends EU summit on Europe's future after Brexit. https://www.baltictimes.com/lithuanian_president_attending_eu_summit_on_europe_s_future_after_brexit/

The Financial Times. (2016, November 13). Baltics fear for any US policy changes to Nato: Possibility of a disengagement has rung alarm bells in states. https://www.ft.com/content/0036b09a-a825-11e6-8898-79a99e2a4de6

The Guardian. (2016a, February 5). Polish PM backs some parts of Cameron's EU renegotiation plans. https://www.theguardian.com/politics/2016/feb/05/polish-pm-backs-parts-david-cameron-eu-renegotiation-beata-szydlo

The Guardian. (2016b, July 28). Donald Trump reiterates he will only help Nato countries that pay 'fair share'. https://www.theguardian.com/us-news/2016/jul/27/donald-trump-nato-isolationist

The Guardian. (2017, February 14). Plans for two-speed EU risk split with 'peripheral' members. https://www.theguardian.com/world/2017/feb/14/plans-for-two-speed-eu-risk-split-with-peripheral-members

The Irish Times. (2018, January 3). EU defence co-operation is no threat to Irish neutrality. https://www.irishtimes.com/opinion/eu-defence-co-ope ration-is-no-threat-to-irish-neutrality-1.3343293

The New York Times. (2016, April 2). Donald Trump Says NATO is 'Obsolete,' UN is 'Political Game'. https://www.nytimes.com/politics/first-draft/2016/04/02/donald-trump-tells-crowd-hed-be-fine-if-nato-broke-up/

The Telegraph. (2011, October 24). David Cameron's statement on the European Council: In full. https://www.telegraph.co.uk/news/worldnews/europe/eu/8846553/David-Camerons-statement-on-the-European-Council-in-full.html

The Telegraph. (2014, April 1). Ukraine crisis: Poland asks Nato to station 10,000 troops on its territory. https://www.telegraph.co.uk/news/worldnews/europe/ukraine/10737838/Ukraine-crisis-Poland-asks-Nato-to-station-10000-troops-on-its-territory.html

The Times. (2016, September 15). EU army plan sets alarm bells ringing on Nato's front line.://www.thetimes.co.uk/edition/world/eu-army-plan-sets-alarm-bells-ringing-on-nato-s-front-line-5q9gxw3ng

TheJournal.ie. (2017, December 7). 'We're being asked to sell out our neutrality': Government accused of trying to rush EU defence deal vote. http://www.thejournal.ie/eu-army-pesco-3734034-Dec2017/

Time.com. (2016, November 14). Can NATO Survive a Donald Trump Presidency? http://time.com/4569578/donald-trump-nato-alliance-europe-afghanistan/

UK Foreign and Commonwealth Office, & UK Ministry of Defence. (2014, July 28). NATO exercise to reassure allies. https://www.gov.uk/government/news/nato-exercise-to-reassure-allies

UK Ministry of Defence. (2016, January 20). Defence Secretary announces UK commitment to Poland. https://www.gov.uk/government/news/defence-secretary-announces-uk-commitment-to-poland

V4. (2016, July 21). Joint Statement of the Heads of Governments of the V4 Countries. https://budapeszt.msz.gov.pl/resource/eb5de611-3c86-413b-b7a1-d389d79fb63f:JCR

V4. (2017a, March 2). Joint Statement of the Heads of Governments of the V4 Countries: "Strong Europe—Union of Action and Trust". https://www.vlada.cz/en/media-centrum/aktualne/joint-statement-of-the-heads-of-governments-of-the-v4-countries-_strong-europe-_-union-of-action-and-trust_-154008/

V4. (2017b, November 10). Poland to join EU's military partnership. http://www.visegradgroup.eu/news/poland-to-join-eu-171110

Vidmajer, S. (2017, November 10). Z oddajo suverenosti si bolj suveren, kot če si sam suveren. https://www.delo.si/sobotna/z-oddajo-suverenosti-si-bolj-suveren-kot-ce-si-sam-suveren.html

Waszczykowski, W., & Macierewicz, A. (2017, November 17). Poland to join PESCO (Letter).

PART IV

Assessment

CHAPTER 9

Confronting Contenders

This chapter is devoted to discussing two alternative explanations derived from well-established approaches to European defense cooperation, *neorealism*, and *neofunctionalism*. To do justice to both theoretical competitors, that is, to represent them adequately and not treat them as "straw men," I draw on the initial empirical puzzle that motivated this study. Why did two similar EU institutions, the EDA and PESCO, exhibit varying degrees of authority in a similar issue area? More specifically, why did EU member states create the EDA and integrate the WEAG/WEAO's functions only to then divert their resources to OCCAR? Conversely, why did the EU member states neglect PESCO as an institution in European defense planning for over a decade until they finally activated it in 2017? Both neorealism and neofunctionalism provide partial answers to these questions. Yet, as we will see, neither of them can account entirely for the variation in, and the timing of, the EU member states institutional choices. Contrasting this book's rationalist argument with two theoretical alternatives will help to distinguish its value-added and increase confidence in its explanatory power.

Since the focus of this book is on international security and defense, realism is the elephant in the room. Is it possible that the different trajectories of the EDA and PESCO can be explained by a purely power-based approach? I will focus on the strand of neorealist literature that is

© The Author(s), under exclusive license to Springer Nature Switzerland AG 2023
F. Biermann, *The Battle for Authority in European Defence Cooperation*, Palgrave Studies in European Union Politics,
https://doi.org/10.1007/978-3-031-30054-7_9

specifically concerned with the development of the CSDP. Dyson and Konstadinides (2013), Rosato (2011), and Posen (2006) build on a defensive reading of structural realism (Schweller, 1994; Waltz, 1979) and expect progress or stagnation in European defense cooperation to depend on how EU member states navigate the *alliance security dilemma* (Snyder, 1984) steering between entrapment on the one hand and abandonment on the other. Depending on what kind of trade-off they opt for, the states will decide whether to engage in bandwagoning or balancing behavior (Dyson & Konstadinides, 2013). Balancing refers to further EU integration and the creation of independent EU military capabilities to act as a counterweight to US hegemony, while bandwagoning signifies reliance on NATO primacy and the rejection of deeper EU cooperation. In consequence, the success of both the EDA and PESCO will, following this reading, depend primarily on the EU–US relationship and EU member states' fear of entrapment, which could undermine their bandwagoning strategy.

Neofunctionalism, by comparison, is not an obvious choice; yet there are good reasons to consider this theoretical approach a serious competitor to the rationalist intergovernmental framework I put forward. Relevant questions here are concerned with the conditions under which EU member states pool and delegate authority to supranational institutions and thus integrate defense markets and defense planning. Framed this way, neofunctionalism, as an important EU integration theory, may help explain the trajectories of the two CSDP institutions. While defense cooperation in the European Union is predominantly intergovernmental, some recent publications have highlighted the influence of the Commission on the development of this policy area (Biermann & Weiss, 2021; Blauberger & Weiss, 2013; Fiott, 2015; Weiss & Blauberger, 2015). The creation of supranational facilities, such as the recently established European Defense Fund, also points in this direction (European Commission, 2017a; Haroche, 2019). Therefore, I will evaluate empirical evidence in light of the neofunctionalist expectations that emerge from the key concepts of *functional, political, and cultivated spillovers* (Haas, 1961, 2004 [1958]; Haroche, 2019; Niemann, 1998; Niemann & Schmittner, 2009; Stone Sweet & Sandholtz, 1997). Neofunctionalist theorizing would expect the EDA and PESCO to be established and regularly used if functional pressure for pooling and delegation is high and supranational actors incentivize the member states to do so.[1]

This chapter is divided into three sections. The first analyzes the EDA and PESCO's genesis through the theoretical lens of neorealism and the alliance security dilemma. This perspective can account for the creation of the EDA as part of the ESDP, a reaction to EU member states' entrapment during the Yugoslav and Iraq Wars, as well as for the fragmentation of European defense planning as a byproduct of Atlanticists' opportunistic bandwagoning. However, the marginalization of the EDA does not follow the logic of the alliance security dilemma—pooling resources across all EU member states would have made balancing more effective, and there were no observable reasons for a change toward an avant-gardist bandwagoning strategy. Moreover, considering then US President Donald Trump's threats to abandon NATO, we should have expected intensified bandwagoning rather than the creation of PESCO as a balancing tool. The second section is devoted to the neofunctionalist account of the trajectory of the EDA and PESCO. While fear of a Commission initiative for a European Armaments Agency might account for the timing of the EDA's creation, and while the setting up of the European Defense Fund may provide an explanation for some of the states originally opposing PESCO finally participating in it, supranational entrepreneurship was not the decisive variable explaining differences between the two institutions. Similarly, functional pressure cannot account for these differences, as it was constant in both cases. The final section concludes by arguing that both neorealism and neofunctionalism add important insights to the empirical subject. Yet neither of them provides a convincing explanation for the observed variation.

---

[1] LI (Moravcsik, 1993b, 1998) comes to mind as an additional theoretical competitor. However, this choice would have done little to advance the plausibility of my framework, as LI, with its focus on intergovernmental bargaining, is complementary to my account. The theoretical framework developed in Chapter 3 extends beyond the EU's confines and takes institutional alternatives outside the EU into account. I discussed the advantages of this approach for the analysis of the relative authority of both PESCO and the EDA in their respective policy areas in the introduction. LI fails to notice the differences between the EDA's marginalization and PESCO's resilience but treats both as expressions of the same integration level. Therefore, testing the plausibility of my framework is best achieved by comparing its explanatory power to two theories that rely on different independent variables.

Neorealism and CSDP Institutions

At the heart of neorealist theorizing is the assumption that power dynamics are the independent variable that explains policy outcomes (Waltz, 1979). More recent neorealist approaches understand EU integration in defense cooperation and the CSDP as the attempt to navigate the alliance security dilemma arising from two concerns, fear of entrapment and fear of abandonment, which are central to the strategic calculations of European states (Dyson & Konstadinides, 2013, p. 154; Jones, 2003, 2007; Snyder, 1984). These fears imply contradictory strategies: either balancing (Posen, 2006; Rosato, 2011) or bandwagoning (Dyson & Konstadinides, 2013; Schweller, 1994). When states fear that being in an alliance with the hegemon undermines their policy discretion and thus entraps them, the counter strategy would be to engage in balancing behavior, that is, to create independent institutions to maintain a certain degree of autonomy in foreign and defense policy decision-making (Rosato, 2011). This behavior is risky, however, as it might provoke dissatisfaction in the hegemon and encourage it to abandon the alliance. The fear of being abandoned by the hegemon which, in the worst case, might terminate the alliance and thus become a veritable threat, suggests another strategic behavior, bandwagoning, which consists in supporting the hegemon politically and financially and fully relying on its guidance without creating independent capacities (Dyson & Konstadinides, 2013).[2] This strategy, in turn, fuels the risk of becoming entrapped once again; "The risks of abandonment and entrapment tend to vary inversely" (Snyder, 1984).

These strategies are rarely clear-cut, however, and neorealist scholars have come up with concepts combining parts of both strategies, such as "reformed bandwagoning" (Dyson & Konstadinides, 2013) or "soft balancing" (Rosato, 2011) to describe the EU member states' approach of neither overtly confronting nor fully giving in to the United States. The EU member states, as rational actors, adjust their strategy whenever either balancing or bandwagoning no longer brings about the desired effects. From the neorealist literature on the CSDP, the following two hypotheses regarding the EU member states' strategies can be deduced:

---

[2] Bandwagoning can also be conducted for profit, i.e., in order to free-ride on the goods provided by the hegemon (Schweller 1994).

NR1: The EU member states create independent defense institutions as part of a soft balancing strategy when they fear entrapment in US foreign policy.
NR2: The EU member states refrain from creating independent structures or disengage from them as part of a reformed bandwagoning strategy when they fear being abandoned by the US.

Neorealism and the EDA

The creation of the EDA, the integration of WEAG/WEAO into the newly created institution, and the EDA's subsequent marginalization can only be reasonably discussed from a neorealist perspective when these things are put into the perspective of the CSDP's overall genesis. The 1998 Franco-British St. Malo declaration for the first time demanded that "the Union must have the capacity for autonomous action, backed up by credible military forces, the means to decide to use them, and a readiness to do so, in order to respond to international crises" (France & United Kingdom, 1998). This declaration, seemingly overcoming the divide in the strategic orientation of Europeanist France and Atlanticist Britain, is the first evidence of EU member states engaging in a balancing strategy vis-à-vis the post-Cold War hegemon. This demand for independent EU capacities arguably arose in reaction to the EU's heavy reliance on US support in dealing with the Yugoslav Wars (Shepherd, 2015). While the EU member states had difficulty in finding a common stance toward this conflict in its immediate neighborhood, it was even more difficult to get the United States involved since it was not interested in supporting military interventions (Hyde-Price, 2006). As the EU was unable to pursue its (not always well-defined) autonomous foreign policy without relying militarily on the United States, the Yugoslav secession wars clearly demonstrated the EU member states' entrapment.

The Franco-British St. Malo declaration that paved the way for the CSDP can thus be understood as expressing a balancing strategy (Posen, 2006). This reading is also supported by the US's reaction to the declaration. In her famous "3Ds" newspaper article, published only three days after the Franco-British declaration, US Secretary of State Madeleine Albright warned the EU member states to refrain from engaging in *decoupling* from NATO decision-making, *duplication* of NATO structures and *discrimination* against non-EU NATO members (Albright, 2001). This warning did not yet correspond to a threat of abandonment but made it unequivocally clear that the United States expected loyalty in return for its security guarantees.

Nonetheless, when the EU member states declared the establishment of the European Security and Defence Policy with the 2001 Nice Treaty, all references to the WEU, the European pillar of NATO, were omitted from the document (Trybus, 2005, p. 101). This step demonstrates that the EU member states again engaged in a balancing strategy intending to create a more autonomous security and defense policy. As the WEAG/WEAO structures were part of the WEU, it was logical to think how these structures might be transferred into an armaments agency within the EU. As the fear of abandonment loomed, however, the 2002 Berlin Plus agreement arguably emerged as a compromise tolerating the EU's ambitions to create more independent but complementary structures to NATO, thus amounting to a "soft balancing" outcome. The agreement "presumes the availability to the EU, if NATO itself does not need them, of NATO capabilities and common assets for use in EU-led operations" (NATO, 2004).

Yet, the divisions among member states on whether to pursue a bandwagoning or a balancing strategy resurfaced with the onset of the Iraq War. In 2003 some EU member states, such as Germany and France, chose not to participate actively in the Iraq War while others, such as the United Kingdom, actively supported the United States on the ground (Hummel, 2007, 16–18, 36). This split reflected the Europeanist vs. Atlanticist divide, which has been thoroughly discussed in the preceding chapters. Parallel to the discussions of the Iraq crisis, the Europeanists lobbied for a potent European armaments agency as a further step toward independence from NATO, while the Atlanticists made efforts to prevent any development in that direction.

Neorealism can explain why there was an impetus stemming from the EU–US relationship, which led the EU member states to transfer the WEU and its subsidiary bodies, the WEAO and the WEAG, to the EU in the first place (Weiss, 2009). Yet it cannot take a clear stance on why the Atlanticists finally gave in and agreed to the establishment of the European Defense Agency. The Europeanists and avant-gardists were at the forefront of plans to balance the United States in light of repeated entrapment. Thus, hypothesis *NR1* is at least partially fulfilled in the case of the WEAG/WEAO's transfer to the European Union.

Yet what about the EDA's subsequent marginalization through OCCAR, an institution outside the EU? Recalling that France, the most enthusiastic supporter of an independent CSDP, was among the first states to promote a bandwagoning strategy toward the United States, suggesting the AA between the EDA and OCCAR in 2008, the question arises as to what induced the avant-gardists' change of strategy. The confirmation of *NR2* would require evidence of the United States signaling its intention to abandon the EU. At the least, it would need to be shown that engaging in OCCAR rather than the EDA and thus excluding the bulk of the EU member states from cooperative armaments programs would support efforts to bandwagon on NATO.

Neorealism can account for the Atlanticists' position that the EDA would not undermine the EU–US relationship and their stance that the EDA would not "turn into a supranational body that dictates procurement decisions" and "cannot force the UK to compromise the kit for our armed forces or to accept a 'fortress Europe' defence industrial policy" (House of Commons, 2004). Yet it is not clear why France considerably reduced its ambitions for the EDA and downgraded it to a regulatory agency with no say in armaments procurement when it shifted its focus toward the exclusive OCCAR, as demonstrated in Chapter 6. A well-functioning EDA would have contributed substantially to the reduction of system types, to the enhancement of collaborative R&T projects, and thus to savings in defense spending. The EU spends "about half the US defence budget but for all that expense achieves a much smaller proportion of US capability" (European Parliament, 2006, p. 16). This implies that in order to successfully pursue a balancing approach—however soft—the EDA would be needed as a functioning armaments procurement agency.

A possible explanation of the French change of strategy could be international terrorism. The attacks in Madrid in 2004 and London in 2005 brought international terrorism to the European Union. It thus negatively affected the EU's security situation and might have prompted the avant-gardist states to turn back toward NATO and encouraged their reorientation toward a bandwagoning strategy. This overall trend is certainly traceable, especially in light of France's decision to reintegrate into NATO command structures in March 2009 (CNN.com, 2009). Yet the French decision to reintegrate was driven less by the fear of abandonment by the United States and more by France's involvement in several NATO missions in the early 2000s without any input into NATO's formal decision-making (Pesme, 2010). Moreover, France continued its general support of the CSDP as an independent European framework and thus did not change its general position in the balancing–bandwagoning conundrum (Rieker, 2013). EU–US relations can thus hardly account for the EU member states, especially France's, decision to shift cooperation away from the EDA. As demonstrated in Chapter 6, both the Europeanists and the Atlanticists had stable preferences regarding further integration in security and defense. Considerable doubt remains regarding hypothesis *NR2* as an explanation for the EDA's demise as a means of armaments cooperation.

In sum, neorealism and its focus on the US impact on EU member states' strategy of engaging either in balancing, that is, creating and focusing on independent EU security institutions, or bandwagoning, that is, supporting NATO and refusing independent institutions, can account for the overall trend of EU member states first creating and then poorly maintaining the CSDP framework. Yet, the alliance security dilemma does not provide a convincing answer to the question of why the avant-gardist states focused on OCCAR instead of the EDA and thus weakened the CSDP immediately after its inception. Without going back to the specific economic and security-related preferences of the individual EU member state coalitions and their relative bargaining power, specific institutional outcomes are hard to predict. Consequently, my rationalist framework is commensurable with neorealist reasoning in accounting for the basic member state preferences. But it goes beyond it by specifying how bargaining dynamics among the EU member states translated diverging preferences into distinct outcomes in terms of interinstitutional authority relations.

Neorealism and PESCO

A focus on the reasons why France decided to first balance and then bandwagon the United States and NATO with respect to the creation of independent and well-functioning defense institutions would not be of much help in explaining the genesis of PESCO. As demonstrated in Chapters 7 and 8, as soon as PESCO had been included in the Lisbon Treaty, the avant-gardists tried continuously to activate it. There was no change in strategy. On the contrary, even in light of the heightened threat from terrorism and Da'esh, the avant-gardists maintained their balancing policy. Therefore, when trying to explain why the EU member states first engaged in bandwagoning and then changed to balancing in 2017, it is necessary to focus on the Atlanticist coalition. I contend that neorealism can account for the period of stasis between 2007 and 2016 during which the Atlanticists profited greatly from bandwagoning on NATO and its security guarantee. Yet, contrary to the expectations formulated in NR2, when the United States sent strong signals of abandonment starting in 2016, the Atlanticists did not engage in intensified bandwagoning but, instead, joined the avant-gardists in balancing against the United States.

The EU's security situation after 2007 was generally deemed to be positive as "the threat of a conventional attack against NATO territory [was] low" (Rasmussen, 2010, para. 7). Even in the separatist wars in South Ossetia and Abkhazia in 2008, the EU's engagement as a mediator between Russia and Georgia was evaluated as a "major diplomatic success" by many (Merlingen & Ostrauskaite, 2009). Backed by, but still independent from, NATO's hard power, the EU appeared as an impartial arbitrator while the United States guaranteed the security of the EU's eastern borders. Consequently, for the Atlanticist states, especially those with minor military capacity, the dominant strategy was to further bandwagon on NATO. Engaging in regional cooperation frameworks outside the European Union allowed for minimal investments in exchange for maximal security and helped prevent all Europeanist attempts to engage in further balancing against NATO.

This situation remained stable until 2014 when two events drastically changed the EU's security perception. First, in March 2014, the Russian Federation unlawfully annexed Ukrainian Crimea, which resulted in an outcry, especially from the EU's eastern member states (BBC News, 2014). As the US reaction to the Russian aggression was rather soft, with then US President Barack Obama giving an assurance that the "United States and Nato do not seek any conflict with Russia" (*The Guardian*, 2014), the Atlanticists had to fear abandonment by the United States. In line with hypothesis NR2, the NATO summit in Wales in September 2014 reconfirmed the EU member states' willingness to put their fate in the hands of the United States. The Wales Summit Declaration called upon all NATO members to "aim to move towards the 2% guideline within a decade" (NATO, 2014) and thus expressed the EU member states' willingness to intensify their bandwagoning strategy. They did not engage in independent balancing toward Russia but continued to rely on NATO. There was no fear of entrapment and, consequently, no reason to engage in balancing. Thus, NR2 points in the same direction as the rationalist framework.

However, while the common EU strategy in 2014 was apparently one of bandwagoning, in other words, refraining from taking any further steps toward an independent EU security and defense arrangement, this was not shared by all of its members. France, shocked by two terrorist attacks in January and November 2015, did not call on NATO for help but on 17 November 2015 for the first time invoked Article 42 (7) of the TEU, the mutual defense clause (Council of the European Union, 2015). This provides evidence that France's position at least in the balancing–bandwagoning nexus had remained unchanged in spite of a severe, if diffuse, threat. This fuels some doubt about the overall explanatory power of the alliance security dilemma.

PESCO's activation in 2017 intensified these doubts. I argue that the developments leading to PESCO represent a challenge to NR1, which expects institution-building in the EU to occur as a response to entrapment. US President Donald Trump was overtly questioning the automatic nature of NATO's collective defense mechanism (*The Guardian*, 2016), and flirting with Russia—"Wouldn't it be great if we actually got along with Russia?" (*The Financial Times*, 2016b), which confronted the EU's member states most vulnerable to Russian aggression, the Baltics and Poland, with an indisputable threat of abandonment (*The Financial Times*, 2016a). The alliance security dilemma would expect further concessions to NATO in order to keep the United States engaged. At least, it would not expect any steps toward balancing and thus running the risk of Trump's United States turning even further away from the European Union. Why would the Atlanticist states, especially the eastern European states sharing a border with Russia, agree to a balancing strategy rather than investing all their efforts in trying to keep the United States engaged?

That the Atlanticist states joined PESCO as a first step toward a European Defense Union (Reuters, 2017) without any further offers to the

United States represents an act of balancing[3] rather than bandwagoning and thus contradicts *NR1*. Indeed, in comparison to the 2014 Warsaw NATO Declaration, the 2% spending goal had even been diluted. The Council reiterated a general commitment to "nearing the 2% of total defence spending" (Council Decision establishing Permanent Structured Cooperation (PESCO) and determining the list of Participating Member States, 2017) but erased any reference to 2024 as the deadline for achieving this number. In light of the US threat of abandonment and increased insecurity regarding Russia's intentions, the EU did not try to reinforce the EU–US alliance but rather engaged in balancing measures—not only toward the United States but also with respect to Russia.

One could reasonably argue that the Atlanticists adopted a hedging strategy. While preferring NATO as the framework for security cooperation and the United States as patron, they could not afford to be caught in the crossfire. Yet, without considering intra-EU bargaining dynamics and the threat of exclusion that PESCO represented to the Atlanticists, their orientation toward the CSDP can hardly be explained. It is not evident why the Atlanticists jumped off the NATO bandwagon and onto the PESCO one thus supporting the Europeanists' balancing strategy. Therefore, considerable doubt remains concerning *NR1* as an explanatory approach to PESCO's activation.

Summing up, while neorealism can account for PESCO's stasis and fragmentation in European defense cooperation between 2007 and 2016, this is not the case for PESCO's sudden activation. Without considering intra-European dynamics, for example, Brexit and the Europeanists' threat of exclusion, the Atlanticists' change in strategy cannot be explained. In light of looming abandonment, neorealism would expect— in direct opposition to the actual events—the EU member states to make further concessions to the United States rather than heading toward a European Defense Union.

---

[3] The creation of PESCO and the European Defense Fund even triggered two US undersecretaries in the Pentagon, Ellen Lord and Andrea Thompson, to write a letter to HR Mogherini in May 2019 expressing their disapproval and threatening abandonment, which provides further evidence that PESCO was considered an act of balancing (Spiegel Online, 2019).

Neofunctionalism and CSDP Institutions

Let us now turn to the second theoretical competitor. This section demonstrates that, while neofunctionalism adds important insights to the explanation of the creation of both the EDA and PESCO, this theoretical lens does not capture the variation in the relative authority possessed by these institutions as its competitors do. Neofunctionalism, as an integration theory, is generally better suited to explaining steps *toward* integration than negative instances, such as marginalization or fragmentation. And as a European integration theory, it is built around the key concept of *spillover effects*.

Scholars traditionally distinguish between three different mechanisms—functional, cultivated, and political spillovers (Haas, 2004 [1958]; Lindberg, 1963; Tranholm-Mikkelsen, 1991). *Functional spillovers* rely on the logic that integrating certain tasks in one issue area leads to problems, which can "only be solved by integrating yet more tasks" (Tranholm-Mikkelsen, 1991, p. 5). These spillovers describe a functionalist self-reinforcing, incremental integration dynamic, "in which the original goal can be assured only by taking further actions, which in turn create a further condition and need for more action, and so forth" (Lindberg, 1963, p. 10). In brief, integration leads to more integration. *Cultivated spillovers* in turn rely on the assumption that supranational actors, such as the Commission, can achieve an "upgrading of common interests" (Haas, 1961, p. 386) and thus overcome intergovernmental least-common-denominator solutions by mediating the bargaining process. In addition, supranational actors have a self-interest in integration—more integration implies an increase in their importance and their discretionary operating space and thus ensures their survival as institutional actors (Haas, 1961, p. 368). Cultivated spillovers are, therefore, often equated with supranational policy entrepreneurship (Bergmann, 2018; Haroche, 2019; Stephenson, 2010). Finally, *political spillovers* focus on societal elites, which, through learning processes, realize that, in order to satisfy their interests, they need to shift "their loyalties, expectations, and political activities toward a new and larger center, whose institutions possess or demand jurisdiction over the pre-existing national states" (Haas, 1961, p. 367) and thus create a political impetus for further integration.

Neofunctionalist scholarship has found that the combination of these spillover dynamics has considerable explanatory leverage in accounting for integration in European security and defense (Bergmann, 2018; Bergmann & Niemann, 2018; Guay, 1996). Building on this brief presentation of neofunctionalist theorizing, I deduce two hypotheses regarding the creation and subsequent use of CSDP institutions, which I will then test in the EDA and the PESCO cases.

NF1: When functional, political, or cultivated spillovers are present, EU member states pool and delegate authority to EU security and defense institutions.

Knowing that neofunctionalism primarily accounts for positive instances of integration and the reasons for disintegration are manifold (Schmitter & Lefkofridi, 2016), deducing a hypothesis for cases of marginalization or fragmentation is difficult without misrepresenting the theory. Nevertheless, the absence of spillover dynamics should make further integration and the use of European institutions less likely—without necessarily implying disintegration. Therefore, I can reasonably—and cautiously—also formulate a hypothesis regarding *non-integration*.

NF2: If functional, political, and cultivated spillovers are absent and functional pressure is low, EU member states refrain from transferring additional tasks to European security and defense institutions.

Analogously to my previous discussion of neorealism, in the following two sub-sections, I analyze the explanatory power of spillovers as an independent variable in the case of the EDA's creation and subsequent marginalization through OCCAR on the one hand and the fragmentation of European defense planning and the subsequent activation of PESCO on the other.

Neofunctionalism and the EDA

Throughout the 1990s, the European Union took major steps toward the creation of a single European market. Formally agreed in Maastricht in 1992, the process toward the European Monetary Union (EMU) put considerable budgetary constraints on the EU member states. These developments functionally spilled over to the defense sector, as "defense cuts are driven partly by the need to meet the budgetary criteria of EMU"

(Guay, 1996, p. 414). The general trends of budgetary pressure and market liberalization also affected the European defense industry. A wave of privatizations and mergers changed both the national and the European defense-industrial landscape (Weiss, 2021).

A good example is the restructuring of the military aircraft sector. Dominated by a multitude of minor national companies in the 1980s, national consolidation and European mergers led to a considerable reduction in the number of aerospace companies and the emergence of international champions, such as the British BAE Systems (founded in 1999) or the Franco-Spanish-German EADS (2000) (International Institute for Strategic Studies [IISS], 2017; Weiss & Biermann, 2021). The creation of MBDA, a European missiles manufacturer (2003), or the Italo-British helicopter manufacturer AgustaWestland (2000) (Guay, 2005) provides additional evidence of this consolidation trend. While consolidating the supply of armaments is one possible way of making the market more efficient, consolidating the demand is another. The establishment of a European armaments procurement agency was a way to ease functional pressures. On the one hand, it would allow harvesting synergies from large orders and joint R&T spending while increasing the (collective) consumer power of the national governments vis-à-vis the ever-larger armaments producers on the other.

In addition to the functional spillovers from market integration and the budgetary constraints related to the creation of the EMU, political spillovers were present as well. While OCCAR received legal personality in 2001 and operated as a joint armaments management agency, the EU's largest armaments producers actively lobbied for a truly European agency promoting European products. The leaders of BAE Systems, EADS, and Thales, a comparable French company asked the EU member states in an open letter to match the bottom-up progress achieved through consolidation by going "way beyond" already established frameworks to "create a European Armaments and Strategic Research Agency ... for initiating and developing large scale defense and security programs across Europe" (BAE Systems, EADS, & Thales, 2003).

Finally, in addition to the functional pressure and the industry's push for integration, the Commission engaged in policy entrepreneurship. In its 2003 Communication, it proclaimed the goal of having "a single set of rules for procuring defence equipment in Europe" (European Commission, 2003, p. 15), the abandonment of *juste retour*, and the establishment of an agency that would draw upon "Community mechanisms and instruments where Member States agree that the Community has a contribution to make" (European Commission, 2003, p. 17).

The functional, political, and cultivated spillovers allow the conclusion that, for the EU member states, it was expedient to create the EDA in 2004. The fact that they set up the EDA purely as an intergovernmental agency through a Joint Action rather than waiting for the ratification of the European Constitution, however, suggests that their intention was to prevent any supranational engagement (Biermann & Weiss, 2021). A closer alignment of defense-industrial procurement by reverting to community mechanisms and instruments was interpreted as a risk to national sovereignty (Georgopoulos, 2015). Consequently, while *NF1* provides a comprehensible functional explanation for the creation of an EU armaments agency in general, the intergovernmental design of the EDA leaves some doubt as to whether the spillover mechanisms played out as theorized.

Doubt increases when one looks at the EDA's subsequent marginalization, which contradicts *NF2*. In view of the European defense industry's strong support for the EDA (Mawdsley, 2003; Oikonomou, 2015, p. 55), persistent functional pressure to spend less money more efficiently (Hartley, 2008, 2011), and the Commission's continuous work toward liberalizing the defense market (Blauberger & Weiss, 2013; Weiss & Blauberger, 2015) it is puzzling, for neofunctionalism, that the EDA did not develop into a proper armaments procurement agency, but was marginalized in this issue area instead.

Rather than giving in to unfolding spillover dynamics and delegating tasks and authority to the EDA, the EU member states used the agency to counter Commission attempts and prevent further integration. While the Commission tried to push for a defense procurement directive in 2005 (Commission of the European Communities, 2005), the EU member states mandated the EDA to draw up a non-binding Code of Conduct and thus "play[ed] the Commission and the EDA off against each other" (Fiott, 2015, p. 550). Instead of turning into a supranational procurement agency, the EDA was used as a fortification against supranational interference, while any relevant armaments cooperation took place outside the EU within the OCCAR framework. In clear contradiction to neofunctionalist expectations, the supranational European Parliament instead of supporting the Commission even invited "the Member States to make use of OCCAR's management experience for the implementation of joint programmes" (European Parliament, 2011a, Art. 50).

Although the EDA's marginalization is puzzling in view of strong functional and cultivated spillover effects, in defense of neofunctionalism and hypothesis *NF2* it has to be admitted that the case is not as clear-cut with regard to political spillovers. While the large-scale companies had a strong interest in further integration and the development of cooperative programs, industrial interests varied considerably depending on their competitiveness. SMEs with niche capabilities as well as uncompetitive companies favored a more protectionist and national modus operandi and thus opposed liberalization (Guay, 1996; Moravcsik, 1993a). The presence of political spillovers is less clear than the existence of functional pressure and supranational policy entrepreneurship.

In sum, while neofunctionalism reveals important dynamics underlying the institutional developments in European armaments cooperation, it has difficulties in accounting for the variation in the EDA's relative position in the field. The presence of spillovers was certainly conducive to the creation of the EDA in the first place. However, functional pressure did not decrease, nor did the Commission stop its engagement after 2004. Hence, these factors cannot account for the agency's subsequent marginalization and the upstream states' shift to OCCAR. Without considering individual member states' preferences and their respective bargaining power, it is hard to make sense of this development.

Neofunctionalism and PESCO

This section engages with the neofunctionalist explanation for the awakening of the "Sleeping Beauty of the Lisbon Treaty" (Juncker, 2017), PESCO. I argue that the Commission's policy entrepreneurship in creating budgetary incentives for member states to participate in PESCO through the European Defense Fund offers important insights into the process (Haroche, 2019). However, as both functional pressure and cultivated spillovers to establish PESCO were already present during the era of fragmentation, the Commission's activities cannot be a sufficient cause for activating PESCO but merely an enabling factor for PESCO's inclusive membership. The financial crisis, the Russian annexation of Crimea, and continuous supranational efforts to enhance military integration were not enough to convince the EU member states to integrate their fragmented regional defense cooperation. Thus, while *NF1* predicts the general tendency toward integration correctly, it remains unspecific about the conditions under which an EU institution would be expected to succeed.

When the Lisbon Treaty came into force in 2009, the Euro crisis was in full swing, and EU member states, the Commission, and the EP were all aware of the necessity of cooperation in defense-related R&T and armaments procurement to maintain military capabilities under enormous budgetary pressure. PESCO would have opened the "perspective for savings in national defence budgets" and "engage[ment] in a more coherent development of the desperately needed military capabilities" (European Parliament, 2011b). Then President of the Commission, José Manuel Barroso, demanded the "strengthening" of the CSDP and reminded the member states that "[t]he speed of the European Union [...] cannot be the speed of its slowest member or its most reluctant member" (Barroso, 2011). Yet, as Chapter 7 showed, any attempts to put PESCO on the political agenda were doomed. This is surprising from the perspective of *NF2*.

What is more, not only were functional and cultivated spillovers present, but the European public unequivocally supported further integration in the realm of CSDP, which is an indicator of political spillovers. The Eurobarometer surveys measuring public support for a strengthened CSDP were constantly hovering around 75% during the period of fragmentation (Irondelle et al., 2015; Peters, 2011) and thus consistently exceeded the 59% required for a positive picture of the European Union in general (European Commission, 2011). Support remained constant at 75% in 2017 and thus cannot serve as an explanatory factor—even though Commission President Juncker attempted to make a case for this, claiming, "the momentum behind closer defence cooperation comes first and foremost from the people of Europe" (Juncker, 2017).

Even when functional pressure to engage in strengthening the CSDP further increased in 2014, when Russia annexed Crimea, no action was taken. Commission President Juncker's conviction that the EU "cannot make do in the long run without at least some integrated defence capacities. The Treaty of Lisbon provides for the possibility that those Member States who wish to can pool their defence capabilities in the form of a permanent structured cooperation" (Juncker, 2014) did not change the institutional landscape. Although spillovers of all kinds were present between 2007 and 2016, further integration and the activation of PESCO did not materialize. This contradicts *NF2*, which would have expected the absence of integration to co-vary with the absence of spillover dynamics.

Juncker made the development of the CSDP one of the top priorities for his presidency from 2014 until 2019 (Juncker, 2014). Thus, the fact that PESCO was activated in 2017, after three years of Juncker's presidential term, might be interpreted as a sign of successful policy entrepreneurship. Support for this interpretation is provided by the fact that in 2016, following HR Mogherini's presentation of the EU Global Strategy (EEAS, 2016, p. 46), the Commission suggested the creation of the European Defense Fund as a budgetary incentive to engage in collaborative R&T and armaments programs. Welcomed by the European Council in December 2016 as part of the Commission's "European Defence Action Plan" (European Council, 2016, para. 12), the Commission created the European Defense Fund on 7 June 2017 (European Commission, 2017b). This facility was structured into a research window and a capability window. While the former offered direct research grants for collaborative R&T (total budget 90 million € for the period 2017–20), the latter incentivized member states to engage in a joint development of prototypes by offering co-financing of up to 20% of the total cost (total budget 500 million € for 2017–2020) (European Commission, 2019). The possibility of receiving a 10% bonus if the collaborative development project took place under the auspices of PESCO is arguably that most relevant consideration when making a connection between the Defense Fund and PESCO.

Against the backdrop of the downstream states' concerns regarding the liberalization of the EDEM, as they feared their niche industries would be sidelined and excluded from defense contracts, the prospect of benefitting from additional EU funds was certainly conducive to their decision to participate in PESCO and to transfer their regionally structured cooperation to the EU. Yet, while it may have amplified collaborative defense spending and helped SMEs to gain a foothold in joint programs, the effect of the European Defense Fund must not be overestimated as its size "in an overall context in which Europeans spend over €200 billion on defence is rather insignificant" (Tocci, 2018). Therefore, it is questionable whether policy entrepreneurship in general and the European Defense Fund in particular were the decisive factors in helping the Atlanticist states overcome their resistance to further EU defense integration.

In addition, the avant-gardist states had already communicated their intention to create PESCO even if the reluctant states were against it

(Deutsche Welle, 2017) and the Council had already agreed on the need for PESCO (General Secretariat of the Council, 2017, para. 6) in March 2017. Therefore, the establishment of the Defense Fund was most likely not decisive for the creation of PESCO. While the fund certainly helped the avant-gardists to convince the reluctant states to join, it is scarcely imaginable that they could have done so if France, Germany, Spain, and Italy had not created a threat of exclusion. Moreover, and equally importantly, without the election of Donald Trump, his undermining of NATO, and the concomitant change in the reluctant states' preference toward inclusive cooperation, the stalemate would probably have persisted. While decreased NATO credibility heightened functional pressure for European cooperation, this pressure should not be mistaken for functional spillovers as understood by neofunctionalism. It did not stem from prior integration, but was induced externally. The same holds true for Brexit.

In sum, while there is evidence for relatively stronger cultivated spillover effects in 2016/17 as compared to the years characterized by fragmentation, it is not plausible that these spillovers were the decisive independent variable accounting for PESCO's activation. In other words, although neofunctionalism and the creation of the EDF help to understand PESCO's inclusive design, *NFl* does not plausibly explain the timing of PESCO's establishment in 2017. Considering the functional spillovers generated by economic and financial integration on the need to liberalize the defense market and to cooperate in defense planning and the continuous supranational support for PESCO, it is difficult to understand why PESCO did not materialize earlier.

Summary

This chapter has presented two alternative explanations as to why the EDA and PESCO demonstrate varying degrees of authority in the issue area they are supposed to govern. The goal was to evaluate their respective explanatory power as compared to that of the rationalist regime complexity framework. It became evident that neither neorealism, with its focus on power and the EU–US relationship as explanatory variables, nor neofunctionalism, which put functional, political, and cultivated spillovers center stage, can fully explain the variation demonstrated in EDA's and PESCO's geneses. To have contrasted this framework with two alternative explanations for this variation and demonstrated their respective inadequacies in accounting for the full range of variation involved increases the plausibility and external validity of my approach.

Neorealism underestimates intra-EU dynamics and the EU member states' varying preferences for inclusive or exclusive cooperation while overemphasizing power. It thus has difficulties in accounting for the EU member states' varying institutional choices beyond the CSDP–NATO dichotomy. Conversely, neofunctionalism overestimates the influence of supranational actors and the importance of functional pressure and neglects intergovernmental bargaining (power). It therefore struggles to explain instances of non-integration and interinstitutional contestation.

The explanation for institutional success and failure I put forward is, however, commensurable with and can profit from the insights provided by both theoretical competitors. Neorealism helps understand Atlanticist and Europeanist preferences and thus to evaluate the importance of intra-EU bargaining and the threat of exclusion in overcoming this fundamental divide. Neofunctionalist reasoning assists in comprehending the factors that influenced the EU member states' preferences for inclusive or exclusive institutional membership. But focusing separately on either power or preferences provides an incomplete picture.

While I do not suggest a synthesis of neofunctionalism and neorealism, my framework still combines the insights provided by both. The explanatory power of my regime complexity framework consequently goes beyond both alternative explanations while retaining parsimony. Understanding the CSDP as a regime complex emerging from contestation and taking institutional alternatives beyond both the EU and NATO into account provides a convincing explanation of the observed variation. An institution's relative position in an emerging complex depends on the power *and* preferences of the states challenging the institutional status quo.

References

Albright, M. (2001). The right balance will secure NATO's future (7 December 1998). In Institute for Security Studies (Ed.), *Chaillot Papers* (vol. 47). *From St-Malo to Nice: European defence: Core documents* (pp. 10–12).

BAE Systems, EADS, & Thales. (2003). *Time to Act! Joint Declaration of BAE Systems, EADS and Thales*. http://www.defense-aerospace.com/articles-view/release/3/17409/euro-majors-warn-%22it%27s-time-to-act%22.html

Barroso, J. M. D. (2011). *The State of Europe—Die Europa Rede*. Berlin. http://europa.eu/rapid/press-release_SPEECH-11-738_en.htm

BBC News. (2014, March 12). Poland and Baltics wary over Crimea. https://www.bbc.com/news/world-europe-26526053

Bergmann, J., & Niemann, A. (2018). From neo-functional peace to a logic of spillover in EU external policy: A response to Visoka and Doyle. *JCMS: Journal of Common Market Studies, 56*(2), 420–438. https://doi.org/10.1111/jcms.12608

Bergmann, J. (2018). Neofunctionalism and EU external policy integration: The case of capacity building in support of security and development (CBSD). *Journal of European Public Policy, 355*(3), 1–20. https://doi.org/10.1080/13501763.2018.1526204

Biermann, F., & Weiss, M. (2021). Power without a cause? Germany's conflict avoidance and the integration of European defence procurement. *Journal of European Integration, 43*(2), 227–242. https://doi.org/10.1080/07036337.2021.1877691

Blauberger, M., & Weiss, M. (2013). 'If you can't beat me, join me! ' How the Commission pushed and pulled member states into legislating defence procurement. *Journal of European Public Policy, 20*(8), 1120–1138. https://doi.org/10.1080/13501763.2013.781783

Commission of the European Communities. (2005). *Communication on the results of the consultation launched by the green paper on defence procurement and on the future commission initiatives* (No. COM(2005) 626 final). https://eur-lex.europa.eu/legal-content/EN/TXT/?uri=CELEX%3A52005DC0626

CNN.com. (2009, March 17). Sarkozy wins French NATO re-entry vote. http://edition.cnn.com/2009/WORLD/europe/03/17/france.nato/

Council Decision establishing Permanent Structured Cooperation (PESCO) and determining the list of Participating Member States, *Official Journal of the European Union* (2017).

Council of the European Union. (2015, November 17). Foreign Affairs Council, 16–17/11/2015. https://www.consilium.europa.eu/en/meetings/fac/2015/11/16-17/

Deutsche Welle. (2017, March 6). Merkel backs idea of 'multispeed Europe' at Versailles meet. https://www.dw.com/en/merkel-backs-idea-of-multispeed-europe-at-versailles-meet/a-37833273

Dyson, T., & Konstanidides, T. (2013). *European defence cooperation in EU law and IR theory*. Palgrave Macmillan.

EEAS. (2016). *Shared vision, common action: A stronger Europe: A global strategy for the European Union's Foreign and Security Policy*. Brussels. European External Action Service (EEAS) website: https://eeas.europa.eu/sites/eeas/files/eugs_review_web_0.pdf

European Commission. (2003). *European defence-industrial and market issues: Towards an EU Defence Equipment Policy* (No. 113 final). Brussels. https://eur-lex.europa.eu/LexUriServ/LexUriServ.do?uri=COM:2003:0113:FIN:en:PDF

European Commission. (2011). *Standard Eurobarometer 76: Die Öffentliche Meinung in der Europäischen Union.* http://ec.europa.eu/commfrontoffice/publicopinion/archives/eb/eb76/eb76_agreport_de.pdf

European Commission. (2017a, June 7). A European Defence Fund: €5.5 billion per year to boost Europe's defence capabilities. http://europa.eu/rapid/press-release_IP-17-1508_en.htm

European Commission. (2017b). *Communication from the Commission to the European Parliament, the Council, the European Economic and Social Committee and the Committee of the Regions: Launching the European Defence Fund* (No. COM(2017) 295 final).

European Commission. (2019). *The European Defence Fund: Stepping up the EU's role as a security and defence provider.* https://ec.europa.eu/docsroom/documents/34509

European Council (2016a). *European Council meeting (15 December 2016)—Conclusions* (No. EUCO 34/16). Brussels. http://www.consilium.europa.eu/media/21929/15-euco-conclusions-final.pdf

European Parliament. (2006). *EU and NATO: Co-operation or competition?* (No. EP-ExPol-B-2006–14). http://www.europarl.europa.eu/meetdocs/2004_2009/documents/dv/eunatorelations_/eunatorelations_en.pdf

European Parliament. (2011a). *European Parliament resolution of 14 December 2011 on the impact of the financial crisis on the defence sector in the EU Member States* (2011/2177(INI)). Strasbourg. http://www.europarl.europa.eu/sides/getDoc.do?type=TA&language=EN&reference=P7-TA-2011-574

European Parliament. (2011b). *The impact of the financial crisis on European defence: Study.* https://www.swp-berlin.org/fileadmin/contents/products/fachpublikationen/Moelling_Brune_EU_Studie_2011_Teil1_ks.pdf

Fiott, D. (2015). The European Commission and the European Defence Agency: A case of rivalry? *JCMS: Journal of Common Market Studies, 53*(3), 542–557. https://doi.org/10.1111/jcms.12217

France, & United Kingdom. (1998). *Joint Declaration on European Defence: Joint Declaration issued at the British-French Summit.* Saint-Malo. https://www.cvce.eu/content/publication/2008/3/31/f3cd16fb-fc37-4d52-936f-c8e9bc80f24f/publishable_en.pdf

General Secretariat of the Council. (2017). Council conclusions on progress in implementing the EU Global Strategy in the area of Security and Defence, Brussels. https://www.consilium.europa.eu/en/press/press-releases/2017/03/06/conclusions-security-defence/

Georgopoulos, A. (2015). The EDA and EU defence procurement integration. In N. Karampekios & I. Oikonomou (Eds.), *Routledge studies in European security and strategy. The European Defence Agency: Arming Europe* (pp. 118–136). Routledge, Taylor & Francis Group.

Guay, T. R. (1996). Integration and Europe's Defense Industry. A "Reactive spillover" approach. *Policy Studies Journal, 24*(3), 404–419. https://doi.org/10.1111/j.1541-0072.1996.tb01637.x

Guay, T. R. (2005). *The European Defense Industry: Prospects for Consolidation* (UNISCI Discussion Papers No. 9). https://www.ucm.es/data/cont/media/www/pag-72532/UNISCI9Guay.pdf

Haas, E. B. (2004 [1958]). *The uniting of Europe: Political, social, and economical forces: 1950–1957. Contemporary European politics and society.* University of Notre Dame Press.

Haas, E. B. (1961). International Integration: The European and the Universal Process. *International Organization, 15*(03), 366. https://doi.org/10.1017/S0020818300002198

Haroche, P. (2019). Supranationalism strikes back: A neofunctionalist account of the European Defence Fund. *Journal of European Public Policy, 14*(3), 1–20. https://doi.org/10.1080/13501763.2019.1609570

Hartley, K. (2008). Collaboration and European Defence Industrial Policy. *Defence and Peace Economics, 19*(4), 303–315. https://doi.org/10.1080/10242690802221585

Hartley, K. (2011). Creating a European Defence Industrial Base. *Security Challenges, 7*(3), 95–111.

House of Commons. (2004). *Establishing a European Defence Agency: European Standing Committee B.*

Hummel, H. (2007). *A survey of involvement of 15 European States in the Iraq War 2003* (paks working paper No. 7). http://paks.uni-duesseldorf.de/Dokumente/paks_working_paper_7_rev.pdf

Hyde-Price, A. (2006). 'Normative' power Europe: A realist critique. *Journal of European Public Policy, 13*(2), 217–234. https://doi.org/10.1080/13501760500451634

International Institute for Strategic Studies (IISS). (2017). *The military balance 2017.* Routledge.

Irondelle, B., Mérand, F., & Foucault, M. (2015). Public support for European defence: Does strategic culture matter? *European Journal of Political Research, 54*(2), 363–383. https://doi.org/10.1111/1475-6765.12090

Jones, S. G. (2003). The European Union and the security dilemma. *Security Studies, 12*(3), 114–156. https://doi.org/10.1080/09636410390443107

Jones, S. G. (2007). *The rise of European security cooperation.* Cambridge University Press.

Juncker, J.-C. (2014). *A new start for Europe: My agenda for jobs, growth, fairness and democratic change: Political guidelines for the next European Commission, opening statement in the European Parliament Plenary*

Session. https://ec.europa.eu/commission/sites/beta-political/files/juncker-political-guidelines-speech_en.pdf

Juncker, J.-C. (2017). *In defence of Europe: Speech by President Jean-Claude Juncker at the Defence and Security Conference Prague.* http://europa.eu/rapid/press-release_SPEECH-17-1581_en.htm

Lindberg, L. N. (1963). *The political dynamics of European Economic integration.* Stanford University Press.

Mawdsley, J. (2003). The European Union and Defense Industrial Policy. https://www.bicc.de/uploads/tx_bicctools/paper31.pdf

Merlingen, M., & Ostrauskaite, R. (2009). *EU peacebuilding in Georgia: Limits and achievements* (CLEER Working Papers No. 6). https://www.peacepalacelibrary.nl/ebooks/files/335882102.pdf

Moravcsik, A. (1993a). Armaments among allies: European weapons collaboration, 1975–1985. In H. K. Jacobson, P. B. Evans, & R. D. Putnam (Eds.), *Studies in international political economy* (vol. 25). *Double-edged diplomacy: International bargaining and domestic politics* (pp. 128–167). University of California Press.

Moravcsik, A. (1993b). Preferences and power in the European Community: A liberal intergovernmentalist approach. *JCMS: Journal of Common Market Studies, 31*(4), 473–524. https://doi.org/10.1111/j.1468-5965.1993.tb00477.x

Moravcsik, A. (1998). *The choice for Europe: Social purpose and state power from Messina to Maastricht. Cornell studies in political economy.* Cornell University Press.

NATO. (2004). *Berlin plus information note: Shape support to the EU operational headquarters.* https://shape.nato.int/resources/3/images/2013/althea/berlin%20plus-information%20note.pdf

NATO. (2014). *Wales Summit Declaration: Issued by the Heads of State and Government participating in the meeting of the North Atlantic Council in Wales.* https://www.nato.int/cps/en/natohq/official_texts_112964.htm

Niemann, A., & Schmittner, P. C. (2009). Neofunctionalism. In A. Wiener & T. Diez (Eds.), *European integration theory* (2nd ed., pp. 45–66). Oxford University Press.

Niemann, A. (1998). The PHARE programme and the concept of spillover: Neofunctionalism in the making. *Journal of European Public Policy, 5*(3), 428–446. https://doi.org/10.1080/135017698343901

Oikonomou, I. (2015). Brothers in arms? The European arms industry and the making of the EDA. In N. Karampekios & I. Oikonomou (Eds.), *Routledge studies in European security and strategy. The European Defence Agency: Arming Europe.* Routledge, Taylor & Francis Group.

Pesme, F. (2010). France's 'return' to NATO: Implications for its defence policy. *European Security, 19*(1), 45–60. https://doi.org/10.1080/09662839.2010.507245

Peters, D. (2011). A divided union? Public opinion and the EU's Common Foreign, security and defence policy (RECON Online Working Paper No. 19). http://www.reconproject.eu/projectweb/portalproject/AbstractRECONwp1119.html

Posen, B. R. (2006). European Union Security and Defense Policy: Response to unipolarity? *Security Studies, 15*(2), 149–186. https://doi.org/10.1080/09636410600829356

Rasmussen, A. F. (2010). *Strategic concept for the defence and security of the members of the North Atlantic Treaty Organisation adopted by Heads of State and Government in Lisbon: Active engagement, modern defence.* https://www.nato.int/lisbon2010/strategic-concept-2010-eng.pdf

Reuters. (2017, June 10). Germany, France drafting details of defense fund: German minister. https://www.reuters.com/article/us-eu-defence-germany-france-idUSKBN1910H4

Rieker, P. (2013). The French return to NATO: Reintegration in practice, not in principle. *European Security, 22*(3), 376–394. https://doi.org/10.1080/09662839.2013.767238

Rosato, S. (2011). Europe's troubles: Power politics and the state of the European project. *International Security, 35*(4), 45–86. https://doi.org/10.1162/ISEC_a_00035

Schmitter, P. C., & Lefkofridi, Z. (2016). Neo-functionalism as a theory of disintegration. *Chinese Political Science Review, 1*(1), 1–29. https://doi.org/10.1007/s41111-016-0012-4

Schweller, R. L. (1994). Bandwagoning for profit: Bringing the revisionist state back in. *International Security, 19*(1), 72. https://doi.org/10.2307/2539149

Shepherd, A. J. K. (2015). EU military capability development and the EDA: Ideas, interests and institutions. In N. Karampekios & I. Oikonomou (Eds.), *Routledge studies in European security and strategy. The European Defence Agency: Arming Europe.* Routledge, Taylor & Francis Group.

Snyder, G. H. (1984). The security dilemma in alliance politics. *World Politics, 36*(04), 461–495. https://doi.org/10.2307/2010183

Spiegel Online. (2019, May 14). EU-Außenministertreffen in Brüssel: USA attackieren EU-Pläne für Verteidigungsfonds. https://www.spiegel.de/politik/ausland/usa-attackieren-eu-plaene-fuer-verteidigungsfonds-a-1267291.html

Stephenson, P. (2010). Let's get physical: The European Commission and cultivated spillover in completing the single market's transport infrastructure.

Journal of European Public Policy, 17(7), 1039–1057. https://doi.org/10.1080/13501763.2010.499247

Stone Sweet, A., & Sandholtz, W. (1997). European integration and supranational governance. *Journal of European Public Policy, 4*(3), 297–317. https://doi.org/10.1080/13501769780000011

The Guardian. (2014, March 26). Barack Obama: No cold war over Crimea. https://www.theguardian.com/world/2014/mar/26/obama-no-cold-war-crimea

The Guardian. (2016, July 21). Trump says US may not automatically defend Nato allies under attack. https://www.theguardian.com/world/2016/jul/21/donald-trump-america-automatically-nato-allies-under-attack

The Financial Times. (2016a, November 13). Baltics fear for any US policy changes to Nato: Possibility of a disengagement has rung alarm bells in states. https://www.ft.com/content/0036b09a-a825-11e6-8898-79a99e2a4de6

The Financial Times. (2016b, November 14). Donald Trump, Vladimir Putin and the art of a deal with Russia. https://www.ft.com/content/9bef31a4-aa57-11e6-a0bb-97f42551dbf4

Tocci, N. (2018). Towards a European Security and Defence Union: Was 2017 a watershed? *JCMS: Journal of Common Market Studies, 49*, 57. https://doi.org/10.1111/jcms.12752

Tranholm-Mikkelsen, J. (1991). Neo-functionalism: Obstinate or obsolete? A reappraisal in the light of the new dynamism of the EC. *Millennium: Journal of International Studies, 20*(1), 1–22. https://doi.org/10.1177/03058298910200010201

Trybus, M. (2005). *European Union law and defence integration. Modern studies in European law* (vol. 7). Hart.

Waltz, K. N. (1979). *Theory of international politics*. Addison-Wesley Pub. Co.

Weiss, M., & Blauberger, M. (2015). Judicialized law-making and opportunistic enforcement: Explaining the EU's challenge of national defence offsets. *JCMS: Journal of Common Market Studies*, 1–19. https://doi.org/10.1111/jcms.12290

Weiss, M. (2009). Power and signals: Explaining the German approach to European security. *Journal of International Relations and Development, 12*, 317–348. https://doi.org/10.1057/jird.2009.15

Weiss, M. (2021). Varieties of privatization: Informal networks, trust and state control of the commanding heights. *Review of International Political Economy, 28*(3), 662–689. https://doi.org/10.1080/09692290.2020.1726791

Weiss, M., & Biermann, F. (2021). Networked politics and the supply of European defence integration. *Journal of European Public Policy, 90*(3), 1–22. https://doi.org/10.1080/13501763.2021.1916057

CHAPTER 10

Quo Vadis, CSDP?

This study has pursued three main goals. First, my research was inspired by the observation that the EU's CSDP institutions vary considerably in their ability to fulfill their formal mandate. The European Defense Agency was created to organize joint procurement and management of armaments programs but was later downgraded to a marketplace for ideas. PESCO, contrariwise, was created as a body with institutional potential and suppressed for a decade until it was finally activated and emerged as the new center of authority in European defense planning. Explaining this variation across institutions was the study's first ambition.

Second, I observed that, although not using either the EDA or PESCO, EU member states did not refrain from institutionalized cooperation altogether. Rather, they cooperated in alternative institutional frameworks outside the EU. Taking these institutions, such as OCCAR, NORDEFCO, or the WEAO, into account suggests that European defense cooperation is best understood as an institutional complex in which elemental institutions overlap with respect to the mandate. The second ambition of this study was to go beyond European integration theory and examine the implications of an innovative approach to analyzing the EU by making use of the literature on regime complexity and contested multilateralism.

The third goal was to synthesize these two ambitions. I developed a theoretical framework to explain the observed variation in the relative authority of the CSDP institutions in their respective complex. Having identified four types of interinstitutional relationship, each characterized by a distinct authority distribution, I theorized the conditions leading to each outcome. Finally, I tested whether the theorized framework was useful in explaining the different authority distributions that emerged in European armaments cooperation and defense planning. My goal was to demonstrate that the processes leading to the integration of the WEAG/WEAO into the EDA, the EDA's marginalization through OCCAR, the fragmentation of European defense planning, and PESCO's resilience unfolded along the theorized pathways based on the go-it-alone power and membership preference of a dissatisfied state coalition challenging the institutional status quo.

The four process-tracing case studies and the subsequent congruence analysis contrasting my argument with alternative explanations derived from neorealist and neofunctionalist reasoning providing evidence of the explanatory power of the theoretical framework. In achieving its goals, this book makes four core contributions, which I will recapitulate by summarizing my argument step by step in the remainder of this chapter.

My first contribution, set out in the first section of this concluding chapter, lies in the advancement of the ongoing debate on the causes and consequences of institutional complexity. This study considerably broadens the scope of the regime complexity literature. I take institutional complexes as a starting point and understand the degree of hierarchy between its constituent institutions as an outcome rather than defining such complexes as non-hierarchical. Integration and fragmentation, one fully hierarchical, the other non-hierarchical, can result from the same original situation—depending on the power and preferences of the challengers and defenders of the status quo. Combining the insights provided by contested multilateralism (Morse & Keohane, 2014; van de Graaf, 2013) with theorizing on regime complexity (Faude & Fuss, 2020; Gehring & Faude, 2013, 2014; Pratt, 2018), has allowed me to fan out the varying outcomes of interinstitutional relationships that emerged in regime complexes and to illuminate the conditions and pathways leading to each of them. In sum, I demonstrate that institutional complexes are, in fact, less complicated and unpredictable than they were thought to be.

The second section summarizes the empirical analysis, which represented a dual contribution to the existing literature. On the one hand, applying my framework to the study of the EU allowed me to go beyond Liberal Intergovernmentalism, which turns a blind eye to institutional developments outside the EU treaties. Focusing on grand bargains, LI neglects the subtler dynamics evident in the relative position of EU institutions in comparison to their non-EU competitors and thus overlooks differences in the CSDP institutions' relative authority. Though characterized by the same level of integration, namely, the pooling and delegation of formal-legal authority, the CSDP institutions demonstrate considerable variation in their de facto ability to fulfill their formal mandate. Hence, conceptualizing the CSDP as part of a regime complex and considering its elemental institutions as competitors rather than treating it as a unitary alternative to NATO helps understand the drivers of and obstacles to EU integration that have previously escaped scholarly attention. European integration theory thus benefits from the results of this study as it provides guidance for future research on the prospects of and challenges to European integration.

On the other hand, I entered unchartered empirical territory in setting out an innovative analytical approach to the timing of the EDA's and PESCO's establishment, their design, their (in)ability to fulfill their mandates, and their future prospects. I have offered a new perspective on the EDA's genesis and relevance, which had already been subject to scientific scrutiny (see, for example, Fiott, 2015; Karampekios & Oikonomou, 2015), contrasting it with its—so far neglected—institutional contenders. Substantiating my analysis with new process evidence from primary sources, which have not yet been analyzed, I provide new insights into the underlying conflicts between the EU member states that have characterized EDA's development (Biermann, 2022) for a slightly different take on PESCO's creation and its implications for European integration. Explaining the geneses and difference in relative importance of the CSDP's two flagship institutions, this study might be of interest to all those with a substantial interest in the EU's CSDP—both in—and outside academia.

The third section of this chapter delineates avenues for further research on the CSDP that arise from this study. First, my theoretical framework relies on rational choice institutionalism and thus takes a snapshot perspective on different points in time. I argue that broadening the time horizon and allowing for endogenous processes, in other words, enriching the framework of institutional order with historical institutionalist theorizing (Hall, 2010; Pierson, 2004), could offer intriguing additional insights. It would make it possible to investigate the question of whether all four institutional orders are equally stable and, thus, if some outcomes of institutional order are more likely than others. Taking into account recent institutional developments in the realm of the CSDP, for instance, the decision on a European Intervention Initiative outside the PESCO framework, offers a hint that marginalization might be the most common outcome in the end—at least in the European security and defense policy complex.

Second, I come back to the relationship between the EU and NATO, which I introduced at the very beginning of this book. I discuss the implications this book's arguments have for the future development of their interinstitutional relationship. The claim is that the relationship between the EU and NATO will not depend on the external security situation or the relationship between the EU and the United States, as neorealists might have it. Rather, the weakening of the EU's CSDP and the simultaneous strengthening of NATO during the war in Ukraine in 2022 seems to follow the very same logic that we observed for the EDA and OCCAR: The CSDP—both as a whole and its elemental institutions—has been marginalized; it remains to be seen, however, whether this process is one that produces distributional conflict or if cooperation and work-sharing will be at the front and center of their future relationship.

Interinstitutional Relationships in Regime Complexes

In the following, I summarize the theoretical framework rolled out in Chapters 2 and 3. Chapter 2 took stock of the existing literature on regime complexity and contested multilateralism, discussing the dominant perspectives on the emergence and consequences of overlapping regimes. My approach understands situations of contested multilateralism (Morse & Keohane, 2014) to be the origin of institutional complexity. Dissatisfied coalitions of states, which are unable to reform an institution from within, engage in competitive regime creation or regime shifting to challenge the institutional status quo. Consequently, there are at least two elemental institutions with overlapping mandates to govern the same issue area, constituting an institutional complex.

Departing from the existing literature on emerging order in institutional complexes (Gehring & Faude, 2013, 2014; Hofmann, 2011), I argued that an analysis of the effects of institutional complexes should examine whether there is hierarchy between the elemental institutions. The degree of hierarchy between the elemental institutions characterizing a complex shapes the opportunity structure for both conflict and cooperation (Faude & Fuss, 2020; Pratt, 2018). Some strategies, such as forum shopping or hostage-taking (Hofmann, 2018), are no longer available in a hierarchical setting. Taking the regime complex as a starting point rather than a result, I demonstrated that overlap in membership and resources could vary, contributing to different distributions of relational authority (Lake, 2009, 2010) between the elemental institutions of the complex. Overlaps in membership and resources generate patterns of institutional use that indicate the relative authority an institution has over an issue area. Relational authority can be distributed equally or unequally across the elemental institutions of a complex. In some complexes, a center of authority, a focal institution, emerges; others are fragmented. The degree of hierarchy in an institutional complex should, therefore, be an empirical question rather than a definitional element. My definition of an institutional complex, which treats overlap in the mandate as the only essential feature, thus considerably broadens definitions advanced by Keohane and Victor (2011), Raustiala and Victor (2004), Alter and Meunier (2009), and Alter and Raustiala (2018), which exclude both fragmented regimes and integrated structures.

This broader definition allowed me to fulfill the second task I set myself in Chapter 2, which was to develop a typology of the dependent variable of this research project, namely the distribution of authority within a complex, which constitutes its institutional order. If states create a new institutional alternative in an issue area already populated by another forum, four types of institutional order can emerge.

Elemental institutions with separate membership and resources characterize an order of *fragmented* authority—there is no coordination among the institutions, and no institution has more authority than the others. If the two elemental institutions are *integrated*, they have identical membership and pooled resources, and authority is centralized in one institution. This centralization of both formal and relational authority in an overarching framework is tantamount to hierarchy. Finally, there are two intermediate cases, which emerge when the two institutions' membership and resources overlap and states use one institution more regularly than the other. These situations amount to a semi-hierarchical order in which both institutions maintain the formal-legal authority to regulate an issue area while relational authority over the issue area is distributed unevenly.

This makes one institution focal while the other is sidelined. A situation in which the original institution is sidelined while the newly created institutional competitor becomes focal, I call *marginalization*. One in which the contested institution is refocused because the competitor proves ineffective, I call *resilience*.

Chapter 3 identified the conditions leading to the different outcomes of institutional order in an institutional complex. I argued that the authority distribution between the elemental institutions of a complex depends on the dynamic interaction between the challengers and defenders of the institutional status quo. Within the rational choice institutionalist paradigm, I theorized what dissatisfied states would want and what they would be able to achieve if they challenged an institution through competitive regime creation.

Dissatisfied states without the ability to reform an institution from within pursue the goal of making a more favorable institutional set-up the new center of authority. Whether states are able to achieve a change in the focal institution, that is, to create an institutional competitor that subsequently has more authority over an issue area than the original institution, depends on their ability to create a credible threat of exclusion. Only when a coalition of challenger states is able to go it alone (Gruber, 2000), that is, to unilaterally alter the status quo, will the defenders give in and accept a new center of authority by shifting their resources to the new framework—even against their original preferences. In other words, only if powerful coalitions engage in contestation will the outcome be integration or the marginalization of the original institution. This supports prior research on the effects of institutional complexity: It seems to benefit the most powerful by giving them the ability to choose their most preferred venue (Benvenisti & Downs, 2007; Drezner, 2009, 2013). Yet, importantly, this is only one side of the coin. *While state coalitions that lack go-it-alone power have difficulties in creating new centers of authority, they still have the means to challenge the institutional status quo sustainably and retain the ability to block cooperation they deem not to be beneficial.* This is the case when they have an exclusive membership preference.

Depending on the member surplus–transaction cost trade-off, the challengers will prefer either an inclusive or an exclusive membership for their newly created institution. If the cost incurred by accepting additional members is high in relation to the opportunity cost of non-cooperation, states prefer an exclusive institution. This is the case when the cooperation problem in question is redistributive and member state preferences are heterogeneous. Conversely, if the costs of non-cooperation are high in relation to the costs of inclusion, states prefer an inclusive membership. This is the case when regulatory or standard-setting issues without direct distributive consequences are at stake, and state preferences are homogenous (Snidal, 1994; Thompson & Verdier, 2014).

Building on these insights, I argue that the combination of these two factors—the challengers' go-it-alone power (Gruber, 2000) and their membership preference (Thompson & Verdier, 2014)—determines the four pathways leading to the distinct outcomes of institutional order.

If the dissatisfied challenger coalition possesses *go-it-alone power*, the institutional competitor they have created will represent a credible threat of exclusion to defenders of the status quo. Fearing to be left out, the defenders will attempt to join the new institution. Whether the challenger states have an interest in admitting them will depend on the ratio between member surplus and transaction cost.

1. When the challengers prefer an *inclusive membership* and accept the defenders into the new forum, the two institutions will end up with identical membership—there will be no overlap. What is more, both challengers and defenders will reallocate their entire resources to the new institution as there will be no more benefits from maintaining both of them. The result is the *integration* of the original institution's functions into the newly created alternative.
2. When powerful challengers prefer an *exclusive* alternative to the pre-existing, inclusive institution, membership overlap is the consequence. The challengers are dual members, while the defenders of the status quo are members of the original institution only. Moreover, when the challengers shift their resources to the exclusive institution, it has a detrimental effect on the defenders. The latter, thus, have an interest in coordinating the activities between the two institutions to secure at least some influence for the original venue. Sectorial specialization, expanding the authority of the institutional competitor while limiting the influence of the original institution, is the result. The contested institution is *marginalized*.

If the challengers lack go-it-alone power, the defenders do not fear being excluded and thus make no effort to join the institution. Whether the challengers' undertaking to shift the focus away from the original institution is successful nonetheless depends once again on the membership preference.

3. The challengers' lack of go-it-alone power, in combination with a preference on their part for an exclusive forum, will lead to a quasi-symmetrical power distribution between challengers and defenders. When the challengers prefer exclusive cooperation among themselves, they can block the original institution and shift their resources to the new forum. As a result, the defenders will no longer be able to use their preferred forum but have to create an alternative institution themselves to re-establish their original utility level. Consequently, the *fragmentation* of the institutional landscape will be the outcome.
4. Lacking go-it-alone power and having an *inclusive* membership preference, challengers will not be able to sustain cooperation among themselves and need additional states to retain their utility level. Failure on the part of the challengers to create a credible outside option is tantamount to an ability on the defenders' part to refocus the original institution and generate a threat of exclusion part of their own. The defenders will thus be able to draw the challengers back to the original institution. If the challengers subsequently agree to shift their resources back, the original institution proves *resilient*, and the challengers' attempt to alter the status quo is unsuccessful.

The CSDP Between Preferences and Power

I have argued that the integration of the WEAG/WEAO structures into the EDA and its subsequent marginalization through OCCAR, on the one hand, and the decade-long fragmentation of European defense planning and PESCO's resilience in 2017 were outcomes of similar dynamics of contestation. A coalition of states challenged the institution they were dissatisfied with and attempted to shift the focus to an institutional competitor, while another coalition defended the status quo. In other words, whether the EDA or PESCO emerged or did not emerge as the center of authority in the issue area it (supposedly) governed depended on its challengers' go-it-alone power and membership preference. To verify this claim, I conducted four case studies.

In all four cases, I was able to demonstrate that a coalition of EU member states was dissatisfied with an existing institution and found the way to internal reform blocked by veto players. The scope conditions under which my framework applies were thus present. In each case, the dissatisfied states created an institutional competitor to challenge the original institution, which triggered the mechanisms that subsequently led to the different outcomes in terms of institutional order. Moreover, in each of the four cases, I confirmed the presence of the causal pathways, which unfolded as theorized. The respective combination of the two conditions, go-it-alone power and membership preference, accounted for the distribution of authority among the original institution and its competitors in the complex. Taken together, this strengthens the internal validity of the theorized framework of institutional order.

In order to judge the external validity and enhance the plausibility of my framework, however, it was necessary to contrast it with alternative explanations. Therefore, by means of a congruence analysis, Chapter 9 engaged with competing hypotheses derived from two theoretical contenders, neorealism (Dyson & Konstadinides, 2013, p. 154; Posen, 2006; Rosato, 2011) and neofunctionalism (Niemann, 1998; Stone Sweet & Sandholtz, 1997). The re-evaluation of the empirical evidence through these two lenses made it obvious that neither can fully explain the observed variation. Neorealism underestimates intra-EU dynamics and the EU member states varying preferences for inclusive or exclusive cooperation while overemphasizing power and thus has difficulty in accounting for member states' varying institutional choices beyond the EU–NATO dichotomy. Conversely, neofunctionalism overestimates the influence that supranational actors have and the importance of functional pressure while neglecting (intergovernmental bargaining) power. Hence, this theory struggles to explain instances of non-integration and interinstitutional contestation.

Taken together, the empirical part of this study demonstrated that the theoretical framework I proposed possesses considerable explanatory leverage for the institutional developments in the EU's CSDP and fares significantly better than its theoretical contenders in explaining the variation in the EDA's and PESCO's ability to fulfill their formal mandates. As this empirical subject falls into the domain of application of both neorealism, emphasizing hegemonically induced cooperation, and neofunctionalism, focusing on endogenous spillover effects, the institutional context represents a hard case for my theoretical framework.

Neither hegemonic interference nor endogenous processes nor supranational actors intervened in such a way as to disqualify the causal mechanisms I theorized. In consequence, I am confident that my framework is equally applicable in different, more favorable institutional and issue-specific contexts, where IO bureaucracies and hegemonic power play even less of a role.

Avenues for Further Research: Endogeneity, Marginalization, and the Future of the CSDP

In conclusion, I would like to highlight three implications for future research on institutional complexes in general and the CSDP specifically that arise from this thesis. First, since the EU represents a hard case for my framework, given its social context, spillover dynamics, and the availability of issue linkages that make competitive regime creation less likely, there are good reasons to believe that the theorized causal pathways to different institutional orders are generalizable to institutional complexes outside the EU. Yet, to further refine and enhance confidence in the framework, it would be necessary to engage in further research beyond EU boundaries. A valuable approach would be to test the theorized conditions as independent variables across a larger set of cases or undertake additional theory-testing process-tracing case studies. Examples of such cases are manifold. Prominent examples are the creation of the Asian Infrastructure Investment Bank, which was intended by China to pressure both the International Monetary Fund and the World Bank, or the US exit from the Transpacific Partnership (TPP) and decision to opt for bilateral agreements instead. In order to provide further theoretical refinement, it would be most helpful to investigate institutional complexes consisting of more than two elemental institutions. This would allow the distorting or supporting impact of network effects among the elements of the institutional complex to be examined (Daßler, 2022; Orsini et al., 2013). Finally, future research would profit from selecting cases not only from different institutional complexes beyond the EU but also from different issue areas, such as economic or environmental affairs. Possible examples include, but are not limited to, the often investigated regime complexes for climate change (Karlsson-Vinkhuyzen & McGee, 2013; Keohane & Victor, 2011) or global energy governance (Colgan et al., 2012; van de Graaf, 2013).

A second avenue for further research would involve a promising expansion of the theoretical lens employed for this study. Drawing on RCI, I have so far adopted a comparative statics perspective on institutional complexes and implicitly assumed that each institutional order represents an equilibrium outcome, which can only be punctuated by exogenous shocks (Krasner, 1984). Consequently, this theoretical approach neglects developments over time and does not allow for suboptimal outcomes and unintended consequences, as suggested by Historical Institutionalism (HI) (Pierson, 2000; Stone Sweet & Sandholtz, 1997, p. 299).

As RCI and HI are compatible (Hall & Taylor, 1996) with the proposed framework, it may well benefit from loosening some assumptions regarding the stability of the emerging interinstitutional relationships. Considering endogenous changes over time and emphasizing bounded rationality have important implications for the member surplus–transaction cost trade-off underlying challengers' membership preference. Introducing time into the equation undermines the simplifying assumption that transaction costs and member surplus are constant. States outside an institution have different and changing costs of compliance and their importance to the founders of an institution will vary. Therefore, it is likely that the trade-off between member surplus and transaction costs has an optimum solution as far as the challenger states, the founders of the institutional alternative, are concerned that lies somewhere between full exclusion of additional members and complete inclusion (Thompson & Verdier, 2014, p. 18). Including the optimal number of states is not a simple task, however. There are two reasons for this. First, in light of bounded rationality, there is considerable uncertainty about others' preferences and abilities, which leads challengers to *exclude too many states* when they do not know if the incentives they are willing to offer will lead the new members to comply (Koremenos et al., 2001, p. 784). Second, if the challengers rely on a market mechanism to set a high entry bar, this will not necessarily yield the desired outcome either. Recalling the "bandwagoning" effect induced by the threat of exclusion, even the least competitive defender states might join an institution if others had done so before them. Consequently, the threat of exclusion tends to result in a membership structure that is *too inclusive* (Biermann, 2022).

If membership is either too inclusive or too exclusive and thus suboptimal from the challengers' perspective, this may, in turn, cause dissatisfaction and even stimulate the creation of additional competitors. Indeed, this could be observed in the EDA case: As membership was too inclusive after the WEAG/WEAO integration and decision-making proved cumbersome, dissatisfied avant-gardist states shifted their resources to OCCAR, thereby marginalizing the EDA. The outcome of integration was endogenously unstable, but the subsequent marginalization, in which a coalition of relatively powerful states used an exclusive forum for ambitious cooperative projects while maintaining an inclusive institution with limited authority on the margins, proved stable. Thus, further research following a process-sequencing design (Howlett & Rayner, 2006, p. 7) to investigate the (in)stability of institutional orders might identify interesting regularities, such as marginalization being more likely than others to be a stable outcome.

Third, I would like to emphasize that investigation of the endogenous instability of institutional order is not only theoretically relevant but may help predict an individual institution's relative position in a complex. Considering recent developments in European military cooperation, there is evidence that PESCO might suffer the same fate as the EDA. Its inclusive membership, a consequence of the bandwagon effect stimulated by a group of powerful member states' threatening exclusion, reduces the likelihood of agreement on the measures necessary to achieve convergence and specialization as envisaged.

While PESCO subsumed an impressive 47 projects in 2020, only a few of these were initiated within the new framework; the vast majority pre-existed it and "had been launched or planned before PESCO" (Terlikowski, 2020). What is more, 30 projects have remained at the "ideation phase, including some which were already established in … 2018" (Council of the European Union, 2020, p. 4). In addition, PESCO's inclusiveness distorted the "binding commitments" beyond recognition. As decisions taken by PESCO members require unanimity, commitments equate to minimal consensus in line with the preferences of the least ambitious member states. There were no provisions, for instance, specifying a date by which the 2% defense-spending goal was to be reached (France et al., 2017, Art. III (1, 4)).

France, which desired a more exclusive framework from the outset, was disappointed with this development. Yet, in view of the impossibility of reforming the membership of PESCO, what can we expect a dissatisfied state to do? French President Emmanuel Macron proposed the establishment of the European Intervention Initiative (EII) (Macron, 2017). Dissatisfied with the inclusive character of PESCO and the poverty of its ambition, France intended to add another cooperation forum to the landscape of European defense. Moreover, in order to reintegrate the military capacity of the United Kingdom, the French proposal is set up the initiative outside both NATO and EU structures (Politico, 2018), thus effectively creating an institutional competitor to PESCO. On 25 June 2018, 9 states[1] signed up for the EII and created a competitive regime outside the EU structures once again (*The Guardian*, 2018). Depending on its future participants' willingness to form an exclusive and ambitious framework and their ability to go it alone, the establishment of the EII may well be the trigger for a process that results in PESCO's marginalization. The framework of institutional order predicts that this is precisely what will happen, as the EII's members include four states out of Europe's "big six," which lends considerable weight to the initiative. In addition, both Denmark and the United Kingdom, which are not PESCO members, are participants in the EII. They are thus likely to push for the new institution to become the center of authority in European military cooperation and undermine the influence of the CSDP in organizing European security and defense.

Finally, and in a similar vein, the arguments presented in this study help us understand the recent major trends in the European security and defense complex. As mentioned at the very beginning of this book, in the run-up to the outbreak of the Ukraine war, the EU was already losing authority vis-à-vis its institutional alternative, NATO. EU institutions and member states were only bystanders in the diplomatic attempts to prevent war, and NATO was the only forum for EU member states to get information and transmit their position. Similarly, when Russia eventually attacked Ukraine in February 2022, this marked a watershed moment—the much-cited German *"Zeitenwende"* for security and defense. However, while EU member states considerably increased their military spending, the instinctive reaction was to invest in intergovernmental purchases from the United States (Foreignpolicy.com, 2022) rather than engaging in concerted action.

Even the success of medium-term European programs is questionable. While France, Spain, and Germany reiterated their strong interest in the Future Combat Air System (FCAS) in December 2022, they were unable to bring in Italy as well. Italy, together with the United Kingdom and Japan, had agreed one week earlier to develop a competing system—the Tempest fighter jet (BBC.com, 2022). From an EU perspective,

---

[1] France, Germany, Belgium, Denmark, Netherlands, Estonia, Spain, Portugal, and the United Kingdom.

this was unfortunate. The avant-gardists are divided, and it thus appears unlikely that the FCAS will be able to withstand US competition in the remaining EU member states. The problems that became apparent in the EDA–OCCAR case seem to be reappearing and issues, such as system duplication and lack of interoperability, persist.

The trend to concentrate security and defense cooperation with NATO and the United States rather than by closing ranks in the EU was further cemented through the Finnish and Swedish decision to give up their neutrality and join the alliance. In view of the mandate overlap between the EU and NATO (e.g., both operate a mutual assistance clause, both provide the structures to organize joint missions), the Finnish and Swedish decisions contribute to a considerable weakening of the EU's authority in security and defense vis-à-vis NATO.

How to make sense of these developments? Deviating from a neorealist line of argumentation, which would unfold along the lines of a strictly power-based explanation emphasizing the role of the United States, the theoretical framework presented in this book would conceptualize the EU member states' decisions to focus on their NATO commitments and neglect CSDP institutions as a case of marginalization. Confronted with the various shortcomings of both the EDA and PESCO, which have been discussed in this book at length, and with the reality of Russia's neglect of the EU in the diplomatic arena, EU member states were dissatisfied with the existing CSDP institutions and shifted their resources to NATO—which has induced even traditionally neutral states to join it. NATO has clearly established itself as the center of authority in security and defense matters.

Nonetheless, the dual members still benefit from having two institutions at their disposal to cope with Russia, the war in Ukraine, and security more generally. Indeed, we observe a typical sign of marginalization, as theorized in this book: sectorial specialization. While NATO is the framework in which military-strategic governance takes place, EU member states use EU institutions to flank their hard-power activities (e.g., arms transfers, intelligence) with soft-power measures, such as economic sanctions. Even though the EU member states seem to have accepted NATO as the center of authority, keeping the EU as an alternative in the realm of security and defense is beneficial to maintaining at least a minimum of what has been called "strategic autonomy."

Therefore, a dismantling of the CSDP institutions and their integration into NATO structures is not to be expected. It would not be surprising, however, if the Atlanticist states, together with the United States, were to try to use this window of opportunity to further cement the dominance of the NATO framework and worked toward an update of the 2002 Berlin Plus agreement, further increasing the EU's dependence on NATO. EU and NATO staffs are currently negotiating a "new comprehensive and ambitious document that would strengthen and deepen EU-NATO partnership" (Borrell i Fontelles, 2022). This third EU–NATO declaration is eagerly anticipated and will likely overshadow the prospects of an autonomous CSDP in the years ahead.

REFERENCES

Alter, K. J., & Meunier, S. (2009). The politics of international regime complexity. *Perspectives on Politics, 7*(01), 13–24. https://doi.org/10.1017/S1537592709090033

Alter, K. J., & Raustiala, K. (2018). The rise of international regime complexity. *Annual Review of Law and Social Science, 14*(1), 329–349. https://doi.org/10.1146/annurev-lawsocsci-101317-030830

BBC.com. (2022). https://www.bbc.com/news/uk-63908284. https://www.bbc.com/news/uk-63908284

Benvenisti, E., & Downs, G. W. (2007). The emperor's new clothes: Political economy and the fragmentation of international law. *Stanford Law Review, 60*(2), 595–632.

Biermann, F. (2022). The differentiation paradox of European Integration: Why going it alone produces suboptimal results. *JCMS: Journal of Common Market Studies*, Early view. https://doi.org/10.1111/jcms.13373

Borrell i Fontelles, J. (2022). *Answer given by High Representative/Vice-President Borrell i Fontelles on behalf of the European Commission* (No. P-003903/2022). https://www.europarl.europa.eu/doceo/document/P-9-2022-003903-ASW_EN.html

Colgan, J. D., Keohane, R. O., & van de Graaf, T. (2012). Punctuated equilibrium in the energy regime complex. *The Review of International Organizations, 7*(2), 117–143. https://doi.org/10.1007/s11558-011-9130-9

Council of the European Union. (2020). Council Recommendation of 15 June 2020 assessing the progress made by the participating Member States to fulfil commitments undertaken in the framework of permanent structured cooperation (PESCO). *Official Journal of the European Union, 2020*(C 204). https://eur-lex.europa.eu/legal-content/EN/TXT/PDF/?uri=CELEX:32020H0618(01)&from=EN

Daßler, B. (2022). Good(s) for everyone? Policy area competition and institutional topologies in the regime complexes of tax avoidance and intellectual property. *Journal of International Relations and Development, 54*(3), 421. https://doi.org/10.1057/s41268-022-00267-x

Drezner, D. W. (2009). The power and peril of international regime complexity. *Perspectives on Politics, 7*(01), 65–70. https://doi.org/10.1017/S1537592709090100

Drezner, D. W. (2013). The tragedy of the global institutional commons. In J. Goldstein & M. Finnemore (Eds.), *Back to basics: State power in a contemporary world* (pp. 280–310). Oxford University Press. https://doi.org/10.1093/acprof:oso/9780199970087.003.0013

Dyson, T., & Konstadinides, T. (2013). *European defence cooperation in EU law and IR theory*. Palgrave Macmillan.

Faude, B., & Fuss, J. (2020). Coordination or conflict? The causes and consequences of institutional overlap in a disaggregated world order. *Global Constitutionalism, 9*(2), 268–289. https://doi.org/10.1017/S2045381719000376

Fiott, D. (2015). The European Commission and the European Defence Agency: A case of rivalry? *JCMS: Journal of Common Market Studies, 53*(3), 542–557. https://doi.org/10.1111/jcms.12217

Foreignpolicy.com. (2022). *The arsenal of democracy is back in business*. https://foreignpolicy.com/2022/12/29/arms-sales-united-states-nato-russia-ukraine-war-the-arsenal-of-democracy-is-back-in-business/

France, Germany, Spain, & Italy. (2017). *Permanent Structured Cooperation (PESCO): FR/DE/ES/IT Proposals on the necessary commitments and elements for an inclusive and ambitious PESCO Supported by BE, CZ, FI and NL*. Paris, Berlin, Madrid, Rome. http://club.bruxelles2.eu/wp-content/uploads/2017/08/principescommuns-pesco-propfrallespita@ue170721.pdf

Gehring, T., & Faude, B. (2013). The dynamics of regime complexes: Microfoundations and systemic effects. *Global Governance, 19*, 119–130.

Gehring, T., & Faude, B. (2014). A theory of emerging order within institutional complexes: How competition among regulatory international institutions leads to institutional adaptation and division of labor. *The Review of International Organizations, 9*(4), 471–498. https://doi.org/10.1007/s11558-014-9197-1

Gruber, L. (2000). *Ruling the world: Power politics and the rise of supranational institutions*. Princeton University Press.

Hall, P. A. (2010). Historical institutionalism in rationalist and sociological perspective. In J. Mahoney & K. A. Thelen (Eds.), *Explaining institutional change: Ambiguity, agency, and power*. Cambridge University Press.

Hall, P. A., & Taylor, R. C. R. (1996). Political science and the three new institutionalisms. *Political Studies, 44*(5), 936–957. https://doi.org/10.1111/j.1467-9248.1996.tb00343.x

Hofmann, S. C. (2011). Why institutional overlap matters: CSDP in the European Security Architecture. *JCMS: Journal of Common Market Studies, 49*(1), 101–120. https://doi.org/10.1111/j.1468-5965.2010.02131.x

Hofmann, S. C. (2018). The politics of overlapping organizations: Hostage-taking, forum-shopping and brokering. *Journal of European Public Policy, 13*, 1–23. https://doi.org/10.1080/13501763.2018.1512644

Howlett, M., & Rayner, J. (2006). Understanding the historical turn in the policy sciences: A critique of stochastic, narrative, path dependency and process-sequencing models of policy-making over time. *Policy Sciences, 39*(1), 1–18. https://doi.org/10.1007/s11077-005-9004-1

Karampekios, N., & Oikonomou, I. (Eds.). (2015). *The European Defence Agency: Arming Europe. Routledge studies in European security and strategy.* Routledge, Taylor & Francis Group.

Karlsson-Vinkhuyzen, S. I., & McGee, J. (2013). Legitimacy in an era of fragmentation: The case of global climate governance. *Global Environmental Politics, 13*(3), 56–78. https://doi.org/10.1162/GLEP_a_00183

Keohane, R. O., & Victor, D. G. (2011). The regime complex for climate change. *Perspectives on Politics, 9*(01), 7–23. https://doi.org/10.1017/S1537592710004068

Koremenos, B., Lipson, C., & Snidal, D. (2001). The rational design of international institutions. *International Organization, 55*(4), 761–799. https://doi.org/10.1162/002081801317193592

Krasner, S. D. (1984). Approaches to the state: Alternative conceptions and historical dynamics. *Comparative Politics, 16*(2), 223. https://doi.org/10.2307/421608

Lake, D. A. (2009). *Hierarchy in international relations. Cornell studies in political economy.* Cornell University Press.

Lake, D. A. (2010). Rightful rules: Authority, order, and the foundations of global governance. *International Studies Quarterly, 54*(3), 587–613. https://doi.org/10.1111/j.1468-2478.2010.00601.x

Macron, E. (2017, September 26). *Initiative pour l'Europe: Une Europe souveraine, unie, démocratique.* http://www.elysee.fr/declarations/article/initiative-pour-l-europe-discours-d-emmanuel-macron-pour-une-europe-souveraine-unie-democratique/

Morse, J. C., & Keohane, R. O. (2014). Contested multilateralism. *The Review of International Organizations, 9*(4), 385–412. https://doi.org/10.1007/s11558-014-9188-2

Niemann, A. (1998). The PHARE programme and the concept of spillover: Neofunctionalism in the making. *Journal of European Public Policy, 5*(3), 428–446. https://doi.org/10.1080/135017698343901

Orsini, A., Morin, J.-F., & Young, O. R. (2013). Regime complexes: A buzz, a boom or a boost for global governance? *Global Governance, 19*(1), 27–39.

Pierson, P. (2000). Increasing returns, path dependence, and the study of politics. *American Political Science Review, 94*(02), 251–267. https://doi.org/10.2307/2586011

Pierson, P. (2004). *Politics in time: History, institutions, and social analysis.* Princeton University Press.

Politico. (2018, February 5). *Emmanuel Macron's coalition of the willing.* https://www.politico.eu/article/emmanuel-macrons-eu-defense-army-coalition-of-the-willing-military-cooperation/

Posen, B. R. (2006). European Union Security and Defense Policy: Response to unipolarity? *Security Studies, 15*(2), 149–186. https://doi.org/10.1080/09636410600829356

Pratt, T. (2018). Deference and hierarchy in international regime complexes. *International Organization, 72*(3), 561–590. https://doi.org/10.1017/S0020818318000164

Raustiala, K., & Victor, D. G. (2004). The regime complex for plant genetic resources. *International Organization, 58*(2), 277–309. https://doi.org/10.2139/ssrn.441463

Rosato, S. (2011). Europe's troubles: Power politics and the state of the European project. *International Security, 35*(4), 45–86. https://doi.org/10.1162/ISEC_a_00035

Snidal, D. (1994). The politics of scope: Endogenous actors, heterogeneity and institutions. *Journal of Theoretical Politics, 6*(4), 449–472. https://doi.org/10.1177/0951692894006004003

Stone Sweet, A., & Sandholtz, W. (1997). European integration and supranational governance. *Journal of European Public Policy, 4*(3), 297–317. https://doi.org/10.1080/13501769780000011

Terlikowski, M. (2020, January 23). *PESCO: Two years later.* https://www.pism.pl/publications/PESCO_Two_Years_Later#xd_co_f=YjUwZWNlYjUtZDIwOC00NDkwLWJkZGMtMmVjZmVjY2M1Y2U4~

The Guardian. (2018, June 25). *Nine EU states sign off on joint military intervention force.* https://www.theguardian.com/world/2018/jun/25/nine-eu-states-to-sign-off-on-joint-military-intervention-force

Thompson, A., & Verdier, D. (2014). Multilateralism, bilateralism, and regime design. *International Studies Quarterly, 58*(1), 15–28. https://doi.org/10.1111/isqu.12100

Van de Graaf, T. (2013). Fragmentation in global energy governance: Explaining the creation of IRENA. *Global Environmental Politics, 13*(3), 14–33. https://doi.org/10.1162/GLEP_a_00181

References

Abbott, K. W., Genschel, P., Snidal, D., & Zangl, B. (2020). Competence versus Control: The Governor's Dilemma. *Regulation and Governance, 14*(4), 619–636.
Abbott, K., Green, W., Jessica, F., & Keohane, R. O. (2013). Organizational ecology and organizational strategies in world politics. Discussion Paper 2013–57. Harvard Project on Climate Agreements.
Albright, M. (2001). The right balance will secure NATO's future (7 December 1998). In Institute for Security Studies (Ed.), *Chaillot Papers* (vol. 47). *From St-Malo to Nice: European defence: Core documents* (pp. 10–12).
Alliot-Marie, M., Westerwelle, G., Sikorski, R., Juppé, A., Guttenberg, K.-T. zu, & Klich, B. (2010, December 6). CSDP.
Alter, K. J., & Meunier, S. (2009). The politics of international regime complexity. *Perspectives on Politics, 7*(01), 13–24. https://doi.org/10.1017/S1537592709090033
Alter, K. J., & Raustiala, K. (2018). The rise of international regime complexity. *Annual Review of Law and Social Science, 14*(1), 329–349. https://doi.org/10.1146/annurev-lawsocsci-101317-030830
Altinget. (2017, June 23). Sverige går med i europeiskt försvarssamarbete. https://www.altinget.se/sakerhet/artikel/sverige-gaar-med-i-europeiskt-forsvarssamarbete
Andries, J. (2011). The 2010 Belgian EU Presidency and CSDP. *Egmont Security Policy Brief* (21). http://aei.pitt.edu/32038/1/SPB21-J.Andries-Belgian-EU-Presidency-CSDP.pdf

© The Editor(s) (if applicable) and The Author(s), under exclusive license to Springer Nature Switzerland AG 2023
F. Biermann, *The Battle for Authority in European Defence Cooperation*, Palgrave Studies in European Union Politics,
https://doi.org/10.1007/978-3-031-30054-7

Asmus, R. D., & Vondra, A. (2005). The origins of Atlanticism in Central and Eastern Europe. *Cambridge Review of International Affairs, 18*(2), 203–216. https://doi.org/10.1080/09557570500164439

Assemblée Nationale. (2006). *Rapport D'Information: Déposé en application de l'article 145 du Règlement Par la Commission des Finances, de l'Économie Générale et du Plan en conclusion des travaux de la Mission d'évaluation et de contrôle (MEC) sur les programmes d'armement: l'exemple du véhicule blindé de combat d'infanterie* (No. N° 3254). http://www.assemblee-nationale.fr/12/pdf/rap-info/i3254.pdf

Assembly of Western European Union. (2004). *The Interparliamentary European Security and Defence Assembly: The European defence agency—Reply to the annual report of the Council* (No. Document A/1856).

Augustine, N. R. (1997). *Augustine's laws* (6th ed.). American Institute of Aeronautics and Astronautics.

Axelrod, R. M. (1984). *The evolution of cooperation.* Basic Books.

BAE Systems, EADS, & Thales. (2003). *Time to Act! Joint Declaration of BAE Systems, EADS and Thales.* http://www.defense-aerospace.com/articles-view/release/3/17409/euro-majors-warn-%22it%27s-time-to-act%22.html

Bailes, A., & Guðmundsson, Jón Ágúst. (2009). *The European Defence Agency (EDA) and Defence Industrial Cooperation: Implications and options for Iceland.* https://dokumen.tips/documents/the-european-defence-agency-eda-and-web-view-the-norwegian-precedent-25.html?page=1

Balkan Insight. (2017, March 2). Balkan EU States Reject a 'Multi-Speed' Union. http://www.balkaninsight.com/en/article/balkan-member-states-reject-a-multi-speed-eu-03-02-2017

Baltic Defence Cooperation. (2010). *Joint Communiqué of the Ministerial Committee.* Tartu. http://www.kaitseministeerium.ee/sites/default/files/sisulehed/balti_kaitsekoostoo/2010-12-17_jc_3b_defmin_tartu.pdf

Barcikowska, A. (2013). *EU Battlegroups—ready to go?* (Brief Issue No. 40). http://www.iss.europa.eu/uploads/media/Brief_40_EU_Battlegroups.pdf

Barnett, M. N., & Finnemore, M. (2004). *Rules for the world: International organizations in global politics.* Cornell University Press. http://www.jstor.org/stable/10.7591/j.ctt7z7mx

Barrasa Martín, J. I. (2010). Cooperation in armaments. In Ministerio de Defensa de Espana (Ed.), *European Defence Agency: Past, present & future* (pp. 125–172). CESEDEN, Ministerio de Defensa; Isdefe.

Barroso, J. M. D. (2011). *The State of Europe—Die Europa Rede.* Berlin. http://europa.eu/rapid/press-release_SPEECH-11-738_en.htm

Bátora, J. (2009). European Defence Agency: A flashpoint of institutional logics. *West European Politics, 32*(6), 1075–1098. https://doi.org/10.1080/01402380903230561

BBC News. (2003, February 5). UK and France boost defence ties. http://news.bbc.co.uk/1/hi/world/europe/2726111.stm

BBC News. (2006, March 7). EU keen on defence research fund. http://news.bbc.co.uk/2/hi/europe/4781548.stm

BBC News. (2014, March 12). Poland and Baltics wary over Crimea. https://www.bbc.com/news/world-europe-26526053

BBC News. (2016, November 18). Baltic warning of Russian test for Nato. https://www.bbc.com/news/world-europe-38014997

BBC.com. (2022). https://www.bbc.com/news/uk-63908284. https://www.bbc.com/news/uk-63908284

Beach, D. (2016). It's all about mechanisms—what process-tracing case studies should be tracing. *New Political Economy, 21*(5), 463–472. https://doi.org/10.1080/13563467.2015.1134466

Beach, D., & Pedersen, R. B. (2013). *Process-tracing methods: Foundations and guidelines*. University of Michigan Press. http://site.ebrary.com/lib/subhamburg/Doc?id=10658497

Beach, D., & Pedersen, R. B. (2016). Selecting appropriate cases when tracing causal mechanisms. *Sociological Methods & Research, 47*(4), 837–871. https://doi.org/10.1177/0049124115622510

Belgium, Hungary, & Poland. (2010). *Position Paper by Belgium, Hungary and Poland on Permanent Structured Cooperation*. http://ddata.over-blog.com/xxxyyy/0/50/29/09/Docs-Textes/CoopStructPsdcPap-BeHuPl1006b.pdf

Benvenisti, E., & Downs, G. W. (2007). The emperor's new clothes: Political economy and the fragmentation of international law. *Stanford Law Review, 60*(2), 595–632.

Bergmann, J. (2018). Neofunctionalism and EU external policy integration: The case of capacity building in support of security and development (CBSD). *Journal of European Public Policy, 355*(3), 1–20. https://doi.org/10.1080/13501763.2018.1526204

Bergmann, J., & Niemann, A. (2018). From neo-functional peace to a logic of spillover in EU external policy: A response to Visoka and Doyle. *JCMS: Journal of Common Market Studies, 56*(2), 420–438. https://doi.org/10.1111/jcms.12608

Bickerton, C. J., Irondelle, B., & Menon, A. (2011). Security co-operation beyond the nation-state: The EU's common security and defence policy. *JCMS: Journal of Common Market Studies, 49*(1), 1–21. https://doi.org/10.1111/j.1468-5965.2010.02126.x

Biermann, F. (2022). The differentiation paradox of European Integration: Why going it alone produces suboptimal results. *JCMS: Journal of Common Market Studies*, Early view. https://doi.org/10.1111/jcms.13373

Biermann, F., Guérin, N., Jagdhuber, S., Rittberger, B., & Weiss, M. (2019). Political (non-)reform in the euro crisis and the refugee crisis: A liberal intergovernmentalist explanation. *Journal of European Public Policy, 26*(2), 246–266. https://doi.org/10.1080/13501763.2017.1408670

Biermann, F., & Weiss, M. (2021). Power without a cause? Germany's conflict avoidance and the integration of European defence procurement. *Journal of European Integration, 43*(2), 227–242. https://doi.org/10.1080/070 36337.2021.1877691

Biermann, F., Pattberg, P., van Asselt, H., & Zelli, F. (2009). The fragmentation of global governance architectures: A framework for analysis. *Global Environmental Politics, 9*(4), 14–40. https://doi.org/10.1162/glep.2009.9. 4.14

Billon-Galland, Alice, & Quencez, M. (2017). *Can France and Germany make PESCO work as a process toward EU defence* (Security and Defense Policy Program - Policy Brief No. 33). Washington DC.

Biscop, S. (2008). *Permanent structured cooperation and the future of ESDP* (Egmont Papers No. 20).

Biscop, S. (2017). *Oratio pro PESCO* (Egmont Paper No. 91). Brussels. http://www.egmontinstitute.be/content/uploads/2017/01/ep91.pdf?type=pdf

Biscop, S., & Coelmont, J. (2012). *Europe, strategy and armed forces: The making of a distinctive power.* Routledge.

Biscop, S., Coelmont, J., Drent, M., & Zandee, D. (2015). *European strategy, European defence, and the CSDP* (Clingendael Report). https://www.clingendael.org/sites/default/files/pdfs/European%20Strategy,%20European%20Defence%20and%20the%20CSDP.pdf

BITS. (2004). *Querschnitt 2004.* Berlin.

Blatter, J., & Haverland, M. (2012). *Designing case studies: Explanatory approaches in small-N research.* Palgrave Macmillan.

Blauberger, M., & Weiss, M. (2013). 'If you can't beat me, join me!' How the Commission pushed and pulled member states into legislating defence procurement. *Journal of European Public Policy, 20*(8), 1120–1138. https://doi.org/10.1080/13501763.2013.781783

BMVg. (2016). *4. Bericht des Bundesministeriums der Verteidigung zu Rüstungsangelegenheiten: Teil 1.* Berlin. https://www.bmvg.de/resource/blob/15378/fa614131fc4c41ea34509e756fa8d96c/b-07-01-02-download-4-ruestungsbericht-data.pdf

Borrell i Fontelles, J. (2022). *Answer given by High Representative/Vice-President Borrell i Fontelles on behalf of the European Commission* (No. P-003903/2022). https://www.europarl.europa.eu/doceo/document/P-9-2022-003903-ASW_EN.html

Börzel, T. A. (2005). Mind the gap! European integration between level and scope. *Journal of European Public Policy, 12*(2), 217–236. https://doi.org/10.1080/13501760500043860

Britz, M. (2010). The role of marketization in the Europeanization of Defense Industry Policy. *Bulletin of Science, Technology & Society, 30*(3), 176–184. https://doi.org/10.1177/0270467610367492

Brunnstrom, D. (2010, November 3). Analysis—Anglo-French defence deal could hurt Brussels goals. https://uk.reuters.com/article/uk-europe-defence/analysis-anglo-french-defence-deal-could-hurt-brussels-goals-idUKTRE6A251S20101103

Buchanan, J. M. (1965). An economic theory of clubs. *Economica, 32*(125), 1. https://doi.org/10.2307/2552442

Bundesministerium Landesverteidigung Österreich. (2010, November 9). Konferenz für mehr regionale Kooperation in Zentraleuropa. http://www.bundesheer.at/cms/artikel.php?ID=5362

Business Review. (2017, October 17). Romania to join EU's defence initiative PESCO. http://business-review.eu/news/romania-to-join-eus-defence-initiative-pesco-150010

Cameron, D. (2013, December 20). European Council December 2013: David Cameron's press conference. https://www.gov.uk/government/speeches/european-council-december-2013-david-camerons-press-conference

Cameron, D. (2014, August 2). PM writes to NATO leaders ahead of NATO Summit Wales 2014. https://www.gov.uk/government/news/pm-writes-to-nato-leaders-ahead-of-nato-summit-wales-2014

Centre for European Policy Studies. (2015). *More Union European defence: Report of a CEPS Task Force.* Centre for European Policy Studies.

Chappell, L., & Petrov, P. (2012). The European defence agency and permanent structured cooperation: Are we heading towards another missed opportunity? *Defence Studies, 12*(1), 44–66. https://doi.org/10.1080/14702436.2012.683973

Checkel, J. T. (2006). Tracing causal mechanisms. *International Studies Review, 8*(2), 362–370. https://doi.org/10.1111/j.1468-2486.2006.00598_2.x

CNN.com. (2009, March 17). Sarkozy wins French NATO re-entry vote. http://edition.cnn.com/2009/WORLD/europe/03/17/france.nato/

Coelmont, J. (2017). With PESCO brought to life, will European defence live happily ever after? *Egmont Security Policy Brief* (90). http://aei.pitt.edu/88540/1/SPB90.pdf

Colgan, J. D., Keohane, R. O., & van de Graaf, T. (2012). Punctuated equilibrium in the energy regime complex. *The Review of International Organizations, 7*(2), 117–143. https://doi.org/10.1007/s11558-011-9130-9

Commission of the European Communities. (2005a). *Communication from the Commission to the Council and the European Parliament on the results of the consultation launched by the Green Paper on Defence Procurement and on the future Commission initiatives* (No. COM(2005) 626 final). Brussels. http://www.europarl.europa.eu/RegData/docs_autres_institutions/commission_europeenne/com/2005/0626/COM_COM%282005%290626_EN.pdf

Commission of the European Communities. (2005b). *Communication on the results of the consultation launched by the green paper on defence procurement and on the future commission initiatives* (No. COM(2005) 626 final). https://eur-lex.europa.eu/legal-content/EN/TXT/?uri=CELEX%3A52005DC0626

Committee of Permanent Representatives. (2003). Armaments Agency [Brussels, 4 September 2003]. In A. Missiroli (Ed.), *Chaillot Papers* (vol. 67). *From Copenhagen to Brussels European defence: Core documents* (vol. IV, pp. 208–210). Institute for Security Studies European Union.

Conseil franco-allemand de défense et de sécurité. (2017, July 13). Relevé de Conclusions. https://www.france-allemagne.fr/IMG/pdf/fiche-cfads.pdf

Consilium. (2018). Voting calculator. http://www.consilium.europa.eu/en/council-eu/voting-system/voting-calculator/

Convention on the Establishment of the Organisation for Joint Armament Cooperation (Organisation Conjointe de Cooperation en Matière d'ARmement) - OCCAR, *JORF* 4468 (2001).

Cottrell, P. M. (2016). *The evolution and legitimacy of international security institutions*. Cambridge University Press. http://www.h-net.org/reviews/showrev.php?id=46936

Council of the European Union. Council Joint Action 2004/551/CFSP of 12 July 2004 on the establishment of the European Defence Agency. *Official Journal of the European Union, 2004*(L 245/17).

Council of the European Union. (2003a). General Affairs and External Relations Council [17 November 2003]: Council conclusions. In A. Missiroli (Ed.), *Chaillot Papers* (vol. 67). *From Copenhagen to Brussels European defence: Core documents* (vol. IV, pp. 256–268). Institute for Security Studies European Union.

Council of the European Union. (2003b). *2518th Council meeting: External relations* (Press Release No. C/03/166). Brussels.

Council of the European Union. (2003c). *2541st Council meeting: External relations* (Press Release No. C/03/321). Brussels.

Council of the European Union. (2008). *Council Conclusions on the ESDP* (No. 15465/08). Brussels. http://register.consilium.europa.eu/doc/srv?l=EN&f=ST%2015465%202008%20INIT

Council of the European Union. (2010). *Council Conclusions on Military Capability Development: 3055th Foreign Affairs (Defence) Council meeting*. https://www.consilium.europa.eu/uedocs/cms_data/docs/pressdata/en/esdp/118348.pdf

Council Decision 2011/411/CFSP defining the statute, seat and operational rules of the European Defence Agency and repealing Joint Action 2004/551/CFSP, 16 *Official Journal of the European Union* (2011).

Council Decision (CFSP) 2015/1835 of 12 October 2015 defining the statute, seat and operational rules of the European Defence Agency (recast), *Official Journal of the European Union* (2015).

Council of the European Union. (2015, November 17). Foreign Affairs Council, 16–17/11/2015. https://www.consilium.europa.eu/en/meetings/fac/2015/11/16-17/

Council of the European Union. (2016). *Council conclusions on implementing the EU Global Strategy in the area of Security and Defence* (No. 14149/16). http://www.consilium.europa.eu/media/22459/eugs-conclusions-st14149en16.pdf

Council Decision establishing Permanent Structured Cooperation (PESCO) and determining the list of Participating Member States, *Official Journal of the European Union* (2017).

Council of the European Union. (2017, March 6). *Council conclusions on progress in implementing the EU Global Strategy in the area of Security and Defence* [Press release]. Brussels. Retrieved from http://www.consilium.europa.eu/en/press/press-releases/2017/03/06/conclusions-security-defence/pdf

Council of the European Union. (2017, December 11). *Defence cooperation: Council establishes Permanent Structured Cooperation (PESCO), with 25 member states participating.* Press release 765/17 [Press release]. http://www.consilium.europa.eu/en/press/press-releases/2017/12/11/defence-cooperation-pesco-25-member-states-participating/

Council of the European Union. (2018). *Council Decision establishing the list of projects to be developed under PESCO* (Legislative Acts and other Instruments No. 6393/18). http://data.consilium.europa.eu/doc/document/ST-6393-2018-INIT/en/pdf

Council Decision (CFSP) 2018/1797 of 19 November 2018 amending and updating Decision (CFSP) 2018/340 establishing the list of projects to be developed under PESCO, *Official Journal of the European Union* (2018).

Council of the European Union. (2020). Council Recommendation of 15 June 2020 assessing the progress made by the participating Member States to fulfil commitments undertaken in the framework of permanent structured cooperation (PESCO). *Official Journal of the European Union*, 2020(C 204). https://eur-lex.europa.eu/legal-content/EN/TXT/PDF/?uri=CELEX:32020H0618(01)&from=EN

Council of Western European Union. (2003). WEAO Charter [1997]. In B. Schmitt (Ed.), *Chaillot Papers* (vol. 59). *European armaments cooperation: Core Documents* (pp. 11–22).

Csiki, T., & Németh, B. (2013). Perspectives of Central European Multinational Defence Cooperation: A new Model? In M. Majer & R. Ondrejcsák (Eds.), *Panorama of Global Security Environment 2013* (pp. 11–24). Bratislava.

Cyprus Mail. (2017, November 8). Cyprus move a step closer to being part of an integrated European defence policy. https://cyprus-mail.com/2017/11/08/cyprus-move-step-closer-part-integrated-european-defence-policy/

Daßler, B. (2022). Good(s) for everyone? Policy area competition and institutional topologies in the regime complexes of tax avoidance and intellectual property. *Journal of International Relations and Development, 54*(3), 421. https://doi.org/10.1057/s41268-022-00267-x

Daßler, B., Kruck, A., & Zangl, B. (2018). Interactions between hard and soft power: The institutional adaptation of international intellectual property protection to global power shifts. *European Journal of International Relations, 5*(1). https://doi.org/10.1177/1354066118768871

De France, O., Major, C., & Sartori Paola. (2017). *How to make PESCO a Success?* (Policy paper No. 21). Armament Industry European Research Group (ARES) website: http://www.iris-france.org/wp-content/uploads/2017/09/Ares-21-Policy-Paper-Sept-2017.pdf

DefenceWeb. (2010, November 4). Anglo-French defence deal could hurt Brussels goals. https://www.defenceweb.co.za/industry/industry-industry/anglo-french-defence-deal-could-hurt-brussels-goals/

Defense News. (2018, August 2). These Baltic nations could build Europe's next ground drone. https://www.defensenews.com/global/europe/2018/08/02/these-baltic-nations-could-build-europes-next-ground-drone/

Denmark, Finland, Iceland, Norway, & Sweden. (2009). *Memorandum of understanding on Nordic Defence Cooperation*. https://www.nordefco.org/the-basics-aboutnordefco

Deutsche Welle. (2017, March 6). Merkel backs idea of 'multispeed Europe' at Versailles meet. https://www.dw.com/en/merkel-backs-idea-of-multispeed-europe-at-versailles-meet/a-37833273

Deutscher Bundestag. (2003). *Unterrichtung durch die Bundesregierung: Bericht der Bundesregierung über die Tätigkeit der Westeuropäischen Union für die Zeit vom 1. Januar bis 31. Dezember 2002* (No. Drucksache 15/1485).

de Wijk, R. (2004). Transatlantic relations: A view from the Netherlands. *International Journal: Canada's Journal of Global Policy Analysis, 59*(1), 167–186. https://doi.org/10.1177/002070200405900108

Deutscher Bundestag. (2010). *Antwort der Bundesregierung auf die Kleine Anfrage der Abgeordneten Paul Schäfer (Köln), Jan van Aken, Christine Buchholz, weiterer Abgeordneter und der Fraktion DIE LINKE: Aufklärung über den Stand der Rüstungskooperation Deutschlands auf europäischer Ebene* (No. Drucksache 17/3937). http://dip21.bundestag.de/dip21/btd/17/039/1703937.pdf

Deutscher Bundestag. (2016, June 28). *Protocol Session 181, 18*. Legislature: Government Statement by Dr. Angela Merkel. https://dip.bundestag.de/ple narprotokoll/protokoll-der-181-sitzung-des-18-deutschen-bundestages/827

Deutscher Bundestag. (2017). *Sachstand: Aktuelle Fortschritte bei der europäischen Zusammenarbeit in ausgewählten Bereichen der Sicherheits- und Verteidigungspolitik* (No. WD 2-3000-069/17). Berlin. https://www.bundestag.de/resource/blob/525944/69cccfc49df56f4bf594e1d90b6c2760/WD-2-069-17-pdf-data.pdf

Deutscher Bundestag. (2017, March 9). *Protocol Session 221, 18*. Legislature: Government Statement by Dr. Angela Merkel. https://dserver.bundestag.de/btp/18/18221.pdf

Devine, K. (2011). Neutrality and the development of the European Union's common security and defence policy. *Cooperation and Conflict, 46*(3), 334–369. https://doi.org/10.1177/0010836711416958

Die Presse. (2017, September 7). Doskozil: Österreich beteiligt sich an EU-Militärzusammenarbeit. https://diepresse.com/home/ausland/eu/528 1471/Doskozil_Oesterreich-beteiligt-sich-an-EUMilitaerzusammenarbeit

Drezner, D. W. (2009). The power and peril of international regime complexity. *Perspectives on Politics, 7*(01), 65–70. https://doi.org/10.1017/S1537592709090100

Drezner, D. W. (2013). The tragedy of the global institutional commons. In J. Goldstein & M. Finnemore (Eds.), *Back to basics: State power in a contemporary world* (pp. 280–310). Oxford University Press. https://doi.org/10.1093/acprof:oso/9780199970087.003.0013

Dyson, T., & Konstadinides, T. (2013). *European defence cooperation in EU law and IR theory*. Palgrave Macmillan.

EADS. (2003). *To New Levels: Corporate Presentation 2003*.

EATC. (2017). The member nations. https://eatc-mil.com/en/who-we-are/the-member-nations

European Defence Agency. (2005, April 22). *Latest News: European Defence Agency Steering Board Agrees Transfer of WEAG/WEAO Activities to EDA* [Press release]. Brussels.

EDA. (2006). European Defence Agency steering board agrees transfer of WEAG/WEAO activities to EDA: 22 April 2005. In *EU security and defence: Core documents 2005* (Chaillot Papers No. 87, pp. 85–89).

EDA. (2008). *2007 Financial Report*. European Defence Agency website: https://eda.europa.eu/docs/finance-documents/2007-financial-report.pdf?sfvrsn=0

EDA. (2011a). *2010 Financial Report*. European Defence Agency website: https://www.eda.europa.eu/docs/documents/EDA_2010_Financial_Report_-_AUDITED_lv

EDA. (2011b). *Defence Data 2010*. Brussels. European Defence Agency website: https://www.eda.europa.eu/docs/eda-publications/defence_data_2010

EDA. (2012a). *2011 Financial Report*. https://www.eda.europa.eu/docs/default-source/documents/2012-financial-report.pdf website: https://eda.europa.eu/docs/finance-documents/2011-financial-report.pdf?sfvrsn=0

European Defence Agency. (2012b, July 27). *Latest News: EDA & OCCAR build links, seeking efficiencies through cooperation* [Press release]. Brussels. https://www.eda.europa.eu/info-hub/press-centre/latest-news/2012/07/27/eda-occar-build-links-seeking-efficiencies-through-cooperation

EDA. (2013). *2012 Financial Report*. European Defence Agency website: https://www.eda.europa.eu/docs/default-source/documents/2012-financial-report.pdf

EDA. (2014a). *10 years of working together*. Brussels.

European Defence Agency. (2014b, December 9). *Latest News: EDA signs Security Arrangement with OCCAR* [Press release]. Brussels. https://eda.europa.eu/info-hub/press-centre/latest-news/2014/12/09/eda-signs-security-arrangement-with-occar

EDA. (2016a). *2017 Budget*. https://www.eda.europa.eu/docs/default-source/finance-documents/eda-budget-2017-with-staff-establishment-plan.pdf

European Defence Agency. (2016b, September 28). *Latest News: European MALE RPAS Definition Study contract awarded* [Press release]. https://www.eda.europa.eu/info-hub/press-centre/latest-news/2016/09/28/european-male-rpas-definition-study-contract-awarded

EDA. (2018). *15 years of working together*. https://www.eda.europa.eu/Aboutus/our-history/15-years

EDA. (2019). *15 years of working together: The birth of an agency*. https://www.eda.europa.eu/Aboutus/our-history/the-birth-of-an-agency

EDA, & OCCAR. (2012). *Administrative Arrangement between the EDA and OCCAR concerning the establishment of their cooperation*. https://www.eda.europa.eu/docs/default-source/documents/aa---eda---occar-27-07-12.pdf

EEAS. (2016). *Shared vision, common action: A stronger Europe: A global strategy for the European Union's Foreign and Security Policy*. Brussels. European External Action Service (EEAS) website: https://eeas.europa.eu/sites/eeas/files/eugs_review_web_0.pdf

Eisenhut, D. (2010). *Europäische Rüstungskooperation: Zwischen Binnenmarkt und zwischenstaatlicher Zusammenarbeit*. Univ., Diss.--Augsburg, 2009 (1. Aufl.). *Augsburger Rechtsstudien* (vol. 59). Nomos Verl.-Ges.

EPRS. (2016). *Implementation of the Lisbon Treaty provisions on the Common Security and Defence Policy (CSDP)* (European Council Briefing). www.europarl.europa.eu/RegData/etudes/BRIE/2016/573285/EPRS_BRI(2016)573285_EN.pdf

ERR News. (2017, May 3). *Estonia joins EU defense cooperation initiative.* https://news.err.ee/593552/estonia-joins-eu-defense-cooperation-initiative
EU 27. (2016). *The Bratislava Declaration*. Bratislava. The Bratislava Summit of 27 Member States website: http://www.consilium.europa.eu/media/21250/160916-bratislava-declaration-and-roadmapen16.pdf
EUobserver. (2006, November 14). *UK under French fire over defence*. https://euobserver.com/news/22849
EUobserver. (2016a, February 5). *Poland 'satisfied' with UK demands in EU referendum talks*. https://euobserver.com/political/132158
EUobserver. (2016b, November 11). *Germany: Trump victory to spur EU military union*. https://euobserver.com/foreign/135877
Euractiv. (2017, March 8). *Two-speed Europe highlights East-West divide*. https://www.euractiv.com/section/future-eu/news/two-speed-europe-highlights-east-west-divide/
European Commission. *Commission Decision of 11.4.2017 on the financing of the 'Preparatory action on Defence research' and the use of unit costs for the year 2017* (No. C(2017) 2262 final). https://www.eda.europa.eu/docs/default-source/brochures/decision-on-the-financing-of-the-preparatory-action-on-defence-research-(padr)-and-the-use-of-unit-costs-for-the-year-2017561fa63fa4d264cfa776ff000087ef0f.pdf
European Commission. (2003). *European defence-industrial and market issues: Towards an EU Defence Equipment Policy* (No. 113 final). Brussels. https://eur-lex.europa.eu/LexUriServ/LexUriServ.do?uri=COM:2003:0113:FIN:en:PDF
European Commission. (2011). *Standard Eurobarometer 76: Die Öffentliche Meinung in der Europäischen Union*. http://ec.europa.eu/commfrontoffice/publicopinion/archives/eb/eb76/eb76_agreport_de.pdf
European Commission. (2013). *Commission staff working document on defence accompanying the document communication towards a more competitive and efficient defence and security sector COM(2013) 542 final* (No. SWD(2013) 279 final).
European Commission. (2016). *European defence action plan: Towards a European Defence Fund*. Brussels. http://europa.eu/rapid/press-release_IP-16-4088_en.htm
European Commission. (2017a). *EU expenditure and revenue 2014–2020*. http://ec.europa.eu/budget/figures/interactive/index_en.cfm
European Commission. (2017b, June 7). *A European Defence Fund: €5.5 billion per year to boost Europe's defence capabilities*. http://europa.eu/rapid/press-release_IP-17-1508_en.htm
European Commission. (2017c). *Communication from the Commission to the European Parliament, the Council, the European Economic and Social*

Committee and the Committee of the Regions: Launching the European Defence Fund (No. COM(2017) 295 final).
European Commission. (2018). Defence Industries: The importance of EU defence industries. https://ec.europa.eu/growth/sectors/defence_en
European Commission. (2019). *The European Defence Fund: Stepping up the EU's role as a security and defence provider.* https://ec.europa.eu/docsroom/documents/34509
European Convention. (2002a). *Final report of Working Group VIII - Defence* (No. WG VIII 22). Brussels. https://web.archive.org/web/200706092 35907/http://register.consilium.eu.int/pdf/en/02/cv00/00461en2.pdf
European Convention. (2002b). *Rapport du Président du Groupe de travail VIII "Défense" à la Convention: Rapport final du Groupe de travail VIII "Défense"* (No. CONV 461/02). https://www.cvce.eu/en/obj/final_rep ort_of_working_group_viii_defence_16_december_2002-en-71dbaa92-ac9e-4556-a639-3c7665fd0812.html
European Council. (2003). *Presidency Conclusions* (No. 11638/03). Brussels.
European Council. (2013). *European Council meeting (19/20 December 2013)—Conclusions* (No. EUCO 217/13). Brussels. http://data.consilium.europa.eu/doc/document/ST-217-2013-INIT/en/pdf
European Council (2016a). *European Council meeting (15 December 2016)—Conclusions* (No. EUCO 34/16). Brussels. http://www.consilium.europa.eu/media/21929/15-euco-conclusions-final.pdf
European Council. (2016b). *European Council meeting (18 and 19 February 2016)—Conclusions* (No. EUCO 1/16). Brussels. http://www.consilium.eur opa.eu/media/21787/0216-euco-conclusions.pdf
European Council. (2017). *European Council meeting (22 and 23 June 2017)—Conclusions* (No. EUCO 8/17). http://www.consilium.europa.eu/en/press/press-releases/2017/06/23-euco-conclusions/
European Parliament. (2006). *EU and NATO: Co-operation or competition?* (No. EP-ExPol-B-2006–14). http://www.europarl.europa.eu/mee tdocs/2004_2009/documents/dv/eunatorelations_/eunatorelations_en.pdf
European Parliament. (2011a). *European Parliament resolution of 14 December 2011 on the impact of the financial crisis on the defence sector in the EU Member States* (2011/2177(INI)). Strasbourg. http://www.europarl.europa.eu/sides/getDoc.do?type=TA&language=EN&reference=P7-TA-2011-574
European Parliament. (2011b). *The impact of the financial crisis on European defence: Study.* https://www.swp-berlin.org/fileadmin/contents/products/fachpublikationen/Moelling_Brune_EU_Studie_2011_Teil1_ks.pdf
Treaty of Nice, Amending the Treaty on European Union, the Treaties Establishing the European Communities and Certain Related Acts, *Official Journal C 80 of 10 March 2001; 2001/C 80/01* (2000).

European Union. (2005). *Treaty establishing a constitution for Europe*. Office for Official Publ. of the Europ. Communities. http://europa.eu.int/constitution/index_en.htm

European Union. (2010). *Consolidated versions of the treaty on European Union and of the treaty on the functioning of the European Union: Charter of fundamental rights of the European Union*. Publications Office of the European Union. http://publications.europa.eu/de/publication-detail/-/publication/3c32722f-0136-4d8f-a03e-bfaf70d16349

Faude, B., & Fuss, J. (2020). Coordination or conflict? The causes and consequences of institutional overlap in a disaggregated world order. *Global Constitutionalism, 9*(2), 268–289. https://doi.org/10.1017/S2045381719000376

Fauré, S. (2017). Mapping European defence policy after Brexit: NATO, OCCAR, CSDP, PESCO, etc. https://samuelbhfaure.com/2017/12/03/mapping-european-defence-policy-after-brexit-nato-occar-csdp-pesco-etc/

Fehl, C. (2016). *Forum shopping from above and below: Power shifts and institutional choice in a stratified international society*. Paper prepared for the workshop on "Power Transitions and Institutional Change". Munich.

Fiott, D. (2015). The European Commission and the European Defence Agency: A case of rivalry? *JCMS: Journal of Common Market Studies, 53*(3), 542–557. https://doi.org/10.1111/jcms.12217

Fiott, D. (2018). Strategic autonomy: Towards 'European sovereignty' in defence. *European Union Institute for Security Studies* (12). https://www.jstor.org/stable/pdf/resrep21120.pdf

Foreignpolicy.com. (2022). The arsenal of democracy is back in business. https://foreignpolicy.com/2022/12/29/arms-sales-united-states-nato-russia-ukraine-war-the-arsenal-of-democracy-is-back-in-business/

Fox, L. (2010). *The Armed Forces, NATO and the EU: What should the UK's role be?* London. POLITEIA website: http://www.politeia.co.uk/wp-content/Politeia%20Documents/2010/March%20-%20The%20Armed%20Forces%2C%20NATO%20and%20the%20EU/%27The%20Armed%20Forces%27%20March%202010.pdf

France. (2008). *French Presidency of the Council of the European Union: Work Programme: Europe Taking Action to Meet Today's Challenges*. archive-ue2008.fr/webdav/site/PFUE/shared/ProgrammePFUE/Programme_EN.pdf

France, & Germany. (2002). *Working Document 36—WG VIII: Franco-German comments on the preliminary draft final report of Working Group VIII "Defence" (WD 022)*. http://european-convention.europa.eu/docs/wd8/5925.pdf

France, & Germany. (2003). Franco-German summit—40th anniversary of the Elysée Treaty: Declaration by the Franco-German Defence and Security

Council [22 January 2003]. In A. Missiroli (Ed.), *Chaillot Papers* (vol. 67). *From Copenhagen to Brussels European defence: Core documents* (vol. IV, pp. 22–26). Institute for Security Studies European Union.

France, Germany, Spain, & Italy. (2017). *Permanent Structured Cooperation (PESCO): FR/DE/ES/IT Proposals on the necessary commitments and elements for an inclusive and ambitious PESCO Supported by BE, CZ, FI and NL.* Paris, Berlin, Madrid, Rome. http://club.bruxelles2.eu/wp-content/upl oads/2017/08/principescommuns-pesco-propfrallespita@ue170721.pdf

France, & United Kingdom. (1998). *Joint Declaration on European Defence: Joint Declaration issued at the British-French Summit.* Saint-Malo. https:// www.cvce.eu/content/publication/2008/3/31/f3cd16fb-fc37-4d52-936f-c8e9bc80f24f/publishable_en.pdf

France, Germany, Italy, Spain, Sweden, United Kingdom. (2000). *Framework Agreement concerning Measures to Facilitate the Restructuring and Operation of the European Defence Industry* (Treaty series No. 33 (2001)). Farnborough. https://assets.publishing.service.gov.uk/government/uploads/sys tem/uploads/attachment_data/file/518178/TS0033_2001.pdf

Fromion, Y. (2008). *Les moyens de développer et de structurer une industrie européenne de défense: Rapport final confié par Monsieur François Fillon.* https://www.ladocumentationfrancaise.fr/var/storage/rap ports-publics/084000456.pdf

Future of Europe Group. (2012). *Final Report of the Future of Europe Group: Of the Foreign Ministers of Austria, Belgium, Denmark, France, Italy, Germany, Luxembourg, the Netherlands, Poland, Portugal and Spain.* http://www.cer. eu/sites/default/files/westerwelle_report_sept12.pdf

Gaber, & Slavko. (2002). *Working Document 32 - WG VIII: Comments on the preliminary draft final report of Working Group VIII "Defence".* http://eur opean-convention.europa.eu/docs/wd8/5881.pdf

Gehring, T., & Faude, B. (2013). The dynamics of regime complexes: Microfoundations and systemic effects. *Global Governance, 19*, 119–130.

Gehring, T., & Faude, B. (2014). A theory of emerging order within institutional complexes: How competition among regulatory international institutions leads to institutional adaptation and division of labor. *The Review of International Organizations, 9*(4), 471–498. https://doi.org/10.1007/s11558-014-9197-1

Gehring, T., & Oberthür, S. (2009). The causal mechanisms of interaction between international institutions. *European Journal of International Relations, 15*(1), 125–156. https://doi.org/10.1177/1354066108100055

Genschel, P., & Jachtenfuchs, M. (Eds.). (2014). *Beyond the regulatory polity?* Oxford University Press.

George, A. L., & Bennett, A. (2005). *Case studies and theory development in the social sciences. BCSIA studies in international security.* The MIT Press.

Georgopoulos, A. (2015). The EDA and EU defence procurement integration. In N. Karampekios & I. Oikonomou (Eds.), *Routledge studies in European security and strategy. The European Defence Agency: Arming Europe* (pp. 118–136). Routledge, Taylor & Francis Group.

German News Informations Services. (2010, November 15). Militarizing the Arctic. https://www.german-foreign-policy.com/en/news/detail/5078/

Germany, & France. (2016). *Erneuerung der GSVP—hin zu einer umfassenden, realistischen und glaubwürdigen Verteidigung in der EU: Deutsch-französische Verteidigungsinitiative zur Erneuerung der Gemeinsamen Sicherheits- und Verteidigungspolitik (GSVP)*. https://augengeradeaus.net/wp-content/uploads/2016/09/20160909_DEU_FRA_EU-Verteidigung.pdf

Germany, & Sweden. (2010). *Pooling and sharing, German-Swedish initiative: European Imperative Intensifying Military Cooperation in Europe—"Ghent Initiative"*. Berlin and Stockholm. http://www.europarl.europa.eu/meetdocs/2009_2014/documents/sede/dv/sede260511deseinitiative_/sede260511deseinitiative_en.pdf

Germany, France, Luxembourg, Belgium. (2003). European defence meeting—'Tervuren' [29 April 2003]: Meeting of the Heads of State and Government on European Defence. In A. Missiroli (Ed.), *Chaillot Papers* (vol. 67). *From Copenhagen to Brussels European defence: Core documents* (vol. IV, pp. 76–80). Institute for Security Studies European Union.

General Secretariat of the Council. (2017). Council conclusions on progress in implementing the EU Global Strategy in the area of Security and Defence, Brussels. https://www.consilium.europa.eu/en/press/press-releases/2017/03/06/conclusions-security-defence/

Gholz, E., & Sapolsky, H. M. (2000). Restructuring the U.S. Defense Industry. *International Security, 24*(3), 5–51. https://doi.org/10.1162/016228899560220

Gormley, J. (2002). *Working document 40—WG VIII: Comments by Mr John Gormley on the preliminary draft final report of Working Group VIII "Defence" (WD 022)*.

Greek Presidency. (2003, May 3). Informal General Affairs and External Relations Council (Gymnich), May 2–3: Press Statement. http://www.eu2003.gr//en/articles/2003/5/3/2662/

Gruber, L. (2000). *Ruling the world: Power politics and the rise of supranational institutions*. Princeton University Press.

Guay, T. R. (1996). Integration and Europe's Defense Industry. A "Reactive spillover" approach. *Policy Studies Journal, 24*(3), 404–419. https://doi.org/10.1111/j.1541-0072.1996.tb01637.x

Guay, T. R. (2005). *The European Defense Industry: Prospects for Consolidation* (UNISCI Discussion Papers No. 9). https://www.ucm.es/data/cont/media/www/pag-72532/UNISCI9Guay.pdf

Guillaume, M. (1998). L'Organisation conjointe de coopération en matière d'armement. *Annuaire Français De Droit International, 44*(1), 283–297. https://doi.org/10.3406/afdi.1998.3514

Haas, E. B. (1961). International Integration: The European and the Universal Process. *International Organization, 15*(03), 366. https://doi.org/10.1017/S0020818300002198

Haas, E. B. (2004 [1958]). *The uniting of Europe: Political, social, and economical forces: 1950–1957. Contemporary European politics and society*. University of Notre Dame Press.

Hall, P. A., & Taylor, R. C. R. (1996). Political science and the three new institutionalisms. *Political Studies, 44*(5), 936–957. https://doi.org/10.1111/j.1467-9248.1996.tb00343.x

Hall, P. A. (2010). Historical institutionalism in rationalist and sociological perspective. In J. Mahoney & K. A. Thelen (Eds.), *Explaining institutional change: Ambiguity, agency, and power*. Cambridge University Press.

Haroche, P. (2019). Supranationalism strikes back: A neofunctionalist account of the European Defence Fund. *Journal of European Public Policy, 14*(3), 1–20. https://doi.org/10.1080/13501763.2019.1609570

Hartley, K. (2008). Collaboration and European Defence Industrial Policy. *Defence and Peace Economics, 19*(4), 303–315. https://doi.org/10.1080/10242690802221585

Hartley, K. (2011). Creating a European Defence Industrial Base. *Security Challenges, 7*(3), 95–111.

Hartley, K. (2012). Company survey series I: BAE systems PLC. *Defence and Peace Economics, 23*(4), 331–342. https://doi.org/10.1080/10242694.2011.593353

Hasenclever, A., Mayer, P., & Rittberger, V. (1997). *Theories of international regimes. Cambridge studies in international relations* (vol. 55). Cambridge University Press. https://doi.org/10.1017/CBO9780511521720

Helfer, L. R. (2009). Regime shifting in the international intellectual property system. *Perspectives on Politics, 7*(01), 39–44. https://doi.org/10.1017/S1537592709090069

Henning, C. R., & Pratt, T. (2020). *Hierarchy and differentiation in international regime complexes: A theoretical framework for comparative research*. 13th Annual Conference on The Political Economy of International Organization. PEIO website: https://www.peio.me/wp-content/uploads/2020/01/PEIO13_paper_66.pdf

Heuninckx, B. (Ed.) (2017). *The law of collaborative defence procurement in the European Union*. Cambridge University Press.

Hill, C. (1993). The capability-expectations gap, or conceptualizing Europe's international role. *JCMS: Journal of Common Market Studies, 31*(3), 305–328. https://doi.org/10.1111/j.1468-5965.1993.tb00466.x

Hirschman, A. O. (1978). Exit, voice, and the state. *World Politics, 31*(01), 90–107. https://doi.org/10.2307/2009968

Hoeffler, C. (2012). European armament co-operation and the renewal of industrial policy motives. *Journal of European Public Policy, 19*(3), 435–451. https://doi.org/10.1080/13501763.2011.640803

Hofmann, S. C. (2009). Overlapping institutions in the realm of international security: The case of NATO and ESDP. *Perspectives on Politics, 7*(01), 45–52. https://doi.org/10.1017/S1537592709090070

Hofmann, S. C. (2018). The politics of overlapping organizations: Hostage-taking, forum-shopping and brokering. *Journal of European Public Policy, 13*, 1–23. https://doi.org/10.1080/13501763.2018.1512644

Hofmann, S. C. (2011). Why institutional overlap matters: CSDP in the European Security Architecture. *JCMS: Journal of Common Market Studies, 49*(1), 101–120. https://doi.org/10.1111/j.1468-5965.2010.02131.x

Hollande, F. (2016, February 19). Conférence de presse de François Hollande à l'issue du Conseil européen. https://ue.delegfrance.org/oui-je-suis-pour-une-europe#III-Conference-de-presse-de-Francois-Hollande-a-l-issue-du-Conseil-europeen-nbsp

Hooghe, L., & Marks, G. (2009). A postfunctionalist theory of European Integration: From permissive consensus to constraining dissensus. *British Journal of Political Science, 39*(01), 1–23. https://doi.org/10.1017/S0007123408000409

Hooghe, L., & Marks, G. (2015). Delegation and pooling in international organizations. *The Review of International Organizations, 10*(3), 305–328. https://doi.org/10.1007/s11558-014-9194-4

House of Commons. (1999). *Defence—Minutes of evidence: Taken before the Defence Committee* (Publications on the internet—Defence Committee Publications No. Session 1999–2000). https://publications.parliament.uk/pa/cm199900/cmselect/cmdfence/69/9111001.htm

House of Commons. (2004). *Establishing a European Defence Agency: European Standing Committee B.*

House of Commons (2008). *Defence—Ninth Report.* https://publications.parliament.uk/pa/cm200708/cmselect/cmdfence/111/11102.htm

House of Commons. (2012). *European Scrutiny Committee—Tenth Report: European Defence Agency and the OCCAR.* https://publications.parliament.uk/pa/cm201213/cmselect/cmeuleg/86-x/86x02.htm

House of Lords. (2005a). *European Union Committee Ninth Report of Session 2004–05: European Defence Agency—Report with Evidence* (European Union No. HL Paper 76). https://publications.parliament.uk/pa/ld200405/ldselect/ldeucom/76/7605.htm

House of Lords. (2005b). Examination of Witness: Mr. Nick Witney Chief Executive, European Defence Agency (17 January 2005). In *European Union*

Committee Ninth Report of Session 2004–05: European Defence Agency—Report with Evidence (European Union HL Paper 76).

House of Lords. (2005c). Minutes of evidence taken before the select committee on the European Union (Sub-Committee C)): 10 June 2004. In *European Union Committee Ninth Report of Session 2004–05: European Defence Agency—Report with Evidence* (European Union HL Paper 76).

House of Lords. (2005d). *European Union—Government Responses: 9th Report—The European Defence Agency*. https://publications.parliament.uk/pa/ld2 00607/ldselect/ldeucom/38/38we06.htm

Howlett, M., & Rayner, J. (2006). Understanding the historical turn in the policy sciences: A critique of stochastic, narrative, path dependency and process-sequencing models of policy-making over time. *Policy Sciences, 39*(1), 1–18. https://doi.org/10.1007/s11077-005-9004-1

Howorth, J. (2004). The European Draft Constitutional Treaty and the Future of the European Defence Initiative: A Question of Flexibility. *European Foreign Affairs Review, 9*(4), 483–508. http://www.kluwerlawonline.com/document.php?id=EERR2004039

Hübner, D. (2002). *Working Document 25—WG VIII: Improving the functioning and effectiveness of ESDP in the service of CFSP*. http://european-convention.europa.eu/docs/wd8/5518.pdf

Hummel, H. (2007). *A survey of involvement of 15 European States in the Iraq War 2003* (paks working paper No. 7). http://paks.uni-duesseldorf.de/Dok umente/paks_working_paper_7_rev.pdf

Humrich, C. (2013). Fragmented international governance of Arctic offshore oil: Governance challenges and institutional improvement. *Global Environmental Politics, 13*(3), 79–99. https://doi.org/10.1162/GLEP_a_00184

Hyde-Price, A. (2006). 'Normative' power Europe: A realist critique. *Journal of European Public Policy, 13*(2), 217–234. https://doi.org/10.1080/135017 60500451634

IDET. (2017). *Security Fairs: Final Report*. http://www.bvv.cz/_sys_/FileSt orage/download/6/5813/final-report-idet-pyros-iset-2017.pdf

International Institute for Strategic Studies (IISS). (2017). *The military balance 2017*. Routledge.

Interview #1: Representative of the General Council Secretariat, 30 November 2017 (Munich, via phone).

Interview #2: Former German government advisor, 1 December 2017 in Munich.

Interview #3: EDA representative, 12 December 2017 in Brussels.

Interview #4: EDA representative, 12 December 2017 in Brussels.

Interview #5: German MoD representative, 14 December 2017 in Brussels.

Interview #6: OCCAR representative, 15 December 2017 in Bonn.

Interview #7: OCCAR representative, 15 December 2017 in Bonn.

Interview #8: EEAS representative, 5 January 2017 in Oxford.
Interview #9: EEAS representative, 20 March 2018 in Brussels.
Interview #10: NATO representative, 21 March 2018 in Brussels.
Interview #11: NATO representative, 21 March 2018 in Brussels.
Interview #12: Former President of the European Commission, 22 November 2019.
Irondelle, B., Mérand, F., & Foucault, M. (2015). Public support for European defence: Does strategic culture matter? *European Journal of Political Research*, 54(2), 363–383. https://doi.org/10.1111/1475-6765.12090
Jelusic, L. (2010). Regional security and defence cooperation in South East Europe. https://www.rcc.int/articles/31/regional-security-and-defence-cooperation-in-south-east-europe-by-ljubica-jelusic-minister-of-defence-of-slovenia
Johnson, T., & Urpelainen, J. (2012). A strategic theory of regime integration and separation. *International Organization*, 66(04), 645–677. https://doi.org/10.1017/S0020818312000264
Jones, S. G. (2003). The European Union and the security dilemma. *Security Studies*, 12(3), 114–156. https://doi.org/10.1080/09636410390443107
Jones, S. G. (2007). *The rise of European security cooperation*. Cambridge University Press.
Jordan, G., & Williams, T. (2007). Hope deferred? *The RUSI Journal*, 152(3), 66–71. https://doi.org/10.1080/03071840701470889
Juncker, J.-C. (2014). *A new start for Europe: My agenda for jobs, growth, fairness and democratic change: Political guidelines for the next European Commission, opening statement in the European Parliament Plenary Session*. https://ec.europa.eu/commission/sites/beta-political/files/juncker-political-guidelines-speech_en.pdf
Juncker, J.-C. (2017). *In defence of Europe: Speech by President Jean-Claude Juncker at the Defence and Security Conference Prague*. http://europa.eu/rapid/press-release_SPEECH-17-1581_en.htm
Jupille, J., Mattli, W., & Snidal, D. (2013). *Institutional choice and global commerce*. Cambridge University Press.
Jutarnji List. (2017, October 17). Pejčinović Burić za zadržavanje nadzora nad migracijskim rutama. https://www.jutarnji.hr/vijesti/hrvatska/pejcinovic-buric-za-zadrzavanje-nadzora-nad-migracijskim-rutama/6658404/
Karampekios, N. (2015). Understanding Greece's policy in the European Defence Agency: Between national interest and domestic politics. *Southeast European and Black Sea Studies*, 15(1), 37–52. https://doi.org/10.1080/14683857.2015.1007750
Karampekios, N., & Oikonomou, I. (Eds.) (2015). *The European Defence Agency: Arming Europe. Routledge studies in European security and strategy*. Routledge, Taylor & Francis Group.

Karlsson-Vinkhuyzen, S. I., & McGee, J. (2013). Legitimacy in an era of fragmentation: The case of global climate governance. *Global Environmental Politics, 13*(3), 56–78. https://doi.org/10.1162/GLEP_a_00183
Keohane, D. (2002). *The EU and armaments co-operation* (Centre for European Reform - Working Paper).
Keohane, D. (2004). *Europe's new defence agency* (Policy Brief). London. http://www.cer.eu/sites/default/files/publications/attachments/pdf/2012/policy brief_defence_agency-5618.pdf
Keohane, R. O. (1984). *After hegemony: Cooperation and discord in the world political economy (1st Princeton* (classic). Princeton University Press.
Keohane, R. O., & Victor, D. G. (2011). The regime complex for climate change. *Perspectives on Politics, 9*(01), 7–23. https://doi.org/10.1017/S1537592710004068
Kiljunen, K. (2002). *Working Document 30—WG VIII: Comments on the preliminary draft final report of Working Group VIII "Defence" (WD 022)*. http://european-convention.europa.eu/docs/wd8/5859.pdf
Kiljunen, K. (2004). *The EU Constitution: A Finn at the Convention* (Publications of the Parliamentary Office No. 01). https://www.eduskunta.fi/FI/tietoaeduskunnasta/julkaisut/Documents/ekj_1+2004.pdf
Koenig, N. (2012). The EU and the Libyan Crisis—In quest of coherence? *The International Spectator, 46*(4), 11–30. https://doi.org/10.1080/03932729.2011.628089
Koenig, N., & Walter-Franke, M. (2017). *France and Germany: Spearheading a European Security and Defence Union?* (Policy paper No. 202). Berlin.
Koenig-Archibugi, M. (2004). Explaining Government Preferences for Institutional Change in EU Foreign and Security Policy. *International Organization, 58*(01), 137–174. https://doi.org/10.1017/S0020818304581055
Kolín, V. (2010). *April)*. Defence and strategy. Advance online publication. https://doi.org/10.3849/1802-7199.10.2010.01.021-044
Koremenos, B., Lipson, C., & Snidal, D. (2001). The rational design of international institutions. *International Organization, 55*(4), 761–799. https://doi.org/10.1162/002081801317193592
Král, D., Řiháčková, V., & Weiss, T. (2008). *Views on American foreign policy: The atlanticism of political parties in Central and Eastern Europe*. EUROPEUM Institute for European Policy.
Krasner, S. D. (1982). Structural causes and regime consequences: Regimes as intervening variables. *International Organization, 36*(2), 185–205.
Krasner, S. D. (1984). Approaches to the state: Alternative conceptions and historical dynamics. *Comparative Politics, 16*(2), 223. https://doi.org/10.2307/421608
Lake, D. A. (2009). *Hierarchy in international relations. Cornell studies in political economy*. Cornell University Press.

Lake, D. A. (2010). Rightful rules: Authority, order, and the foundations of global governance. *International Studies Quarterly*, 54(3), 587–613. https://doi.org/10.1111/j.1468-2478.2010.00601.x

Le Monde. (2022). Vladimir Poutine marginalise les Européens. https://www.lemonde.fr/international/article/2022/01/07/face-a-vladimir-poutine-l-inquietude-des-europeens_6108494_3210.html

Leuffen, D., Rittberger, B., & Schimmelfennig, F. (2013). *Differentiated integration: Explaining variation in the European Union* (1. publ). The European Union series. Palgrave Macmillan.

Lijphart, A. (1971). Comparative politics and the comparative method. *American Political Science Review*, 65(03), 682–693. https://doi.org/10.2307/1955513

Lindberg, L. N. (1963). *The political dynamics of European Economic integration*. Stanford University Press.

M2 PressWIRE. (2010, November 15). Desire for broad cooperation in the North.

MacDonald, P. K. (2018). Embedded authority: A relational network approach to hierarchy in world politics. *Review of International Studies*, 44(1), 128–150. https://doi.org/10.1017/S0260210517000213

Macron, E. (2017, September 26). Initiative pour l'Europe: Une Europe souveraine, unie, démocratique. http://www.elysee.fr/declarations/article/initiative-pour-l-europe-discours-d-emmanuel-macron-pour-une-europe-souveraine-unie-democratique/

Maior, L. (2002). *Working document 45—WG VIII: Note by Mr Liviu Maior*.

Malta Today. (2017, December 15). Malta to 'wait and see' before deciding on PESCO defence pact, Muscat says. https://www.maltatoday.com.mt/news/europe/83085/malta_to_wait_and_see_before_deciding_on_pesco_defence_pact_muscat_says#.WsDXUZdpG71

Manners, I. (2002). Normative power Europe: A contradiction in terms? *JCMS: Journal of Common Market Studies*, 40(2), 235–258. https://doi.org/10.1111/1468-5965.00353

Marrone, A., De France Olivier, & Fattibene, D. (2016). *Defence budgets and cooperation in Europe: Developments, trends and drivers*. Istituto Affari Internatzionali website: http://www.iai.it/sites/default/files/pma_report.pdf

Martin, L. L. (1992). Interests, power, and multilateralism. *International Organization*, 46(04), 765. https://doi.org/10.1017/S0020818300033245

Mauro, F., & Santopinto, F. (2017). *Permanent Structured Cooperation: National Perspectives and State of Play*.

Mauro, F., & Thoma, K. (2016). *The future of EU defence research*. European Union, Directorate-General for External Policies, Policy Department.

Mawdsley, J. (2003). The European Union and Defense Industrial Policy. https://www.bicc.de/uploads/tx_bicctools/paper31.pdf

Mawdsley, J. (2008). European Union Armaments Policy: Options for small states? *European Security*, *17*(2–3), 367–385. https://doi.org/10.1080/09662830802525923

Mawdsley, J. (2010). Arms, agencies, and accountability: The case of OCCAR. *European Security*, *12*(3–4), 95–111. https://doi.org/10.1080/09662830390436542

Mawdsley, J. (2013). The A400M Project: From Flagship Project to warning for European Defence Cooperation. *Defence Studies*, *13*(1), 14–32. https://doi.org/10.1080/14702436.2013.774961

Mawdsley, J. (2015). France, the UK and the EDA. In N. Karampekios & I. Oikonomou (Eds.), *Routledge studies in European security and strategy. The European Defence Agency: Arming Europe* (pp. 139–154). Routledge, Taylor & Francis Group.

Mearsheimer, J. J. (1994). The false promise of international institutions. *International Security*, *19*(3), 5. https://doi.org/10.2307/2539078

Mearsheimer, J. J. (2014). Why the Ukraine crisis is the West's fault: The liberal delusions that provoked Putin. *Foreign Affairs*, *93*(5), 77–127.

Mearsheimer, J. J. (2018). *The great delusion: Liberal dreams and international realities*. Yale University Press.

Menon, A. (2011a). European Defence Policy from Lisbon to Libya. *Survival*, *53*(3), 75–90. https://doi.org/10.1080/00396338.2011.586191

Menon, A. (2011b). Power, institutions and the CSDP: The promise of institutionalist theory. *JCMS: Journal of Common Market Studies*, *49*(1), 83–100. https://doi.org/10.1111/j.1468-5965.2010.02130.x

Menon, A., & Lipkin, J. (2003). *European attitudes towards transatlantic relations 2000–2003: An analytical survey: Survey prepared for the informal meeting of EU Foreign Ministers, Rodhes and Kastellorizo, May 2–May 3, 2003* (Research and European Issues No. 26).

Merlingen, M., & Ostrauskaite, R. (2009). *EU peacebuilding in Georgia: Limits and achievements* (CLEER Working Papers No. 6). https://www.peacepalacelibrary.nl/ebooks/files/335882102.pdf

Mill, J. S. (2010 [1843]). *A system of logic, ratiocinative and inductive*: Nabu Press.

Ministère de la Défense. (2009). *M. Marc Dolez - Question Écrite: Union européenne - fonctionnement - présidence française perspectives* (Journal Officiel - 13ème législature No. QE 28821). http://questions.assemblee-nationale.fr/q13/13-28821QE.htm

Ministère des Affaires étrangères et européennes de Luxembourg. (2017). *Lignes directrices de la défense luxembourgeoise à l'horizon 2025 et au-delà*. https://defense.gouvernement.lu/dam-assets/la-defense/lignes-directrices-de-la-defense-luxembourgeoise-a-l-horizon-2025-et-au-dela.pdf

Ministry of Defence of the Czech Republic. (2004). *Národní strategie vyzbrojování: National armaments strategy* (1. vyd). Praha: Ministerstvo obrany České republiky - Agentura vojenských informací a služeb.

Ministry of Foreign Affairs of the Republic of Poland. (2012). Cooperation of defence industries. https://www.msz.gov.pl/en/foreign_policy/security_policy/defence_industries/

Ministry of National Defence Republic of Lithuania. (2017, September 8). Lithuania proposes for EU members to establish a military Schengen and to tighten cyber defence cooperation. https://kam.lt/en/news_1098/current_issues/lithuania_proposes_for_eu_members_to_establish_a_military_schengen_and_to_tighten_cyber_defence_cooperation.html

Mölling, C. (2015). State of play of the implementation of EDA's pooling and sharing initiatives and its impact on the European defence industry. https://op.europa.eu/en/publication-detail/-/publication/5dfb4548-526d-4f33-be3d-ea7a1d4c4ce9/language-en

Moravcsik, A. (1993a). Armaments among allies: European weapons collaboration, 1975–1985. In H. K. Jacobson, P. B. Evans, & R. D. Putnam (Eds.), *Studies in international political economy* (vol. 25). *Double-edged diplomacy: International bargaining and domestic politics* (pp. 128–167). University of California Press.

Moravcsik, A. (1993b). Preferences and power in the European Community: A liberal intergovernmentalist approach. *JCMS: Journal of Common Market Studies, 31*(4), 473–524. https://doi.org/10.1111/j.1468-5965.1993.tb00477.x

Moravcsik, A. (1997). Taking preferences seriously: A liberal theory of international politics. *International Organization, 51*(4), 513–553. https://doi.org/10.1162/002081897550447

Moravcsik, A. (1998). *The choice for Europe: Social purpose and state power from Messina to Maastricht. Cornell studies in political economy*. Cornell University Press.

Morse, J. C., & Keohane, R. O. (2014). Contested multilateralism. *The Review of International Organizations, 9*(4), 385–412. https://doi.org/10.1007/s11558-014-9188-2

Mörth, U. (2005). *Organizing European Cooperation: The case of armaments* (New ed.). Rowman & Littlefield Publishers.

Moustakis, F. (2003). *The Greek-Turkish relationship and NATO*. Routledge.

Müller, P. (2016). Europeanization and regional cooperation initiatives: Austria's participation in the Salzburg Forum and in Central European Defence Cooperation. *Österreichische Zeitschrift für Politikwissenschaft, 45*(2), 23. https://doi.org/10.15203/ozp.1102.vol45iss2

Muzaka, V. (2011). Linkages, contests and overlaps in the global intellectual property rights regime. *European Journal of International Relations, 17*(4), 755–776. https://doi.org/10.1177/1354066110373560

NATO. (2004). *Berlin plus information note: Shape support to the EU operational headquarters.* https://shape.nato.int/resources/3/images/2013/alt hea/berlin%20plus-information%20note.pdf

NATO. (2014a, April 29). Allies enhance NATO air-policing duties in Baltic States, Poland, Romania. https://www.nato.int/cps/ic/natohq/news_109354.htm

NATO. (2014b). *Wales Summit Declaration: Issued by the Heads of State and Government participating in the meeting of the North Atlantic Council in Wales.* https://www.nato.int/cps/en/natohq/official_texts_112964.htm

Németh, B. (2012). How to bridge the 'three islands': The future of European military co-operation. https://kclpure.kcl.ac.uk/portal/files/11764177/Nemeth_How_to_bridge_the_three_islands_The_future_of_European_military_co_operation.pdf

Németh, B. (2014, April 16). Why don't Europeans Use NATO and the EU? http://www.css.ethz.ch/en/services/digital-library/articles/article.html/178665/pdf

News.at. Wie viel kosten Eurofighter? Minister nennen erste Details. https://www.news.at/a/wie-eurofighter-minister-1-details-57115

Niemann, A. (1998). The PHARE programme and the concept of spillover: Neofunctionalism in the making. *Journal of European Public Policy, 5*(3), 428–446. https://doi.org/10.1080/135017698343901

Niemann, A., & Schmittner, P. C. (2009). Neofunctionalism. In A. Wiener & T. Diez (Eds.), *European integration theory* (2nd ed., pp. 45–66). Oxford University Press.

OCCAR-EA. (2016). *OCCAR Business Plan 2017.* Bonn. http://www.occar.int/media/raw/OCCAR_Business_Plan_2017_External.pdf

O'Donnell, C. M. (2011). *Britain and France should not give up on EU defence co-operation* (Policy Brief). London. http://www.cer.eu/sites/default/files/publications/attachments/pdf/2011/pb_csdp_24oct11-3907.pdf

Oikonomou, I. (2015). Brothers in arms? The European arms industry and the making of the EDA. In N. Karampekios & I. Oikonomou (Eds.), *Routledge studies in European security and strategy. The European Defence Agency: Arming Europe.* Routledge, Taylor & Francis Group.

Orsini, A., Morin, J.-F., & Young, O. R. (2013). Regime complexes: A buzz, a boom or a boost for global governance? *Global Governance, 19*(1), 27–39.

Oshri, I., Kotlarsky, J., & Willcocks, L. (2009). *The handbook of global outsourcing and offshoring.* Palgrave Macmillan.

Ostrom, E. (1990). *Governing the commons: The evolution of institutions for collective action.* Cambridge University Press.

Permanent Representation of the Slovak Republic to the EU. (2017, September 7). Ivan Korčok of MFEA SR attends an informal meeting of EU diplomacy heads in Tallinn. https://www.mzv.sk/web/szbrusel-en/news/-/asset_publisher/olsKsIdtEfpB/content/statny-tajomnik-mzvaez-sr-ivan-korcok-na-neformalnom-stretnuti-sefov-diplomacie-krajin-eu-v-tallinne/10182

Pertusot, V. Pragmatic Approach to Defence Cooperation in Europe: Why bi- and minilateral cooperation is not a passing phenomenon. *Paper presented at the EU International Affairs Conference.*

Pertusot, V. (2015). European defence: Minilateralism is not the enemy. In D. Fiott (Ed.), *Egmont Paper* (vol. 79). *The Common Security and Defence Policy: National Perspectives* (pp. 101–104).

PESCO Member States. (2017). *Notification on Permanent Structured Cooperation (PESCO) to the Council and to the High Representative of the Union for Foreign Affairs and Security Policy.* https://www.consilium.europa.eu/media/31511/171113-pesco-notification.pdf

PESCO Member States. (2018). *Permanent Structured Cooperation (PESCO) updated list of PESCO projects.* https://www.consilium.europa.eu/media/37028/table-pesco-projects.pdf

Pesme, F. (2010). France's 'return' to NATO: Implications for its defence policy. *European Security, 19*(1), 45–60. https://doi.org/10.1080/09662839.2010.507245

Peters, D. (2011). *A divided union? Public opinion and the EU's Common Foreign, security and defence policy* (RECON Online Working Paper No. 19). http://www.reconproject.eu/projectweb/portalproject/AbstractRECONwp1119.html

Pierson, P. (2000). Increasing returns, path dependence, and the study of politics. *American Political Science Review, 94*(02), 251–267. https://doi.org/10.2307/2586011

Pierson, P. (2004). *Politics in time: History, institutions, and social analysis.* Princeton University Press.

Pierson, P. (2016). Power in historical institutionalism. In O. Fioretos, T. G. Falleti, & A. Sheingate (Eds.), *The Oxford handbook of historical institutionalism* (pp. 124–141). Oxford University Press.

Piks, & Rihards. (2002). *Working Document 29—WG VIII: Comments to the preliminary draft final report of Working Group VIII "Defence".* http://european-convention.europa.eu/docs/wd8/5848.pdf

Platteau, E. (2015). *Defence Data 2013.* https://issuu.com/europeandefenceagency/docs/eda_defence_data_2013_web/1?e=4763412/12106343

Politico. (2016a, August 25). Angela Merkel: Brexit won't dominate Bratislava summit. https://www.politico.eu/article/angela-merkel-brexit-wont-dominate-bratislava-summit-european-union-priorities-agenda-estonia/

Politico. (2016b, September 15). EU needs 'Schengen for defense'. https://www.politico.eu/article/italian-foreign-minister-eu-needs-schengen-for-defense-paolo-gentiloni-islamic-state-migrants-security/

Politico. (2017a, June 3). In Versailles, EU's big 4 back multispeed Europe. https://www.politico.eu/article/in-versailles-eus-big-4-back-multispeed-europe-italy-france-germany-spain/

Politico. (2017b, November 11). EU defense pact tests Portugal's left-wing government alliance. https://www.politico.eu/article/eu-defense-pact-tests-portugals-left-wing-government-alliance/

Politico. (2018, February 5). Emmanuel Macron's coalition of the willing. https://www.politico.eu/article/emmanuel-macrons-eu-defense-army-coalition-of-the-willing-military-cooperation/

Politico. (2021). Von der Leyen finds EU's soul—and its weakness—in State of Union address. https://www.politico.eu/article/ursula-von-der-leyen-eu-soul-weakness-state-of-union-address/

Porter, M. E. (1990). *The competitive advantage of nations*. Free Pr.

Posen, B. R. (2006). European Union Security and Defense Policy: Response to unipolarity? *Security Studies, 15*(2), 149–186. https://doi.org/10.1080/09636410600829356

Pratt, T. (2018). Deference and hierarchy in international regime complexes. *International Organization, 72*(3), 561–590. https://doi.org/10.1017/S0020818318000164

Rasmussen, A. F. (2010). *Strategic concept for the defence and security of the members of the North Atlantic Treaty Organisation adopted by Heads of State and Government in Lisbon: Active engagement, modern defence*. https://www.nato.int/lisbon2010/strategic-concept-2010-eng.pdf

Raustiala, K., & Victor, D. G. (2004). The regime complex for plant genetic resources. *International Organization, 58*(2), 277–309. https://doi.org/10.2139/ssrn.441463

Reuters. (2016a, January 3). Exclusive: Poland wants Britain's help over NATO troops in Brexit talks. https://www.reuters.com/article/us-britain-eu-poland-idUSKBN0UH0IE20160103

Reuters. (2016b, November 14). Europeans agree defense plan after campaign swipes by Trump. https://www.reuters.com/article/us-eu-defence/europeans-agree-defense-plan-after-campaign-swipes-by-trump-idUSKBN1391HH

Reuters. (2016c, December 14). Baltic states urge strong U.S. defense commitment to region. https://www.reuters.com/article/us-baltic-security-usa-trump/baltic-states-urge-strong-u-s-defense-commitment-to-region-idUSKBN14321O

Reuters. (2017, June 10). Germany, France drafting details of defense fund: German minister. https://www.reuters.com/article/us-eu-defence-germany-france-idUSKBN1910H4

Rieker, P. (2013). The French return to NATO: Reintegration in practice, not in principle. *European Security, 22*(3), 376–394. https://doi.org/10.1080/09662839.2013.767238

Rosato, S. (2011). Europe's troubles: Power politics and the state of the European project. *International Security, 35*(4), 45–86. https://doi.org/10.1162/ISEC_a_00035

Rynning, S. (2011). Realism and the common security and defence policy. *JCMS: Journal of Common Market Studies, 49*(1), 23–42. https://doi.org/10.1111/j.1468-5965.2010.02127.x

Salmon, T. C., & Shepherd, A. J. K. (2003). *Toward a European army: A military power in the making?* Rienner.

Sandler, T., & Tschirhart, J. (1997). Club theory: Thirty years later. *Public Choice, 93*(3/4), 335–355. https://doi.org/10.1023/A:1017952723093

Sanfourche, J.-P. (1999). The WEAG and the Future European Armaments Agency: Interview with Major General Andries Schlieper. *Air & Space Europe, 1*(3), 6–9.

Sartori, P., Marrone, A., & Nones, M. (2018). *Looking through the fog of Brexit: Scenarios and implications for the European Defence Industry* (DOCUMENTI IAI No. 18). https://www.iai.it/sites/default/files/iai1816.pdf

Scharpf, F. W. (1997). *Games real actors play: Actor-centered institutionalism in policy research*. Theoretical Lenses on Public Policy.

Schelling, T. C. (1960). *The strategy of conflict*. Harvard University Press.

Schilde, K. (2017). *The political economy of European Security*. Cambridge University Press.

Schimmelfennig, F. (2001). The community trap: Liberal norms, rhetorical action, and the Eastern enlargement of the European Union. *International Organization, 55*(1), 47–80. https://doi.org/10.1162/002081801551414

Schimmelfennig, F., Leuffen, D., & Rittberger, B. (2015). The European Union as a system of differentiated integration: Interdependence, politicization and differentiation. *Journal of European Public Policy, 22*(6), 764–782. https://doi.org/10.1080/13501763.2015.1020835

Schmitt, B. (2003). *The European Union and Armaments: Getting a bigger bang for the Euro*. https://www.iss.europa.eu/sites/default/files/EUISSFiles/cp063e.pdf

Schmitter, P. C., & Lefkofridi, Z. (2016). Neo-functionalism as a theory of disintegration. *Chinese Political Science Review, 1*(1), 1–29. https://doi.org/10.1007/s41111-016-0012-4

Schneider, C. J., & Urpelainen, J. (2013). Distributional conflict between powerful states and international treaty ratification 1. *International Studies Quarterly, 57*(1), 13–27. https://doi.org/10.1111/isqu.12024

Schweller, R. L. (1994). Bandwagoning for profit: Bringing the revisionist state back in. *International Security*, *19*(1), 72. https://doi.org/10.2307/2539149

Seawright, J., & Gerring, J. (2008). Case selection techniques in case study research. *Political Research Quarterly*, *61*(2), 294–308. https://doi.org/10.1177/1065912907313077

Senato della Repubblica. (2007). *4a Commissione Permanente (Difesa): Indagine Conoscitiva Sullo Stato Attuale e Sulle Prospettive Dell'Industria Della Difesa e Sulla Cooperazione in Materia di Armamenti* (Giunte e Commissioni No. 68a seduta). http://www.senato.it/documenti/repository/commissioni/stenografici/15/comm04/04a-20070529-IC-0431.pdf

Shepherd, A. J. K. (2015). EU military capability development and the EDA: Ideas, interests and institutions. In N. Karampekios & I. Oikonomou (Eds.), *Routledge studies in European security and strategy. The European Defence Agency: Arming Europe*. Routledge, Taylor & Francis Group.

Simon, H. A. (1957). *Models of man: Social and rational mathematical essays on rational human behavior in society setting*. Wiley.

SIPRI. (2008). *Armaments, disarmament and international security 2008*. Oxford University Press. https://books.google.de/books?id=EAyQ9KCJE2gC

SIPRI. (2022). Explainer: The proposed hike in German military spending. https://www.sipri.org/commentary/blog/2022/explainer-proposed-hike-german-military-spending

Slovakia. (2010). Program of the Slovak Presidency of the Visegrad Group July 2010–June 2011: Efficient Visegrad—Continuity, coehsion, solidarity, awareness. http://www.visegradgroup.eu/documents/presidency-programs/2010-2011-slovak-110412

Snidal, D. (1994). The politics of scope: Endogenous actors, heterogeneity and institutions. *Journal of Theoretical Politics*, *6*(4), 449–472. https://doi.org/10.1177/0951692894006004003

Snyder, G. H. (1984). The security dilemma in alliance politics. *World Politics*, *36*(04), 461–495. https://doi.org/10.2307/2010183

Spiegel Online. (2016, November 16). 'Extreme and unprecedented uncertainty': NATO prepares for Trump Presidency. http://www.spiegel.de/international/world/worry-grows-over-trump-threat-to-european-security-a-1121536.html

Spiegel Online. (2019, May 14). EU-Außenministertreffen in Brüssel: USA attackieren EU-Pläne für Verteidigungsfonds. https://www.spiegel.de/politik/ausland/usa-attackieren-eu-plaene-fuer-verteidigungsfonds-a-1267291.html

Stahl, B., Boekle, H., Nadoll, J., & Jóhannesdóttir, A. (2004). Understanding the Atlanticist-Europeanist divide in the CFSP: Comparing Denmark, France,

Germany and the Netherlands. *European Foreign Affairs Review*, 9(3), 417–441.

Steketee, M. (2001, January 13). 'Defensie negeert alternatief voor nieuw pantservoertuig'. https://www.nrc.nl/nieuws/2001/01/13/defensie-negeert-alternatief-voor-nieuw-pantservoertuig-7525823-a535462

Stephenson, P. (2010). Let's get physical: The European Commission and cultivated spillover in completing the single market's transport infrastructure. *Journal of European Public Policy*, 17(7), 1039–1057. https://doi.org/10.1080/13501763.2010.499247

Stoltenberg, T. (2009). *Nordic Cooperation on Foreign and Security Policy: Proposals presented to the extraordinary meeting of Nordic foreign ministers in Oslo on 9 February 2009*. Oslo. https://www.regjeringen.no/globalassets/upload/ud/vedlegg/nordicreport.pdf

Stone Sweet, A., & Sandholtz, W. (1997). European integration and supranational governance. *Journal of European Public Policy*, 4(3), 297–317. https://doi.org/10.1080/13501769780000011

Stuart, G. (2002). *Working document 23—WG VIII*. http://european-convention.europa.eu/docs/wd8/5452.pdf

Taylor, C. (2003). *UK Defence Procurement Policy* (RESEARCH PAPER No. 03/78).

Taylor, C. (2008). *Priorities for ESDP during the French Presidency of the EU* (No. SN/IA/4807).

Teissier, G., & Rohan, J. de (Eds.) (2011, September). *9 ème Université d'été de la Commission de la Défense nationale et des Forces armées de l'Assemblée nationale et de la Commission des Affaires étrangères, de la Défense et des Foces armées du Sénat: Etat-industries: de l'urgent opérations aux grands systèmes de Défense*. http://testleni2.site.exhibis.net/Data/ElFinder/s4/UD/universit%C3%A9s/actes_mars_ix.pdf

Terlikowski, M. (2016). Defence policy in the European Union: Multi-speed security? https://www.pism.pl/publications/bulletin/no-74-924

Terlikowski, M. (2020, January 23). PESCO: Two years later. https://www.pism.pl/publications/PESCO_Two_Years_Later#xd_co_f=YjUwZWNlYjUtZDIwOC00NDkwLWJkZGMtMmVjZmVjY2M1Y2U4~

The Baltic Times. (2016, September 16). Lithuanian president attends EU summit on Europe's future after Brexit. https://www.baltictimes.com/lithuanian_president_attending_eu_summit_on_europe_s_future_after_brexit/

The Financial Times. (2016a, November 13). Baltics fear for any US policy changes to Nato: Possibility of a disengagement has rung alarm bells in states. https://www.ft.com/content/0036b09a-a825-11e6-8898-79a99e2a4de6

The Financial Times. (2016b, November 14). Donald Trump, Vladimir Putin and the art of a deal with Russia. https://www.ft.com/content/9bef31a4-aa57-11e6-a0bb-97f42551dbf4

The Guardian. (2008, June 7). European HQ heads Sarkozy plan for greater military integration. https://www.theguardian.com/world/2008/jun/07/eu.france

The Guardian. (2014, March 26). Barack Obama: No cold war over Crimea. https://www.theguardian.com/world/2014/mar/26/obama-no-cold-war-crimea

The Guardian. (2016a, February 5). Polish PM backs some parts of Cameron's EU renegotiation plans. https://www.theguardian.com/politics/2016/feb/05/polish-pm-backs-parts-david-cameron-eu-renegotiation-beata-szydlo

The Guardian. (2016b, July 21). Trump says US may not automatically defend Nato allies under attack. https://www.theguardian.com/world/2016/jul/21/donald-trump-america-automatically-nato-allies-under-attack

The Guardian. (2016c, July 28). Donald Trump reiterates he will only help Nato countries that pay 'fair share'. https://www.theguardian.com/us-news/2016/jul/27/donald-trump-nato-isolationist

The Guardian. (2017, February 14). Plans for two-speed EU risk split with 'peripheral' members. https://www.theguardian.com/world/2017/feb/14/plans-for-two-speed-eu-risk-split-with-peripheral-members

The Guardian. (2018, June 25). Nine EU states sign off on joint military intervention force. https://www.theguardian.com/world/2018/jun/25/nine-eu-states-to-sign-off-on-joint-military-intervention-force

The Irish Times. (2018, January 3). EU defence co-operation is no threat to Irish neutrality. https://www.irishtimes.com/opinion/eu-defence-co-operation-is-no-threat-to-irish-neutrality-1.3343293

The Netherlands. (2002, December 4). Working Document 28—WG VIII: Dutch comments on the preliminary draft final report of Working Group VIII "Defence" (WD 022). http://european-convention.europa.eu/docs/wd8/5837.pdf

The New York Times. (2016, April 2). Donald Trump Says NATO is 'Obsolete,' UN is 'Political Game'. https://www.nytimes.com/politics/first-draft/2016/04/02/donald-trump-tells-crowd-hed-be-fine-if-nato-broke-up/

The Telegraph. (2011, October 24). David Cameron's statement on the European Council: In full. https://www.telegraph.co.uk/news/worldnews/europe/eu/8846553/David-Camerons-statement-on-the-European-Council-in-full.html

The Telegraph. (2014, April 1). Ukraine crisis: Poland asks Nato to station 10,000 troops on its territory. https://www.telegraph.co.uk/news/worldnews/europe/ukraine/10737838/Ukraine-crisis-Poland-asks-Nato-to-station-10000-troops-on-its-territory.html

The Times. (2016, September 15). EU army plan sets alarm bells ringing on Nato's front line.://www.thetimes.co.uk/edition/world/eu-army-plan-sets-alarm-bells-ringing-on-nato-s-front-line-5q9gxw3ng

TheJournal.ie. (2017, December 7). 'We're being asked to sell out our neutrality': Government accused of trying to rush EU defence deal vote. http://www.thejournal.ie/eu-army-pesco-3734034-Dec2017/
Thompson, A., & Verdier, D. (2014). Multilateralism, bilateralism, and regime design. *International Studies Quarterly*, 58(1), 15–28. https://doi.org/10.1111/isqu.12100
Time.com. (2016, November 14). Can NATO Survive a Donald Trump Presidency? http://time.com/4569578/donald-trump-nato-alliance-europe-afghanistan/
Times of Malta. (2004, July 19). European Defence Agency membership "could be in violation of constitution".
Tocci, N. (2018). Towards a European Security and Defence Union: Was 2017 a watershed? *JCMS: Journal of Common Market Studies*, 49, 57. https://doi.org/10.1111/jcms.12752
Toje, A. (2008). The consensus expectations gap: Explaining Europe's Ineffective Foreign Policy. *Security Dialogue*, 39(1), 121–141. https://doi.org/10.1177/0967010607086826
Tranholm-Mikkelsen, J. (1991). Neo-functionalism: Obstinate or obsolete? A reappraisal in the light of the new dynamism of the EC. *Millennium: Journal of International Studies*, 20(1), 1–22. https://doi.org/10.1177/03058298910200010201
Treaty on European Union. (1992). Luxembourg: Office for Official Publ. of the Europ. Communities.
Trybus, M. (2005). *European Union law and defence integration. Modern studies in European law* (vol. 7). Hart.
Trybus, M. (2006). The New European Defence Agency: A contribution to a common European Security and defence policy and a challenge to the community acquis? *Common Market Law Review*, 43, 667–703.
Trybus, M. (2014). *Buying defence and security in Europe: The EU defence and security procurement directive in context*. Cambridge University Press.
Tsebelis, G. (1995). Decision making in political systems: Veto players in presidentialism, parliamentarism, multicameralism and multipartyism. *British Journal of Political Science*, 25(03), 289. https://doi.org/10.1017/S0007123400007225
Tuomioja, E. (2003). 'Europe needs to work as a whole on defence': Article by Erkki Tuomioja, Finnish Foreign Minister [*The Financial Times*, 28 October 2003]. In A. Missiroli (Ed.), *Chaillot Papers* (vol. 67). *From Copenhagen to Brussels European defence: Core documents* (vol. IV, pp. 424–425). Institute for Security Studies European Union.
UK Foreign and Commonwealth Office, & UK Ministry of Defence. (2014, July 28). NATO exercise to reassure allies. https://www.gov.uk/government/news/nato-exercise-to-reassure-allies

UK Ministry of Defence. (2001). *Maximising the benefits of defence equipment co-operation (HC 300 2000–2001)—Full Report (665 KB): Report by the Comptroller and Auditor General* (Session 2000–2001 No. HC 300). London.

UK Ministry of Defence. (2012, December 12). Letter of intent: Restructuring the European defence industry: Overview of the work of the Letter of Intent (LoI) group. https://www.gov.uk/guidance/letter-of-intent-restructuring-the-european-defence-industry

UK Ministry of Defence. (2016, January 20). Defence Secretary announces UK commitment to Poland. https://www.gov.uk/government/news/defence-secretary-announces-uk-commitment-to-poland

UK Prime Minister's Office. (2010, December 2). UK–France summit 2010 declaration on defence and security co-operation. https://www.gov.uk/government/news/uk-france-summit-2010-declaration-on-defence-and-security-co-operation

United Kingdom. (2003). British non-paper: "Food for thought". In A. Missiroli (Ed.), *Chaillot Papers* (vol. 67). *From Copenhagen to Brussels European defence: Core documents* (vol. IV, pp. 204–207). Institute for Security Studies European Union.

United Kingdom, & France. (2003). Declaration on strengthening European cooperation in security and defence [4 February 2003]: Le Touquet. In A. Missiroli (Ed.), *Chaillot Papers* (vol. 67). *From Copenhagen to Brussels European defence: Core documents* (vol. IV, pp. 36–39). Institute for Security Studies European Union.

United Kingdom, & France. (2011). *Treaty between the United Kingdom of Great Britain and Northern Ireland and the French Republic for defence and security co-operation: London, 2 November 2010. Treaty series: no. 36 (2011)*. Stationery Office.

United Kingdom, & Italy. (2003). Declaration Defence and Security [31 February 2003]. In A. Missiroli (Ed.), *Chaillot Papers* (vol. 67). *From Copenhagen to Brussels European defence: Core documents* (vol. IV, pp. 40–45). Institute for Security Studies European Union.

V4. (2014). *Long term vision of the Visegrad Countries on deepening their defence cooperation*. Visegrad. Visegrad Group website: www.visegradgroup.eu/calendar/2014-03-14-ltv

V4. (2016a, July 21). Joint Statement of the Heads of Governments of the V4 Countries. https://budapeszt.msz.gov.pl/resource/eb5de611-3c86-413b-b7a1-d389d79fb63f:JCR

V4. (2016b, September 16). Joint Statement of the Heads of Governments of the V4 Countries, Bratislava. https://www.vlada.cz/en/media-centrum/aktualne/joint-statement-of-the-heads-of-governments-of-the-v4-countries--bratislava--16-september-2016-148913/

V4. (2017a, March 2). Joint Statement of the Heads of Governments of the V4 Countries: "Strong Europe—Union of Action and Trust". https://www.vlada.cz/en/media-centrum/aktualne/joint-statement-of-the-heads-of-governments-of-the-v4-countries-_strong-europe-_-union-of-action-and-trust_-154008/

V4. (2017b, November 10). Poland to join EU's military partnership. http://www.visegradgroup.eu/news/poland-to-join-eu-171110

Vabulas, F., & Snidal, D. (2013). Organization without delegation: Informal intergovernmental organizations (IIGOs) and the spectrum of intergovernmental arrangements. *The Review of International Organizations, 8*(2), 193–220. https://doi.org/10.1007/s11558-012-9161-x

Valášek, T. (2005). New EU Members in Europe's Security Policy. *Cambridge Review of International Affairs, 18*(2), 217–228. https://doi.org/10.1080/09557570500164454

Van de Graaf, T. (2013). Fragmentation in global energy governance: Explaining the creation of IRENA. *Global Environmental Politics, 13*(3), 14–33. https://doi.org/10.1162/GLEP_a_00181

Van Eekelen, W. F., & Kurpas, S. (2008). *The evolution of flexible integration in European defence policy: Is permanent structured cooperation a leap forward for the common security and defence policy? CEPS working document* (vol. 296). CEPS.

Van Langenhove, L., & Maes, L. (2012). The role of the EU in peace and security. https://unu.edu/publications/articles/the-role-of-the-eu-in-peace-and-security.html

Vestel, P. (1995). *Defence markets and industries in Europe: time for political decisions?*

Vidmajer, S. (2017, November 10). Z oddajo suverenosti si bolj suveren, kot če si sam suveren. https://www.delo.si/sobotna/z-oddajo-suverenosti-si-bolj-suveren-kot-ce-si-sam-suveren.html

Von Ondaraza, N. von (2011). Common security and defence policy: Bilateral vs. structured cooperation? Flexible cooperation in and outside the EU framework as a tool for advancing European capabilities. In E. Fabry (Ed.), *Think Global—Act European (TGAE): The contribution of 16 European Think Tanks to the Polish, Danish and Cypriot Trio Presidency of the European Union* (pp. 322–326). Notre Europe.

Vukadinović, L. Č. (2014). The Croatian View on the EU Common Security and Defence Policy (CSDP). *Austria Institut für Europa- und Sicherheitspolitik* (1).

Wagner, W. (2003). Why the EU's common foreign and security policy will remain intergovernmental: A rationalist institutional choice analysis of European crisis management policy. *Journal of European Public Policy, 10*(4), 576–595. https://doi.org/10.1080/1350176032000101262

Waltz, K. N. (1979). *Theory of international politics*. Addison-Wesley Pub. Co.
Waszczykowski, W., & Macierewicz, A. (2017, November 17). Poland to join PESCO (Letter).
Weiss, M. (2009). Power and signals: Explaining the German approach to European security. *Journal of International Relations and Development*, *12*, 317–348. https://doi.org/10.1057/jird.2009.15
Weiss, M. (2011). *Transaction costs and security institutions of the state institutions: Unravelling the EDSP*. Palgrave Macmillan.
Weiss, M. (2019). State vs. market in India: How (not) to integrate foreign contractors in the domestic defense-industrial sector. *Comparative Strategy*, *37*(4), 286–298. https://doi.org/10.1080/01495933.2018.1497323
Weiss, M. (2021). Varieties of privatization: Informal networks, trust and state control of the commanding heights. *Review of International Political Economy*, *28*(3), 662–689. https://doi.org/10.1080/09692290.2020.1726791
Weiss, M., & Biermann, F. (2018). Defence industrial cooperation. In H. Meijer & M. Wyss (Eds.), *The handbook of European defence policies and armed formces* (pp. 693–709). Oxford University Press.
Weiss, M., & Biermann, F. (2021). Networked politics and the supply of European defence integration. *Journal of European Public Policy*, *90*(3), 1–22. https://doi.org/10.1080/13501763.2021.1916057
Weiss, M., & Blauberger, M. (2015). Judicialized law-making and opportunistic enforcement: Explaining the EU's challenge of national defence offsets. *JCMS: Journal of Common Market Studies*, 1–19. https://doi.org/10.1111/jcms.12290
Weiss, M., & Heinkelmann-Wild, T. (2020). Disarmed principals? Institutional resilience and the non-enforcement of delegation. *European Political Science Review*, *12*(4), 409–425. https://doi.org/10.1017/S1755773920000181
Western European Armaments Group. (2003). EUROPA MoU [2001]. In B. Schmitt (Ed.), *Chaillot Papers* (vol. 59). *European armaments cooperation: Core Documents* (pp. 95–107).
Western European Armaments Group. (2005, March 30). Information on the Spring 2004 Meeting of the WEAG National Armaments Directors: Dublin, 26 February 2004. http://www.weu.int/weag/whatsnew.htm
Western European Union. (1997). *Erfurt Declaration*. http://www.weu.int/weag/
Western European Union. (1998). *Rome Declaration*. Retrieved from http://www.weu.int/weag/
Western European Union. (2000). *WEU Today*. Brussels. Retrieved from http://www.weu.int/
Western European Union. (2002). *Rome Declaration*. http://www.weu.int/weag/Rome_Declaration.pdf

Western European Union. (2004). *Assembly of Western European Union—The Interparliamentary European Security and Defence Assembly: The European Defence Agency—Reply to the Annual Report of the Council* (No. A/1856). Paris. http://stopwapenhandel.org/sites/stopwapenhandel.org/files/imported/projecten/Europa/EDA/WEU_on_EDA.pdf
Williamson, O. E. (1985). *The economic institutions of capitalism: Firms, markets, relational contracting*. Free Press. http://www.loc.gov/catdir/bios/simon051/87011901.html
Witney, N. (2008). *Re-energising Europe's security and defence policy. Policy paper*: European Council on Foreign Relations.
Wivel, A. (2005). The security challenge of small EU member states: Interests, identity and the development of the EU as a security actor. *JCMS: Journal of Common Market Studies, 43*(2), 393–412. https://doi.org/10.1111/j.0021-9886.2005.00561.x
Zandee, D. (2017). *Developing European defence capabilities: Bringing order into disorder* (Clingendael Report). https://www.clingendael.org/sites/default/files/2017-10/Developing_European_Defence_Capabilities.pdf
Zangl, B., Heußner, F., Kruck, A., & Lanzendörfer, X. (2016). Imperfect adaptation: How the WTO and the IMF adjust to shifting power distributions among their members. *The Review of International Organizations, 11*(2), 171–196. https://doi.org/10.1007/s11558-016-9246-z
Zelli, F., & van Asselt, H. (2013). Introduction: The institutional fragmentation of global environmental governance: Causes, consequences, and responses. *Global Environmental Politics, 13*(3), 1–13. https://doi.org/10.1162/GLEP_a_00180
Zürn, M. (1992). *Interessen und Institutionen in der internationalen Politik: Grundlegung und Anwendungen des situationsstrukturellen Ansatzes*. VS Verlag für Sozialwissenschaften.
Zürn, M. (2017). From constitutional rule to loosely coupled spheres of liquid authority: A reflexive approach. *International Theory, 9*(2), 261–285. https://doi.org/10.1017/S1752971916000270
Zürn, M., & Faude, B. (2013). Commentary: On fragmentation, differentiation, and coordination. *Global Environmental Politics, 13*(3), 119–130. https://doi.org/10.1162/GLEP_a_00186

INDEX

A
A-400M, 6, 141
Ad hoc Group, 129
Administrative Arrangement, 95, 141, 157
AA, 95, 141–143, 149–151, 153, 157–161, 241
aircraft, 6, 124, 141, 150, 153, 248
alliance security dilemma, 24, 236–238, 242, 244
armaments agency, 6, 20, 111–116, 118–120, 122–124, 133, 142, 145, 148–150, 156, 240, 249
Atlanticists, 23, 100, 102, 103, 106, 160, 173, 177, 189–191, 193, 199, 201, 202, 204–210, 216–218, 224, 237, 240–243, 245
Austria, 101, 111, 148, 180, 190, 206, 215, 216
authority, 38, 74, 237
  formal-legal authority, 8, 11, 12, 15, 38, 112, 263, 265

relational authority, 8, 11–16, 39, 43, 50, 52, 53, 56, 57, 63, 71, 82, 83, 134, 157, 162, 201, 218, 265
avant-gardist states
avant-gardists, 103, 120, 145, 147, 149, 151, 161, 170, 171, 182, 189, 205, 206, 208–215, 218, 224, 240–243, 253, 274

B
BAE Systems, 119, 248
balancing, 24, 236–245
Baltic Defence Cooperation, 180, 182, 209
bandwagoning, 24, 74, 81, 211, 236–245, 271
Battlegroup, 173, 181
Belgium, 11, 101, 111, 116, 118, 124, 152, 155, 177, 179, 186, 214, 215, 273
Berlin Plus, 103, 240, 275

© The Editor(s) (if applicable) and The Author(s), under exclusive license to Springer Nature Switzerland AG 2023
F. Biermann, *The Battle for Authority in European Defence Cooperation*, Palgrave Studies in European Union Politics,
https://doi.org/10.1007/978-3-031-30054-7

INDEX

big six, 102, 192, 273
Brexit, 22, 193, 200, 202, 204–210, 218, 245, 253
Bulgaria, 101, 191, 213, 215

C

Cameron, David, 191, 202
capabilities, 69
capabilities–expectations gap, 8, 10
capability gaps, 21, 127, 142, 158, 160, 161
center of authority, 12, 16–18, 21–23, 38, 39, 63, 68, 70, 71, 74, 83, 111, 224, 261, 265, 266, 268, 273, 274
Central European Defence Cooperation (CEDC), 6, 7, 180, 182, 188, 209, 214
Common Foreign and Security Policy (CFSP), 112, 131, 146
Common Security and Defence Policy (CSDP), 3, 4, 6–14, 19, 23–25, 27, 99–101, 103, 131, 146, 158, 162, 169, 173, 177, 178, 181, 184, 186, 187, 190, 203, 205, 206, 209, 210, 236, 238, 239, 241, 242, 245–247, 251, 252, 254, 261–264, 268–270, 273, 274
competition, 9, 22, 44, 46–48, 51, 102, 103, 115, 119, 148, 175, 274
compliance, 66, 74, 76–78, 98, 271
congruence analysis, 19, 23, 26, 86, 95, 96, 99, 262, 269
consensus, 5, 10, 11, 76, 115, 116, 122, 147, 188, 208, 212, 272
contested multilateralism, 14, 15, 19, 26, 40, 49, 50, 57, 66, 68, 74, 94, 96, 97, 261, 262, 264
cooperation, 48, 113, 182
costs of exclusion, 64, 78
costs of inclusion, 17, 64, 78, 267
Council of the European Union, 122, 125
Council, 98, 193
Croatia, 101, 180, 182, 191, 213, 215
Cyprus, 70, 101, 149, 151, 159, 215
Czech Republic, 101, 111, 148, 152, 180, 188, 213, 214

D

Defence Technological and Industrial Base (DTIB), 192
Defense Union, 3, 6, 218, 244, 245
Denmark, 101, 111, 112, 121, 125, 131, 134, 173, 179, 190, 199, 216, 217, 273
Danish, 202
dissatisfaction, 45, 64, 65, 69, 86, 95, 98, 100, 116, 144, 145, 172, 179, 238, 271
distribution of authority
  authority distribution, 14–17, 37, 39, 40, 49, 53, 54, 63, 64, 162, 204, 265, 269
distributive concerns, 17, 64
distributive effects, 78, 154
downstream states, 102, 112, 115, 116, 118, 119, 121–123, 125–131, 133, 134, 142–144, 146–154, 156, 157, 159–161, 210, 211, 252
drone, 6, 141, 162

E

EADS, 248
Estonia, 101, 213, 217, 273
Euro crisis, 22, 177, 187, 251
European Commission, 102
  Commission, 10, 24, 98, 217

INDEX 317

European Convention, 5, 98,
  120–123, 127, 170, 172, 173
European Council, 124, 125, 129,
  190, 202, 203, 206, 252
European Defence Agency (EDA),
  5–7, 10–13, 15, 19–21, 24–27,
  38, 95, 98, 100, 111–113, 119,
  121–123, 125–134, 141–154,
  156–162, 170, 172, 173, 178,
  187, 201, 211, 235–237, 239,
  241, 242, 246, 247, 249, 250,
  253, 261–264, 268, 269, 272,
  274
European Defence Technological and
  Industrial Base (EDTIB), 9, 25,
  117
European Defense Fund, 24, 217,
  236, 237, 245, 250, 252
European Intervention Initiative, xv,
  264, 272
EII, 272, 273
Europeanists, 100, 106, 160, 171,
  173, 177, 186–193, 200, 202,
  204, 206, 240, 242, 245
European Monetary Union
  EMU, xv, 247
European Parliament, xv, 10, 209,
  213, 249
EP, xv, 10, 251
externalities, 42, 44, 55, 65, 74, 75,
  77, 98
external validity, 19, 24, 94, 95, 254,
  269

F
federalist states
  federalists, 103, 124, 171, 189,
    214, 216, 217
Finland, 4, 101, 111, 153, 161, 174,
  179, 209, 214, 215, 217
fortress Europe, 120, 241
Forum-shopping, 48

fragmentation, 17–19, 22, 23, 26,
  38–40, 47, 50, 53, 54, 56, 63,
  68, 70, 71, 75, 80, 82, 83,
  95–97, 128, 162, 169–172, 178,
  187, 188, 191, 192, 199, 202,
  204, 205, 224, 237, 245–247,
  250, 251, 253, 262, 268
France, 11, 99, 101–103, 111, 116,
  120, 123, 129, 133, 142, 145,
  149, 150, 154, 157, 158, 161,
  162, 171, 175, 176, 179, 182,
  186, 189, 192, 207, 208,
  212–214, 216, 218, 240–242,
  244, 253, 272, 273
free riding, 64
Future Combat Air System (FCAS),
  141, 273

G
generalizability, 95–97
geopolitical, 65–67, 94, 100
Germany, 3, 11, 23, 69, 99,
  101–103, 111, 116, 120, 123,
  154, 162, 171, 175, 176, 179,
  182, 186–189, 192, 202, 207,
  212–216, 218, 224, 240, 253,
  273
Ghent initiative, 172
global balance, 117, 124, 152
governance, 15, 38, 40, 41, 46, 48,
  54, 67, 68, 83, 211, 270, 274
Greece, 100, 101, 111, 118, 124,
  149, 151, 159, 215

H
hierarchy, 15, 16, 38, 39, 41, 42, 44,
  48–50, 54–56, 262, 265
Historical Institutionalism, xv, 271
HI, 271
hostage-taking, 48, 51, 81, 265
House of Commons, 148

Hungary, 101, 111, 148, 178, 180, 188, 191, 215

I
India, 145
industry, 65, 66, 102, 103, 118, 119, 122, 124, 125, 145, 148, 149, 158, 161, 178, 185, 216, 224, 248, 249
institution
  focal institution, 17, 19, 21, 23, 37, 56, 63, 64, 67, 68, 70, 71, 75, 79, 80, 142, 159, 170, 171, 181, 200, 212, 217, 218, 224, 265, 266
integration, 5, 7, 9–13, 17–19, 25–27, 38–40, 50, 53, 54, 56, 63, 68, 71, 74, 75, 80, 81, 83, 95–97, 111, 112, 117, 119, 126, 133, 152, 153, 159, 169, 171, 173, 180, 184, 185, 192, 193, 201, 202, 205, 207, 210, 213, 236–239, 242, 246–254, 261–263, 266–269, 272, 274
interdependence, 44, 67, 68, 83, 97, 98
interinstitutional relationship, 15, 19, 26, 39, 40, 49, 54, 82, 83
Ireland, 101, 216
Italy, 11, 99, 101–103, 111, 116, 120, 123, 154, 162, 176, 182, 186, 206, 212, 214–216, 218, 253, 273

J
juste retour, 103, 115, 117, 118, 121, 122, 124, 147, 148, 152, 248

L
Lancaster House Treaties, 186, 187

Latvia, 101, 174, 209, 215, 217
Le Touquet, 119, 121, 123
Liberal Intergovernmentalism, xv, 7, 263
LI, 7, 237, 263
Lithuania, 101, 215, 217
LoI, 20, 116–118, 120, 123, 126, 129, 130, 133, 153, 156
Luxembourg, 69, 101, 111, 124, 186, 215

M
Maastricht, 112
Maastricht Treaty, 112, 113
Macron, Emmanuel, 272
Malta, 101, 126, 199, 216, 217
marginalization, 16–19, 21, 26, 38–40, 53, 54, 56, 57, 63, 68, 71, 74, 75, 80, 81, 83, 95–97, 141–144, 149, 151, 157, 159–161, 237, 239, 241, 246, 247, 249, 250, 262, 264, 266, 268, 270, 272–274
membership, 38, 111, 112
membership preference, 17, 18, 20, 22, 23, 25, 26, 64, 75, 79, 80, 82, 85, 94, 98, 100, 112, 126, 127, 129, 142, 154, 157, 170, 182, 184, 191–193, 200–202, 204, 207, 208, 211, 214, 218, 224, 262, 266–269, 271
member surplus, 64, 75–81, 85, 126, 127, 155–157, 185, 208, 218, 266, 267, 271
Merkel, Angela, 202, 206, 207, 212
migration, 202
military capabilities, 6, 23, 24, 97, 124, 172, 176, 184–186, 205, 209, 224, 236, 251
military headquarters, 206
mixed-motive situation, 47

INDEX 319

N

negative spillovers, 77, 78
neofunctionalism, 24, 27, 86, 95, 235–237, 246, 247, 249
neorealism, 4, 24, 26, 95
Netherlands, 100, 101, 106, 111, 152, 160, 174, 175, 186, 214, 273
neutrality, 101–103, 175, 216, 274
Nordic Defence Cooperation (NORDEFCO), 6, 7, 13, 15, 179, 180, 182, 209, 214, 261
North Atlantic Treaty Organization (NATO), 4, 5, 7, 9, 12, 13, 22–25, 27, 66, 69, 70, 99–101, 103, 106, 113, 114, 120, 145, 148, 149, 170, 173, 175–177, 179–181, 183, 184, 187, 190–192, 199, 200, 203, 204, 206–209, 211, 214, 215, 224, 236, 237, 239–245, 253, 254, 263, 264, 269, 273, 274
nuclear weapons, 69

O

opt-out, 131, 179, 202, 217
Organisation Conjointe pour la Coopération en matière de l'Armement (OCCAR), 6, 7, 11–13, 15, 19–21, 26, 95, 99, 116–118, 120, 121, 123–126, 129, 130, 133, 134, 141–144, 148–162, 235, 241, 242, 247–250, 261, 262, 264, 268, 272, 274
overlap, 12, 16, 18, 37–39, 41, 42, 44, 48–57, 76, 80, 82, 85, 98, 121, 142, 180, 206, 217, 261, 265, 267, 274

P

Permanent Structured Cooperation (PESCO), 5–7, 10–13, 15, 19, 20, 22–27, 38, 95, 98, 100, 162, 169–182, 184–193, 199–202, 204–208, 210–219, 224, 235–237, 242, 244–247, 250–253, 261–264, 268, 269, 272, 274
Poland, 101, 106, 111, 148, 152, 153, 161, 174, 178, 180, 189, 190, 203, 206, 212, 215, 244
populist, 202
Portugal, 69, 101, 111, 216, 273
power
  bargaining power, 63, 66, 69, 73, 97, 204, 242, 250
  go-it-alone power, 17–19, 25, 26, 63, 64, 70, 71, 73–75, 80–82, 85, 86, 94, 98, 122, 142, 157, 162, 181, 185, 189, 191, 193, 199–201, 208, 211, 262, 266–269
  hard power, 6, 8, 141, 243
  power-based, 48, 70, 71, 97, 235, 274
power distribution, 68, 86, 268
preferences, 5, 11, 13, 17, 18, 21, 23, 24, 26, 45, 63–66, 69, 71, 74–76, 79, 80, 86, 97–100, 121, 123, 133, 151, 161, 193, 200, 204, 206, 211, 213, 215, 224, 242, 250, 254, 262, 266, 268, 269, 271, 272
process tracing, 19, 94–96, 99

Q

Qualified Majority Voting (QMV), 146, 175, 176, 204

R

R&T, 6, 111, 114, 118, 127, 128, 132, 142, 143, 145, 149, 150, 156, 157, 217, 241, 248, 251, 252
Rational Choice Institutionalism, 17
RCI, 64, 271
regime complex, 7, 14, 16, 19, 25, 26, 38–40, 42–44, 46–51, 54, 57, 65, 75, 80, 83, 189, 200, 254, 263, 265
reluctant states, 103, 106, 123, 126, 170, 173, 174, 176, 181–186, 188, 189, 191–193, 200, 202, 204, 205, 208, 209, 211–215, 218, 224, 252
resilience, 16, 17, 19, 23, 26, 38, 40, 54, 56, 57, 63, 68, 71, 75, 80, 83, 96, 199, 200, 204, 217, 218, 224, 237, 262, 266, 268
Romania, 101, 123, 213, 215
Russia, 3, 4, 179, 203, 208, 243–245, 251, 273, 274
Russian, 4, 69, 202, 203, 209, 243, 244, 250

S

sectorial specialization, 274
selective states
selectives, 145
Slovakia, 101, 148, 180, 188, 215
Slovenia, 101, 148, 174, 180, 191, 215
Spain, 11, 100–103, 111, 116, 153, 155, 162, 176, 177, 182, 186, 212, 214, 216, 218, 253, 273
spillovers
cultivated spillovers, 246
functional spillovers, 246
political spillovers, 246, 248, 250, 251

standard, 17, 64, 66, 76, 128, 161, 267
Steering Board, 130–132, 146
St. Malo declaration, 3, 116, 169, 239
strategic inconsistency, 48, 53
strategic orientation, 65, 66, 100, 174, 239
Sweden, 4, 101–103, 111, 153, 161, 171, 174, 175, 179, 187, 188, 200, 206, 209, 215, 216

T

threat of exclusion, 17, 18, 20, 22, 23, 26, 63, 65, 71, 74, 75, 80–83, 85, 112, 122, 126, 133, 142, 151, 152, 162, 170, 171, 182, 188, 192, 201, 208, 211–213, 216, 217, 224, 245, 253, 254, 266–268, 271
transaction cost(s), 47, 64, 65, 76, 78–82, 85, 126, 127, 129, 130, 156, 157, 208, 209, 266, 267, 271
Treaty of Lisbon, 6, 10, 169, 218, 251
Lisbon Treaty, 9, 95, 169, 171–173, 175–177, 180, 190, 205, 207, 210, 242, 250, 251
Treaty of Nice, 169, 174
Treaty on European Union, 172, 212
TEU, 130, 169, 172, 173, 244
Trump, Donald, 22, 193, 199, 200, 202, 208, 210, 224, 237, 244, 253

U

Ukraine, 3, 25, 69, 264, 273, 274
Ukrainian, 4, 203, 243
unanimity, 7, 10, 11, 45, 70, 76, 118, 146, 175, 272
unilateralism, 67

United Kingdom, 11, 21, 69, 99,
  101, 111, 119, 145, 150, 175,
  204, 211
United States (US), 4, 8, 24, 69, 100,
  101, 115, 119–121, 145, 149,
  170, 175, 177, 184, 185, 193,
  199, 200, 208–210, 236–245,
  253, 264, 270, 273–275
upstream states, 102, 112, 115–119,
  121–130, 132–134, 141, 142,
  144–146, 149, 151, 153–162,
  250

V
variable geometry approach, 11, 118
Visegràd states, 148
  V4, 148, 181, 185, 188, 205, 206,
  209, 212

W
Western European Armaments Group
  (WEAG), 5, 7, 15, 19–21, 26,
  95, 99, 111–123, 125, 128–134,
  143, 144, 156, 235, 239, 240,
  262, 268, 272
Western European Union, 5
  WEU, 5, 113, 116–118, 131, 152,
  240
Witney, Nick, 122, 125, 145, 160,
  187

Z
Zeitenwende, 3, 273

Printed in the United States
by Baker & Taylor Publisher Services